Making IT happen

Critical Issues in IT Management

Wiley Series in Information Systems

CURRENT VOLUMES IN THE SERIES

Making IT Happen

Critical Issues in IT Management

JAMES D. McKEEN and HEATHER A. SMITH

Queen's University, Kingston, Ontario, Canada

WILEY

Other Wiley Editorial Offices

John Wiley & Sons Inc., 111 River Street, Hoboken, NJ 07030, USA

Jossey-Bass, 989 Market Street, San Francisco, CA 94103-1741, USA

Wiley-VCH Verlag GmbH, Boschstr. 12, D-69469 Weinheim, Germany

John Wiley & Sons Australia Ltd, 33 Park Road, Milton, Queensland 4064, Australia

John Wiley & Sons (Asia) Pte Ltd, 2 Clementi Loop #02-01, Jin Xing Distripark, Singapore
129809

John Wiley & Sons Canada Ltd, 22 Worcester Road, Etobicoke, Ontario, Canada M9W 1L1

Wiley also publishes its books in a variety of electronic formats. Some content that appears in
print may not be available in electronic books.

British Library Cataloguing in Publication Data
A catalogue record for this book is available from the British Library

ISBN 0-470-85087-6

Project management by Originator, Gt Yarmouth, Norfolk (typeset in $10\frac{1}{2}$/12pt Palatino)
Printed and bound in Great Britain by T.J. International Ltd, Padstow, Cornwall
This book is printed on acid-free paper responsibly manufactured from sustainable forestry
in which at least two trees are planted for each one used for paper production.

Wiley Series in Information Systems

Editors

RICHARD BOLAND   Department of Management Information and Decision Systems, Weatherhead School of Management, Case Western Reserve University, 10900 Euclid Avenue, Cleveland, Ohio 44106-7235, USA

RUDY HIRSCHHEIM   Department of Decision and Infomation Systems, College of Business Administration, University of Houston, Houston, Texas 77202-6283, USA

Advisory Board

NIELS BJØRN-ANDERSEN	Copenhagen Business School, Denmark
D. ROSS JEFFERY	University of New South Wales, Australia
HEINZ K. KLEIN	State University of New York, USA
ROB KLING	Indiana University, USA
BENN R. KONSYNSKI	Emory University, Atlanta, USA
TIM J. LINCOLN	IBM UK Limited, UK
FRANK F. LAND	London School of Economics, UK
ENID MUMFORD	Manchester Business School, UK
MIKE NEWMAN	University of Manchester, UK
DANIEL ROBEY	Georgia State University, USA
E. BURTON SWANSON	University of California, USA
ROBERT TRICKER	Warwick Business School, UK
GEOFF WALSHAM	University of Cambridge, UK
ROBERT W. ZMUD	University of Oklahoma, USA

Praise for McKeen and Smith's earlier book, *Management Challenges in IS*

"... this is a valuable and practical review, written with academic thoroughness but delivering practical information which is immediately usable by the manager at work."

The Computer Bulletin (five-star rating and Book of the Month)

"The book ... should be compulsory reading for anybody involved at the decision-making end of IS/IT ... I found it impossible to put down and am seriously thinking of suing the authors for loss of sleep caused by HAVING to read their book!"

IMS Journal

"Shorn of all the jargon, buzzwords and hype typical of the computing field, this book speaks in business management language."

New York Review of Books

Contents

Part D   People and Productivity   265

Foreword by Robert Zmud

Today, the tasks associated with the strategic and tactical management of information technology (IT) are becoming incredibly difficult, and the effectualness by which these tasks are handled can have profound impact on business success as well as on the personal careers of IT executives. Further, IT has become an omnipresent force driving business operations and strategies; the IT environment (emerging technologies, networks of service providers, competitor's actions) has become volatile; and IT management has become both exceedingly complex and, visibly intrusive regarding its influence in heightening (or dampening) business success.

For those executives charged with managing IT the challenges are imposing. How does one confront this complexity while adding value through this intrusiveness? McKeen and Smith, in taking on this challenge themselves by offering guidance to today's IT executive, have produced a book that should be both insightful and helpful to readers. Thankfully, the book is neither a "how-to" guide (that would be just about impossible to pull off in such a complex domain) nor a generalized treatise on IT management (that would be unlikely to add value for executives seeking pragmatic advice). Instead, the book provides a template—targeted at the executive level—of the technology and organizational issues that need to be dealt with and well-grounded means (decision structures and decision processes) for handling these issues. A particular, and very unique, strength of the book is the manner in which McKeen and Smith skillfully blend and leverage the best thinking of leading scholars and successful IT executives. As a consequence the book should prove valuable both for IT executives confronting today's IT management challenges and for scholars seeking to better understand this dynamic and elusive context.

Robert Zmud
Michael F. Price Chair of MIS, University of Oklahoma
and Research Director, Advanced Practices Council of SIM, International

Series Preface

The information systems community has grown considerably since 1984, when we began publishing the Wiley Series in Information Systems. We are pleased to be a part of the growth of the field, and believe that this series of books is playing an important role in the intellectual development of the discipline. The primary objective of the series is to publish scholarly works that reflect the best of the research in the information systems community. These works should help guide the IS practitioner community regarding what strategies it ought to adopt to be successful in the future. Books in the Series should also help advanced students— particularly those at the graduate level—understand the myriad issues surrounding the management of IS.

To this end, the current volume—*Making IT Happen: Critical Issues in IT Management*, written by Jim McKeen and Heather Smith—provides a key addition. The authors have done an excellent job tying together three critical parts of making IS successful. First, IS must provide efficient and effective infrastructure. Second, IS must possess skilled staff who can interact with both technologists and business units. Third, IS must constantly scan the horizon looking for future technologies that might be used by the corporation to gain a competitive advantage. The book is well grounded, based on the views of key IS managers in 15 leading-edge organizations. The focus of these views is on critical IS management issues, and the authors have tied together these views into a coherent picture of how IS organizations should proceed in the future.

McKeen and Smith's book is a welcomed addition to our Series, and should be of interest to practitioners, students and academics alike.

Rudy Hirschheim

Preface

Information technology (IT) presents many challenges to managers. Constant change, e-business, massive amounts of information, global operations, and building new alliances and capabilities are just some of the transformations being driven by the use of IT in business today. No modern manager can afford to ignore IT or to leave it to the professionals. As too many companies have found out the expensive way, effective IT doesn't just *happen*. It is a lot of hard work. Every single IT project involves complex decisions about selecting the appropriate technology for a particular business strategy, redesigning the business processes of which the technology is part, and ensuring that anticipated benefits are actually achieved. But perhaps the more challenging part of the IT job is the work that goes on behind the scenes to ensure that the many different applications on which company operations and strategies are built will be able to work at all. Existing software must operate reliably and securely, new applications must be developed on time and on budget, and integrated and useful information must be made available to the business. Putting these pieces in place requires leadership, prescience, planning, technical savvy, and good business sense, to name just a few of the many qualities an IT manager needs today.

To make IT happen, managers must function simultaneously in three modes. First, they must provide efficient, cheap, reliable infrastructure and operations that rarely break down and always provide the functionality needed to run the present and near-future business. Second, they must provide competent, skilled staff and project-leaders who not only understand and work well with the business and who are capable of working with a multitude of (sometimes incompatible) technologies but who can also be counted on to bring complex and risky projects in on time and on budget. Third, they must be futurists, scanning the business and technical environments to bring the best ideas forward for incorporation into the firm's business and technology strategies. And they must accomplish this in an environment of constant change.

This book tackles the tough issues of managing in an environment where IT is everywhere. Based on the real-life experiences of senior IT managers in leading-edge businesses and incorporating thorough research, *Making IT Happen* separates fact from fad, shows where managers can make a real difference, brings real-world insight regarding IT issues into the office or the classroom, and provides useful and practical advice for coping in the fast-paced world of IT.

GENESIS OF THE BOOK

As part of their overall research program, the authors convened a group of senior IT managers on an ongoing basis. This *focus group* (from 15 leading-edge organizations from different industry sectors including retail, manufacturing, banking, insurance, government, and automotive) meets regularly to identify and discuss *critical IT management issues*. Once an issue is selected, focus group members research it within their own organization and then attend a full-day session where the issue is discussed by all members. Following the session, the authors write a report based on the discussion. Each report has three parts: (1) a description of the issue; (2) the introduction of models derived from research to position the issue within a contextual framework; and (3) the identification of near-term strategies (i.e., those that can be implemented immediately) that have proven successful in dealing with the specific issue. This book is organized around these critical IT issues—one per chapter.

We have learned over the years that the specific issues vary little across organizations—even in organizations with unique IT strategies. However, each organization tackles a specific issue differently. It is this diversity that provides the richness of insight regarding each issue. Because "everyone has part of the solution", the focus group provides an opportunity for different individuals (representing different organizations) to share their understanding and experiences (both successful and otherwise) so that collectively a thorough understanding of each issue can be developed and strategies for how it can be managed most successfully can be identified. Finally, it is important to recognize that this book is focused on the *management* of IT. It is not about technology *per se*. Technology is explored only to a depth sufficient to identify the management issues it presents.

This book is a sequel to *Management Challenges in IS: Successful Strategies and Appropriate Action* (John Wiley & Sons, UK, August 1996). Both books are based on the identification and management of critical issues in IT. It is interesting to note that, with the exception of the chapter describing the *impending* Y2K problem, most of the issues described within the first book—such as "Marketing IS within the Organization", "Enhancing Development Productivity", and "Managing Legacy Systems"—remain as vital today as they were then. Technology changes frequently and unrelentingly. In contrast, IT issues and their management are much more enduring.

MULTIPLE AUDIENCES

Because of its focus and format, *Making IT Happen* will be of interest to three different audiences—business managers, IT managers, and university/college professors. Each have their own unique motivation and need for understanding IT.

1. *Business managers* need to understand critical IT issues and how they impact their organizations and decision-making. At Queen's School of Business, we offer executive-level, one-week programs on "IT for non-IT Executives". Attendee feedback on draft chapters of this book has been overwhelmingly positive. One wrote, "this is the first time I have really understood the world of IT . . . now I can relate much more effectively with my partners in IT."
2. *IT managers* need a strategic approach to the management of IT and day-to-day guidelines for managing IT successfully. IT managers tend to learn "on the job". Formal training tends to be technology-focused. Gaining an understanding of the big picture of IT can therefore take a long time and be largely based on personal experience. *Making IT Happen* explores the whole gamut of critical IT issues, explaining each and positioning them within a broad organizational context. As such, it exposes IT managers to the full breadth and depth of the management actions involved in deploying IT effectively.
3. *University/College professors* need a vehicle for teaching advanced courses in Management of IT and IT Strategy to enable their students to understand the real world of business and technology management. Based on the authors' personal experiences in the classroom, it is felt that the book is most appropriate for executive programs, MBA programs, and senior-level, undergraduate management information systems (MIS) courses covering topics of Management of IT and IT Strategy. It is particularly well suited to courses whose pedagogy is case-based. Appropriate chapters within the book can be assigned as preparatory reading for the discussion of each case. Because of the proposed format of this book (stand-alone, issues-focused chapters), it lends itself particularly well to "cut and paste", electronic text/case books.

ANTICIPATED USAGE

For business managers and IT practitioners, usage of the book will depend on your specific needs. If your goal is to fully understand how and why the IT role is changing, it is recommended that you read all the chapters within the first part, which collectively describe all aspects of the impending change. Alternatively, if you are struggling with how to launch a CRM (customer relationship management) initiative, you would go straight to Chapter 9 where you would find a full description of the issues and a number of useful frameworks plus selected near-term strategies, which you implement. Our experience over the years has indicated that *Making IT Happen* will be most beneficial to managers about to assume a senior position within IT such as chief information officer (CIO), VP Strategy, VP Development, chief technology officer (CTO), VP Planning, or VP Infrastructure. At this stage in one's career, it is necessary to have a broad understanding of the full range of management issues within IT. It will also be beneficial for business managers whose role brings them into contact with IT issues and decision-making (e.g., members of the Executive Committee, the IT Steering Committee, or business unit leaders).

For academics, *Making IT Happen* is targeted for the capstone course in IT Strategy (or Management of IT). These courses are typically offered to under-graduate seniors in Business and Commerce programs and to final-year master in business administration (MBA) students. Given the grounding of the book in the actual practice of IT management, its value is directly related to the experience level of the student. The authors have found that it is most successful for executive MBA programs and executive development programs within business schools. Here the students/attendees are typically mid-career executives with a substantial experiential base. The IT management issues raised in the book are, in some cases, all too real and current ... which makes for lively classroom discussion!

OUR PHILOSOPHY

We have been working in the field of IT as researchers, educators, practitioners, and consultants for many years. Over that time, we have built a number of successful bridges to industry—the direct result of our adherence to a philosophy with four main tenets:

- *Industry should be our laboratory*—organizations represent a hotbed of ideas, problems looking for solutions, test-beds for new approaches, and a ready source of motivated and resourceful individuals willing to take chances.
- *Theory should be grounded in practice*—theory without application and practice without theoretical guidance are both impoverished.
- *Insight regarding IT issues is best achieved by experiencing them within the context of an organization*—if you fail to understand why individuals do the things they do, you haven't spent enough time "in their shoes".
- *Academics and practitioners need each other*—organizations are rife with vexing problems calling out for attention; academics enjoy the freedom to focus their research on whatever topic they find personally intriguing. Clearly the overlap can be mutually beneficial.

This book is a direct result of putting this philosophy into play. We have had the opportunity to work with literally hundreds of IT managers over the years. The topics we have explored have all been selected by practitioners as being important to their work. Where we felt existing research could inform, we have introduced it into our analysis. Without doubt, we could not have accomplished the writing of this book without the collective efforts on the part of all the members of the focus groups. Their wisdom, insights, experiences, and demonstrated willingness to share in order to gain a better understanding is acknowledged. To them, we owe a great deal of gratitude. We sincerely hope the end product is found to be of significant value.

A GUIDE TO THIS BOOK

Making IT Happen is organized into four parts covering the changing role of IT, methods for leveraging the business with IT, strategies for managing technology, and issues pertaining to people and productivity. Each part contains a number of chapters each addressing a specific management issue in IT. There is no logical hierarchy among chapters, thus permitting the maximum degree of flexibility. That is, the reader is not required to read the first three chapters in order to understand the issue described in the fourth chapter.

Part A, *The Changing Role of IT*, looks at how the mandate of the IT function has evolved over time and discusses some of the new responsibilities it is being asked to take on in the future. We have found that practicing IT managers often need to have a strong focus on the future in order to anticipate and guide their organization's transformation with technology. As a result, it is not uncommon to see IT managers considering issues that have not yet become concerns in organizations. Thus, in this section you will see a range of new IT roles examined—from those that are just now being taken seriously by the rest of the business world (e.g., change management, risk management, and knowledge management) to those that still haven't truly made it onto their radar screens (e.g., managing external relationships and the social impacts of technology).

Part B, *Leveraging Business with IT*, takes a comprehensive look at the perennial question of IT value, but at a whole new level. Today, as anyone who has been involved in a merger or acquisition can attest, IT affects every part of a business. Both customer-facing functions and back office integration are now within the scope of IT and the emergence of large-scale off-the-shelf products, such as ERP (enterprise resource planning) and CRM systems, is dramatically changing how business operate. Other IT investments are strategic (e.g., e-business) requiring close cooperation between technology and multiple business areas. As a result of this growing scope and impact, it is increasingly critical that IT and business be closely aligned in their goals and that the overall good of the enterprise is considered paramount in determining which technology projects to undertake. It is also essential that IT's benefits be seen in a much larger context than in the past and take the full range of potential business value, from cost reduction to competitive positioning into consideration.

Part C, *Managing Technology*, explores a topic that is more traditionally the purview of the IT manager. However, even here IT managers face much bigger challenges than in the past. As the number of technologies available proliferates, selecting and managing the right hardware and software for an organization has become, in the words of one IT manager, "a minefield". Managing an ever-increasing portfolio of technology and continually evaluating emerging new technologies requires not only technical and managerial capabilities but excellent strategic and political skills as well. Today's IT manager must navigate between the often conflicting demands of business managers and the "hype" of vendors and consultants to chart a technical path for his or her organization. Similarly, there are many complex decisions to make about how, where and how much to source technology services. Ideally, an enterprise architecture guides all these decisions without limiting the organization to a particular technological direction. However, while much of an organization's competitiveness relies on a flexible architecture that can respond to rapidly changing business needs, flexibility can also conflict with the growing need for higher degrees of technical integration. Therefore, IT managers are often called to make difficult trade-offs between these two goals.

Part D, *People and Productivity*, addresses two of the most challenging issues facing IT managers today. Every IT leader wants to hire and retain the right people for his or her organization. Identifying these skills and working with HR (human resources) departments to put the programs in place that will attract and keep these people often "pushes the envelope" of what organizations are willing to do for their staff. In spite of much innovation in this area, it is especially difficult to hire effective project-managers and IT leaders. Two chapters in this part therefore address how companies are developing their own leadership talent in-house. IT organizations are also pioneering new forms of working such as work from home and virtual teams. Their experiences with managing virtual work serve as a window into what will be a growing phenomenon in the early 21st century. The final chapter of this section, and the book, explores issues surrounding IT measurement. All too often, organizations spend a considerable amount of time and effort in this area without getting the results they are seeking. As with everything else about IT management, measurement is an art, not a science, and one that requires judgment and astuteness to do properly.

This book does not offer any "silver bullets" or panaceas for the problems and challenges of IT management today. However, readers *will* find perspective and practical advice on how to handle them. The real world of IT is full of complexity and compromise, not textbook solutions. We hope this book will provide a clearer picture of the fascinating world of IT management and offer insight and guidance about how to make IT happen effectively in an organization.

Acknowledgments

The work contained in this book is based on numerous meetings with many senior IT managers. We would like to acknowledge our indebtedness to the following individuals who willingly shared their insights as based on their experiences "won the hard way":

Michael Abbott, Prem Agrawal, Rick Ashall, Tim Aubrey, Chuck Bailey, John Bailey, Maria Benedek, Bob Betts, Diane Bezdikian, Nancy Blackstad, Don Blake, Steve Boily, Ray Brennan, Gary Brooks, Kevin Butcher, Gary Charlton, Christine Cheung, Ray Chin, Michael Cole, Gary Davenport, Drew Davison, Danny Deacetis, Cathy Decker, Art D'Silva, Ken Dschankilic, Reg Elliott, Brian Gill, Rick Haier, Ron Hartnoll, Mark Hatfield, Karen Hilton, Caroline Hogwood, Kelly Kanellakis, Jay Kembhavi, Gerry Kestenberg, Deborah Kinread, Greg Kowal, Gerry Krups, Jim Lambert, Bruce Lauckner, David Londry, Karen Mason, Roy McCatty, Lena McDonell, David Mitchell, Mel Mitzel, Bob Noseworthy, Terry O'Toole, Brian Patton, Penny Prazak, Clyde Rajack, Karey Reilly, Mohammad Rifaie, Eugene Roman, Darlene Ross, John Rudd, Linda Siksna, Kathy Simpson, Robbin Sinclaire-Chenier, Martin Small, Irene Sobolewski, Phil Surtees, Jennifer Thompson, Vanda Vicars, Igal Volach, Rob Wharton, Doug Wolfe, and Norma Wright.

We would also like to recognize the contribution of Queen's School of Business to this work. The School has facilitated and supported our vision of better integrating academic research and practice and has helped make our collaborative approach to the study of IT Management and Strategy an effective model for interorganizational learning.

James D. McKeen
Heather A. Smith
School of Business, Queen's University,
Kingston, Ontario
January, 2003

Part A
The Changing Role of IT

Information technology (IT) sits squarely at the intersection of two massive forces of change—relentless business pressures and a rapidly evolving technology landscape. As a result, more than any other organizational function, the IT organization has faced continual pressure to change and expand its role over the past 30 years. In the 7 years since our previous book, IT's responsibilities have grown to include new technologies (e.g., enterprise resource planning [ERP], customer relationship management [CRM]), new ways of doing business (e.g., business-to-business [B2B], business-to-consumer [B2C]), enabling new ways of working (e.g., knowledge management, business integration), and different methods of carrying out their mandate (e.g., change management, risk management). Increasingly, the chief information officer (CIO) is included in a company's executive team and IT is considered fundamental to any business strategy. Today, IT's influence encompasses much of the traditional organization and is extending beyond the walls of the firm to its customers, suppliers, and partners.

This part looks at some of the newer responsibilities IT is now taking on within an organization. Chapter 1, "A Look at IT in the Next Five Years", tries to make sense of the challenges that are facing IT and how they are changing the department that everyone loves to hate. Here, we look at some of the early warnings managers are receiving from their business and technical environments and predict how IT's mission, mandate, and responsibilities will change in the near to mid-term. Chapter 2, "Managing the Social Impacts of Technology", explores how IT is transforming our work, our working relationships, our organizations, and our behavior and identifies some trends with which IT managers and others will have to deal in the very near future. Chapter 3, "Managing External Relationships", discusses IT's interactions with the increasingly large number of suppliers, vendors, and partners, whose services have become essential to the delivery of effective IT solutions to the organization. Chapter 4, "Knowledge Management and IT", looks at how organizations are moving beyond mere information management to the development of several different types of intellectual capital and explores the role IT is playing in this new field that we are only beginning to understand. In Chapter 5, "Risk Management in IT: Problems and Potential", we examine the complexities and uncertainties IT organizations must face when assessing and implementing new IT opportunities. It suggests that understanding and coping with risk on an ongoing basis is fundamental to being able to take advantage of technology while controlling for its potential problems. Finally, Chapter 6, "Achieving Effective Change with IT", explores IT's new responsibilities as an agent of change and the implications these have for how new technology is implemented.

1

A Look at IT in the Next Five Years

Yet another revolution has begun in the field of information systems. When it is over, IS departments as they are currently constituted will be dismantled. Independent software specialists will dominate the development of systems, programming and other software. Users will completely control individual information systems. (Dearden, 1987)

Business processes will take center stage in eBusinesses, forcing the IT organization as we know it to disappear. Technology management will become the responsibility of business process owners—both inside and outside the corporation. (Cameron, 2000)

At the beginning of the fifth (or sixth) decade of the "information age"—depending on how you count—it is both amusing and frustrating to see the consistency of the pundits on information technology (IT). Predicting the demise of IT seems to be a theme. At the start of the current decade, they're still at it. Articles with titles like "IT department faces extinction" (Marron, 2000) and "Are CIOs obsolete?" (Maruca, 2000) are challenging the concept of a separate IT department within organizations. The experts cite trends such as the growth of e-business and the rise of application service providers as well as the increasing technical sophistication of users as the reasons that IT, as a separate entity, will likely disappear into the rest of the organization in the future.

Conversely, other research groups are predicting dire shortages of IT staff. The GartnerGroup (1999c) writes:

Through 2004, market demand for relevant and specialized IT skills and know how will continue to outstrip supply.

By 2006, nearly half the workers in developed global economies will be employed by industries that either produce IT or use IT intensively.

Similarly, it has been found that the scope and depth of the chief information officer (CIO) role is expanding, the status of IT is rising in most organizations, and that the CIO's formal power is increasing (Maruca, 2000).

This chapter tries to make sense of the challenges that are facing IT, particularly over the next five years, and how they will shape the organization that everyone loves to hate. We selected a five-year term as being the best time frame in which to predict meaningful change. This has proven to be remarkably accurate in the past (see McKeen and Smith, 1996). We believe that to look further ahead than five years is not only extremely difficult, but is ineffective given the pace and rate of change in the business and IT environment. This chapter presents the findings of this focus group. After a brief overview of the environment in which IT will find itself in the not-so-distant future and a look at how IT has changed over time, we then discuss IT's evolving role and responsibilities in each of these areas.

THE CHANGING IT FUNCTION

More so than any other organizational function, IT has had to face pressures for continual change and challenge. For example, in the mid-1990s we wrote: "It is evident that a more sophisticated mechanism for delivering IS to the organization is now required. Like the process of retooling an outdated factory to turn out products faster and more efficiently, the IS function must undergo a change that is no less comprehensive it if is to fulfill its organizational mandate . . . the risk of not doing so is increasing inadequacy and eventual obsolescence" (McKeen and Smith, 1996). Five years later, we read, "IT needs to transform itself, the way it operates, the way it does business. Those who are not successful will disappear" (Marron, 2000).

This kind of pressure stems from two sources: the changing business environment and the changing technology landscape. Ten years ago, globalization, merger mania, deregulation, and electronic commerce not only didn't exist, no one had even predicted them (Maruca, 2000). Similarly the relentless improvements in all forms of technology, many of which *were* predicted, have led to a huge variety of applications that have continually surprised and challenged IT and business managers alike. Just keeping up with these vast and varied changes has left everyone breathless. And it is unlikely that the pace of change is going to abate. In fact if there is one thing that everyone agrees on it's that change is going to increase.

While every organizational function has been affected by these business and technology changes, none has faced more of them than IT. This is because as the function charged with delivering technical solutions to business problems, it sits squarely at the intersection of these two massive forces. One way the IT organization has coped is by dramatically expanding the scope and number of its responsibilities. Table 1.1 illustrates how these have changed over the last two

Table 1.1   *IT's growing list of responsibilities.*

1980s' responsibilities	1990s' responsibilities	2000s' responsibilities
Systems development	Systems development	Systems development
Operations management	Operations management	Operations management
Vendor relationships	Vendor relationships	External relationship management
	Data management	Knowledge management
	End-user computing	Infrastructure management
	Education and training	Change management
	Managing emerging technologies	Environmental scanning
	Corporate architecture	Corporate architecture
	Strategic systems	Strategic leadership
	Systems planning	Strategy implementation
		Network management
		E-commerce
		Business integration (CRM, ERP, etc.)
		Resource management
		Risk management

decades. This "add-on" feature is one of the most characteristic features of the changes affecting IT over the last 20 years. It also explains why IT is becoming increasingly more difficult and complex to manage. In fact, some organizations represented in the focus group are beginning to recognize that the demands of managing such an entity are so great that they require more than one person and have created a chief technology officer (CTO) as well as a chief information officer (CIO). Others are creating an "office of the CIO" staffed with several senior people, each with very specific responsibilities (Maruca, 2000).

Whatever the future holds for the IT department itself, it is clear that IT and its central place in the organization will get more important in the foreseeable future. To cope, IT departments will have to adapt. As Table 1.1 shows, IT's influence now encompasses not only much of the traditional organization, but is also expanding to include the new forms of organization toward which the world is evolving. Looking ahead to the next five years, our focus group managers saw a critical and important role for IT in both these areas, helping companies to adapt to the new business and technological realities they are facing.

THE IT ORGANIZATION IN FIVE YEARS' TIME

Focus group members faced a wide variety of challenges in their day-to-day jobs and each placed a different emphasis on what would be the most important one for their particular IT organization in the future. For example, one manager

Table 1.2   *IT in five years will be different from the previous two decades.*

	1980s' view	1990s' view	2000s' view
IT mission	Technology management	Corporate change	Corporate transformation
IT function	System automation	Corporate re-engineering	Mobilize strategy
IT management	Reactive	Proactive	Anticipatory
IT self-image	Service provider	Facilitator	Catalyst
External controls	Balkan states	Federated republic	Federated network
Internal controls	Metrics	Impact	Value
Staffing	Specialists	Skilled generalists	Business technologists
Systems development	Structured	Evolutionary	Assembled
Hardware/Software management	Planned	Confused	Minefield
In the workplace	Office automation	Automated office	Boundary-less office

believed that IT staffing would be a driving issue behind the future of IT, while others felt it would be e-commerce or the major new technologies that are just hitting the market (i.e., wireless and unlimited bandwidth). However, together the members painted a compelling picture of the shape and face of the IT organization in the next five years. Table 1.2 summarizes their vision and contrasts it with that of the previous two decades. The remainder of this chapter will discuss each of the features of the IT organization of the future.

IT Mission

The concept of the IT organization leading or driving *corporate change* was introduced in the early 1990s, along with the notion of re-engineering. It was the first time that organizations had realized that technology could be used to dramatically change how company processes worked. Instead of "paving the cow paths", IT could be used to eliminate or short-circuit many time-honored practices. With this realization came a growing recognition that it wasn't enough to simply change a process with technology, one also had to change the human practices that supported it. Thus was born the concept of IT as a corporate change agent or change manager. However, although corporate change has become increasingly significant during the last decade, what has remained constant is the concept of the organization itself. Today, most organizations are still the same recognizable entities they have always been. This is about to change.

Whereas in the 1990s change focused around processes, in the next five years we will see the beginning of the radical transformation of organizations themselves. The advent of the Internet in the mid-1990s has opened up new possibilities for doing business across organizational boundaries. Tapscott et al.

(2000) suggest that as businesses come to recognize and exploit these opportunities, they will soon realize that technology can be used to create and enhance inter-enterprise effectiveness and efficiency. Over the next five years, companies will initiate major experiments with inter-organization ventures to explore new ways of structuring enterprises to deliver value. Tapscott et al. (2000) predict that several new, inter-enterprise business structures will emerge in the coming decade, such as those that integrate across a value chain (e.g., Dell Computers) or that aggregate goods for other companies (e.g., Amazon.com). IT will provide the means to facilitate such *corporate transformations*, and IT staff will be instrumental both in identifying the possibilities available and establishing the mechanisms whereby these new ways of business will operate.

Internally too, businesses will begin to look significantly different, due to improving applications of technology, integration, and knowledge and to management's increasing need for structures and processes that can respond rapidly to external pressures and growing customer demands. There will thus be a significant broadening of IT's change management responsibilities as companies realize that technology can not only be used to make its processes more effective and efficient but can also fundamentally transform the way business operates.

In short, IT's mission will grow to be more than facilitating change. Over the next five years, we will see organizations expecting IT to be front and center in the drive to transform almost every aspect of the business: from how it delivers value, to how it is structured, to how it operates internally.

IT Function

In the 1990s, business automation for individual departments became increasingly passé. Instead, IT organizations were asked to work with business managers at higher and higher levels in the corporation to develop corporate-wide applications to improve organizational work processes. This involved changing many of the fundamental ways in which work was done—eliminating steps altogether, simplifying processes, integrating them with related processes or by restructuring them. This *corporate re-engineering* function gave IT a new mandate to seek broader corporate-wide synergies and to link existing functional areas in new ways. In the process, businesses cut layers of management and began to see themselves in terms of processes rather than functions. As the decade progressed, it became clear to senior managers that the IT organization and its staff had a much broader corporate perspective than other functional areas, and were thus able to suggest worthwhile new ways of deploying technology across departmental "stove-pipes" to benefit the organization as a whole. Thus, CIOs and IT staff came to be seen as having an increasingly strategic role to play in the organization. By 2000, more than three-quarters of CIOs were either on the board or the executive committee of their respective organizations (Maruca, 2000).

Over the next five years, the IT function will increasingly come to be valued for its unique perspective on both the corporation and technology and its ability to use this perspective to facilitate strategy development and *mobilize strategy* for the business. IT will have two key contributions to make to strategy formation. First, as the Internet and electronic commerce become a greater and greater portion of a business, IT will be expected to play a key role in developing and implementing the organization's e-business strategies. Second, as technology continues to evolve and diversify rapidly, IT will be expected to become more strategic about its technology policy and to present this strategy to senior management in ways that can be effectively integrated into business strategy.

These new strategic functions will require IT staff and management to develop new competencies, such as business acumen and leadership skills. They will also mean that, for the first time, IT decisions and actions will be in an area where they will have a direct impact on the corporate bottom line. Whereas in the past, the influence of systems has been mediated by other company staff, increasingly over the next five years, through the Internet and other customer-facing technologies, IT systems will interact directly with customers. Thus, the IT function will, of necessity, become more outward-looking and more concerned with business value than previously. It will also become more visible both within the organization and externally. For example, focus group members noted that they have already begun to see their stock prices vary as market analysts assess their company's e-commerce strategies. This pressure can only increase in the near term as both customers and the market vote with their dollars on the quality of IT's work.

IT Management

Focus group members believe that there is no question that the job of the IT manager has got increasingly complex. As Table 1.1 demonstrates, over the years more and more responsibilities have been heaped on IT's plate. But the *tone* of management is also changing. In the 1980s, responding to user criticisms that it was inflexible and bureaucratic, IT tried to *react* to users' needs by creating support functions and adopting client-centered methodologies. However, in the 1990s this style of management was no longer enough. Many IT managers were dismayed to discover that their users expected them to be *proactive* in their vision for how IT could help the company respond to business change by improving processes and developing new products and services. During this decade, IT managers explored a variety of ways to develop this skill. For example, they looked for ways to effectively combine a client-centered business orientation with the knowledge of how IT can change and improve company processes.

In the future, however, even more will be expected of IT managers. In the rapidly changing business and technical environment in which they will be operating, IT managers will be expected to *anticipate* coming trends and to propose business strategies to take advantage of them. As business cycles shorten to become almost spontaneous and technology outstrips the ability to assimilate it, IT managers will be expected to look even further forward and develop strategies that will enable the company to fulfill needs *as they develop*. Thus, the key skill that IT managers will have to develop is the ability to "get ahead and stay ahead of the curve" in both business and technology strategy.

To do this, IT managers will have to dramatically increase their environmental scanning skills so they can learn about new technologies and the new applications of those technologies. They will also have to develop their research and development capabilities to explore and gain experience with these technologies and what they can do. Because of the difficulties involved in predicting the future in such an unpredictable area, many IT managers will begin to use "real options" thinking (Amram and Kulatilaka, 1999) to develop and design hedging strategies for their organizations. This will require a more flexible approach to technology policy and architecture than has been used previously.

IT managers will also need a more in-depth knowledge of business than in previous decades. As they realize that they need to better understand the business trends facing the company, IT managers will develop new links with the parts of the business designed to monitor customer feedback and business trends, and develop new products. Initially, IT will do this by assisting the business to develop better tools to analyze and identify business information, such as customer reactions, patterns, incipient trends, and consumer needs. As they acquire a clearer understanding of what business is looking for, a much tighter IT–business partnership will develop than has existed in the past.

IT Self-image

How IT views itself internally is key to how it performs. In the 1980s, IT saw itself as a service provider to the business community and designed its processes, structure and metrics accordingly. In the 1990s, however, IT saw its major role to be that of a *facilitator* of business. Its main job became providing the technology and tools that the business needed to do its work. Thus, IT infrastructure became much more important in the last decade. IT organizations developed PC "workbenches" or suites of software for users to access as needed in their work, and large, integrated databases were developed (i.e., data warehouses) for users to explore and do their own analysis, rather than having to rely on preformatted information from an IT system. Over the last decade as well, IT organizations came to recognize that facilitation of business did not necessarily mean that IT itself had to provide all IT services. Thus, IT organizations began to help users to find consultants and to outsource non-core functions (e.g., operations). By the end of the decade, many IT organizations saw themselves as coordinators of technology delivery to the business, rather than the sole providers of it.

In the future, IT will have to change its self-image yet again to accommodate the more active role it will be taking in business. To underscore its responsibilities for business transformation, IT will come to see itself as more of a *catalyst* in identifying and delivering new forms of value to business. In adopting this self-image, IT will have to be careful if it is not to be perceived as arrogant. IT in and of itself will never be solely responsible for business transformation and new business strategy, no matter how important technology is to the business. Instead, IT must view itself as a chemical agent that, when added to other substances, will cause something completely new and different to occur. As a catalyst, IT can start things happening in organizations that would never have occurred without it; it can stimulate new ideas and start people thinking about new possibilities. This is an exciting role, but it is also one that requires considerably more business acumen and leadership skill than being a mere facilitator. Therefore, it is essential that IT groom and develop its people to be prepared for the role. An effective catalyst must pay more attention to the mixture of relationships, politics, finance, business reality, and technology potential than it has in the past and use its judgment as to whether a new idea will create something new and valuable or merely result in a chemical disaster.

External Controls

As the IT function matured in organizations during the 1980s, companies experimented widely with different forms of governance structures. By the end of that decade, IT functions typically had a wide range of relationships with different departments, and very few controls and standards had been established. Over the 1990s, most IT functions adopted some form of *federal model* of governance, which operated much like a country of united states. In this model, individual user groups were free to make their own IT decisions until they wanted to use the corporate infrastructure. Then, they had to follow corporate standards. By the end of the decade, the need for corporate IT standards and controls over such things as security, communications, and data for new applications had been accepted by most business groups, although IT organizations were still playing catch-up with legacy systems developed in earlier years.

Over the next five years, the need for corporate standards will grow as companies pursue ever greater levels of integration. The adoption of enterprise-wide software packages, such as enterprise resource planning (ERP) and customer relationship management (CRM) will reinforce this need, as will the need for hardware and software to be "plug and play". However, the new challenge IT will face will be how to establish such standards and controls across the network of businesses and customers with which the company will increasingly interact. This will reinforce the need for intra-organizational standards and controls so data and transactions can be easily exchanged. Already some industries, such as the oil and gas industry, have adopted a common data model that greatly facilitates mergers and acquisitions. Architecture standards are growing increasingly "open" too. This process will ultimately lead to a *federated network* of standards and controls to which all groups must ascribe. There will however be no single set of external controls. Instead, they will be established in a variety of places according to the type of control involved. Industry and technology groups will lead some standards efforts as will major players in a particular field (e.g., Microsoft, the US government). In addition, concerns for security and privacy will hasten legislation and both government and self-regulation in these areas. Organizations of all types will begin to cooperate, especially in the area of security. Companies can expect some form of federal government coordinating body will be established in this area by 2005. In short, standards and controls will increasingly come from a variety of places *outside* the organization for any type of computing that involves using the network. While internal standards and controls will still have a place, they will be relatively diminished by the greater need to establish an open network.

Internal Controls

In the 1980s, fed up with expensive systems disasters and unresponsive IT organizations, it was the accepted wisdom among managers that IT had to be brought under control (McKeen and Smith, 1996). Thus began a fascination with IT performance metrics that has lasted (in some form) up until the present day. In the 1990s, however, it became increasingly obvious that focusing on metrics alone resulted in some very poor systems with great metrics. Therefore, executives and researchers alike began to look at what *impact* information technology was actually having on the firm. They realized that simply delivering systems was not enough. The systems actually had to be beneficial to the organization. Thus, over the last decade, both IT and business departments have been increasingly held accountable for what a system contributes to the bottom line of the business. Unfortunately, this has all too often been interpreted as cost savings, which are considerably easier to measure, than to increased revenues or new opportunities, which are often more nebulous and more difficult to attribute to the use of IT alone.

In the next decade, it is likely these simplistic measures will be refined and made more sophisticated. IT will be assessed not only according to its impact on the bottom line or even according to whether or not applications were delivered on time and on budget, although these will still be important. The major, internal yardstick in IT's future will be the *value* that it delivers to the enterprise. This will take many forms, such as the ability to offer new products and services, to become more competitive, to participate in new markets, to operate more effectively, and to develop new capabilities. While value will frequently be defined as new value, companies will also begin to realize that the ability to *leverage* existing people, technologies, and information more effectively also delivers value. In the past, once a system was developed IT management saw very little significance in the ongoing effort to maintain and upgrade it. Maintenance was seen largely as an overhead function—a necessary evil. Over the next five years, IT management will begin to recognize that companies can frequently exploit current applications of technology more extensively. IT organizations will therefore look for ways to use existing infrastructure and applications more fully to deliver some "quick hits" of value to the business.

Increasingly, delivering value will come to be seen as a team effort—something that cannot be done without the unique skills and abilities of both the IT and the business members of the team. Interestingly, however, identifying value in advance will continue to remain an elusive skill. While there will be great successes in installing a particular piece of hardware or functionality in a particular company, there will be no guarantees that adopting it will yield the same value in another company. This will refocus management's attention more fully on the non-technical aspects of value. Capabilities, cultures, and management themselves will increasingly come under the microscope to determine how they contribute to the value that can be derived from IT.

IT Staffing

It has always been a challenge for IT to acquire the right mix of skills in its IT staff. During the 1980s, a number of different *specialists* were developed as technology became more and more complex. Unfortunately, handoffs between them became problematic. In the 1990s, therefore, there was a move to develop more *skilled generalists* who would be able to bring a set of systems skills and disciplines to specific situations and adapt, by learning, the specialized tools and techniques that are required. While this helped certain business-facing parts of IT (e.g., project management and systems analysis), the need for highly skilled specialists in certain "hot" areas remained. In 1996, we suggested that "careful attention must be paid to the people resource if IT is to excel." Today, the rash of material around the IT "staffing crisis" (GartnerGroup, 1999b), combined with the focus group's personal experiences, suggests that these warnings have not been heeded. Staffing IT is and will continue to be a growing problem over the next five years.

With the explosion of IT work taking place at present, most organizations will face serious skills shortages over the next five years. As in the past, management will have to resort to hiring specialists from consulting firms to fill the need for high-demand technical skills. Over the next five years it will be essential for IT organizations to develop individuals' professional skills and recognize different career paths for different types of IT staff. The experts are predicting a growth in demand for such "soft" skills as relationship management, strategic and analytical thinking, and portfolio management (GartnerGroup, 1999a). They also suggest that the competencies needed by IT staff are expanding rapidly and include both technical and business skills. While focus group members agreed that these are and will be required, they also noted an ongoing need for specialists in key technology fields. Thus, over the next five years, it appears that, while the majority of IT staff in any particular organization will evolve to become *business technologists*, there will also remain a strong need for technical specialists, which companies will increasingly fill with skilled contractors.

Systems Development

In the last two decades, systems development has moved from a highly structured process to one that is more flexible and fluid according to the circumstances. During the 1990s, businesses placed increasing amounts of pressure on IT organizations to develop more adaptable systems in shorter delivery cycles. IT organizations responded by developing systems in smaller pieces, making greater use of prototypes, and providing users with more dynamic control over discretionary items, such as report and display formats, and even process logic. Thus, systems came to be developed in a more *evolutionary* fashion. During this time, the older style, structured systems development life cycle has been gradually abandoned in favor of an approach that marries strong project management disciplines with a much more eclectic and modular development approach that may include: packaged software, custom software, legacy software, and end-user tools. Development teams, also, look very unlike those of the past. Increasingly they are composed of equal numbers of users and technical staff (including contractors). Pieces of systems are often developed separately by teams of consultants or specialists in a particular area (e.g., telecommunications, Web-development) and then plugged in. Proprietary data files, owned by a system, are mostly things of the past.

In the new decade, these trends in systems development will continue to escalate as the pressures increase for faster development and more functionality. To address these, over the next five years systems development will increasingly become a matter of *assembling* system pieces rather than coding new software. More and more systems developers will try to cobble existing software and tools together with new technology to create new value for the organization. In addition, knowledge management will become more and more important and a significant amount of development effort will revolve around acquiring or building the means to manipulate corporate and customer information. To this end, ongoing efforts will be made to standardize corporate data and processes so that the entire company has one look and feel to its systems. As bandwidth becomes less of a restriction, companies will begin to add more multimedia features to their systems. This, however, will not be a major feature of systems over the next five years. And, naturally, the Internet and its intranet and extranet siblings will play a huge part in all future development. Over the next five years, substantial efforts will be made to retrofit most existing corporate systems to make them accessible over the Internet and to make the company available to its customers around the clock.

With the IT staffing crisis looming large, IT organizations will also have to modify their development teams—making increasing use of external contractors for technological components and users to work on business requirements and interface issues. IT staff, with their strategic perspective and business technologist skills, will be required for their "big picture" view of the overall initiative. More and more, they will be used to maintain the linkages between the various parts of the development team through relationship management, coordination skills, and intelligent integration. A company's development staff will come to be utilized more to pull a variety of disparate people and platforms together to achieve a desired result and to identify and resolve problems and issues that threaten the delivery of the system than for the actual development of software. Thus, they will come to be seen much as general contractors in the construction industry. These people may do some of the actual building work, but they may not. However, they always assume responsibility for deadlines, relationship management, project management, and risk management.

Hardware/Software Management

Over the last decade, hardware and software management has become increasingly *confusing* for IT managers. The proliferation of hardware available and the increasing number of vendors has kept managers running hard just to keep up. Today, most IT organizations interact with a network of vendors for a variety of purposes. This has meant that the task of managing all the relationships involved, and sometimes managing the relationships between two vendors, has become a larger and larger challenge for IT.

Over the next five years, these trends will grow to a different level of intensity because of the impact that IT architectural decisions will have on the business. In the past, infrastructure was largely seen as a technical decision and best left to the experts. As organizations come to view infrastructure as strategic to the enterprise, hardware and software management decisions will become more and more visible in the organization. Thus, it will become a *minefield* for IT management, which could blow up in its face if it makes the wrong technology decision. For this reason, IT managers will begin to pay more serious attention to the development of technology strategy. This strategy will not simply make architectural decisions for the organization, however. It will also be devised to hedge against the wrong choices being made. Rather than investing in a single technology direction, organizations will begin to explore and develop options— to various degrees—in multiple technologies. Risk management will become much more fully refined in this area as a result, and companies will begin to look at their technology strategy as a portfolio of options rather than as a static, cast-in-concrete architecture.

In the Workplace

During the 1990s, IT organizations focused on developing an *automated office*. They ensured that all users were connected electronically in some way and had access to the basic software they needed in order to function. Many IT organizations developed a standard suite of office software and integrated corporate systems into office PCs when and where they were needed. Policies and standards were established to ensure that systems were kept secure and that viruses and non-approved software were not introduced. These practices worked reasonably well until the later part of the decade when the Internet opened organizations up to the world. Almost overnight, not only could employees communicate electronically with others outside the firm, customers and other companies could access the company—both its people and its systems. All of a sudden, the concept of a self-contained automated office appeared both quaint and dangerously out of date.

Over the next five years, the Internet will be the catalyst for changing the workplace. While many features of the future workplace have already been introduced (e.g., email, online access, multi-media, integrated software, partnerships with external organizations), they have not yet come together to change most offices in dramatic ways. This is about to change. In the near future, offices will open up more and more to the outside world until the workplace becomes truly *boundary-less*, and work is conducted in cyberspace rather than the workplace. Remote workers, mobile workers, home workers, networked workers, virtual workers will all become a reality over the next five years in many companies. Similarly, as companies themselves become boundary-less, the space in which they do business will also change from "bricks and mortar" to "clicks and mortar". IT will be kept busy enabling not only company functions, but also office support anywhere, anyplace, anytime since existing security and infrastructure will not be adequate to cope with the new demands. The workplace will perhaps see some of the most observable changes in organizations over the next five years. By 2005, through IT, the entire look and feel of a company to both its customers and its workers will be fundamentally changed and the virtual office will have arrived.

CONCLUSION

This chapter has explored the ongoing evolution of the IT function in the organization. In particular, it has tried to identify the ways in which key elements of the IT function will be different in the future than in the past. It has shown that IT is becoming increasingly central to corporate strategy in many ways. Not only will IT be making a major contribution to a firm's business and technical strategic visions for the future, it will also have a primary role in implementing and mobilizing these strategies. IT will therefore increasingly need to anticipate the company's future direction and to provide the information and infrastructure to ensure that the business will be in the right place at the right time. With the walls of the organization beginning to crumble and firms exploring new ways of working and delivering services to their customers, IT will be expected to act as the catalyst for this transformation. IT itself will also be changing to accommodate these needs with new ways of developing systems and partnering with other companies to deliver value to the organization. The pressures involved will place a significant strain on IT staff, and it is expected that recruiting the right types of business technologist for a company will be a considerable challenge. The next five years will not be easy ones, but they will be exciting as IT managers experiment with and explore ways to facilitate the organization of the 21st century.

REFERENCES

Amram, M. and N. Kulatilaka (1999) *Real Options: Managing Strategic Investment in an Uncertain World*, Harvard Business School Press, Boston.
Cameron, R. (2000) "The death of IT," *The Forrester Report*, January.
Dearden, J. (1987) "The withering away of the IT organization," *Sloan Management Review*, Summer 1987, **28**(4), 87–92.
GartnerGroup (1999a) "The role of the IS professional in the new millennium," Conference Presentation, ITxpo99, Orlando, Florida, 11–15 October.
GartnerGroup (1999b) "Workforce strategies," Conference Presentation, ITxpo99, Orlando, Florida, 11–15 October.
GartnerGroup (1999c) "Compelling workplace," Conference Presentation, ITxpo99, Orlando, Florida, 11–15 October.
Marron, K. (2000) "IT department faces extinction," *The Globe and Mail*, 30 March.
Maruca, R.F. (2000) "Are CIOs obsolete?" *Harvard Business Review*, March–April.
McKeen, J. and H. Smith (1996) *Management Challenges in IS: Successful Strategies and Appropriate Action*, John Wiley & Sons, Chichester, UK.
Tapscott, D., D. Ticoll and A. Lowy (2000) *Digital Capital: Harnessing the Power of Business Webs*, Harvard Business School Press, Boston.

Material for this chapter has been taken from previously published work by Smith and McKeen in *The Make or Break Issues in IT Management: A Guide to 21st Century Effectiveness* (edited by Dan Remenyi and Anne Brown), Butterworth-Heinemann, Oxford, 2002, pp. 157–174. Reproduced by permission of Elsevier Science, Ltd.

2
Managing the Social Impacts of Technology

The future of our organizations and our social institutions is, in many ways, in the hands of IT managers.

While most people would have rejected this statement out of hand even five years ago, today, many recognize that it now reflects a significant grain of truth. What has made the difference in our understanding? The short answer is: pervasive systems. Today, it is difficult to avoid information technology (IT). The Internet and mobile computing as well as technology's increasing power have vastly increased both the reach and the depth of technology in our lives. They are entering into human lives and relationships in an unprecedented fashion, and it is frequently IT managers who first grasp the implications of the changes resulting from new forms of technology.

The most obvious impact is on work. IT not only changes *how* we work, it changes *where* we work and with whom. Increasingly, work involves interacting with technology in some way, and often our working relationships are mediated through technologies such as email, groupware, mobile computing, and the Internet. Thanks to technology, work itself is moving beyond traditional company boundaries to include an increasing number of external electronic interactions such as transactions and supply chain integration. As a result, our external working relationships with partners, contractors, vendors, and even competitors are becoming more significant.

With these changes in work come a new set of changes in organizational behaviors and values that companies frequently don't recognize or manage well, at least initially. First, there are a whole series of issues around managing work when it is done outside the office. Then, there are the challenges of family–work balance. When a worker can be available 24/7 anywhere, where and how should the line be drawn between the two? Increasingly, too, there are questions concerning an employee's use of company technology for personal use. The recent case of an officer who was disciplined for using an armed services computer on his own time and with his own Internet account to view pornography illustrates the fine moral line that organizations must walk. Finally, there are privacy issues to consider. How much should a company intrude on its employees' private emails and other activities, now that technology is available to do so? These and many other questions are leading us to develop new social expectations as well as new human resource (HR) practices and policies surrounding technology.

This chapter explores how organizations are handling these social issues. The first section describes IT's impact on work—both on how and where it is done—and on how it is managed. The second section describes IT's impact on the organization, including its internal and external structures. Finally, the effects these changes are having on company policies, norms, and values and as well as the work–life balances are examined.

IT'S IMPACT ON WORK

As IT takes over most routine types of processing, we are increasingly moving into an information economy where knowledge is becoming a larger part of all aspects of organizational life. This is fundamentally changing the nature of work. Much professional work today is already knowledge work. In the near future, the sphere of knowledge work will enlarge until most workers will be responsible for contributing new insights and facilitating the implementation of new ideas. Analysis and sense-making will be key skills to leverage the knowledge of a company (Horwitt and Condon, 1996; Webber, 1993). Some experts suggest that, as computers become more intuitive, skill with particular kinds of technology will become less important and new disciplines of questioning and improving on how things are done will become more important (Solomon, 1998). Clearly, however, information-sharing and critical thinking will be essential capabilities for all workers (Drucker, 1988a).

To facilitate such new kinds of insight and question, work is becoming less structured and the company organization chart fuzzier. The ways people interact and go about work are changing. Jobs today require multiple skills, tasks, and responsibilities, and competencies are changing. Now and in the future, the tasks, projects, and alliances of organizations will take place in a radically different conceptual framework where people will be linked by technology and by what they know rather than by their job titles or ranks (Barner, 1996; Jones et al., 1995; Greengard, 1998).

The combination of IT and increasing business pressures is also driving organizations to experiment with a variety of alternatives to the traditional office environment. Alternative forms of work are being touted as ways to attract and motivate talented staff, make existing staff more productive, and save money. For example, some firms are dispensing with the office and becoming either partially or completely virtual. (A virtual organization presents its customers with the appearance of being a traditional company but may not in reality be a single company, or operate out of a single office.)

Alternative forms of work are growing rapidly. In 1998, approximately 40 million people in the USA were either telecommuters (i.e., working part-time from home) or full-time home-based workers, and these numbers are growing annually (Apgar, 1998). Many others are fully or partially mobile. Furthermore, a large number of firms are now also using a blended workforce—a mix of core and temporary staff combined with personnel from their suppliers and partners (Crandall and Wallace, 1998). In this, IT departments have led the way, but other parts of the organization are rapidly catching on. Today, an organization's workforce can consist of many different types of staff including: full-time, part-time, mobile, telecommuting, global, contract, consultants, and outsourcers.

Traditional workplaces are changing too—whether they like it or not—because organizations that are networked through email and other technologies work fundamentally differently from those that aren't. These technologies irrevocably alter the nature of managerial authority and work, and inspire a new, informal style of operations that circumvents old-style hierarchies, supercharges social networks, and crosses functional boundaries (Stewart, 1994).

Today, most organizations are trying to develop an appropriate mix of traditional and alternative working arrangements (Davenport and Pearlson, 1998). Technology or cost-saving should never be the sole justification for implementing new ways of working. Changes must be made for the right reasons, and people must be able to put them in the context of their company's purpose, mission, and values (Alford, 1999). Most focus group companies are finding that the successful and effective use of new ways of working requires careful analysis of how and where traditional jobs as well as management policies and practices need to be adapted and modified. Typically, making the change to an alternative form of work will be both a management and an HR decision.

Companies utilize one or more of the following alternative working arrangements (Davenport and Pearlson, 1998):

Telecommuting. With this alternative, workers do occasional work from home. This is by far the most common alternative and requires the least amount of managerial change.

Hoteling. In this arrangement, workers who only need to come to an office occasionally do not have fixed office space. They work where they are needed and can reserve a space in the office when necessary.

Tethering. Here, while workers come regularly to an office, mobile technology enables them to roam around the office or nearby, as needed.

Home work. In this alternative, workers function from a home office and only meet with their co-workers on a periodic basis.

Mobile work. Here, workers are on the road almost constantly and interact largely with customers at their offices.

IT'S IMPACT ON MANAGEMENT

While IT is clearly both a driver and a facilitator of new ways of working, it is a common misconception among many managers that providing the right electronic tools, such as email and databases, is all they need to do to make them happen. However, nothing could be further from the truth:

> Business is . . . a highly personal activity and we don't yet have tools that can fully replace the richness of face-to-face contact. When you lose the synergy that comes from daily informal contact, you risk alienating workers from one another and from the company's goals (Pape, 1996).

As a result, already companies are discovering that it is the "human factors" associated with modern work that make the difference between success and failure on most initiatives (Geber, 1995). They are also learning that failure to manage work effectively in a contemporary organization with its wide variety of working relationships can lead to disastrous results (Pape, 1996; Fritz and Manheim, 1998). Conversely, if properly managed, new ways of working can also be the source of significant business benefits (Fritz and Manheim, 1998).

As companies grow increasingly dependent on their human assets, several management capabilities are becoming more and more critical:

• *Making connections.* A key fear of workers who operate outside company boundaries is the loss of visibility. Remote workers often feel they are missing out on critical business advances. Effective managers therefore work actively to counteract this feeling. They provide frequent updates about what's happening in the company; they give all individuals a chance to participate in planning processes; and they communicate what individuals are doing to the rest of the group. As one manager commented on how his people management style has changed as a result, "I have to do things differently now. I can't just walk around to supervise people and call a meeting whenever I think one is needed . . . This would favor team members working in my office and alienate those who work at other sites" (Geber, 1995). People still working in the office also need to be trained how to work with and include those working outside the office (Davenport and Pearlson, 1998), and efforts need to be made to include enough face-to-face contact between dispersed workers to build relationships and trust (Greengard, 1998).

- *Leading and modeling.* Managers (and the company through its HR policies) need to make a clear personal commitment to making alternative working arrangements successful (Alford, 1999). They must give people time to consider the experience of change and to understand its implications. They should also recognize that not everyone is able to adapt to changes in working conditions and give individuals an accurate picture of the opportunities, implications, and expectations involved (Grenier and Metes, 1995).
- *Communicating.* Many companies have found that the managerial skills that become most important in new forms of working are those that revolve around old-fashioned human contact (Stewart, 1994). As working arrangements become more varied, focus group members noted that it becomes easy for managers to slip into task-oriented communication and to omit relationship-building communication. Managers need to design ways to improve all forms of communication and information flow when not all staff members are working the same hours or in the same locations. Staff need to be trained how to access and use electronic tools, share information virtually, and to become more effective providers and consumers of information (Davenport and Pearlson, 1998). Managers must also recognize that the new and more numerous communications pathways of networked organizations may bypass them and the traditional corporate hierarchy. They need to let staff know that this type of communication is okay and that they have the right to seek out whatever information they need to do their job effectively. Conversely, managers also need to deal with "info glut" where they receive so much information they cannot deal with it all. Finally, it is interesting to note that, as workplaces become more flexible, there is a corresponding need to *increase* traditional forms of communication (e.g., newsletters, visits).
- *Building trust.* Focus group members agreed that trust forms the basis for almost all new ways of working. The foundation of effective teamwork is the ability of people to develop personal trust in each other. In order for an organization to truly exploit the potential of workplace flexibility therefore, it must trust its employees and they must trust each other (Stewart, 1994). Trust has at least two dimensions: *personal trust*—the understanding that people must establish with each other to deal with the issues and challenges that inevitably arise during work; and *competence*—the trust that comes from performance (Geber, 1995). Managers must facilitate both kinds of trust. They must find ways to ensure that all staff members have both the opportunities they need to interact and develop personal trust relationships and the abilities to do what they are expected to do. Managers also have a responsibility to develop measurements to make sure people are meeting their commitments (i.e., a philosophy of "trust but verify"). And when this is not the case, managers must deal with the problem quickly and firmly.
- *Relationship building.* No matter how remotely people work, managers must find ways to develop good relationships between team members. The most important means of doing this is through face-to-face contact. At Verifone, a

completely virtual company, for example, senior managers meet personally every six to eight weeks. Some firms, such as PricewaterhouseCoopers, have people work together for a few weeks before moving into a virtual situation. Others arrange regular times for dispersed team members to get together. Indeed, many practitioners do not believe that a virtual team can be successful without personal contact (Geber, 1995). When necessary, managers should also find other ways to compensate for the loss of daily face-to-face contact. Videoconferencing and telephone calls are common means of doing this. Other tactics include developing an online chat area for informal employee schmoozing and allowing the creation of personal home pages. Furthermore, teams also need norms and facilitation about how to disagree virtually, when the inevitable conflicts arise (Pape, 1996; Geber, 1995).

Advice for managers

- *Alternative work must be designed for a particular organization.* There is no one right answer for every company as to what forms of alternative work to adopt. Instead, organizations should aim for a mix of work arrangements that are tailored to their needs.

- *Invest in tools, training, and techniques to support new forms of work.*

- *Aim for a holistic approach to alternative work.* Isolated efforts such as empowerment, self-directed teams, re-engineering, total quality management, telecommuting, job sharing, networking, and flattening the organization are not going to work in and of themselves.

- *Expect staff members to do their parts.* Workers themselves have important roles to play. Changes can be killed just as effectively from below as above (Shostak, 1998). Traditional staff and organized labour attitudes to work (e.g., "It isn't in my job description") must also adapt to changing times.

IT'S IMPACT ON ORGANIZATIONS

According to some authors (Ruhleder et al., 1996; Tapscott, 1993), new technology, new enterprise models, a new business environment, and a new geopolitical environment are converging and recreating almost everything we have traditionally "understood" about organizations. In the next decade, we will increasingly work differently, run companies differently, change how we measure and achieve organizational value, and even transform our products.

Why is this happening? To understand this, we must understand the key role that technology and information are playing in business transformation. Change at all levels is being driven by the transformation of our society from an industrial economy to an information economy (Vogt, 1995). Networked, modular, and open (i.e., interconnectable) technology is leading to a freer and freer exchange of information between people, businesses, and nations. This, in turn, is leading to increasingly interconnected global economic development, new economic alliances and rules, and the liberalization of developing economies (Hitt et al., 1998; Rondeau, 1999), commonly referred to as *globalization*. Together, information technology and globalization are reinventing marketplaces, threatening regulatory environments, challenging the traditional ways business has been conducted (Tapscott, 1993, 1995; Hitt et al., 1998) and driving deregulation of industry and instability in the old political order (Rondeau, 1999; Tapscott, 1993).

Faced with these new conditions, businesses have little choice but to change both internally and externally (Drucker, 1988b; Tapscott, 2000). Internally, the advent of massive amounts of information and technology has meant that organizations *must* engage in information analysis or risk being swamped by data. However, "as soon as a company takes the first tentative steps from data to information, its decision processes, management structure, and even the way work gets done begin to be transformed" (Drucker, 1988a). This transformation began slowly; the information economy is already about 40 years old, and it is only just now coming to fruition with its own economic and organizational models (Davis, 1996). What has been missing until recently is the networking of technology and information beyond the boundaries of the organization (Tapscott, 1993, 1998). With the advent of the Internet and other networking technologies, the last pieces of the puzzle are now available. Thus, in the future, the impact of the information economy will be increasingly revolutionary, as new infrastructures are developed to harness the power of worldwide information. While more traditionally based organizational models most likely will not collapse overnight, they will decline in scope and importance and find themselves increasingly left behind.

IT's Impact on Internal Structures

The hierarchical, industrial corporation of the 20th century was designed for the technologies of the time. With the introduction of personal computing devices and networking—the technologies of the 21st century—the mechanisms of coordination began to change, leading in turn to a change in the shape and nature of the organization (Malone, 1998). Some of the areas in which this is occurring in organizations include size, design, and function:

- *Size.* The ability to share information instantly and inexpensively across time and space decreases the importance of centralized decision-making and bureaucracy for delivering value (Malone, 1998). Smaller organizations will thus become "better" because they are less expensive and more flexible. New coordination technologies will enable smaller companies to enjoy many of the benefits of larger ones without giving up the leanness, flexibility, and creativity of being small (Malone, 1998). In spite of the current spate of mergers and acquisitions, many people believe that large companies will tend to disintegrate into smaller businesses or at least semi-autonomous business units as they attempt to focus on what they do well and get out of doing commodity-like work that can be given away to someone else (Caldwell, 1996).

- *Design.* The three primary structures of the 21st century organization—Internetworked enterprises, teams and individuals, and business webs—will each be facilitated by technology (Tapscott, 2000). Instead of being designed around functions, departments, and individuals, they will be organized around networks, teams, competencies, and infrastructures both internally and across organizational boundaries. This will lead to a variety of new business models all designed to put together the capital—especially the knowledge capital—of the organization in new ways.

- *Function.* Technology facilitates the development of new structures and enables them to draw upon the resources they need regardless of where they are located and who owns them. Thus, managing and developing human capital will play a relatively more important role than in the past. A second, significant organizational function will be the development of the internal and external environments where work takes place. Finally, firms will have to learn how to aggregate, disaggregate, and reconfigure assets quickly in order to respond to competitive conditions (Hitt et al., 1998).

IT's Impact on External Structures

Technology also facilitates new levels of coordination beyond company boundaries (Matthews, 1996). As a result, companies are today viewing their role, responsibilities, and interactions in a much broader setting than in the past. Organizations now participate in a variety of relationships with other organizations, both inside and outside their industries, to accomplish a number of operational and strategic goals, such as:

1. *External sourcing and alliances.* Using technology as an interface, many companies are seeking the integration of functions that reach beyond the organization's boundaries. For example, there could be substantial customizing of products or services by suppliers. At the other end of the value chain, companies are also linking themselves much more tightly to their customers to better anticipate demand and provide improved customer service. Both trends result in an organization that is much more responsive to its customers and more adaptable to market conditions.

2. *Partnerships and joint ventures.* This type of external structure involves setting up an external entity with one or more partner organizations for the benefit of all the partners. Typically, this entity is focused on developing and supplying a product, a service, or a technology. The companies involved are frequently

competitors who work together, sharing expertise and costs, to develop or create something they all need.

3. *Networks.* In a network structure, common business functions typically conducted within a single organization are performed by independent organizations working in collaboration. Activities are coordinated by information systems and a generally agreed structure of payment for value added. Technology also monitors performance.

4. *Business webs.* Ultimately, as electronic communication and e-commerce become ubiquitous, networks will grow and develop increasingly complex forms. Tapscott (2000) suggests that we will increasingly see companies identify a customer value proposition and build an appropriate system of suppliers, distributors, commerce services providers, infrastructure providers, and customers to make it profitable. A lead firm will control core elements of the value proposition, such as customer relationships, value creation coordination, management processes, and intellectual property. Partners will take care of everything else.

Advice for managers

The business, technology, and social changes now occurring will shape and constrain the necessities and possibilities for all future organizational activity. They are inextricably intertwined with each other and with the picture of the organization of the 21st century. While we can see the broad outlines of where organizations are going, managers still face a daunting task of trying to fill in a huge number of blank spaces and of transforming generic trends into something that works for their particular enterprise. To learn more about what will affect this future state, IT managers should:

- continually assess their environment not only from a technological point of view but also from a social and competitive perspective;

- experiment with new coordination mechanisms both internally and externally.

IT'S IMPACT ON HUMAN RESOURCE (HR) POLICIES AND BUSINESS BEHAVIOR

IT's Impact on HR policies

Most new forms of working arrangement have a significant number of human implications making HR's job more complex (Fritz and Manheim, 1998). Many organizations have concerns about controlling and coordinating what gets accomplished when people work non-standard hours and in a wide variety of locations. They worry about how to structure, control, and evaluate work and managing such things as communications, security, and productivity at a distance or across functional or organizational boundaries. Traditional HR policies are obviously inadequate for managing new forms of work, although many senior managers and HR departments are only gradually becoming more aware of the HR implications of alternative forms of work and new organizational structures. Unfortunately, focus group members felt that many HR policies still directly mitigate against the effective use of new ways of working. For example, compensation systems often reward individual success while companies are trying to encourage and promote teamwork. HR departments will have to reassess their policies continually to ensure that they are in keeping with how work and organizations are changing (Greengard, 1998). Table 2.1 gives an overview of the areas that HR should monitor.

Work–Life balance

New forms of work and organization have important implications for people's personal lives as well. New technologies have a tendency to speed up the pace of life. This was noticed as long ago as the 1870s with the introduction of the telegraph (Standage, 1998). While technology is often blamed for a host of ills, in many cases, how people react to new technologies can be found in age-old human tendencies rather than in the technologies themselves. Typically, the potential of a new technology to change things for the better is invariably overstated, while the ways in which they will make things worse are usually unforeseen. IT's impact on work–life balance is a case in point. While there are obvious benefits to having more mobile, flexible work, there are also down sides, which organizations and individuals are just beginning to recognize.

New ways of working require considerable individual self-discipline in dealing with the work–life balance. Although many people are initially concerned that they might give the company short shrift if they are not in an office, research shows that the opposite is more often true. Many home-based and mobile workers feel considerable stress at never being able to leave their jobs behind (Davenport and Pearlson, 1998). Thus, they are having to learn how to cope with this *mobility paradox* and decide when and where they should disconnect electronically (Apgar, 1998).

Maintaining a healthy work–life balance requires honesty by both workers and the company to ensure that alternative forms of work are effective for both. However, focus group members have found that a successful work–life balance lies largely in the staff member's ability to draw the line between work and home and to be confident that the line is in the right place. Often employees feel guilty about the amount of freedom they have; sometimes they feel that they are never free of the "electronic leash"; others find alternative work to be liberating. Experts agree that achieving an appropriate work–life balance requires an ongoing effort until both sides are comfortable it has been reached (Apgar, 1998).

Table 2.1   *Areas of HR responsibility that need to be assessed and/or redeveloped.*

Responsibility	HR should develop	Goal
Staffing	Improved recruiting, evaluation, and termination processes for different types of staff	The right mix of skills and flexibility
Compensation	"Soft" performance measures for workers. Pay for value delivered, rather than on an hourly or a salaried basis according to hierarchical position	New ways of overseeing employee productivity and of measuring and compensating workers' contributions
Orientation	Policies and practices that reflect and reinforce the organization's culture	To unify an organization's culture with a diverse workforce operating out of many locations. To make it easier to change
Monitoring	Appropriate use of electronic monitoring and performance enhancement systems	Employee motivation and development, *not* increased stress
Training	Programs in how to work from home, planning, and maintaining good communications	To make new ways of working function effectively
Infrastructure	Redesigned/More flexible job descriptions, methods of promotion, means of determining who qualifies for a job and benefits	To accommodate the needs of a mobile and dispersed workforce
Checks and balances	Means to identify how and where alternative work is successful and under what conditions it should be terminated or modified	To ensure productive and satisfied staff
Human interaction	Mechanisms to promote and encourage human interaction	To build the relationships and trust on which a 21st century organization will thrive

IT's Impact on Business Behavior

With work becoming more transitory and mobile, companies have to find ways to rapidly educate all types of staff on company values and culture and to provide a context for understanding the work of the organization. When workers are not located in a central office, this task becomes even more challenging. It is now clear to most companies that enabling flexible work technically is just the beginning.

Companies are finding that most people need coaching in the basic protocols of alternative work as well (Apgar, 1998). Therefore, many organizations have developed formal policies and guidelines dealing with the company's expectations for alternative forms of work; others provide formal training. Most firms offer flexible work as a privilege, not a right, and monitor performance closely. If either the staff member or the manager believes the job is not working, flexibility is reduced or terminated.

O'Shea (2001) suggests that businesses will move through five stages in their use of technology:

1. *Plaything*. Here, a few people try out the technology and it is seen as essentially a toy (e.g., data phones).
2. *Substitution*. At this stage, new technology is used occasionally as a substitute for other ways of working, but use is heavily restricted and requires strong justification (e.g., videoconferencing).
3. *Enhancement*. Here, the technology becomes normal equipment for certain workers because it is recognized that it extends availability and improves productivity. Work is carried on in much the same way as always but the accessibility of staff has improved (e.g., the mobile phone).
4. *Transformation*. At this stage, work (and living) is done differently as a result of technology (e.g., telecommuting).
5. *Transparency*. Here the technology becomes ubiquitous and is so well integrated into how we live and work that it is no longer remarkable (e.g., email).

New forms of technology are frequently implemented before norms and values can be established as to how to deal with them in a business environment. As a result, awkward situations can arise, such as the one mentioned above where the officer and his employer, each acting in good faith, conflicted on the appropriate standards of behavior for Internet usage. By now, most companies have found it necessary to establish formal policies for what is and is not suitable to view on the Internet and have enforced them with electronic monitoring. Similarly, all focus group member firms have policies governing the ownership of email. However, behavior for other forms of technology is still up in the air. For example, most firms are still uncertain about controlling personal use of business technology such as mobile phones and laptops. While some ban personal use altogether, others recognize that the melding of home and personal life mean that some non-business use is acceptable. The newest challenge is the use of instant messaging and cell phones in meetings, which some find rude and disruptive. Some companies have banned them outright from meetings; others are using informal methods, such as disapproval to control this practice. And all focus group members expressed the need for staff to control themselves regarding the indiscriminate use of email, resulting in a glut of unnecessary messages that must be read.

Technological networks broaden the number of business relationships possible and tend to make them more superficial and task-oriented (Stewart, 1994). Therefore, today companies are having to rediscover the importance of relationship-building to success. Whether these are relationships inside the firm or with external partners or service providers, personal contact is the key. Thus, firms are beginning to realize the importance of socialization among widely dispersed groups of workers to help co-workers size each other up and develop trust. Today, socializing is becoming recognized as a valuable exercise that creates a sense of belonging and develops the necessary relationships to make remote and cross-functional work successful.

Advice for managers

- Identify and document HR policies that mitigate against new forms of working.

- Monitor satisfaction with work–life balance—especially among mobile and home-based workers.

- Ensure that time for socialization is built in to meetings and gatherings.

- Make behavioral expectations for the use of technology explicit.

- Use electronic monitoring judiciously and only after thorough testing. While not always possible, employees should be involved in most performance-monitoring.

- Monitor the effectiveness of new HR policies and have a mechanism to evolve them as needed.

No matter how a workforce is organized, communication is fundamental to its effectiveness. "How [team members] communicate and what they voluntarily communicate are as important as the advanced knowledge [they] may have" (Quinn et al., 1996). Widely dispersed teams need both more formal mechanisms of communication than co-located teams and a range of informal opportunities to force communication to take place. Tactics such as making people overlap on different teams, keeping hierarchical roles purposely ill-defined, using the compensation system to encourage information-sharing, and having team evaluations are all methods that are recommended for motivating ongoing communication (Quinn et al., 1996; Despres and Hiltrop, 1996).

With work itself becoming more flexible and workers more empowered to make decisions, the organization's role is changing. Its job is increasingly to establish the "rules of the game" without which business cannot take place. By creating the common vision, sense of direction, and understanding of values, ethics, and standards, it can establish an environment within which people will be able to organize themselves, with technology, in a variety of different ways to deliver value to the firm (Webber, 1993).

CONCLUSION

We often hear that science and technology will reshape society over the next 30 years, and that the convergence and ubiquity of information technologies will have a huge impact on the nature of work. It would be understandable therefore if some managers were skeptical about the extent of these claims given the limited impact of IT in organizations over the past 30 years (Tapscott, 1993). However, in the future we will see dramatic changes in technology that will fundamentally alter what can be done with it. As we have seen, new technological capabilities are behind most if not all business changes that are occurring today. However, it is important to note that technology is facilitating these changes, not causing them. Technology and business change go hand in hand; it is *how* technology is used in business and how people interact with and manage it that will determine the ultimate impact of technology (Sommet sur la TI et l'économie du savoir, 1997; Vogt, 1995; Coates, 1994). This is why the decisions made now in implementing technology in organizations will make such a difference to organizations in the future.

REFERENCES

Alford, R.J. (1999) "Going virtual, getting real," *Training & Development*, January, 34–44.

Apgar, M., III (1998) "The Alternative Workplace," *Harvard Business Review*, May–June 1998, 121–136.

Barner, R. (1996) "The new millennium workplace: Seven changes that will challenge managers and workers," *The Futurist*, March–April, **30**, 14–18.

Caldwell, B. (1996) "Computer services—the new outsourcing partnership—vendors want to provide more than just services. They'll help you create a virtual corporation," *Techsearch Results*, June, **585**.

Coates, J. (1994) "83 assumptions about the year 2025," *The Highly Probable Future*, 1–7.

Crandall, N.F. and M.J. Wallace (1998) "Getting to the new deal in the virtual workforce," *Work and Rewards*, 239–250.

Davenport, T.H. and K. Pearlson (1998) "Two cheers for the virtual office," *Sloan Management Review*, Summer, **39**(4), 51–65.

Davis, S. (1996) "Rumble, rumble," *Training & Development*, November, **50**, 44–45.

Despres, C. and J.M. Hiltrop (1996) "Compensation for technical professionals in the knowledge area," *Research Technology Management*, September–October.

Drucker, P.F. (1988a) "Management and the world's work," *Harvard Business Review*, September–October, 2–9.

Drucker, P.F. (1988b) "The coming of the new organization," *Harvard Business Review*, January–February, 3–11.

Fritz, M.B. and M. Manheim (1998) "Managing virtual work: A framework for managerial action," in P. Sieber and J. Griese (eds), *Organizational Virtualness*, pp. 123–132, Simona Verlag Bern, Bern, Switzerland.

Geber, B. (1995) "Virtual teams," *Training*, April.

Greengard, S. (1998) "How technology will change the workplace," *Workforce*, January, 74–78.

Grenier, R. and G. Metes (1995) *Going Virtual*, Prentice Hall, Englewood Cliffs, NJ.

Hitt, M., B. Keats, and S. DeMarie (1998) "Navigating in the new competitive landscape: Building strategic flexibility and competitive advantage in the 21st Century," *Academy of Management Review*, **12**(4), 22–42.

Horwitt, E. and R. Condon (1996) "Right here, right now," *Computerworld*, 9 September, 20–24.

Jones, J., R. Reid, and R. Moomaugh (1995) "A look into the future: The 2020 organization," *Reid Moomaugh & Associates*, http://www.improve.org/2020org.html#The 2020 Organization Context (current July 2002).

Malone, T.W. (1998) "Inventing the organization of the twenty-first century: Control, empowerment, and information technology," in Bradley and Nolan, *Sense and Respond*, Harvard Business School Press, Boston.

Mathews, J. (1996) "Holonic organisational architectures," *Human Systems Management*, **15**(1), 1–29.

O'Shea, D. (2001) "The 3G mobile phone: A manager's guide," *Harvard Management Communication Letter*, Reprint No. C0101D.

Pape, W. (1996) "Remote control," *INC—The Magazine for Growing Companies*, 15 September.

Quinn, J.B., P. Anderson, and S. Finkelstein (1996) "Managing professional intellect: Making the most of the best," *Harvard Business Review*, March–April, 25–27.

Rondeau, A. (1999) "Transformer l'organisation. Comprendre les forces qui façonnent l'organisation et le travail," *Revue Gestion*, **24**(3), Autumn, 148–157 [in French].

Ruhleder, K., B. Jordan, and M. Elmes (1996) "Wiring the new organization: Integrating collaborative technologies and team-based work," presented at the 1996 Annual Meeting of the Academy of Management.

Shostak, A.B. (1998) "Virtual corporations and American labor unions: So many unknowns, so much potential," in M. Igbaria and M. Tan (eds), *The Virtual Workplace*, pp. 360–367, Idea Group Publishing, Hershey, PA.

Soloman, C. (1998) "Sharing information across borders and time zones," *Workforce*, March.

Sommet sur la TI et l'économie du savoir (1997) "Le Canada et l'économie du savoir," *Strategis*, décembre, **3**.

Standage, T. (1998) *The Victorian Internet*, Berkeley Books, New York.

Stewart, T.A. (1994) "Managing in a wired company," *Fortune*, 11 July, 44–56.

Tapscott, D. (1993) *Paradigm Shift: The New Promise of Technology*, McGraw-Hill, New York.

Tapscott, D. (1995) *The Digital Economy: Promise and Peril in the Age of Networked Intelligence*, McGraw-Hill, Toronto.

Tapscott, D., D. Ticoll, and A. Lowy (2000) *Digital Capital, Harnessing the Power of Business Webs*, Harvard Business School Press, Boston.

Vogt, E. (1995) "The nature of work in 2010," *Telecommunications*, International edition, September.

Webber, A.W. (1993) "What's so new about the new economy?" *Harvard Business Review*, January–February, 4–11.

3
Managing External
Relationships*

The need to manage external relationships is not new. What is new is that managing external relationships has become much more complex and critical to an organization's success. Three factors are primarily responsible for these changes. The first is the organizational trend toward the expansion of IT activities and responsibilities. The second factor is the proliferation of technology platforms (both software and hardware) that have worked their way into organizations. The third factor is the change within the IT industry—IT organizations are stocked with legacy staff, experienced staff are difficult to hire, and the demand for specialized skills/services is enormous. Because of these factors, IT managers have come to the realization that they can no longer be all things to all people and that IT should, in many cases, be a service *coordinator* as well as a service *provider*. The result has been the necessity for IT organizations to deal with a veritable host of suppliers.

One IT organization discovered that it was currently managing 147 different relationships with various independent service providers including hardware vendors, body shops, service bureaus, skills trainers, consultants, and boutique firms ... not to mention a multitude of software product vendors. Without a management structure in place to direct these activities, they were getting out of control. In one instance, they had two independent ongoing projects—one being done by a hardware vendor and the other by a systems integrator. The two projects needed to be integrated. When that time arrived, it was discovered that the two suppliers had used different approaches, different conventions, different methodologies, and different languages.

This chapter describes the nature of external relationships, groups them into

* A version of this chapter appeared in the *Proceedings of the 34th Hawaii Conference on Systems Science*, Maui. HI, 5–8 January 2001, IEEE Computer Society, NJ.

categories, and presents a number of strategies for managing external relationships effectively.

THE IMPETUS FOR EXTERNAL RELATIONSHIPS

Before discussing the nature of external relationships, it is important to understand the main reasons that organizations are establishing so many relationships with so many different providers. The push toward building external relationships springs from two opposing forces: the need for greater functionality from the IT department in ever-shortening cycles coupled with the reluctance to expand the IT staff on a permanent basis. These two forces provide the organizational context within which the decision to look externally for help is taken.

The need for increased functionality is driven by the level of competition in the marketplace. Organizations can no longer afford to wait 12 to 18 months for delivery of IT solutions. The organization may not survive that long. One group member pointed out that his industry faces seasonal deadlines for many of their products. Delivery deadlines of 12 to 18 months would dictate "flying two years ahead of their customers" and his business was not able to do this. With information technology playing such a major role in the delivery of today's services and products, few business initiatives are able to go forward without the support of IT.

One obvious way to meet the need for increased functionality is to expand IT staff. With few exceptions, the focus group felt that this was not a viable option. Expansion of the *permanent* IT staff is not in keeping with the restructuring initiatives in place throughout their organizations. At the same time, it is clear that the business expects to have to pay more for faster delivery of IT functionality. That is, the case against expanding the permanent workforce is not necessarily financial. Despite its slightly incongruent appearance, this organizational bias exists and predisposes organizations to view the establishment of external relationships favorably. According to a member of the focus group, the driving factor is "the need to be flexible, not frugal."

THE NATURE OF EXTERNAL RELATIONSHIPS

"External relationships" is a very general term and encompasses many different types of negotiated arrangement (Lacity and Willcocks, 1998). The decision to adopt this term reveals our intention to understand the full range of external arrangements in which IT departments are engaging. We decided against the term "outsourcing" or its more recent counter-position of "insourcing" (Hirschheim and Lacity, 2000; Lacity and Hirschheim, 1995). Despite their popularity, there appears to be little agreement regarding these definitions. Furthermore, outsourcing appears to imply specific types of external relationships—Lacity and Hirschheim (1993) classify outsourcing into the following taxonomy: body shop, project management, and total outsourcing—and, because of this, we felt that its use might unduly limit the breadth of this discussion. It is important therefore to be clear about the term "external relationship".

Members of the group were asked to outline the types of IT function that were provided to their organizations by external suppliers. The list is varied and includes such activities as systems planning, training, application development, application support, computing, data entry, POS (point of sale) maintenance, security disaster recovery, network management, help desk, data communications, voice communications, PC support, and data center operations. A closer examination of these functions suggests they can be classified into an organizing framework whose two primary dimensions are *relationship type* and *delivery mechanism*. Three different types of external relationship emerged:

1. *Product-based* relationships having deliverables with physical attributes (e.g., an installed network).
2. *Service-based* relationships having deliverables that are process-oriented (e.g., training).
3. *Partnership-based* relationships having deliverables as the result of joint ventures where the parties involved work to deliver a product or a service. Unlike either a product-based relationship or a service-based relationship, neither party "hires" the other in a partnership-based relationship (e.g., two organizations co-develop a system for product-tracking).

Delivery mechanisms were categorized into two types:

1. *Project-based* delivery mechanisms referring to those relationships established and managed as a project (e.g., creating a customer database).
2. *Time-based* delivery mechanisms referring to those relationships established and managed according to the calendar (e.g., staffing a help desk for a year).

Table 3.1 categorizes various external relationships along these two dimensions and highlights some of the nuances among external relationships. For example, contracting externally to replace all the workstations in one area of a firm would be a product-based relationship with a project-based delivery mechanism. Contracting externally to keep all the workstations current (i.e., *evergreening*) would constitute a product-based relationship with a time-based delivery mechanism. Movement from cell to cell within the table has ramifications for contractual choices. Table 3.1 highlights the variety of external relationships into which organizations can enter. The extent of this variety shows why the term "outsourcing" is somewhat nebulous and why managing external relationships has taken on such importance for IT organizations.

INTERNAL VERSUS EXTERNAL?

It was clear from the group that the question was not whether organizations should be looking outside for support. All organizations represented within the

Table 3.1 *Classification of external relationships.*

Relationship type	Delivery mechanism	
	Project-based	Time-based
Product	Application development Network installation Purchased packages	Buying transactions Printing operations Credit report acquisition
Service	Skills training Systems planning Application support Overload programming	Help desk Security Disaster recovery Hardware maintenance Data entry
Partnership	Joint product development Acquisitions/Mergers Systems integration	Network sharing Data center management Research and development (R&D) Data communications

group were actively engaged in external contracting for various activities. As suggested previously, these organizations simply could not afford to wait for the additional functionality to be delivered by internal resources. The real question these organizations are wrestling with is *how to decide what should be kept internal and what should be negotiated externally.*

There has been an ongoing and sometimes heated debate surrounding this issue for some time. Current wisdom suggests that the best candidates for external suppliers are non-core activities. But what is a core activity? For some organizations, core activities are those that define the very nature of their business. For a retailer whose motto is "having the right goods at the right price at the right time", core activities would imply the buying function, the marketing function, the distribution function, and the service function. This seems simple, but how would this retailer classify POS systems, 7/24 service call centers, logistical routing systems, order replenishment systems, store inventory systems, network management activities, or in-store radio frequency systems? At the detail level, distinctions between core and non-core activities become problematic.

Some organizations have taken a different approach. They distinguish "strategic competitive" systems from "strategic necessity" systems. This explicitly recognizes the fact that *all* systems are vital for the continued health of the organization—it is just that strategic competitive systems are expected to provide competitive advantage by generating additional revenues via new products/services or by significantly altering cost structures. Many systems do not do this, but are strategically necessary to the business. In a bank, for example, millions of transactions are enacted overnight—referred to as the "overnight miracle"—and every bank has to do this. Arguments can then be made for contracting those systems that are strategic necessities externally and keeping those that are strategic–competitive internal. This approach results in different decisions than would be made following the "core versus non-core" approach. Few would argue that updating banking transactions is a non-core activity for a bank, particularly when the sole function that a bank provides to the majority of its customers is the provision and maintenance of saving and checking accounts.

There were additional factors—cost savings and specialization—highlighted by the forum members. Organizations have come to the realization that, faced with a highly competitive marketplace and a dramatic rate of change, they can no longer be best at everything. Most organizations now realize that there are external providers who can accomplish certain tasks much more effectively, sometimes with remarkable cost savings possibly due to economies of scale. An example of this is the payroll function. Until fairly recently, the majority of organizations handled their own payroll function. Now, it has become common for these activities to be handled externally by banking institutions. Similar to the cost savings argument is the specialization argument. That is, most organizations now realize that they cannot have all the specialized skills they need in-house. The reasons for this are varied. In some cases, these specialties are fleeting (i.e., we need them to perform a certain function, but not on a continuing basis) while in other cases there is reluctance to expand the size of the IT function to accommodate extra areas of specialization.

Although the preceding arguments help to frame the discussion, they fail to move us closer to actually deciding what to keep inside and what to move to an outside provider. The remaining challenge is to develop decision criteria to establish the basis for this involvement. While it is easy to state that "core activities must be done internally", it is much more difficult to decide what actually constitutes a core activity. How should this be decided? Furthermore, whose decision is it to make? Should IT decide what a core activity is? Or should the business?

One group member felt that the distinction between core and non-core or between strategic–necessity and strategic–competitive was a business strategy issue, not an IT issue. Therefore, the business was asked to identify their key activities (i.e., those things they feel they must excel at in order to remain competitive). Using this list, IT then identified their internal processes that they need to excel at in order to support these key business activities. IT then staffed these key processes with the best IT people. Much of the work that was not deemed to be a key process/activity was offered to external suppliers to deliver. The IT organization was still accountable for ensuring service delivery to the business, but was not necessarily the provider of the actual service.

In order to determine the best resources available within IT, this organization assessed the skills and behaviors that they believed they required in the future. As part of performance reviews, the individual's future marketability (that is, his or her ability to meet the demands of a new competitive business environment where significant change in both the business and technology was the norm) was also assessed. Each IT employee was characterized with respect to his or her ability to:

- Embrace change—pushes the boundaries; challenges with suggestions and better ideas; fosters innovation; and moves the organization forward.
- Take responsibility for self-development—has an aptitude for technology and learns quickly; is motivated to succeed; cares about the IT organization; and can tie personal success to organizational success.
- Be team-oriented—coaches others and shares knowledge; is a team player; uses a participative style of leadership; shares team accountabilities; builds effective working relationships; and utilizes strong communication and listening skills.
- Deliver results—has a track record of delivering; conveys a sense of urgency in completion of assignments; and makes decisions readily.
- Understand the technical environment—displays IT organizational awareness; has significant business knowledge; and is recognized in IT and by the business partners for IT technical skills.

Making these assessments was not an easy task and involved feedback on performance, results delivered, skills, behaviors, and team leadership. The assignment of staff to best work reflected these assessments of resources. By assigning their best IT personnel to the processes judged to be most vital by the business and by freeing these people from other less important tasks, they felt that they could deliver change faster and improve the quality of the systems that were implemented at the same time. Although they are not far along this road, the early evidence appears to suggest that this is happening.

This is one organization's approach. It is not being suggested as the favored solution. It serves only to illustrate the types of decision criteria to be established and the types of process to be followed. The point is that each IT organization must establish its own rationale for deciding what to handle internally and what makes a good candidate for an external provider. Because of the individuality of organizations, it may be unreasonable to expect a best or even preferred approach.

STRATEGIES FOR MANAGING EXTERNAL RELATIONSHIPS

As a group, the members of the forum represented a significant experiential base regarding the issues of managing external relationships. As a result, we used the forum to extract a number of strategies that the forum members felt would constitute a beneficial set of guidelines for IT management. The strategies that emerged are presented below.

1   Learn from the Business about External Relationships

One group member felt that a fruitful way to think about external relationships was to view them in the same manner that the business views IT. His argument follows. Since the business has been "outsourcing" their systems development to the IT organization for years, it is likely that they have developed a level of expertise in managing external relationships—at least with the IT organization. In his organization, business users are regularly asked to assess their relationship with IT on the basis of the following six questions:

- Do they understand your business?
- Do they have the same priorities?
- Do they understand the "non-specified" issues?
- Do they have the urgency?
- Do they anticipate what you need?
- Do they care for your budgetary constraints?

These questions relate to the level of intimacy between buyers and providers. While it is not always necessary to have an intimate relationship with external providers, it is probably true that the degree of alignment between any two parties usually plays a key role in the conduct of the eventual relationship. For this reason, these questions (or similar ones) could be used to assess the nature of the relationship between IT organizations and external providers. Furthermore, answers to these questions could provide the basis for deciding which external provider is chosen. If nothing more, these questions raise interesting questions regarding external relationships—questions that are not easily quantifiable and that never appear on a contractual agreement. This omission, however, does not in any way diminish their relevance and importance to the topic.

2   Make Relationship Management Part of Your Strategy

Many group members felt that it is not enough just to be involved in external relationships. IT management needs to formally recognize external relationships as part of the overall strategy. Taking this step is necessary to ensure that adequate resources are committed and that positions are created to manage this activity. The organizations represented by group members share a common history regarding their involvement with external relationships—each had experienced haphazard growth over a number of years and each allowed the situation to evolve to the point of needing critical management attention. Contract management is handled in non-uniform ways: no single person or office had full responsibility for managing external relationships, the number of external contracts had grown dramatically, and contract management was becoming a part-time job for too many people within IT.

Step 1 is to make external relationship management a recognized part of your IT strategy. This step is in recognition of external relationship management as an increasingly critical activity in ensuring the well-being of the IT organization. Organizations should be clear about their objectives with respect to external relationships. In support of these objectives, there should be a document that clearly outlines such things as the organization's mandate, its assumptions, its preferred approaches, its procedures of conduct, a list of preferred suppliers, contract templates, a set of rules and procedures, and areas of responsibilities.

Step 2 is the creation of a locus of responsibility. Someone within the organization must be assigned to the task of external relationship management. Each member of the forum underlined the importance of a centralized function in order to coordinate the activities involved with external relationship management. This office would maintain copies of contracts, lists of preferred vendors, and past ratings of various suppliers and vendors. The importance of a designated focal point was emphasized by one group member who acknowledged that one area of her organization had hired an external consultant who had been fired by another area of the organization! The person(s) in this office are charged with the *responsibility* of relationship management—that is, they coordinate all relationship management activities but not necessarily perform them all.

Step 3 is to educate the IT organization regarding matters of external relationship management. This is done through communication. The IT organization must understand the nature and details of external relationships. They must understand the boundaries of the work being handled externally and its relationship to the work that is handled internally. The IT organization must understand the terms of the contracts set between the IT organization and the external provider in order that they work most effectively with the provider. In one organization, an external provider spent weeks preparing design specifications for an application only to discover that complete design specifications existed within the organization. After the fact, it was discovered that the internal team was simply unaware of the external activity. This turned out to be a costly oversight and should not have happened.

3   Make Contract Management a Core Competency

Contract management is an emerging set of activities that, when done well, can result in rather significant gains for organizations. It involves many activities beginning with the selection process and continuing through the satisfaction of the terms of the contract. One company has an evaluation team set up to handle all requests for questions (RFQs), requests for information (RFIs), and requests for proposals (RFPs). They feel that this gives them a degree of consistency that results in a much better selection process. No longer are contracts discovered in people's desks!

One of the key tasks is contract development and administration. The importance of the contract cannot be underestimated—especially in the event of disagreement between the two parties. It seems that, the longer the term of the contract, the greater the chance of disagreement. In essence, the contract sets the tone for the negotiation and provides the basis for the ongoing management of the external relationship. The trick is to develop a contract that strikes the correct balance between being too detailed and being too vague.

Contract management should be centrally controlled and managed. This practice ensures that organizations learn from their experiences as a party to external relationships. It also ensures that vendor information is accessible and current. The information that is held should, in addition to the details specified as part of the contract, contain experiential information even if anecdotal. This type of information can prove to be invaluable during the process of managing the external relationship as well as during future negotiations with this or other providers. One organization has even hired a *contract consultant* from another organization. As the title suggests, this person's primary duty is to oversee contract management for all external relationships.

Because of the increasing number of external providers to firms today, it is easy to miss the opportunity to learn over time, particularly if a centralized strategy for managing vendor contracts is not in place. An effective technique used by one company is to hold integrated review meetings on a regular basis. These meetings are attended by senior level executives (in addition to the account level managers) to deal with all the business the organization is doing with each vendor (whether vendors are on a time-based delivery mechanism or a project-based mechanism). The impetus for this strategy came when IT realized that the business had their own dealings with one of their external vendors (previously unknown to IT).

The message is simple—contract management should not be haphazard or even casual. It is as important to be excellent at this management task as it is at other IT activities. Contract management should be made a core competency.

4   Consolidate Your External Relationships

Most IT organizations face the same (or at least a similar) situation described in the introduction of this chapter; that is, their use of independent contractors (particularly in maintenance of legacy systems) is increasing; they have numerous third-party services firms involved in a variety of technologies and projects (from body shops of 20-member teams to day-to-day independents); and they are heavy users of boutique firms used for specialized and often scarce expertise (i.e., architecture). In order to cope with this reality, many IT organizations are seeking ways to consolidate their external relationships in an effort to make them more manageable. The group, as a whole, recommended adopting the following guidelines:

- reduce the number of service providers;
- encourage longer term partnerships (i.e., move toward the bottom of Table 3.1);

- form time-based rather than project-based partnerships (i.e., move toward the bottom right cell in Table 3.1);
- contract out complete projects (when it makes sense);
- assemble external resources to be accountable for all activities;
- consider outsourcing whole portions of the applications portfolio where possible (not just projects);
- utilize vendor's staff for modifications and integration when packages are purchased;
- continue to buy rather than build wherever possible.

The aim of this strategy is two-fold: to reduce the number of projects handled by external providers (because the projects are larger), and to reduce the number of external providers (because each has a larger share of the business). Like the US marines, the need is for "a few good strategic partnerships", not a bevy of independent relationships. Consolidating your external providers encourages allegiance and loyalty, and provides an organizational lever to make providers much more accountable.

5   Establish the Terms of Reference for Consulting Partners

The group felt that each organization should develop a standard document that establishes the terms of reference for consulting partners to be agreed to by both parties. This document should outline each of the following:

- the principles of the relationship;
- the external provider's role and responsibilities;
- the organization's role and responsibilities;
- the service and quality expectations;
- fees and expenses; and
- the mechanisms for managing the relationship.

Once established, this document becomes the template for all external relationships and forms the basis for effective partnership. Combined with the promise of a long-term continuing partnership, providers are motivated to agree to the terms of the document. This strategy plays a key role in bringing many aspects of external relationship management back under control.

6   Build a Preferred List of Partners

Reducing the number of external providers requires a strategy of its own. The group recommended the following approach. On an annual basis, solicit proposals from those external providers wishing to be considered for your preferred list of suppliers. These proposals should include an outline of the supplier's IT skills inventory, their guaranteed rates, their volume discounts, and their willingness to sign your "Terms of Reference for Consulting Partners". From these submissions, select three to five companies for your preferred list and place the rest on your backup list. Membership on the preferred list is reviewed annually and those failing to perform satisfactorily are replaced.

On an ongoing basis, project-managers (when they have secured permission to use external resources) contact those providers on the preferred list directly and request submissions (RFPs) to meet their specific needs. Based on these submissions, the provider that best meets the needs of the project-manager is selected. If necessary, the project-manager may approach those providers on the backup list. Once detailed negotiations are completed, a contract is signed. From that point forward, all performance on the contract is tracked and reported by the project-manager until the completed project is delivered. At that point, the product goes through a formal acceptance procedure and the appropriate skills transfer and support responsibility are enacted. All contract performance information is retained centrally (see Strategy 3 above).

7   Beware the Potholes

In many ways, establishing external relationships is a necessary evil. Benefits are derivable by reallocating resources, speeding up delivery of systems, acquiring specialized skills, offloading routine activities, and sharing the costs of development through partnership, but there are dangers. The group listed the following potholes to beware when dealing with external providers:

- *Losing IT staff to external providers.* Because external IT personnel often command higher salaries, the internal IT staff can be hired away by the provider. Alternatively, the internal IT staff may be motivated to demand that their contracts be renegotiated. In one case, an internal IT person, whose skills were in a high-demand area, successfully negotiated a 30% jump in salary.
- *External providers are "booked up".* Reliance on external providers means dependence on their availability. Unless specifically covered contractually, organizations can find themselves unable to secure external providers with the willingness and/or capability to react to the organization's time-frame.
- *Losing expertise.* One organization has outsourced approximately 95% of its legacy systems. It was advantageous to do so particularly when few internal IT staff saw any career in working with these systems. Without the continuance of internal expertise, however, the organization now feels vulnerable due to its dependence on the external provider. The ramifications of the external provider discontinuing support are serious.
- *Losing control.* Many people feel that you can "outsource anything but policy and planning." The argument is that the organization could legitimately question IT's ability to add value if its total operation (including policy and planning) were transferable to external providers. The counter-argument is

that policy establishment and planning are activities that can benefit from external expertise. Indeed, architecture-planning is frequently outsourced. The trick is to maintain the control of these activities internally.

- *Culture collision.* External providers are typically hired for their needed technical skills. Often they lack the specific business insight and rarely do they have the same culture as the organization hiring them. Sometimes their different cultures are found to be complementary and sometimes not. As a result, the organization can experience a significant degree of challenge in coordinating with the external provider even with respect to such seemingly minor issues as work ethic. This often results in significant problems that must be addressed very early in negotiation. In one organization, the problem was worsened when the business was forced to interface directly with the external provider without the IT organization playing a liaison role. Unfortunately, the business did not choose the external provider, had not agreed to work with them directly, and quite frankly, felt that IT was offloading its rightful duties and obligations to the business. This leads to the last potential pothole.
- *Shirking responsibility.* There is the possibility that, with many different external relationships in place, the IT organization could forget that it is charged with the ultimate responsibility for the proper functioning of the technological side of the organization. To shirk this responsibility is organizational suicide. When the system goes down, it is inconsequential to senior management that IT has outsourced the data center to an external provider. Furthermore, it is inconsequential to senior management that this external provider has breached the contract. What is consequential to senior management is IT's liability for whatever actions they take. The previously stated rule should be amended in the following manner—IT can "outsource anything except accountability."

CONCLUSION

The proliferation of external relationships has given rise to a new organizational mandate. This mandate is to transform the management of external relationships into a core competency. Those organizations who are successful at this task will undoubtedly gain advantage over those who fail to meet the challenge. A well-focused strategy, if formulated and adhered to, should guide IT organizations in establishing productive external relationships.

REFERENCES

The following articles are useful references for understanding the breadth of issues involved with managing external relationships:

Hirschheim, R. and M.C. Lacity (2000) "The myths and realities of information technology insourcing," *Communications of the ACM*, **43**(2), 99–108.

Lacity, M.C. and R. Hirschheim (1993) *Information Systems Outsourcing: Myths, Metaphors and Realities*, John Wiley & Sons, Chichester, UK.

Lacity, M.C. and R. Hirschheim (1995) *Beyond the Information Systems Outsourcing Bandwagon: The Insourcing Response*, John Wiley & Sons, Chichester, UK.

Lacity, M.C. and L.P. Willcocks (1998) "An empirical investigation of information technology sourcing practices: Lessons from experience," *MIS Quarterly*, **22**(3), September, 363–409.

McFarlan, F.W. and R.L. Nolan (1995) "How to manage an IT outsourcing alliance," *Sloan Management Review*, Winter, 9–23.

4
Knowledge Management and IT

To most of us, it comes as a surprise to learn that we entered the information age in 1956. Since the turn of the 20th century, the proportion of the work force employed in agriculture has been in steep decline. The same is true for manufacturing. In 1956, for the first time in North American history, more people were employed in knowledge work than in any other activity. It's not that we have declining needs for food, shelter, and physical goods (in fact, it is quite the contrary). It's just that fewer and fewer workers supply our need for these items due to increasing levels of automation (that is, the industrial age). The industrial age, which substituted machines for human muscle, began in the late 19th century and continued to dominate well into the last century . . . or at least until 1956. In contrast, the mission of the information age is to augment our brains, not our muscles. Unlike the physical limitations of our muscles, our ability to think, conceive, and imagine is without bounds. The engine of the information age—the computer—simply allows us to remember more, communicate faster, analyze more thoroughly, and test our ideas quicker than ever before.

But with every new age comes change. The arrival of the steam engine soon ushered in the massive development of railroads and their accompanying infrastructure (coal-mining, engineering, hotels, travel, and urbanization). With the information age, we have seen the emergence of software development, the Internet, and the massive international flow of people, goods, services, and ideas via new multinational and transnational organizations. Change requires accommodation and management. Every age experiences dislocations where old skills become obsolescent and new skills evolve. Typically each age is associated with the emergence of a new class of leaders—the "new centurions"—those with the foresight and ability to grasp the impact of the new order and seize the reins of power. Andrew Carnegie and Henry Ford were the centurions of the industrial age. One wonders who will be seen as the dominant leaders of the information age.

The upheaval of change—particularly change as massive as a new age—creates new problems, forces new thinking, and requires new forms of management. With the information age, we are faced with information overload (often referred to as information glut) and the phenomenon of being data-rich and information-poor. We appear to be creating two classes in our society—those with access to information and those without. We are struggling with the whole concept of the information economy. For the most part, knowledge represents an intangible asset: one that is difficult to measure and one that bucks the laws of accepted economic principles. Nevertheless, we are starting to appreciate the economic value of information/knowledge; some would argue that it is becoming the dominant form of wealth creation (Stewart, 1997). These authors point out that, in many situations, the *knowledge* of *assets* is more valuable than the actual *assets*.

The challenge then is to understand the role of knowledge so that we can manage it effectively. While knowledge management is an intrinsically human activity, information technology will certainly play a dominant role. How do we use information technology (IT) most effectively? Which technology is most advantageous? What is the role of IT management in knowledge management? How do we use IT to leverage the people in our organization most effectively? In order to find answers to these questions, we first need to cover some definitional attributes of knowledge management. This is done in the next section. Following that is a discussion of the process of managing knowledge. The final section of the chapter presents a number of strategies that IT managers can adopt in order to foster a climate that encourages and rewards effective knowledge management.

KNOWLEDGE AS AN ASSET

A few years ago we learned to differentiate "data" (e.g., 6135332360) from information (e.g., 613-533-2360). Well, guess what? We now have a new term—knowledge!

> Knowledge is about imbuing data and information with decision- and action-relevant meaning. This is the vital role of human intervention. Information about customers becomes knowledge when decision-makers determine how to take advantage of the information. In this way, knowledge is inseparable from thinking and acting (Fahey and Prusak, 1998).

From this definition, we start to understand the role of knowledge as an asset. In many ways, knowledge is similar to other corporate assets. Like capital and labor, it has no value until it is used. Like the steam engine, it empowers people to accomplish feats that would otherwise be impossible. Finally, like our natural resources, leveraging knowledge enables the development of new services, products, and markets. At the same time, knowledge is significantly different from other more familiar assets (e.g., cash, labor, resources, and/or machinery). In fact, Stewart (1997) refers to knowledge as the "weird resource" by identifying four major characteristics that cause knowledge to differ from other economic resources. We quote from him below.

First, he claims that knowledge is a "public" good—that is, it can be used without being consumed:

- It is non-subtractive—my obtaining a piece of knowledge in no way diminishes your ability to obtain it too. It follows from this that the cost of producing knowledge is unaffected by how many people eventually use it.
- Knowledge exists independently of space—it can be in more than one place at a time.
- The fact that information is sold to someone does not prevent it (the same item) from being sold to someone else.
- Knowledge is extremely sensitive to time—much more so than other assets. An example would be predicting the weather, political polling, or a "hot tip" on the next horse race.

Second, knowledge is abundant. In fact, knowledge is overwhelmingly abundant. But the contemporary laws of economics suggest that value is derived from scarcity, not abundance.

Third, most knowledge-intensive goods and services have a cost structure that is dramatically different from the cost structure of physical assets. Costs are heavily front-end-loaded—the costs of producing the first one may be extraordinarily high while the costs of producing subsequent copies may be virtually negligible. A good example is software.

Finally, when it comes to creative work, there is no meaningful correlation between knowledge input and knowledge output. The value of knowledge isn't necessarily related to the cost of acquiring it. This fact alone, notwithstanding the others, creates havoc for accountants in their attempts to value knowledge as a corporate resource.

It is obvious that knowledge is quite unlike other economic resources with which we are familiar. That being said, it is our challenge to understand it in order to be able to manage it. To do otherwise would be to leave our organizations vulnerable to those that discover how to effectively leverage their knowledge assets.

THE KNOWLEDGE ORGANIZATION

According to Mall (1996):

> . . . there is no standard profile of what a knowledge-based firm looks like. In general service firms have recognized greater benefits from knowledge management

initiatives than have manufacturing firms. However, this is not surprising given the intellectual-intensive work of most service industries. Many small companies have implemented knowledge management principles in an attempt to develop new products faster than firms with greater physical or financial resources. Many large firms have revamped their knowledge and information systems in an attempt to simultaneously realize both economies of scale efficiencies and mass customization flexibility. Although knowledge objectives run the gamut from increased innovation to decreased overhead, the strategic consequences of exploiting intellect typically result in a knowledge-based competitive advantage not easily duplicated by competitors.

It is perhaps safe to conclude that every organization is knowledge-based with the difference being the degree to which they are currently reaping the advantages of their knowledge base. Knowledge can (and will) undoubtedly play an ever-increasing role even in organizations that historically have not considered themselves to be knowledge-based. It is often the knowledge of resources that is of more value than the actual resources. Consider the following:

- About four out of five of the dollars Levi Strauss spends to make a pair of blue jeans go to information, not to make, dye, cut, and sew denim.
- It used to need three or four man-hours of labor to make a ton of steel. Now the business of sheet steel has been revolutionized with a process that requires sophisticated computers—it can't work without them—and requires only forty-five man-minutes of labor per ton. The intellectual component has grown and the physical component shrunk (Stewart, 1997).

To understand the knowledge organization, we need to explore the concept of "intellectual capital". A member of the focus group provided the following definition:

> Intellectual capital consists of information, knowledge, experience, methods, techniques, code, and/or best practices that are structured to enable sharing for reuse to deliver value to customers and shareholders.

There are three types of intellectual capital—human, structural, and customer (Stewart, 1997):

- *human capital* is "the capabilities of the individuals required to provide solutions to customers";
- *structural capital* is "the capabilities of the organization to share and transport knowledge—that is, to leverage knowledge—to meet market requirements"; and
- *customer capital* is "the value of an organization's relationships with the people with whom it does business".

Although all forms of intellectual capital are equally important, this chapter will focus its attention on the management of structural capital—that is, knowledge management—where IT plays a major role.

KNOWLEDGE MANAGEMENT

Davis and Meyer (1998) makes the distinction between an *organization* and a *business*. Organizations are defined from the inside out—they are described by who reports to whom, by departments, processes, matrices, and perks. A business, on the other hand, is defined from the outside in, by markets, suppliers, customers, and competitors. The distinction is important. According to Stewart (1997), "there is money to be saved by improving knowledge management in the *organization* ... but there is money to be made by managing the knowledge of the *business* ... thus knowledge management should really be about linking people to people to serve customers, people needing expertise with people who have expertise. They should be about connection, not collection."

The notion of knowledge management is further clarified by highlighting the importance of leveraging knowledge to enable organizations to become more than just the sum of the knowledge of individuals. It has often been said that a university is a collection of brilliant people that rarely demonstrates collective brilliance. Because there is little knowledge flow, the university is not intelligent as a whole. Knowledge management, according to Mall (1996), is:

> the process of systematically and actively managing and leveraging the vast stores of knowledge and information that exist within a typical company ... The product of the knowledge management process is intellectual capital ... Proponents of knowledge management assert that knowledge assets can be identified, that management processes can enhance them, that tangible knowledge metrics can be developed, and that managing knowledge improves financial performance.

This last quote really presents the challenge of this chapter—to identify knowledge assets, to enhance them, to develop knowledge metrics, and to link all these activities to the financial performance of the organization (rather, the *business*). Before proceeding on this task, however, we need to distinguish an important aspect of structural capital—stocks and flows. At any point in time, there is a *stock* of knowledge and, during any period of time, there is a *flow* of knowledge. This distinction is analogous to the difference between a balance sheet and an income statement. We can see from this that knowledge management will consist of two highly interconnected activities—that is, what knowledge to stock and how to make it flow. The challenge of knowledge management can then be seen to be two-fold: first, to codify bodies of knowledge that can be transferred so as to preserve information that might otherwise be lost; and, second, to connect people to data, experts, and expertise—including bodies of knowledge—on a just-in-time basis (Stewart, 1997).

In the next section, we take up the challenge of outlining strategies for managing knowledge; that is, creating structural capital.

STRATEGIES FOR KNOWLEDGE MANAGEMENT

The process of knowledge management begins with identifying the knowledge "gaps" within the company. Knowledge gaps are categories of knowledge needed to support the company's strategy that are currently not found within the organization. Knowledge gaps are identified by first determining the role that professional intellect *should* play in the company's business strategy. Next, managers should assess how the company currently utilizes knowledge. The major knowledge gaps should be rather apparent after completing these two steps (Mall, 1996).

The key word here is strategy. It is theoretically and physically impossible to identify knowledge gaps without first having delineated a corporate strategy. The corporate strategy guides the search for knowledge gaps. It provides the road map to suggest which direction to take and, more importantly, which direction to avoid. The following case demonstrates the strength of linking strategy with knowledge management (Davenport, 1996).

> In 1993, Roger Nelson, Managing Partner of Ernst & Young's US management consulting practice, announced a new strategic plan called "Future State '97". The emphasis was on knowledge processes including capturing and leveraging knowledge from consulting engagements, having every consultant contribute to the firm's stock of knowledge, and becoming known by clients as a valued source of knowledge and thought leadership. Another key aspect of the strategy was to use knowledge to speed up the process of providing consulting solutions for clients. By 1995 the strategy had been formalized into an approach called the Accelerated Solutions Environment (ASE), which involved the rapid application of E&Y knowledge, models, and approaches to client situations in facilitated large group settings.

This example demonstrates the advantages of performing an orchestrated gap analysis for knowledge management. Albeit, Ernst & Young competes in a knowledge-intensive industry, but, nevertheless, those in less knowledge-intensive industries can benefit by adopting similar activities. Ernst & Young enhanced its structural capital (that is, systems to capture knowledge, models, outcomes, and expertise) that leveraged its human capital (worldwide consultants in client engagements benefiting from past similar engagements by other consultants) and built customer capital (understanding the clients' business, needs, challenges, and goals in order to forge stronger relationships). Ernst & Young accomplished this by taking three proactive steps: (1) they explicitly recognized the value of intellectual capital to their business, (2) they meshed this opportunity with their corporate strategy, and (3) they built the infrastructure to make knowledge management a reality.

Subsequent to performing a gap analysis, managers should focus on five primary knowledge management tasks (Mall, 1996). They are: (1) generating knowledge, (2) accessing knowledge, (3) representing and embedding knowledge, (4) facilitating knowledge, and (5) generalizing knowledge. Focus group members were asked to suggest various strategies and techniques that they had found to be successful in managing knowledge. Their strategies are grouped under these five primary activities. Their ideas follow.

1   Generating Knowledge

Organizations must continually cultivate the creation of new ideas, the development of new processes, and the recognition of previously unseen patterns. There are many ways to accomplish this. One obvious strategy is to hire the best and the brightest—that is, to build up your human capital. This strategy ensures that you have the people with the capability to spawn new ideas, to question current practices, and to spot new opportunities. As long as your complement of human capital is energized, refreshed, challenged, rewarded, renewed, and retained, the generation of new knowledge should be ensured.

Establishing and nourishing strong partner relationships with buyers, suppliers, and/or customers generates the other obvious source of new knowledge. It is through this linkage that customer capital is created. One focus group member outlined his approach to generating new customer capital. He formed semi-permanent customer task forces with members representing various specialized areas of knowledge and expertise. Each task force was assigned to different customer groups and given the challenge of developing new business solutions for that customer group. By focusing entirely on the customer's business needs and through the collaboration of many diverse people, creative solutions soon emerged. The focus member pointed out that "through customer intimacy they gained a level of understanding of mutual business needs that allowed innovative solutions."

The most creative companies continue to develop new ideas by rewarding innovation, encouraging experimentation and reflection, and applying new knowledge as soon as it is generated. With the customer task forces described above, all new business ideas were fast-tracked through a management review process and incentives were established to reward the successful adoption of these new ideas. Recognition (and financial reward) for a new idea was made if (and only if) the idea was successfully implemented. In that case, both the customer task force and the business unit implementing the idea shared in the reward. Furthermore, incentives were established for other business units to adopt these ideas to encourage organizational learning. If the idea was adopted elsewhere within the organization, the originating customer task force and the new business unit shared an additional financial award. This procedure encouraged the task forces and the organization as a whole to explore these new ideas. Via this reward structure, new knowledge was encouraged to "flow" throughout the organization. Within the first six months of operation, three new business solutions had been implemented and were producing results. It was interesting to note that many of these solutions were very simple and easily achieved with only modest changes to existing processes.

2   Accessing Knowledge

It is one thing to *have* knowledge somewhere in the organization and it is an entirely different matter to be able to *access* that knowledge. It is the old lament: "we know that someone in this organization can solve the problem if only we could find that person." There are two aspects of accessing knowledge within an organization. The first includes developing policies and processes for initial knowledge capture and the second includes developing tools for the subsequent use of knowledge.

The first aspect of accessing knowledge—capturing knowledge—is difficult to engrain in professionals. These are typically high-performance individuals who are busy developing marketing plans, closing sales, meeting production deadlines, or developing new procedures. They are not necessarily interested in assisting in the capturing of knowledge for future applications. Capturing knowledge is often seen as non-productive work. It takes time to fill out reports and document your activities. Besides, the individual doing the capturing may feel he or she has little to gain personally by this endeavor. It may be beneficial for the organization as a whole, but not everyone is so altruistic. Capturing knowledge must be a recognized part of everyone's job. There must be expectations, policies, and deliverables for this activity. It must be seen as beneficial to the individual as well as the organization. Without such effort, knowledge will not be captured.

The sales force in most organizations is notorious for its distaste for accurate record-keeping. Yet, selling opportunities are frequently mismanaged (or indeed lost) due to lack of good customer information. There are many possible reasons for this. The needed information may be available but inaccurate or out-of-date, it may be available but cannot be found, it may be available but the sales force is unaware of this fact, the sales force may not know whom to contact to get the needed information, or some member of the sales force is guarding his or her contact information as privileged and confidential and therefore not to be shared.

One focus member described how his organization has set a process in place to capture and manage sales knowledge. An internal sales representative works in partnership with an *external* sales representative to manage all selling. The external sales representative is responsible for all client meetings—forging the contacts and prospecting new clients, obtaining preferences, learning of future plans, presenting quotes, and managing the negotiations. The *internal* sales representative is responsible for recording all sales-related information, setting schedules for his or her external representative, performing required research, maintaining phone contact with clients, and ensuring all internal processes are tracked and completed. Since the internal representative is managing the external representative's schedule, they are in continual contact throughout the day (typically six to seven times). The external sales representative receives the customary commissions for sales but the inside representative also receives sales-related incentives for such things as the number of calls, the number of entries made to the customer database, and the number of inside/outside sales. This approach explicitly recognizes the differential skill requirements of each partner—it relieves the external sales representative to "do the selling" and empowers the internal representative to "manage the customer capital". Working together makes both more productive and maximizes the benefits for the organization. All customer information is now centralized, well managed, and can be accessed easily by anyone needing the most up-to-date information. Mining this customer knowledge base has produced substantial rewards (e.g., sales leads, new products, differential service options, and customized packages) for the organization as well as for the internal/external representatives. It was the clear sense of the focus group that knowledge capture requires two organizational changes; first, a cultural shift away from "knowledge is power" to "knowledge sharing is power" and, second, well-structured and well-defined organizational processes.

The second aspect of accessing knowledge is the development of tools for knowledge exchange; that is, tapping into and unlocking the individual's tacit knowledge. Most researchers (e.g., Holtshouse, 1998) believe that this requires a highly interactive social process between workers in a co-located, face-to-face work environment. Co-location is critical because tacit knowledge is shared and exchanged through direct first-hand observation, interaction with others, subtle body language, and so on.

Physical co-location, however, is becoming more the exception than the rule. The onslaught of outsourcing, partnering, alliances, and mergers coupled with downsizing initiatives has left little room for water cooler exchanges. Today, the challenge is to create an equivalent level of informal exchange and socializing, without workers necessarily interacting face-to-face. One large consultancy, realizing that its far-flung consultants had lost some of the collective whole, has orchestrated "fly-in Fridays" in order to provide an opportunity to share experiences, build personal ties, and work collaboratively on corporate strategic matters. Could we go to the next step of virtual exchanges? Would they be as effective?

3　Representing and Embedding Knowledge

Knowledge assumes different forms. It is represented in skills and experience as well as brainpower. Much knowledge is tacit—that is, understood but not expressed. The crack software troubleshooter may have a lot of tacit knowledge that is difficult to express in typical policy manuals. Nevertheless, this knowledge must be represented and embedded within the organizational structure if for no better reason than to protect the organization should any of their key knowledge-workers decide to leave.

Representing and embedding knowledge is really about encoding knowledge to enable others to learn and benefit. Our time-honored approach has been to make new recruits "serve an apprenticeship". The new recruit, over some period of time, hopefully obtains insight and knowledge from the master through experiential learning. As an example, the yardmaster who was responsible for all railroad car movements through a rail yard took years to learn his trade and the task was frequently passed down from father to son. Today, that job is performed by an expert system—a system that outperforms even the very best yardmaster. Somehow the knowledge of the yardmaster has been represented and embedded within a system, the organization is no longer indebted to a single knowledge-worker, every rail yard is operated as effectively and uniformly as all others, and this knowledge-worker (the yardmaster) has been declared redundant.

Can expert systems be used elsewhere? The answer is a qualified: "yes, in knowledge domains that are well defined." There are numerous examples of expert systems for medical diagnosis, network troubleshooting, airline flight control, exploration site selection and drilling, optimal truck-routing, credit analysis, and even chess-playing. Because these systems have the ability to explain the logic they use in arriving at a decision, they are effective teachers as well. Using an expert system for credit analysis might be the best way to train a new lending officer. For these well-structured domains, expert systems will undoubtedly play a large role given their ability to represent and embed knowledge structures.

But much organizational knowledge is not of the well-structured type. And many of the difficulties with organizational knowledge relate to access. It can be that you simply don't know where to seek information, whom to ask, or what to ask. Often, you don't know what you don't know and therefore would never think to ask for it. These situations require a different approach to representing and embedding knowledge—a simpler and more flexible approach. One such approach is email. With the touch of a few keys, it is possible to mass-mail a request for help—"Has anyone out there ever encountered a problem like this?"—often referred to as the "chaos model" or the "broadcast model". Since there is no structure for this knowledge, the person inquiring has no real options other than broadcasting. Furthermore, those with the ability to answer may not see this as their job and thus have little if any incentive to respond.

Another approach is the chat board. This system allows anyone within the organization to join an ongoing "chat" about various topics of interest. It is typically voluntary, and individuals may be regular contributors to many chat boards. Focus members, as a whole, felt that chat boards were for the most part a failure with respect to effective knowledge management. This failure arose, not from the technology, but from the (lack of) organizational procedures. No-one was assigned responsibility to manage the chat boards. Given that information has a very short life expectancy, much of the information found on the chat boards was outdated or, worse yet, inaccurate. Many of the chat board topics were not directly tied to organizational outcomes such as customer needs or new products/services. Without the "outside-in" orientation, there was little connection to the value chain of the organization and, without ongoing management and direction, these chat boards soon wallowed in "misinformation".

A member of the focus group suggested another similar but more successful approach. In his organization, "communities of interest" are formed around key products or technologies. Individuals are assigned to these communities and someone is given ownership of the list of members. Membership in a community of interest is recognized explicitly as part of the member's job description. Members are responsible for entering information in "free-form"—that is, posting magazine articles, providing uniform resource locators (URLs) that point to good discussions, and correcting any information that is not accurate. Each entry on the system is assigned as (1) read and respond, or (2) considered subject matter input. A knowledge-manager is appointed and his or her duties are to take information off the community of interest exchange daily and place it in an organized knowledge base. Everyone in the organization has access to this knowledge base. A search engine is used to scan the knowledge base to find information of interest. Owners assume responsibility for knowledge content and can elect to terminate the committee's activities whenever appropriate. Involvement in a community of interest is seen as a positive career step whereby individuals receive technical depth and recognition for their contributions.

As with many organizational initiatives, IT plays a dual role in knowledge management. First, IT is responsible for the operational aspects of knowledge management—that is, building the structural capital of the organization—including the capture, assimilation, coding, update, and transmission of knowledge. Here, the technology of choice is clearly the Internet/intranet platform. The advantages are its universality, availability, ease of use, multiplicity of usage, and the ability to work with free-form knowledge. This last advantage is vital. It permits individuals to enter information in any form including text, hyperlinks, graphics, video, and audio. One member organization links telephony with its intranet to enable an individual to contact an expert by "touching a button". The second role played by IT is to develop the knowledge bases for its own internal usage. These knowledge bases are typically organized around specific technologies (such as intranet), various processes (such as project management), and a set of management practices (such as centers of excellence).

4   Facilitating Knowledge

The primary goal of facilitating knowledge is to create a culture that emphasizes the key role knowledge plays in day-to-day corporate success. Mall (1996) suggests three general guidelines to accomplish this:

First, companies should encourage constant experimentation, team-based learning, and socialization. Secondly, the leader must empower the process and serve as the driver of ongoing renewal of intellectual capital. Finally, and most importantly, there must be a transparent articulation of the value of knowledge to the firm's long-term competitive posture.

When asked to assess the priority attached to knowledge management, most members of the focus group felt that the importance of knowledge management within their organizations was already well established. Not surprisingly, the need for knowledge management was driven more from failure than success. Members had little difficulty in citing examples of the "mismanagement" of knowledge—new product ideas that got waylaid in someone's drawer, parallel development of similar products within the organization, failure to adopt common branding across all markets, and missing opportunities already available in the marketplace due to ignorance of their existence. In creating the appropriate culture for knowledge management, focus group members felt the role of incentives is key. They differentiated incentives that recognized the "successful application of knowledge" from the "successful attainment of knowledge". Rewarding both is critical.

One member organization has attempted to facilitate a knowledge culture within IT by creating a number of knowledge centers. It has developed career centers and communities of interest to augment its centers of excellence. A "leading practitioner" manages each center. They have segregated knowledge into two categories: operational and technological. Under operational knowledge are defined processes for things like project management, and each process has a process-owner who looks for best practice. Under technological knowledge, individuals are assigned to be experts in various specific domains and they are responsible for gathering knowledge to populate the knowledge databases. Interestingly, they view their role as "managing knowledge about knowledge" as opposed to "managing knowledge". The appointment of a full time leader to each domain is an important and explicit signal to the organization of the recognized importance of knowledge management.

One focus member's organization has advanced knowledge management to the point of having developed a comprehensive and integrated approach. This approach combines three key elements: (1) a well-articulated executive vision and strategy with (2) a value system of knowledge-sharing and (3) a management system for knowledge management. This organization begins by classifying its customer knowledge into one of four categories: novelty, mass production, continuous improvement, and mass customization. For each type of knowledge, they identify a distinct management system (process, organization, and technology). Knowledge is organized around competencies—competencies that the organization already has, competencies that customers currently need, and emerging competencies. Around these competencies are formed knowledge networks described by the organization as:

... global knowledge networks of practitioners focused on client needs responsible for the valuation and structure of knowledge for sharing among peers and across client projects ... established where the business sees requirements for intellectual capital management, not organizational units.

These knowledge networks have core members with various subject matter expertise and responsibility. The networks are the cornerstone for knowledge management. It is their duty to work with practitioners to solicit and acquire knowledge, to verify and authenticate each submission, to structure the knowledge for entry into the knowledge base, to publish its availability to the organization, to facilitate the usage of the knowledge in new applications, and to retire outdated information. The success of this knowledge management activity is measured against outputs and deliverables in a continuous feedback loop—that is, the results of the application of knowledge (e.g., a new marketing approach) are evaluated and the gained experience is added to the competency network database, which then is available for reuse. Success is achieved by creating a culture of awareness—awareness of knowledge as the source of wealth, the recognized benefits of sharing and building this knowledge, and awareness of the impact of knowledge management on everyone's career interests.

5　Generalizing Knowledge

This is a vital stage of knowledge management. According to Mall (1996), "the only real sustainable competitive advantage is the rate at which a company is able to learn. This learning is only valuable, however, if it can be transferred from one department or situation to another. Therefore a firm's learning capability can be defined as $G * G$, or the ability to generate new ideas (discussed above) multiplied by the ability to generalize these ideas throughout the company and in various situations." The challenge is two-fold: how do you do this and whose job is it?

The goal of organizational learning is to create an organization that can learn from its environment, be flexible and responsive when the market demands it, and be able to differentiate "knowing when to apply the rules" from "knowing when the rules don't apply". In most organizations, unfortunately, organizational learning remains a goal, not an achievement. This will have to change. Organizational learning and knowledge management exist hand-in-hand. If organizations are to build and leverage their intellectual capital—an intrinsically human activity— they will have to enhance their ability to learn both individually and collectively.

One focus group member described the initiatives taken to transform her organization into a learning organization. The change was driven by three key elements: (1) speed to market, (2) avoiding potential employee turnover, and (3) the realization that intellectual assets are a major part of the overall company's value. Because of the dominant role of people in learning organizations, they decided that the change would have to be orchestrated by the human resources

(HR) function, renamed "Organization Development". In order to accomplish this task, many of the typical, "operational" HR functions such as pensions and benefits were outsourced to free up resources to create the learning culture. The learning culture was based on three premises: (1) there should be no bounds on employee-learning (that is, allow learning that is not limited to a current job), (2) the initiative should focus on the "whole" employee, and (3) knowledge management is the key component. IT employees embarking on specific career paths are supported by learning centers (which function like small libraries where people go to learn), training programs, 360-degree feedback sessions, and performance evaluations based on outputs. In addition, there are various incentive programs that reinforce the need to share information. Although this organization admits that much remains to be done, they believe that they have identified the three prerequisites for success:

- building a knowledge culture (management commitment, an individual performance evaluation process, and incentive programs);
- capturing the right knowledge content (relevant information, external sources, and media choices); and
- adopting the right technology (network architecture, software tools, and security/accessibility standards).

Information-intensive organizations have only two resources—people and IT. Because of the nature of knowledge as an economic resource (as previously described), it is possible to achieve a $G * G$ effect by creating an organizational environment that supports learning. The road to a true learning organization is not well charted, but the significance of the rewards makes the trip worth taking.

CONCLUSION

The role of creating the structural capital of the organization (i.e., knowledge management) has been given to IT by default. It is therefore up to IT to accept this challenge and begin the work. It will not be easy. It will require a dramatic reorientation in management thinking. Never before have organizations been created to manage an intangible asset such as knowledge. There are new rules and new behaviors. The rewards are enormous.

REFERENCES

Davenport, T. (1996) *Knowledge Management at Ernst & Young, May 1996*, Center for Business Innovation, Ernst & Young, Boston.
Davis, S. and C. Meyer (1998) *Blur: The Speed of Change in the Connected Economy*, Warner Books, New York.

Fahey, L. and L. Prusak (1998) "The eleven deadliest sins of knowledge management," *California Management Review*, **40**(3), Spring, 265–276.

Mall, S. (1996) "Knowledge management", Unsourced chapter, May.

Stewart, T.A. (1997) *Intellectual Capital: The New Wealth of Organizations*, Bantam Doubleday Dell, New York.

5

Risk Management in IT: Problems and Potential*

Risk can be perceived to be a negative word in information technology (IT) organizations because it implies that something could go wrong with an IT project. This negative perspective conflicts with many IT professionals' traditionally optimistic worldview and with a management philosophy that makes it seem harsh and disloyal to talk about a plan's down sides. Where risk is addressed in IT, it is commonly utilized only as a factor to modify a system's potential financial returns, rather than as a management practice (KPMG Study, 1999). Thus, to date, risk assessment and management is something that has been done minimally if at all in IT, and studies show that only one-third of senior executives feel that they understand IT risks well (Wah, 1998). Even those companies that have formal, risk management processes for other parts of their business demonstrate consistently poor IT risk management and take a fragmented approach to it (Hoffman, 1998). Typically, organizations do not make IT risk management a priority, don't link IT risks to business strategy, and don't put enough effort into anticipating problems (Wah, 1998). Therefore, the practice of IT risk management in organizations varies greatly (KPMG Study, 1999).

Risk management can be an extremely powerful approach to dealing with the complexities and uncertainties that increasingly surround technological change and its management. Conventionally in IT projects, risks have been narrowly defined; for example, would a project meet all its objectives or would it be implemented on time? Today, with IT becoming integral to a company's existence, the stakes are considerably higher and broader in scope. As systems have become more interconnected, the things that can go wrong have increased exponentially. As well, with companies adding new partners, untried tech-

---

* Smith, H.A. and J.D. McKeen (2001) "Risk management in IS: Problem and potential," *Communications of the Association of Information Systems*, August, **7**(13), 1–28 (reproduced by permission of the Association for Information Systems).

nologies, and challenging business strategies to the mix, senior executives are beginning to realize that there are serious human and organizational risks associated with the use of IT. Finally, with our rapidly changing business and technology environments, some companies are being required to take bigger and bigger risks to remain competitive. Therefore, effective risk management has now become a much more important issue to both IT and business managers.

This chapter first examines the nature of risk and provides an overview of the process of risk management. It then explores the three steps of this process in more detail. They look at identifying risk in IT initiatives, determining appropriate levels of risk, and dealing with unacceptable types and levels of risk.

WHAT IS RISK AND HOW IS IT MANAGED?

IT managers and researchers have traditionally defined risk as something that has only negative consequences. For example, Aubert et al. (1998) use Boehm's definition: "the possibility of loss or injury." Focus group managers described it similarly as "the possibility of loss or damage" and "the possibility of suffering harm or loss". Although this view of risk is widely used, Billington (1997) points out that when examined closely, "risk" can actually lead to both positive *and/or* negative consequences. In any particular initiative, he notes, the risks involved could represent different things to an organization. A risk can be:

1. A *hazard* that must be minimized or eliminated.
2. An *uncertainty* about which path should be taken and which must be studied to reduce the variance between anticipated outcomes and actual results.
3. An *opportunity* for growth or improvement, which must be assessed to determine *how much* innovation, initiative, and entrepreneurship should be exercized.

Viewing risk as something more than a hazard is highly applicable to risk management in IT. Although IT risks *can* lead to negative results, they can also represent significant opportunities for savings or business development. As well, since technology and its application are changing so rapidly, the vast uncertainty surrounding IT is one of the biggest challenges an IT manager faces these days. Thus, this chapter will explore IT risk and its management in all its dimensions, recognizing that not all risk leads to negative consequences and not all risk needs to be eliminated.

Levels of Risk

Several members of the focus group saw IT risk as operating largely on IT projects. They defined it as, "The cumulative effect of the changes of uncertain occurrences which may adversely affect project objectives" and "the potential event or occurrence that may jeopardize the success of a project or cause it not to achieve one or more of its objectives." However, the discussion also made it plain that companies are now perceiving that IT risk can exist at two other broader levels. First, IT can have an impact on a company's operations. The consequences of technology failure or declining service, and how systems work with business processes, can affect both a company's internal and external effectiveness and efficiency. Second, a firm's use of technology is often central to its overall business strategy. IT can dramatically influence a company's reputation and relationships, as well as its competitiveness and profits. Because risk works at all three levels simultaneously, it has qualities that cut across them. For example, the uncertainty involved in a project or an operating environment can affect business performance just as an uncertain business climate can affect a project's success. Similarly, an IT project can represent either a hazard or an opportunity to a business or its operations.

Risk Management

The different dimensions and levels of risk each need to be properly understood and managed. Carnegie Mellon's Software Engineering Institute website (www.sei.cmu.edu) explains that without risk management, companies are continually "fire fighting". With a risk management program in place, companies shift to proactive decision-making, which tries to anticipate and avoid problems before they occur. It notes: "A successful risk management practice is one in which risks are continuously identified and analyzed for relative importance. Risks are mitigated, tracked and controlled to effectively use resources." Risk management can provide managers with insights into what *could* happen. Consequently, without risk management more effort is spent correcting problems that could have been avoided sooner, success and failure can occur without warning, and decisions are made without complete information or adequate knowledge of future consequences.

Risk management involves three steps. The first step is to identify the risks involved in a particular initiative to determine what could go wrong. Often risk management stops at this step, which accounts for the overwhelmingly negative impression of what it is all about. Typically, risks are narrowly defined and focused primarily on schedule, budget, and technology. While these are important, as the next section makes clear, risk comes in many sizes and shapes. Identifying *all* the risks involved—especially digging out the ones that are masked by assumptions or hidden by imperfect knowledge—is therefore an essential first step to determining how to manage them.

The second step is to assess the company's exposure to the identified risks. This includes determining both the likelihood of the risk occurring and the potential impact if it occurs. Not all risks will occur and not all risks will have a significant effect on an initiative or a strategy. Thus, risk exposure is a function of how these two aspects work together. While risk assessment tends to focus on the consequences of a failure (i.e., what will be lost?), focus group managers also pointed out that corporate impacts can be generated by extreme success as well as failure (i.e., too much demand on a system).

Dealing with risk is the third step. Effectively addressing risk involves utilizing a continuum of strategies depending on the nature and amount of risk involved. In some cases, simply monitoring the risk is adequate, in others, action should be taken to mitigate or reduce risk. Sometimes, anticipation of risk can lead to plans to deflect impacts (as with insurance) or contingency-planning may be necessary where rapid recovery is essential (Aubert et al., 1998).

In short, risk management is a forward-looking activity that makes the potential problems, opportunities, uncertainties, and threats implicit in an initiative explicit to management. It is a formal process by which risk can be brought under control and whereby surprises are minimized. The next three sections of this chapter explore these three steps of risk management in more detail.

IDENTIFYING RISK

In order to assess the risks involved in an initiative, it is essential to understand where they can come from. Risk arises from many different, general sources. In this section, we will explore these sources of risk and illustrate how one source of risk can have one or more dimensions (i.e., it can represent a hazard, uncertainty, or opportunity) and operate simultaneously at the project, operations, and business strategy levels in an organization.

Financial Risk

It has long been understood that the financial return of an IT project should be greater than the amount invested in it. This is why return on investment (ROI) is usually computed for IT projects. Dué (1996) notes that, typically, an IT investment's estimated return needs to be adjusted by between 10% and 25% to account for the chance that it will not pay off as expected. The risk of overestimating benefits and underestimating costs is a real one, as many companies can attest. However, a straightforward cost–benefit analysis is only appropriate for situations where the value of IT derives primarily from operational efficiencies. Venkatramen (1997) points out that, although companies have historically managed most IT activities on the basis of rigid, quantitative payback criteria, they can be vulnerable financially from sources that are not quantifiable using ROI. For example, at a *business strategy* level, companies may need to invest simply to keep opportunities open or to support new organizational strategies (Luehrman, 1998; Venkatramen, 1997). *Operationally*, investment may be needed to support current business capabilities or create new ones. Furthermore, even at a project level, the risks of being over budget or behind schedule must be balanced with the longer term cost of errors if a system is installed too rapidly. Thus, while ROI continues to be an important element of financial risk, it should not be the only financial factor considered in risk assessment.

Technology Risk

New and untried technology increases the risk of project failure because neither IT professionals nor users understand it well (McFarlan, 1981). Technology performance, scalability, reliability, and stability are other sources of risk that can impact a project's success. However, organizations are now recognizing that technology can represent a risk at other levels as well. Several focus group managers pointed out that their companies consider technology to be both an operating risk (i.e., that general technology failures could prevent business from being conducted) and a strategic risk (i.e., that outdated technology will result in a loss of market share and render the company non-competitive). *Operationally*, with more and more business functions being automated, an effective technology infrastructure (i.e., hardware, software, networks, and processes)—or the lack of one—is now a significant factor in how a company conducts its business (Wah, 1998). Champey (1998) points out that operational failure of technology has brought new meaning to the term "killer application" at some companies. *Strategically*, there is not only the risk of choosing the wrong technology but also of implementing it poorly and thereby awakening the competitive instinct of other organizations, raising the cost of doing business (Prakash, 1998), or losing new business opportunities.

Security Risk

Security is the ability for a business and its customers to trust the electronic environment in which the company operates and offers its services (Garigue and Mackie, 1999). In the past, security risk has most often referred to the hazards represented by unauthorized system access or by general disasters. Today, application security (including user authentication, control and authorization, and data integrity) continue to be risks at a *project* level. However, with the increasing electronic interaction between companies and with individuals, network defensibility (local, wide area, and global) is today a major *operating* hazard. Network, system, and file protection have all become general security risks that must be addressed at an organization level, and even beyond. Thus, security management and security awareness also contribute to the levels of operating risk a business faces. Companies must assess whether passive protection mechanisms (e.g., virus-scanning, encryption, and firewalls) are adequate for their needs, or whether more active protection, such as vulnerability analysis and intrusion detection, is needed.

Information Risk

Commonly, information risk is perceived to arise from data that are inaccurate or missing in a system. However, there is growing recognition that information risk is broader than this, cutting across all levels of organization management and control. Newer information risks include privacy, decision-making, and strategy development. Privacy has become a more important hazard recently with the advent of privacy legislation in many jurisdictions, which regulates what information can be collected about individuals and how it can be used (Smith and McKeen, 1999). Peladeau (1995) points out that the most common sources of information risk in this area are collecting too much information and not disposing of unneeded or outdated material.

A second source of risk is that information can be used to make improper decisions about business situations (i.e. decision-making risk). Knowledge embedded in systems and organization controls as assumptions or internal logic is often not apparent to decision-makers. This type of knowledge, if improperly understood or represented, can produce an illusion of control for managers while affecting many aspects of business operations such as model assumptions, human resources (HR), accounting, liquidity, credit, legal, and other operating processes (Marshall et al., 1996).

Since knowledge is the means by which managers deal with uncertainty and complexity, there is also a risk that they will not have the information they need, in the right format, and at the right time, in order to make strategic decisions (Marshall et al., 1996).

People Risk

In a bizarre and now prophetic sense, Russell Gates, managing partner of (the former) Arthur Andersen's Computer Risk Management practice, comments that, while it is often easy to see technological risks, people must be factored in to risk management just as much (Wah, 1998). People are a source of uncertainty because of the variety of ways they can react to IT and its challenges. Because people respond subjectively to change, their reactions can be difficult to predict. Thus, users at all levels can respond either positively or negatively to a new system, as can external customers. Both can create risk for a company, especially if the reaction is extreme and unanticipated.

Other sources of people risk in a *project* that are sometimes ignored, according to focus group participants, include inadequate project resource management, poor decision-making competency at all levels, poor expectations management, lack of relationship-building with all the people involved in an initiative, and failure to match the pace of change to the staff's ability to cope with it. Pressure, burnout, and loss of face are other risks that are sometimes not apparent in a company's haste to implement new IT projects. At the *operational* and *strategic* levels, people risk may be less obvious, but is equally uncertain. The influence of corporate power politics cannot be ignored in business decision-making around IT as many IT managers have found out to their dismay. For example, one focus group manager noted that conflict is a major reason why risk is not adequately addressed in organizations at senior levels.

Business Process Risk

Information systems are frequently used to make changes in business processes to reduce operating costs. The greater the change being made, the greater will be the risk involved. Major transformations in a number of business areas typically require the large-scale transformation of jobs, competencies, procedures, work flow, management, and decision-making. If successful, these changes can make an organization more effective and efficient. However, if not properly managed, they can represent a threat to organizational survival (Yetton et al., 1994). Often, the impact of a change (and hence, the type of risk involved) is not clearly visible to senior management. Simons (1999) explains that people at the top of an organization are usually less aware of risk in this area than those lower down. He notes that when processes change, information flows change, and this often creates operational havoc. Internal reporting systems measuring critical performance variables can be affected as well. Focus group managers also cited lack of technology usability, poor help desk and support problems, inadequate training, and unanticipated results as all contributing to risk in this area.

Management Risk

Every project has its own special set of vulnerabilities and dependencies that need to be managed (e.g., schedule, budget, functionality, compatibility, relationships, expectations, and communication). The quality of the management brought to bear on these issues, including how they are planned for, identified, assessed, dealt with, and balanced against each other, will do a great deal to enhance or detract from the success of a project (Dieckmann, 1996). Similarly, the quality of IT management as a whole will contribute strongly to the hazards, uncertainties, and opportunities facing an organization's operations and business strategies. For example, if a company has weak IT assets, particularly if it is in a competitive industry, it can easily become a corporate liability.

External Risk

Risk from external sources has received considerably more attention recently with the advent of IT outsourcing, IT subcontracting, enterprise resource planning (ERP) systems, and other forms of pre-packaged software (Champey, 1998; Aubert et al., 1998). Companies can also find it very tempting to buy a "shrink-wrapped" solution off the shelf. Focus group managers pointed out that these projects need to be assessed and managed for risk just like any other system development project, since they face many of the same schedule, budget, and implementation problems. In addition, risk can come from making too many customized changes, assumptions embedded in the software, poor contract management, limited understanding of the business requirements to be addressed, the stability of the software development company, and its responsiveness to the unique needs of the purchasing company. As the size of the software package increases, risk increases in all areas. ERP systems affecting many business divisions and business processes are more risky than applications that are more single-purpose.

When a company decides to outsource some or all its IT functions, overall business risk can also increase. Aubert et al. (1998) identified three key risk factors in outsourcing. Client capacity, including lack of experience and expertise with contracts and contract management, can create risks. Supplier capacity, including supplier stability, size, and expertise, also are risks that need to be recognized. The nature of the outsourcing activities, including their interdependence with internal activities, their proximity to core competencies, the availability of competitors, and clarity of success factors and measures, may also introduce risks that should be assessed. With outsourcing, companies are not only vulnerable to increased costs but also to such things as increased rigidity, poor support, and technological lock-in. Each of these risks can seriously impact both an organization's ability to operate effectively and efficiently and its implementation of business strategy.

Risk of Success

A source of risk that is frequently neglected but which can have equally devastating consequences for a company is the risk of success. Focus group managers explained that projects can be as unprepared for success as they are for failure. Success can mean a higher volume of transactions than expected or that users see more potential in an application than was originally anticipated leading to demand for expansion of a project. Thus, scalability of volume and function are two key risks of success at a *project* level. Simons (1999) explains that success can increase the level of *operational* risk because rapid expansion can mean that the resources, processes, and structures of a company are inadequate to the change. Performance measures, controls, and jobs may all have to be redefined as a result.

Risk identification is fundamental to risk management. If managers do not know where risk exists in an organization, they cannot act. Almost all the focus group managers reinforced this point as being a significant limiting factor in their ability to manage risk effectively. Unfortunately, they stated, the biggest problems arise not from being unable to identify risk, but from being unable to incorporate it into their project, operations, and strategic plans.

ASSESSING RISK

Risk is endemic in business and IT initiatives, and cannot be eliminated altogether. The challenge for IT managers is to determine how much risk they are facing with an IT initiative and to assess whether or not this level of risk is appropriate

Table 5.1   *Sample risk evaluation checklist for external dependencies.*

Risk factor	Likelihood of occurrence	Potential impact
Risk #1		
Risk #2		
Risk #3		
Risk #4		
Risk #5		

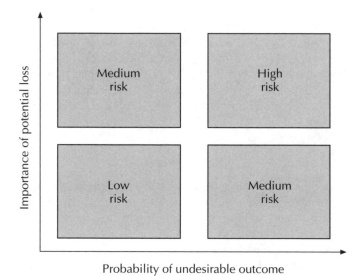

Figure 5.1   *Possible levels of risk (data from Aubert et al., 1998, used with kind permission).*

for their business. Evaluating risk exposure is an art, not a science. Most assessment methods involve evaluating each individual risk factor on scales of impact and probability (e.g., 1 = no impact, 3 = high impact; and 1 = very unlikely to occur, 7 = extremely likely to occur). These can be documented using such tools as a checklist (see Table 5.1) or a graph (see Figure 5.1). Multiplying impact by probability will then yield an overall risk exposure figure that can be compared with a predetermined degree of acceptable risk.

Since risk exposure is a subjective measure, what is more important than what method is used to assess it is ensuring that everyone involved in an IT venture— at all levels—agrees on the level of risk involved and can accept it. It seems that developing common understanding about risk is at least as important in managing it as the actual levels of risk involved. McFarlan (1981) writes:

> Often fiascoes occur when senior managers believe a project has low risk and IS managers know it has high risk. In such cases, IS managers may not admit their

assessment because they fear that the senior executives will not tolerate this kind of uncertainty ... and will cancel a project of potential benefit to the organization.

Others believe that it is IT that is always searching to eliminate risk and that business is more comfortable with higher levels of risk exposure (Maccoby, 1997; Knowles, 1996). Focus group participants saw misalignment of how risk is viewed as a major inhibitor of effective risk management, as the following comments demonstrate. One focus group participant stated, "Management blocks out risk messages. It's not safe to send them. It's better to say everything's okay." Thus, while the concept of risk is well established and is understood as a prerequisite for success in business, in IS, risk and its management are usually seen as a problem to be avoided. "If you take a risk and fail," said another participant, "you could lose your job." "If you identify a risk, you'd better have a solution," said a third.

Acceptable levels of risk need to be continuously monitored. The key to risk assessment is not to identify an arbitrary risk exposure number that is "too high", but to ensure that there is agreement about how much risk is involved and then to work to make sure that the levels of risk involved are appropriate for the business. One of the best ways to do this is to "package" risk into some sort of graphical format so that everyone can clearly view and understand the risk involved in key areas. Some organizations in the focus group categorize risk exposure by the major sources of risk (e.g., technical, external, etc.) and color-code them green, yellow, and red for the levels of risk involved. These can then be linked in a table or in a web-diagram, which show all the types and levels of risk together.

DEALING WITH RISK

Once risks have been identified and an appropriate level of exposure has been agreed on, the final step in risk management is to determine what to do about each risk. Again, there is a great deal of variation in specific risk management strategies by company. From the focus group participants, the authors collected over 50 practices used by IT managers today (see Table 5.2 for the list). When these were analyzed, a number of more general principles for dealing effectively with all types of risk emerged. These would be advisable for any organization to implement, regardless of industry or degree of risk tolerance, and are presented below:

- *Take a holistic approach to risk.* Risk management cannot be effective unless it is understood in all its dimensions and seen as intrinsic to projects, operations, and business strategies. Risk management is a cycle that must be repeated continually. Focus group managers were clear that risk management is an ongoing process that requires continuous follow-up. New hazards, uncertainties, and opportunities regularly appear on the horizon even as others are

Table 5.2   *Selected risk management practices.*

(A) PROJECT PRACTICES

Risk identification
- brainstorm risk as a team
- work with clients to develop a "what if" plan
- employ risk checklists and templates
- calculate return on investment
- do an anonymous survey of users and IS staff
- conduct a project post-mortem

Risk assessment
- update risk assessments after every project phase
- undertake a formal impact assessment

Risk mitigation/control
- document and monitor the business case
- establish clear objectives and requirements
- spend time and money upfront with vendors to clarify requirements
- document requirements in vendor contracts
- use a project methodology
- hold project reviews
- enforce project-planning
- ensure proper testing
- create a project support office
- develop worksheets for all documentation needed
- use estimating tools
- establish a SWAT team of experienced staff to help if the project gets stuck
- pay vendors by deliverables, not time and materials
- create a support-and-maintenance plan for packaged software
- get references for vendors and suppliers
- create contingency plans for high-risk items
- implement in small pieces
- increase project management competencies
- provide a mentor for inexperienced project-managers
- develop a training strategy

(B) OPERATIONS PRACTICES

Risk identification
- research technology changes
- appoint a chief risk-officer
- establish a lessons-learned database

Risk mitigation/Control
- develop contingency plans for high-risk situations
- create risk management plans for computer operations and data management
- implement architectural reviews of all technology initiatives
- hold security and technology reviews

- establish technical and quality assurance groups
- monitor defects
- investigate and implement estimating tools
- develop risk metrics
- establish access, security, and privacy standards
- keep organizational changes relatively small

(C) BUSINESS STRATEGY PRACTICES

Risk identification
- monitor political, social, and technology trends
- monitor the company's reputation, competition, and regulation

Risk mitigation/control
- design the organization to deal with risk
- establish a clear business vision
- monitor business cases
- assign all IT initiatives a business executive sponsor
- once a vision has been agreed, move quickly
- take responsibility for risk
- integrate risk management into all business management activities.

---

effectively managed. Risk assessments too will change as more knowledge becomes available, technologies improve, and the business environment changes.
- *Develop a risk management policy* Companies should develop a framework to establish the standards and protocols needed to manage risk in their particular business. Such a policy aims to integrate IT risk management with the general strategies and policies of managing the business and to make risk both visible and acceptable to talk about. It also develops a common understanding of what is an appropriate level of risk and ensures consistency in its assessment. Finally, it identifies specific mechanisms to manage IT risk within the organization. This could mean creating a technology policy committee, enhancing the role of the internal audit group, or developing templates that ensure that IT work as a whole can be properly monitored by senior management.
- *Establish clear accountabilities and responsibilities.* Once risks have been identified, it is extremely important to assign responsibility for managing and monitoring individual risks. At a project level, the project-manager is an obvious candidate for overall responsibility. Many of the focus group participants' organizations also assign more general, risk management functions to an audit team, an architecture review team, or a quality assurance group. Focus group managers pointed out that, because these external groups tend to be knowledgeable in specific areas of risk management, they can be extremely helpful in managing risk if they are involved early in the project's development.

- *Balance risk and controls.* It's easy to slip into a risk-averse mentality with IT since there is so much uncertainty and so much that can go wrong (Knowles, 1996). But managing risk into the ground is a guaranteed way to kill innovation (Maccoby, 1997). There are many risks in IT initiatives that only need to be monitored, not controlled (Aubert et al., 1998). While controls are essential in the case of some risks, the use of formal controls should always be balanced against the level of risk exposure involved.

- *Be open and reduce conflict.* One of the surest ways to inhibit risk management, agreed the focus group participants, is to get into a negative spiral of conflict and fear. Once this happens, trust is destroyed and damage escalates (Maccoby, 1997). A key, risk management principle is therefore to create an environment of openness. While trust cannot be decreed, it can be built by management through such things as strategic leadership, good coaching, and treating people with respect (Maccoby, 1997). A positive attitude toward risk management not only takes pressure off staff, it enables them to share hard news with senior management when it is necessary.

- *Enforce risk management disciplines.* As companies begin to pay more attention to risk, it will become clear which practices are most helpful in managing risk at the project, operations, and strategic levels. These practices need to be adopted as disciplines within the overall risk management framework. Disciplines such as architectural reviews, reviews with a project management office, budget and schedule controls, and audit controls need to be enforced consistently and rigorously. Properly designed, they can serve as an early warning system to senior management, address commonly understood risks that may arise due to inexperience or inattention, and help reduce uncertainty at all levels.

- *Learn what works and what doesn't.* Finally, extracting lessons learned in risk management can enhance an organization's effectiveness in this area. Learning how to identify and document lessons learned in a way that is relevant to others, repeatable, and accessible when needed is not easily done. However, implementing learning disciplines will have a considerable impact on reducing risk at both a project and operations level.

CONCLUSION

Risk management is a way of thinking that continually seeks to ensure that the risk-to-reward ratio is in balance for a company. In this paper, we have looked at risk management as a means to an end—whether it is a successful IT project, stable, secure technical operations, or a properly implemented business strategy using technology. It is not a one-time activity, but rather an ongoing process of identification, assessment, and action, which needs to be well-integrated into every part of IT management. The pace of change in IT and business today means that risk cannot be ignored or dealt with only when it arises. IT organizations cannot afford to deal with it through fire fighting mode. Instead, IT managers must learn to control both the problems and the potential that risk represents.

REFERENCES

Aubert, B., S. Dussault, M. Patry, and S. Rivard (1998) "Managing the risk of IT outsourcing," *Proceedings of the 31st Hawaii International Conference on Systems Sciences*, January, IEEE Computer Society, NJ.

Billington, J. (1997) "A few things every manager ought to know about risk," *Harvard Management Review Update Article*, March, #U9703D.

Champey, J. (1998) "Killer technologies," *Forbes*, **162**(5), 7 September, 180–181.

Dieckmann, M. (1996) "Making new technology investments pay off," *Managing Office Technology*, **41**(7), July, 14–26.

Dué, R. (1996) "The value of information," *Information Systems Management*, Winter, 68–72.

Garigue, R. and A. Mackie (1999) "From provincial action to national security: A national information protection agenda for securing government in cyberspace," Paper prepared for the Third Lac Carling Conference on Electronic Service Delivery, held in Bromont, Quebec, 24–26 May.

Hoffman, T. (1998) "Risk management still a wild frontier," *Computerworld*, **32**(7), 16 February, 10.

Knowles, J. (1996) "Learn to bungee jump," *Datamation*, **42**(16), October, 29.

KPMG Study (1999) *The Risk Survey Report*, Risk Strategy Services, KPMG Consulting, Toronto.

Luehrman, T. (1998) "Strategy as a portfolio of real options," *Harvard Business Review*, September–October, 89–101.

Maccoby, M. (1997) "Building trust is an art," *Research Technology Management*, **40**(5), September–October, 56–58.

Marshall, C., L. Prusak, and L. Shpilberg (1996) "Financial risk and the need for superior knowledge management," *California Management Review*, **38**(3), Spring, 77–101.

McFarlan, W. (1981) "Portfolio approach to information systems," *Harvard Business Review*, **59**(5), September–October, 142–150.

Peladeau, P. (1995) "Principles of personal data protection," *Risk Management*, **42**(12), December, 35–40.

Prakash, A. (1998) "Leveraging the potential of strategic systems," *Information Systems Management*, **15**(1), Winter, 58–63.

Simons, R. (1999) "How risky is your company?" *Harvard Business Review*, **77**(3), May–June, 85–94.

Smith, H. and J. McKeen (1999) "The CIO brief on privacy," *CIO Brief*, **5**(1), Queen's School of Business.

Software Engineering Institute (SEI) (1999) "SEI risk management frequently asked questions," www.sei.cmu.edu, Carnegie Mellon University (referenced 14 April).

Venkatramen, N. (1997) "Beyond outsourcing: Managing IT resources as a value center," *Sloan Management Review*, **38**(3), Spring, 51–64.

Wah, L. (1998) "The risky business of managing IT risks," *Management Review*, **87**(5), May, 6.

Yetton, P., W. Johnston, and K. Craig, (1994) "Computer-aided architects: A case study of IT and strategic change," *Sloan Management Review*, **35**(4), Summer, 57–68.

6
Achieving Effective Change with IT

We hear a lot these days about how organizations are changing—how they *must* change if the management gurus are to be believed (Arena, 2002). By this time, most senior business managers have bought into the idea that information technology (IT) is going to be *the* primary means of effecting change and the heat is on the information systems (IS) group to make the new organization happen (Kanter et al., 1992; Benjamin and Levinson, 1993; Castle and Sir, 2001). But change is difficult, as most of us know from both our personal and professional experience. Like a diet, it's relatively easy to start, but incredibly difficult to develop the new habits that will allow us to achieve permanent success.

Part of the reason for this is that change is typically viewed as a negative in organizations. One IT manager described it as "a bitter pill for the front line workers" and "very frustrating". Change is unsettling at best, and frequently frustrating, demoralizing, and confusing. Is it any wonder that as soon as we have stopped paying attention to it, the old, comfortable, satisfying ways slowly creep back in? Documented success rates of change projects in organizations are between 20% and 50% (Strebel, 1996).

While change has been with us for a long time—Heraclitus in 500 BC noted, "Nothing endures but change"—there is a general consensus that change these days is bigger, faster, and different from what it used to be. Price Pritchett points out that, in the 1980s, nearly half of all US companies were restructured, over 80,000 firms were acquired or merged, and several hundred thousand companies were downsized (Pritchett and Pound, 1994). That's a lot of change to deal with! And the velocity of change is different too. A chief executive officer (CEO) of a large company commented to us recently, "it used to be a lot of fun to work ten years ago. You could almost cope. Today, it's almost impossible because things happen at such a rapid rate."

For better or worse, IT is frequently the means through which change is implemented in a company. The key drivers of change—increasing information flow, technological discontinuity, new business practices, and increasing customer expectations—are each significantly facilitated by IT. Even though the actual changes may have much more to do with work flow, culture, and management than technology, IT is often seen as a miraculous remedy that can magically transform the organization into a lean, trim version of its former self with a minimum of effort. IT staff members are therefore "agents of change" because they initiate, design, and build this powerful technology (Markus and Benjamin, 1997). Unfortunately, just as fad diets rarely achieve a lasting impact, IT is no panacea for organizational change. In reality, IT is only one element of the organization's metabolism that must be aligned with others to achieve productive and permanent change.

This chapter looks at how organizations are approaching organizational change using IT. It looks first at the two dimensions of becoming a change-ready organization: the *what* and the *how* of change. It then offers a way of determining whether or not an organization is ready for the changes it is facing. Finally, it examines the actual regimen of change and how to plan, implement, and maintain permanent change using IT.

THE C-ZONE: WHAT IT TAKES TO BE A CHANGE-READY ORGANIZATION

Barry Sears' (1995) popular diet book, *The Zone*, describes the conditions necessary to achieve a desirable metabolic balance of protein and carbohydrates. This balance, he says, provides the individual with optimal health, greater energy, weight loss, and improved mental focus and productivity. Life outside this Zone is "its normal self—sometimes rewarding, mostly frustrating, filled with perplexing problems, missed opportunities, and illnesses great and small." One focus group member suggested that there is a similar zone for optimal organizational health—the change-ready zone (or C-zone)—within which companies are better prepared for and able to deal with change. Companies in the C-zone find change positive, look forward to the benefits it brings, and are better able to cope with its challenges. Those outside it tend either to be in a heightened state of panic, or are overly complacent or skeptical about change. Both these states are dangerous to the health of the organization.

Change feeds on two key components of the organization's metabolism: challenges and resources (see Figure 6.1). In companies where the challenge requires greater knowledge, effort, skill, or speed than people can cope with, change can cause chaos and panic. Conversely, where the time, people, and technology available exceed the challenge, an organization becomes complacent. What's needed therefore is a balance of the two. When it has been found, the organization is in the C-zone, and ready to make permanent changes. In the next three sections, we will look at these two components, and how to assess whether or not they are in balance.

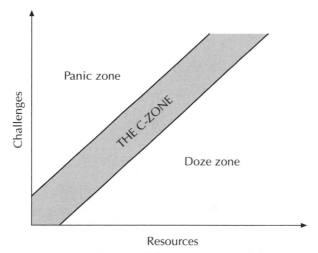

Figure 6.1   *The C-zone balances resources and challenges.*

THE CHALLENGES OF CHANGE

Challenges are what stimulate an organization to change, so they should not always be reduced or avoided. However, challenges also incorporate difficulties and risks for individuals and organizations. Therefore, it is important that IT managers understand the extent of the challenges involved in a particular change and that they ensure the necessary resources and leadership are provided to make it happen. Underestimating the challenges involved, as frequently happens, will lead to an imbalance in the effort devoted to making the change and thus increase the likelihood of failure. When considering how much challenge an organization is facing, leaders should assess four different dimensions of a change:

1. *Vision.* By definition, change means doing something differently. The first step toward change is determining *what* needs to be done differently. A vision for change involves more than a simple "vision statement" and more than a new system. If leaders perceive change to be a single silver bullet the result will be "thousands of cynical employees" (Brill and Worth, 1997). Nevertheless, a compelling picture of what could be will reduce the amount of difficulty involved in change because it will be attractive to the people involved. This is particularly true if this picture can be immediately perceived as being the right thing to do. One focus group member commented that, contrary to the popular belief that change must come from the top down, change is considerably less difficult to implement when there is a demand for it among the front-line workers. He remarked: "If you can get thousands of users to say 'I want this', you can create a drive for change that can't be challenged."

Change visions must therefore be able to communicate across the internal cultures within the organization and appeal to the actual recipients and implementers of change. Schein (1996) comments that, until executives and IT staff learn how to properly communicate a vision for change, users in an organization will always be working at cross-purposes. Thus, for certain individuals and groups, a vision should emphasize such things as usability and practicality for getting the job done, rather than financial survival, shareholder returns, or technical potential (even though such things may also be part of the vision).

2. *Mode.* A second challenge of change is the mode in which it is implemented. Many experts feel that change can only come about as the result of a crisis (Brill and Worth, 1997). Without it, they say, there is not enough motivation for people to move out of their present comfort zone. A crisis promotes change because it galvanizes staff and shakes them out of their complacency, encouraging them to align behind common organizational goals. However, a crisis can also overwhelm staff into helplessness and inertia. Using a crisis to promote change can therefore be a dangerous balancing act for an organization's leadership.

   Can an organization be galvanized into change without a crisis? Focus group members believed this is not only possible, but desirable, since change should be a continual way of life in the modern organization. They believe that change can also be stimulated if there is a dynamic change-leader in the organization, with a strong record of credibility, who can convince users to follow him or her and to put up with the ups and downs of the change process.

3. *Type.* There are two extreme types of change in organizations and many variations in between. At one end of the spectrum change is evolutionary, such as when the organization adapts to growth or to its environment. Here, change occurs in small steps and is therefore less dramatic (e.g., continuous improvement). The other extreme type is revolutionary change. Here, change is designed to quickly and radically transform one or more fundamental aspects of an organization (e.g., power structures, management, or business assets: Kanter et al., 1992). Many leaders believe that evolutionary change is too slow and cumbersome and that culture is too entrenched to accept evolutionary change. Revolution and chaos are the only ways to make change, they believe, because a crisis is the only thing that will shake an organization out of its self-balancing complacency (Browne, 1997). Again, the challenge involved must be carefully judged. Strebel (1996) points out that what senior managers see as one type of change (e.g., an opportunity to strengthen the business or take on new opportunities), employees at the mid- to lower levels may see as another because it is highly disruptive and intrusive. He notes senior managers consistently misjudge this gap in perception, and this is why change is more difficult than they expect.

4. *Impact.* The final challenge of change is found in how it affects an organiza-

tion. Change operates at two levels at least. It has both superficial and fundamental impacts. For example, a technological change could lead to a superficial change in staffing levels. What is often not seen or anticipated is the fact that it can also lead to changes in the psychological or social dimensions of the jobs that are left (Benjamin and Levinson, 1993; Strebel, 1996). While surface changes are usually obvious, fundamental changes can remain hidden or take time to become visible. Thus, our ability to recognize the impact of a change may be limited to the immediately obvious and superficial ones, while more powerful factors can be hidden, leading us to overlook elements of the change that can cause problems.

The discrepancy between what we anticipate the impact of technological change will be and how it actually affects organizations contributes significantly to the difficulties businesses face as they attempt to introduce IT change effectively.

Orlikowski and Hofman (1997) believe that we should recognize that not all impacts can be anticipated when making technological change. They suggest that many of the difficulties of change arise when we only plan for and manage anticipated changes and anticipated impacts. This increases the complexity of change because we don't recognize the unanticipated changes that can occur and deal effectively with their impacts. These include:

- *Emergent changes*—changes that arise spontaneously in response to planned change. Their impacts can be either positive or negative for the organization.
- *Opportunity-based changes*—changes that are introduced intentionally during the change process in response to unexpected impacts that arise (e.g., opportunities, events, or breakdowns).

THE RESOURCES OF CHANGE

Resources are the tools through which change is implemented. Organizations have three main resources at their disposal: technology, people, and processes. Leaders must provide the *right combination* of these resources to address a particular set of change challenges. Just as a single tool, such as a hammer, is not adequate for most building jobs, so any one of these tools is unlikely to be appropriate to deal with all the challenges involved in a change.

Technology

Like all resources, technology can be used to promote or hamper change. Change-readiness therefore depends on the role IT plays in the change process. Interestingly, none of the managers in the focus group saw it as being the most important resource of change implementation. In fact, they tended to underplay its significance. "Technology is the easy part," they agreed. "People and culture are the hardest aspects of change." Nevertheless, technology does have a part to play in helping organizations to change. Focus group members noted that an organization must have its technology fundamentals right (e.g., infrastructure, architecture, and technology leadership) in order to facilitate change. Conversely, the wrong technology can slow down what changes can be accomplished.

In some companies, IT is viewed as the *only* resource necessary for change. This may be a convenient self-deception that actually hinders change (Markus and Benjamin, 1997). For example, when IT staff and executives package new ideas as technologies, it helps them to distance themselves from the more difficult people aspects of change. Users too can find it easier to criticize technology rather than criticize the ideas embedded in it (e.g., "We'd use the technology to cut costs if we could but this software is a real dog"). Thus sometimes IT can be a scapegoat in organizational change and an excuse for not confronting the real issues involved.

The design of technology too can play an important role in facilitating change. Often, the assumptions made by IT staff can virtually design humans out of systems rather than into them. Schein (1996) notes that linear, cause-and-effect quantitative thinking can result in a worldview where "machines and processes work in perfect precision and harmony without human intervention" and leads to technology that is not useful for solving operational problems or promoting changed behavior. Conversely, IT that addresses real needs can create enthusiastic users.

People

We frequently hear about how "people" can make change a success or failure. However, there are at least three different factors involved in determining how people respond to change. Each must be considered an important element in mobilizing this resource:

1. *Culture.* The set of assumptions a group of people make about how the world is and ought to be, is known as culture. All organizations have at least three different cultures operating within them at all times: the culture of operators (i.e., the people who actually do the work in organizations), the culture of engineers (i.e., the people who design and implement the technology of organizations), and the culture of executives (i.e., the people who manage the financial survival and growth of the organization: Schein, 1996). Having a change-ready culture means ensuring the different languages and assumptions of these three groups are recognized and understood and that each are treated as providing a valid and useful perspective on the organization. To be ready to change, people must focus on mutual understanding, rather than on

mutual blame (Schein, 1996). One effective way of doing this is to develop "expert-users" or "super-users". These are people whose job bridges the semantic and skills gap between users and IT and who bring these two cultures to a common understanding of what is needed. Change can therefore be presented in ways that each understands and is willing to accept. Similarly, they can also play a bridging role between the executive culture and IT. In this way cultural alignment can be used to facilitate change.

2. *Skills.* Change also requires mental disciplines that help shape people's actions and govern their behavior (Pascale et al., 1997). The presence of these skills can transform the attitudes of everyone in the organization toward change. They include:

   - *Teamwork.* People must work in an environment where they can set aside hierarchy, apply their skills and intelligence to a larger goal, exercise self-criticism, and operate as true partners with each other, sharing equally in successes and failures. One company has set the following priorities for its organization: customer, company, business unit, and, lastly, the individual. It feels that these promote the spirit of teamwork and establish the context for effective team behavior and decision-making.

   - *Straight talk.* Staff and organizations must be willing to face the truth about themselves and able to engage in a healthy give-and-take (Pascale et al., 1997). Too often in change, conflict is seen as a negative. In fact, it can be constructive and supportive of change if it produces new ideas and possibilities (Kanter et al., 1992).

   - *Questioning.* Focus group members suggested that to promote change, people must be knowledge-hungry. Successful learning organizations are moving away from command-and-control forms of leadership to a discipline of relentlessly questioning everything. Once internalized, this discipline reveals itself in repeated questions about how things can be done better, faster, or cheaper. For example, the US army has found that this attitude has resulted in improvements in every level of performance (Pascale et al., 1997).

   - *Perspective.* Change-ready people act with the big picture in mind. They have a sense of meaning in their work, which results from understanding the value of a change. The ability to influence the nature of a change (Pascale et al., 1997) involves making sure people have a thorough understanding of the business and where it is going.

3. *Communication.* A third factor, which can be a significant resource in change, is communication. Focus group members emphasized that communication is so important that one or more full-time professionals should be dedicated to this work when any major transformation is taking place. John Kotter (1995) calls under-communicating a major cause of why transformation efforts fail. "Without credible communication, and a lot of it, the hearts and minds of the troops are never captured." Unfortunately, most change-leaders under-communicate by a factor of 10.

The real challenge facing organizations is to develop these three factors of culture, skills, and communication synergistically. All three are essential; neglecting one negates the others.

Processes

The last resource of a change-ready organization is the processes that support change. Processes accomplish two things. First, they help model how we view change and therefore shape our expectations. Second, they ensure that, in the midst of upheaval, critical things do not get forgotten. Some of the processes that an organization in the C-Zone should have in place include:

1. *A change management process.* The ability to view change systematically provides an organization with an approach to understand and better manage its realities in the modern organization (Orlikowski and Hofman, 1997). Traditionally, change has been viewed as a life cycle with sequential steps for envisioning, planning, implementation, consolidation, and institutionalization (Kotter, 1995; Benjamin and Levinson, 1993). However, because of the difficulty of predicting the organizational impacts of IT, a life cycle may not be the most effective change management model for IT to use. Furthermore, traditional change models suggest that change will end at some point in time. In fact, organizations are continually absorbing change, responding to unexpected events, and adapting to evolving technological capabilities, emerging practices, and unanticipated outcomes (Orlikowski and Hofman, 1997). An improvisational model of change management may therefore be a better way of viewing IT change because it takes into consideration the fact that change is an ongoing process rather than a discrete event. This type of model recognizes that only anticipated change can be planned. Emergent and opportunity-based changes must be *responded to*. Thus, it sees technological change not as a predefined program charted by management ahead of time, but as an iterative sequence of plans and responses. Through it, "rather than predefining each step and then controlling events to fit the plan, management creates an environment that facilitates improvisation ... and supports and nurtures the expectations, norms, and resources that guide the ongoing change process" (see Figure 6.2).

2. *Analytic processes.* To effectively cope with change, focus group members identified several analytic processes that IT organizations should have in place, including:
   - *Stakeholder analysis.* This is used to learn who will be affected by a particular change and who will be expected to be involved in making it a success. One IT manager commented, "It is often surprising to find out who the real stakeholders in a change are."
   - *Risk assessment and management.* Formal risk assessment and management procedures must be in place to address the down sides of change. Organizations that have implemented these practices have found themselves

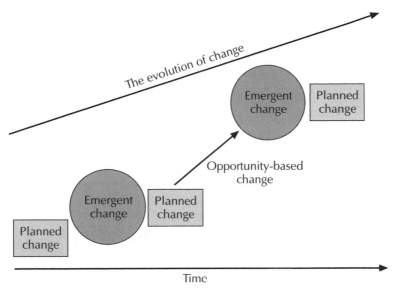

Figure 6.2   *An improvisational model of change incorporates all three types of change as needed.*

significantly better able to identify and mitigate the potential negative impacts of change (Aubert et al., 1998).

- *Usability analysis.* Many IT organizations have found they can generate considerable user support for change through involving them in assessing the usability of proposed technology changes. Focus group members have found that usability labs are well worth their cost in helping prevent change problems and positioning changes positively with users.
- *Root-cause analysis.* As problems with change arise, as they will inevitably, a change-ready organization must be prepared to cope with them. This involves looking for and addressing the underlying causes of problems, not simply their symptoms.

3. *Personal compact analysis.* Changes alter the status quo in organizations and with it the relationship between employees and organizations. Strebel (1996) calls this the *personal compact* a company has with its staff. There are formal (i.e., contractual) as well as social and psychological dimensions of this compact that can be affected by change. Managers who neglect to redefine the compact's new terms and persuade employees to buy into them can find themselves with disaffected employees who can undermine well-designed plans. Organizations should have the resources to assess employee concerns about the personal compact, such as:

- What am I supposed to do for the organization?
- What help will I get to do the job?
- How and when will my performance be evaluated and what form will the feedback take?

- What will I be paid and how will pay relate to my performance?
- How hard will I really have to work?
- What recognition, financial reward, or other personal satisfaction will I get for my efforts?
- Are the rewards worth it?
- Are my values similar to those of others in the organization?
- What are the real rules that determine who gets what in this company?

. Focus group members noted that if the incentives associated with change are not aligned with the behaviors management wants to promote, employees will resist the change. Assessment of the personal compact should therefore not only include evaluation of the formal incentives of an organization but also of the informal, social, and psychological incentives that make work worthwhile for an employee.

The resources an organization devotes to change should match the challenge of the changes it wants to make. Clearly, a company making process improvements of a limited scope needs fewer resources than one attempting fundamental change across several business units. Effective change leadership therefore involves assessing the challenges involved in the changes the company wants to make and ensuring that adequate resources are available for dealing with them.

IS YOUR ORGANIZATION IN THE C-ZONE?

To assess whether or not your organization is well equipped to cope with change, use the questionnaires in Tables 6.1 and 6.2 to determine whether or not you are in the C-zone. These questionnaires are scored as follows. For each

Table 6.1 *How much change challenge do you face?*

In my organization, *most* change ...	Not at all	Sometimes	Most of the time
1. Comes from the top down			
2. Is significant in scope			
3. Is urgently needed by the business			
4. Objectives are frequently unclear at lower levels in the organization			
5. Is not effectively implemented			
6. Affects the organizational hierarchy (from supervisor up)			
7. Affects how we run our business			
8. Affects employee staff and skill levels			
9. Affects more than one business unit			
10. Involves new ways of doing work			

Table 6.2   *How many resources are devoted to managing change?*

In my organization . . .	Not at all	Sometimes	Most of the time
1. The IT infrastructure effectively supports most applications			
2. There are specialists who can effectively provide a bridge between IT staff and users			
3. Straight talk about change is valued even if it is negative			
4. Staff are encouraged to actively question why and how things are done and to seek answers			
5. Everyone involved in change understands the big picture			
6. Teamwork is effective			
7. Communication is excellent			
8. Change is implemented following a formal model			
9. There are formal processes for risk assessment, root-cause analysis, stakeholder analysis, and usability analysis			
10. Change is accompanied by formal assessment of employee jobs and working conditions			

answer in the "Not at all" column, count 0 points. For each answer in the "Sometimes" column, count 5 points. For each answer in the "Most of the time" column, count 10 points. Total the points for Challenge (Table 6.1) and Resources (Table 6.2) separately and plot them on the graph in Figure 6.3. Their position indicates how much challenge your organization is facing from change and how ready your organization is to deal with it (i.e., whether or not you are in the C-zone).

THE CHANGE REGIMEN: EXECUTING AND MAINTAINING SUCCESSFUL CHANGE

Once your organization is in the C-zone, change with IT will be easier, but individual changes will still have to be implemented and maintained. Just as a successful weight loss program involves a specific regimen of eating and exercise, so successful change involves adhering to certain proven guidelines. As well, like a diet, change is a discipline. In order to have a long-term impact, change involves ongoing vigilance until the new habits have been completely integrated into the lifestyle of the corporation. Focus group managers pointed out that true and lasting change involves "guts, fortitude, and commitment" on behalf of the

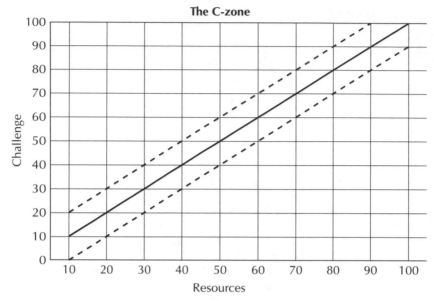

Figure 6.3   *Balancing challenges with available resources to achieve change.*

change team since change itself can be complicated and sometimes messy. They suggested that every change project undertaken should plan to do the following:

- *Go on a journey.* Changing expectations about change is the first step in effective change management. As noted above, change with IT is not likely to follow a systematic step-by-step process and have clearly defined impacts. One focus group member remarked, "You can no more manage change than a sailor can manage the wind." You can however use the wind to help reach an objective, adapting to conditions as they arise. A change project is therefore best conceived of as an iterative and ongoing process of opportunities and challenges that are not always predictable at the start. Plans should be developed but viewed as guides rather than blueprints. Deviations should not be considered failures, but as events to be expected and actively managed.
- *Build relationships.* We actually know a lot about how to change, say the experts, but we don't always use what we know. For example, the most important change practice is personal contact: "Change flows across a helping relationship ... It is a contact sport" (Markus and Benjamin, 1997). However, it is not sufficient to simply tell people how and why they must change. Users must be able to behave mindfully and with commitment to and understanding of the technology so they can use it to accomplish the desired results. Thus, ultimately, change management cannot be separated from the IT used.
- *Obtain results.* Focus group members agreed that, because change can be

uncomfortable, it is essential that results come quickly and be highly visible. Successful change breeds more success when people begin to see its benefits. Thus, large changes should be broken down into smaller deliverables. Kotter (1995) states that not systematically planning for and creating short-term wins is a key reason why transformation efforts fail. Actively looking for ways to obtain clear short-term improvements and recognizing the people involved boosts the credibility of the change effort. It can also keep urgency levels up and force detailed analytical thinking to clarify or revise visions. As well, specific, measurable results achieved within a few months of a change can lead to a subtle but profound shift in mind-set that promotes other learning and change initiatives throughout the company (Schaffer and Thompson, 1992).

- *Assign responsibilities.* Most focus group members stated that their companies identify a specific person or persons as being responsible for achieving change. (They cautioned that this person should not be the same as the project- or program-manager who has specific IT deliverables to develop.) A change-agent is typically someone who works cross-functionally to manage and guide the process of change. Often he or she is an expert-user, but a change-agent could also be an IT person with relationship management responsibilities. There are other important change management roles as well. A change-sponsor is the person who initiates and legitimizes the change. He or she mobilizes the change-champions, ensures alignment of the change with the corporate culture, and removes any obstacles to change. A change-champion is a person who co-creates the strategy for change and enables it. He or she provides the necessary resources to implement the change and also offers ongoing guidance and support. Change-recipients, also known as stakeholders, are the people who are affected by the change and whose involvement is key to its success. A change-recipient is a person who uses and adapts changes and who actually achieves results. Feedback from recipients is essential in the change management process. In spite of everyone performing their assigned role, however, failure can occur. To ensure success, both IT and user staff must recognize that change is really everyone's job and that they need to do whatever it takes to get it done.

- *Provide leadership.* Being an effective change-leader requires a variety of skills. Technical knowledge is needed to know IT's capabilities, to understand the IT implications of business decisions, to communicate value, and to deploy processes and technology. Visioning is required to provide the creative thinking behind the change and to communicate it effectively. Analytic and negotiating skills are important to develop and manage effective change plans and to build relationships and gain people's support for change. And personal credibility attributes such as self-confidence, a willingness to change, and a willingness to take risks are necessary to encourage others to follow. But leadership does not always mean providing the solutions to change problems. Studies of organizations that have transformed themselves suggest that successful change requires "leading from a different place" (Pascale et. al., 1997). This means leaders must resist the temptation to always provide the answer. These companies have found that to develop the learning behaviors that will promote true change in an organization, "the solutions and the commitment to deliver on them must come from the ranks" (Pascale et al., 1997).

- *Make use of setbacks.* Setbacks *will* occur in a change project. Real change never runs smoothly because of the emotions and social issues involved. No matter how perfectly a technology works, the people and processes involved in IT change are inherently unpredictable. This is why effective change-leaders must see setbacks as windows to learning (Pascale et al., 1997; Orlikowski and Hofman, 1997). This is easier said than done, since humans are conditioned to react to mistakes in negative ways. However, with discipline, setbacks can be recontextualized as breakthroughs and opportunities. At the very least, setbacks must force the change team to deal with whatever issues are causing them. Focus group members were unanimous that problems cannot be ignored. True change will only result when *all* issues and concerns are declared and dealt with.

CONCLUSION

This chapter has explored the process of change in organizations using IT, and how to ensure that it is implemented effectively. Rather than focusing on a sequential procedure for individual changes, it has looked at what it takes for an organization to be *change-ready* and continually changing as necessary. Viewing change as an ongoing process is a better way to manage the realities of change in most organizations today. But this requires that IT managers change the way they change—how they conceptualize and implement it, the resources they use, and the competencies they develop. It is only when IT managers realize that technology is not a silver bullet for change that they will be able to take advantage of the opportunities presented by individual and corporate reactions to it. In this way, they will be able to unlock the real value *behind* IT change for the organization.

REFERENCES

Aubert, B., S. Dussault, M. Patry, and S. Rivard (1998) "Managing the risk of IT outsourcing," *Proceedings of the 31st Hawaii International Conference on System Sciences*, January, IEEE Computer Society, NJ.

Benjamin, R.I. and E. Levinson (1993) "A framework for managing IT-enabled change," *Sloan Management Review*, Summer.

Brill, P. and R. Worth (1997) *The Four Levers of Corporate Change*, American Management Association, New York.

Browne, J. (1997) "Unleashing the power of learning", *Harvard Business Review*, September–October.

Castle, D. and M. Sir (2001) "Organization development: A framework for successful information technology assimilation," *Organization Development Journal*, Spring, **19**(1), 59–72.

Kanter, R.M., B.A. Stein, and T.D. Jick (1992) *The Challenge of Organizational Change*, The Free Press, New York.

Kotter, J.P. (1995) "Leading change: Why transformation efforts fail," *Harvard Business Review*, March–April, 59–67.

Markus, L. and R.I. Benjamin (1997) "The magic bullet theory in IT-enabled transformation," *Sloan Management Review*, Winter, 55–68.

Orlikowski, W.J. and J.D. Hofman (1997) "An improvisational model for change management: The case of groupware technologies," *Sloan Management Review*, Winter, 11–21.

Pascale, R., M. Millemann, and L. Gioja (1997) "Changing the way we change," *Harvard Business Review*, November–December, 127–139.

Pritchett, P. and R. Pound (1994) *Change: The Employee Handbook for Organizational Change*, Pritchett & Associates, Dallas, TX.

Schaffer, R. and H.A. Thompson (1992) "Successful change programs begin with results," *Harvard Business Review*, January–February, 80–89.

Schein, E.H. (1996) "Three cultures of management: The key to organizational learning," *Sloan Management Review*, Fall, 9–20.

Sears, B. (1995) *The Zone*, Regan Books, New York.

Strebel, P. (1996) "Why do employees resist change?" *Harvard Business Review*, May–June, 86–92.

Part B
Leveraging Business with IT

Today, information technology's (IT's) potential for delivering value to an organization is widely acknowledged, if not universally realized. "Leveraging the business" is a relatively recent term that describes IT's ability not only to enable a firm to do more with less but also to uncover new sources of organizational value. Thus, technology can be a fundamental component of new goods and services, facilitate new ways of interacting with customers, or lead to more integrated organizations and information. However, leverage does not come easily. As many companies have discovered with the recent dotcom bubble, it is extremely easy to invest millions and receive very few benefits. New ideas, enabled by technology, can be enticing, but leverage will only be achieved if they are part of a larger corporate strategy, properly conceived in conjunction with the business and effectively implemented.

This section examines several aspects of what it means to leverage a business with IT. Chapter 7, "Aligning IT with the Business", looks at how to develop a viable fit between an organization's business and IT functions to achieve an effective strategic, structural, and cultural fusion of interests and activities. The next chapter, "Mergers and IT: Making the Most of an Arranged Marriage", looks at the role of IT in a corporate merger and presents strategies for achieving a merger as quickly and painlessly as possible.

The next two chapters discuss how to derive value from an enterprise-wide technology package. Chapter 9, "Leveraging CRM with IT", discusses customer relationship management software and strategies for its successful implementation. Chapter 10, "ERP Systems: What a Manager Needs to Know", examines the effort it will take and the types of decision necessary to realize the benefits these large, complex suites of software promise.

The final two chapters in this part look at the processes involved in determining which IT projects should be undertaken by the organization. Chapter 11, "Estimating the Benefits of IT", addresses the ongoing challenge of how best to assess the potential value of an IT project and to actually engineer optimal benefits. Chapter 12, "IT Project Prioritization", maps the process that governs IT projects from their initial conceptualization through to project launch. It suggests that project prioritization is a critical linkage mechanism between IT and business. When done effectively, it ensures that investments are focused on high-potential applications that will truly leverage the business.

7
Aligning IT with the Business

In the last decade, developing a viable fit between an organization's strategies and its information technology (IT) resources has come to be seen as essential to a company's performance. Traditionally, IT has been seen as a means of reducing administrative expenses, rather than a strategic resource. However, research has shown that where there is a strong match between business and IT plans and strategies, companies tend to be top achievers in their industries. IT on its own is not sufficient to create performance or competitive advantage. It is only when IT is effectively *aligned* with corporate strategies, processes, and practices that it can enable companies to achieve their performance goals (Chan and Huff, 1993).

Alignment is therefore a state in which the goals and activities of a business are in harmony with the information systems that support them. Perfect alignment between IT and business would be similar to a marriage where each partner understands the tastes and needs of the other to such an extent that either could make decisions that match the decision that the other would make. Clearly, perfect alignment is an ideal, rather than a realistic objective!

Nevertheless, good alignment can have an important impact on both IT effectiveness and business performance. Business strategy can enhance or diminish the impact of IT. Similarly, IT strategy can enhance or diminish the impact of business strategy. Achieving a fit or synergy between IT and business is therefore a worthwhile goal for IT managers.

However, while a great deal is already known about alignment *in theory*, in practice it is difficult to achieve and measure. This chapter therefore discusses how organizations have applied the theory of business–IT alignment to their current operations. It first outlines the different elements of alignment, and how alignment can be recognized. Then, it describes forces in the organization that can work in favor of alignment or against it. Finally, it examines ways organizations are actually working to achieve alignment.

WHAT IS ALIGNMENT?

Alignment is a complex concept, and there are many different approaches to understanding it. Furthermore, business and IT do not necessarily align in a one-to-one fashion. The collective fit between the two is more important to performance than individual fits across single items (Zahra and Covin, 1993). Research has identified three dimensions of alignment—*strategic, structural,* and *cultural*—each of which plays an important role in determining the degree of alignment in an organization.

1 Strategic Alignment

Strategic alignment exists when the goals and activities of a business are in harmony with the information systems that support them. The most effective and sustainable uses of IT are those that occur when IT is tightly integrated into every aspect of the firm's strategic thinking. Alignment is the degree to which IT resources are directed toward a company's unique strategic thrust. In general, the stronger a company's strategic orientation, the more important alignment is (Henderson and Venkatramen, 1999).

IT can play an important role in many business strategies—building relationships with customers and suppliers, enlarging a business's competitive domain, and creating new products, services, and markets. However, before this can happen, IT planning must be linked in some way to the organization's planning, and senior business managers must also understand the capabilities and potential of IT.

Formulation of formal strategic plans is the first aspect of ensuring strategic fit. To do this, both IT and business managers must have an understanding and an appreciation of the processes and methods involved. Companies can adopt four different approaches to planning (Henderson and Venkatramen, 1991):

- *strategy execution*—where a business strategy is developed first and directs the development of an IT strategy;
- *competitive potential*—where managers first actively consider how to take advantage of IT to achieve major business change, and this then sets the business's strategic direction;
- *service level*—where IT and business strategies are developed separately and then scrutinized to achieve matches and modified;
- *technology potential*—where the IT strategy is developed first and business strategy is evolved out of what the technology enables it to do.

However, formal planning alone is insufficient to ensure strategic alignment. To be effective, strategies must be communicated and implemented throughout the organization by all levels of business and IT management (Lederer and Mendelow, 1986). Top managers must ensure that strategies fit with the organization as a whole and take into consideration the changes in the firm's external environment. Middle managers must work to ensure that strategies are turned into practical and effective blueprints for action. And operational managers need to focus on actually implementing and monitoring projects.

2 Structural Alignment

An organization's structure is an outcome of the interaction between technology and organizational design. Organizations can capitalize on IT's capabilities and use it to facilitate certain kinds of organization structure (e.g., decentralization), but there is no one *best* structure for a particular firm. Research shows that IT can have a variety of impacts on a firm's organizational structure, but no single predictable impact (Brown and Magill, 1994). This suggests that managers need to understand and anticipate the ways in which IT and organizational design interact to minimize negative impacts and to ensure that an organization's structure emerges in conjunction with, not despite, the IT that is implemented.

Historically, companies have been organized hierarchically. Today, however, IT makes new and different modes of organizing more practical. For example, IT can remove restrictions on access to information, such as those pertaining to time and geography, and can enable information to be formalized and diffused across a broad population. Enabling organizations to communicate differently in turn alters decision-making processes. In this way, IT can be used either to support existing organizational designs or to promote new work models and processes (Rockhart and Short, 1989).

Some of the impacts that IT can have on organization structure include: changes in managerial structure, roles, and processes; the development of new methods of organizing work; the creation of electronically integrated organizations; the integration of processes and data; increasing management interdependence; and changing control systems. The impact of IT on control systems is especially significant since these types of system are utilized extensively in organizations to reorganize information for a variety of different uses. This can lead to the *consolidation, centralization,* or *decentralization* of information and decisions in a firm (Bruns and McFarlan, 1987).

Structure is also a key factor in how firms organize to promote IT innovation and adoption to get returns from their IT investments. Organizations need to balance the degree of slack that is needed to encourage innovation with the degree of control needed to infuse innovation into the organization and manage any unintended consequences of change. It is therefore important to consider the *structure of the IT function* and its relationship to the organization as a whole. The trend in maintaining this balance is toward recentralization of infrastructure decisions and further decentralization of applications and project management decisions within organizations (Huber et al., 1990). Such an approach requires a high degree of sharing between the IT group and functional areas of a company.

3 Cultural Alignment

Culture is pervasive throughout an organization and colors the meaning that individuals ascribe to all organizational acts. It is the pattern of basic assumptions, which are taught as the "correct" way to perceive, think, and feel by members of an organization. Culture is therefore a stabilizing influence in the organization and, once in place, an inherently conservative force, which can inhibit change.

IT can have profound effects on organization strategies and structure, but only if the organizational culture can accept change. Three cultural visions have grown up around the way IT should be implemented in organizations (Wolfe, 1993; Schein, 1985):

- *the vision to automate*—where IT is used to enable routine kinds of work (e.g., document preparation) to be done largely by machines with little human intervention;
- *the vision to informate*—where IT is used to create information about organizations and activities that never existed previously or could not be accessed easily. This information is used to enrich jobs and to create new jobs. Informating's primary purpose is to support and enhance decision-making, not to replace human intervention.
- *the vision to transform*—where IT is used to integrate human and technical capabilities, thus achieving radical transformations in work.

Culture directly affects the nature and deployment of IT because it is the means whereby organizations and their members both cope with the environment and innovate. Innovative cultures will propagate IT to transform thinking, production, and managerial processes. The most innovative organizations are those that emphasize consensus and consistency on an organization-wide basis. These organizations can adapt most readily to changing environmental conditions. They tend to have adaptive, flexible, responsive information systems and flexible, equitable and participative leadership (Schein, 1994). A resistive culture, on the other hand, can virtually prevent the successful implementation of IT-led change (Zammuto and O'Connor, 1992).

Fortunately, culture can be directly influenced by management action. To do this, managers need to be coherent and consistent in their communications, selectively choose a few crucial interventions that will make a difference, and develop formal and informal networks within the organization (Nixon, 1992).

ORGANIZATIONAL FORCES AFFECTING ALIGNMENT

The focus group first discussed forces in organizations that could encourage or discourage business–IT alignment. The participants stressed that none of these supporting factors will lead to alignment in and of themselves. However, together they can create an *environment* that can lead to greater alignment or discourage efforts to create greater alignment, despite the best efforts of IT or senior managers.

Forces Promoting Alignment

There was strong agreement on the factors that supported alignment. At a strategic level, a clear, common vision about where the enterprise is going is essential. The most important thing senior executives can do to promote alignment in their organizations is to agree among themselves about the business's strategy and philosophy and to communicate it consistently to all parts of the company.

A corollary to this is that working with IT as an equal partner can ensure the company's technical and strategic directions complement each other rather than work against each other. Regardless of how business and technical strategies are developed (see above), both groups must recognize that, without the other at the table and able to participate fully, there can never be effective alignment.

Finally, business must take ownership of IT projects. With IT an integral part of most business strategies today, an "us and them" mentality where IT is blamed for ineffective technology and systems is clearly inappropriate. While IT has the mandate to deliver technology to the organization, it is the business's responsibility to ensure it gets what it needs. It can only do so by taking overall responsibility for all aspects of strategy, including the technological ones. Many group members found that the best way to ensure business becomes accountable for the technology it asks for is to completely expose the costs of all parts of the technical strategy. When these are made clear, business managers are much more likely to work to ensure that they receive value for the money being spent.

At a structural level, alignment can be encouraged by having good organizational definitions about who is responsible for what in the organization. The ability to easily match business and IT subunits on an organization chart also facilitates structural alignment. Interestingly, several members noted that having common titles and HR policies enhanced this type of alignment. Knowing that a "director" or a "manager" means the same thing in both IT and business makes it easier for members of both groups to relate to each other. This, in turn, develops cross-functional relationships that promote informal communication and, ultimately, alignment.

Two organizational policies strongly foster structural alignment. Centralization of decision-making and an emphasis on integration both make alignment easier to achieve by reducing the numbers of people involved and emphasizing cross-functional integration. However, such policies can also have negative effects on the organization, and many companies therefore choose not to implement them or adopt a hybrid organization structure. As one manager noted:

Centralization is good for alignment with corporate strategy and for integration across business units. But decentralization makes it easier to build relationships, trust, and accountability throughout the organization rather than just at senior levels.

Another reason not to be totally centralized is that it discourages innovation. A large number of legacy systems may also mean that centralization is not appropriate for an organization.

Culturally, a recognition of the mutual dependence of business and IT, as well as a fundamental appreciation of the value of IT, go a long way to encouraging business and IT to truly work together to achieve alignment.

Forces Inhibiting Alignment

Group members also identified a number of factors that limit or detract from good business–IT alignment. Initially, these appeared to be more organization-specific than the supporting factors (e.g., politics). However, when examined more closely, they fell into a number of common themes, suggesting that limiting factors are more typical than many IT managers realize. If these are stronger than the supporting forces, then efforts to promote alignment can be negated (Spier, 1973).

Most damaging to strategic alignment is the failure of senior management to focus their organizational and IT priorities. One company (Smith and McKeen, 1996b) had over 470 projects under way at one time! With so many competing priorities, it is unlikely that a company or an IT organization can support any strategic direction. A related factor, which can detract from alignment, is making too many tradeoffs between strategic and tactical projects. This can result in strategic projects being continually postponed.

One mistake that companies sometimes make is encouraging a strong alignment with individual business units rather than with the enterprise as a whole. Not surprisingly, this results in projects that optimize business unit strategies at the expense of corporate strategies. Finally, naivety about the true costs of IT can lead businesses to adopt unrealistic strategies.

Structurally, alignment can be negatively affected when IT and business subunits have either a one : many or a many : many relationship. This leads to confusion and to disagreements over ownership and decision-making. Similarly, a strong emphasis on departmental independence and decentralized decision-making makes it harder to ensure that agreement can be reached on enterprise-wide business or technical issues. Within IT, isolating different skills into different structural groups (e.g., development, maintenance, and support) requires business units to deal with different groups, and can lead to unclear lines of responsibility and accountability. Finally, the physical isolation of groups can also lead to misalignments by discouraging interaction between them, in turn discouraging the development of informal relationships and knowledge—which can overcome some types of structural misalignment.

Cultural alignment can be discouraged, group members strongly agreed, by a lack of accountability for decisions. When this happens, decision-makers feel no strong sense of commitment to a particular decision (e.g., an IT project) and, thus, do not feel responsible for its success. Viewing IT as a support function can also negate alignment because this belief can lead to a lack of true partnership between business and IT.

ACHIEVING ALIGNMENT

Achieving alignment is first and foremost "a lot of hard work" according to IT managers. Even with a supportive environment, companies must still take proactive steps toward alignment and to ensure that it is occurring at all levels. The managers in the group had the following advice for others seeking to align themselves better:

- *Place a strong emphasis on planning and modeling at all levels.* At a minimum, a business plan and IT architecture must be developed. Most members felt that planning should be rigorous and should link the business architecture with the IT architecture. Because of the interaction between them, neither plan should be cast in concrete before the other—even if one is considered the driving force. Four types of plan are possible:

  1. *An enterprise business plan,* which includes a marketing strategy, business technology plan, and a future mode of business operation.
  2. *Specific business unit plans,* which include business unit strategies, new products, and business transformation projects.
  3. *An information systems plan,* which includes a business process architecture, an IT architecture, and projects.
  4. *An enterprise technology plan,* which includes technology architecture, standard products, design principles, and a data model.

  Different organizations use different mechanisms to ensure plans are effectively aligned (e.g., steering committees, technical and business councils). In one innovative approach described by a group member, IT develops a *business* plan and the business develops a *technical* plan and then they work together to perfect them. This helps each group to understand the other's area more clearly and to identify gaps in knowledge and awareness of the other's field of expertise:
- *Focus on the business's bottom line.* To counteract the natural tendency to trade off strategic for tactical projects and to undertake too many projects, every IT project should be associated with a strong business case, including *measurable benefits*. If business units are held accountable for the benefits to be achieved,

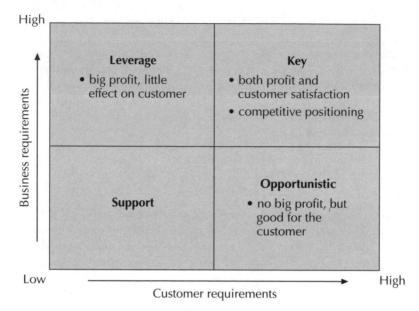

Figure 7.1   *Project classification for performance (data from McKeen and Smith, 1996, used with kind permission).*

and if post-implementation audits are held, then a clear linkage between IT and business benefit can be realized. Another way to achieve this focus is to classify every project according to its business and customer requirements (see Figure 7.1). Emphasis is placed on increasing the percentage of projects that have high value for the customer and high business payback and those that are high-leverage projects for the company that would not be apparent to the customer (i.e., Quadrants 1 and 2). By assessing *every* project in this way, it is easy to demonstrate to the business that the greatest returns to the organization come from investments that are strategically focused. Using this approach, one company was able to reduce its priority projects from 470 to 23 in two years.

- *Move up the value chain.* Typically, the IT function covers the gamut of technology services from equipment provisioning and communications services to applications development and strategic planning. Increasingly, IT managers are realizing that their true value to the organization comes from providing the "higher end" services; that is, those that require specialized knowledge of the business and that emphasize the partnership between business and IT. Operations, maintenance, and equipment and communications management, while they must be done, provide very little distinctive value to the company. Aligning IT with business therefore means identifying those areas of IT where it provides unique value and focusing on them, while spending as little time as possible on the others. In short, this means focusing here on IT *has* to be the best.

- *Standardize.* Wherever possible, standards should be developed and followed. A standard IT operating environment is essential and eliminates numerous integration and upgrading problems. Many organizations are now insisting on a common configuration of technology and a common suite of software for the desktop. This promotes efficiency—so every department doesn't operate its own mini-IT function—and saves the cost of maintaining multiple technical environments. Most organizations forbid the use of any non-standard hardware or software. This ensures that different subunits of the organization can communicate with each other and eliminates differences in technical strategy—both of which can seriously hamper alignment between business subunits and cause significant alignment problems for IT. Similarly, using standard data helps both business and IT subunits to keep enterprise concerns first and foremost in their minds. Sharing data promotes integration and discourages the development of narrow-focus business applications. The focus group pointed out that standardization is not always popular with individual business units. They may not want to spend the money to upgrade to a standard environment; they may wish to go their own way (and spend their own money) to implement the applications and technology they want. The group emphasized that senior management must strongly support standards—to the point of insisting that they be followed even if there is no immediate business value for an individual business unit.
- *Insist on business accountability and ownership.* The most effective method of promoting alignment is one where business takes accountability for the results of the IT that is implemented and IT takes the responsibility for its delivery. In organizations where they are considered responsible for the IT they get, business managers take more time with business cases, participate more in the decisions that are made, and pay more attention to the work being done. One way some companies encourage accountability is to formally monitor the business benefits achieved by every project, removing savings after the project is successfully implemented. Focus group managers were unanimous that business ownership of IT is essential to achieving effective alignment.
- *Adopt a consulting model for IT.* IT must be considered to be a part of the business management team. To do this, IT staff must develop both consulting skills and business knowledge. In many cases, the informal relationship that develops between an IT manager and his or her business counterpart is more important to alignment than any formal planning and decision-making processes. Focus group members stressed repeatedly that trust, a good track record, and a strong personal relationship between a chief information officer (CIO) and a chief executive officer (CEO) or between division heads, was a key reason behind good alignment in their organizations. To achieve this level of relationship, one organization assesses all its IT staff according to a "partnership model" of the *role* they play vis-á-vis their counterparts in

business. Individuals (regardless of their formal title) are assessed as to whether they *act* as a junior partner (i.e., providing services), partner (i.e., having a vote and being a contributor to the management team), or a senior partner (i.e., someone to whom all decisions are referred and who is considered integral to the success of the business unit). Ideally, IT staff should be so tightly integrated with the business that they understand and are able to anticipate the business's needs.

- *Measure alignment.* Although alignment is an elusive quality more noticeable in its absence than in its presence, there are some tools and techniques that companies can use to monitor and measure strategic, structural, and cultural alignment. One of the most common approaches is a regular customer satisfaction survey. IT managers disagree about the effectiveness of such surveys. However, a properly designed survey can reveal a great deal about alignment. Not only should such a survey reveal how satisfied users are with IT currently, it should also assess how well positioned they feel their IT is making them for the future (McKeen and Smith, 1996). Several researchers have also developed instruments for assessing strategic and cultural alignment. These include Chan's (1996) study of structure and alignment, the Fletcher Cultural Audit (Fletcher and Jones, 1992), and the Organizational Cultural Profile (Chatman and Jehn, 1994). Focus group participants pointed out that, often, an external consultant can be more effective in assessing alignment and identifying the root causes of misalignment than internal staff. This is because consultants are presumed to be less biased than business managers. Finally, several organizations have found that the use of a group decision support system (GDSS) using force field analysis (Spier, 1973) can be very useful in quantifying the strength of factors that support and limit alignment within the organization.

- *Promote Successes.* Business's *perception* of IT's capabilities is a fundamental factor in determining the quality of an organization's alignment. If IT is perceived to be incompetent, it is highly unlikely that it will ever be consulted or treated like a partner (Smith and McKeen, 1996a). Recognition of successful IT implementations serves several purposes. *First*, it underscores the importance of IT to the business. *Second,* as one CIO recently noted, both IT and business people need to be reminded of their accomplishments in systems. Both groups tend to be somewhat negative when things go wrong, not seeing all the progress that is being made. External and internal presentations along with articles make these links explicitly for people and present a positive image of what has been achieved. Positive feelings can then translate into a more productive work environment (Smith and McKeen, 1996a). *Third,* it promotes trust between the two groups. This is the essence of an effective relationship. When each knows that the other can be trusted to deliver, it is more likely to seek to establish the necessary relationships and attitudes that promote good alignment.

CONCLUSION

Aligning IT and corporate goals has been a top priority for IT managers for at least 10 years (Anonymous, 1996). In spite of this, IT organizations everywhere are continuing to struggle with this issue. As we have shown, the concept of "alignment" strikes at the heart of many of the problems faced by IT in organizations—how decisions are made, who makes them, and who is responsible for the benefits of technology. Furthermore, business–IT alignment is much more than coordinated planning. It is nothing less than the complete fusion of the two functions strategically, structurally, and culturally. Finally, alignment is not simply an IT problem. While in some organizations, business managers have recognized their role in ensuring business–IT alignment, in too many others it is still the responsibility of IT managers to promote it. The focus group made it clear that it is only when both IT and business managers face such issues head-on, and clearly address them *together*, that the problem of alignment can be resolved.

REFERENCES

Anonymous (1996) "Aligning technology and corporate goals IT top concern," *SimNetwork*, July.

Brown, C. and S. Magill (1994) "Alignment of the IT function with the enterprise: Toward a model of antecedents," *MIS Quarterly*, December.

Bruns, W. and F.W. McFarlan (1987) "Information technology puts power in control systems," *Harvard Business Review*, September–October.

Chan, Y. and S. Huff (1993) "Strategic information systems," *Business Quarterly*, **57**, Autumn.

Chan, Y. (1996) "Business and information systems strategy, structure and alignment: An APC-sponsored study," *SimNetwork*, February, 15–16.

Chatman, J. and K. Jehn (1994) "Assessing the relationship between industry characteristics and organizational culture: How different can you be?" *Academy of Management Journal*, **37**(3).

Fletcher, B. and F. Jones (1992) "Measuring organizational culture: The cultural audit," *Managerial Auditing Journal*, **7**(6).

Henderson, J.C. and N. Venkatramen (1991) "Understanding strategic alignment," *Business Quarterly*, **55**, Winter.

Henderson, J.C. and N. Venkatramen (1999) "Strategic alignment: Leveraging information technology for transforming organizations," *IBM Systems Journal*, **32**(1).

Huber, G., C. Miller, and W. Glick (1990) "Developing more encompassing theories about organizations: The centralization–effectiveness relationship as an example," *Organization Science*, **1**(1).

Lederer, A. and A. Mendelow (1986) "Issues in information systems planning," *Information & Management*, **10**.

McKeen, J. and H. Smith (1996) *Management Challenges in IT: Successful Strategies and Appropriate Action*, John Wiley & Sons, Chichester, UK.

Nixon, B. (1992) "Developing a new culture for organizations in the '90's," *Management Education and Development*, **23**(1).

Rockhart, J. and J. Short (1989) "Information technology and the new organization: Towards more effective management of interdependence," *Sloan Management Review*, **30**(2), Winter.

Schein, E.H. (1985) *Organizational Culture and Leadership*, Jossey-Bass, San Francisco.

Schein, E.H. (1994) "Innovative cultures and organizations," in T.J. Allen and M.S. Scott Morton (eds), *Information Technology and the Corporation of the 1990's*, Oxford University Press, New York.

Smith, H. and J. McKeen (1996a) "The CIO Brief on Sears Canada," *The CIO Brief*, **2**(1), February.

Smith, H. and J. McKeen (1996b) "The CIO Brief on Canadian Tire," *The CIO Brief*, **2**(2), May.

Spier, W.C. (1973) "Kurt Lewin's 'force field analysis'," in J.E. Jones and J.W. Pfeiffer (eds), *The 1973 Annual Handbook for Group Facilitators*, University Associates, San Diego.

Wolfe, R. (1993) "The path to strategic alignment," *Information Strategy*, Winter.

Zahra, S. and J. Covin (1993) "Business strategy, technology policy and firm performance," *Strategic Management Journal*, **14**.

Zammuto, R.F. and E.J. O'Connor (1992) "Gaining advanced manufacturing technologies' benefits: The roles of organization design and culture," *Academy of Management Review*, **17**.

8
Mergers and IT: Making the Most of an Arranged Marriage

As if all the challenges facing a modern organization aren't enough to keep an information technology (IT) manager busy, today many IT shops are finding themselves being joined in corporate matrimony with an unfamiliar IT partner as a result of a merger. Those who have been through the adjustments associated with such arranged nuptials know that a true marriage of technology, systems, and culture can literally take years to develop. In the meantime, productivity and morale can decline as IT staff on both sides try to cope with new ways of doing things, uncertainty about their work and jobs, and deep resentments over the upheaval in their lives. At the same time, IT is expected to present a "business as usual" image of the new corporate entity to the public. As one IT manager put it:

> The deal gets closed and everybody is sitting around a table at an office somewhere sipping champagne, saying, "We closed the deal." And your IT staff, on both sides, is back in their office with a gun to their heads (Francis, 1998).

Unfortunately, it appears that an era of mergers is just beginning. IT organizations are therefore going to need to know how to effectively manage and make the most of an arranged marriage. This chapter explores what general lessons can be learned about managing mergers from the IT perspective and how to achieve a harmonious union of IT organizations as a result of a corporate merger. It first examines the corporate parents and their roles in the merger process. Then it looks at some of the different impacts a merger can have on their IT offspring. Next, it explores the challenges of integrating two different IT organizations once the marriage has been arranged. Finally, it looks at the key issues that must be addressed in achieving an effective IT integration and provides guidelines for managers on how to deal with them.

THE CORPORATE PARENTS: AN OVERVIEW OF MERGERS

Corporate mergers seem to be becoming increasingly common. While mergers and acquisitions (M&As) have been part of the business landscape for decades, their number and size are growing (Gillooly, 1998; Greenberg, 1997). Why are so many mergers happening *today*? To understand this, one must understand *why* mergers take place at all. Day (1997) suggests the one over-riding reason for corporate consolidation is to remove excess capacity from an industry (i.e., there are too many companies vying for too little business). Weaker players get shaken out and markets coalesce around a small number of powerful consolidators. However, there are two distinct syndromes that create this excess capacity:

- *The boom-and-bust syndrome.* This occurs in hot, emerging markets or highly cyclical businesses. When a growing market begins to slow, falling margins drive the weaker players out of business. The ultimate winners survive by adapting to slower growth through putting a premium on operational effectiveness. A bust can be triggered by disappointing growth, the emergence of a dominant design, or scarce resources. These are the traditional drivers of mergers.
- *The seismic-shift syndrome.* This strikes stable, mature industries that have enjoyed protected prosperity and relatively high profit levels. Protection comes from isolating mechanisms (e.g., government regulations), which have deterred competition and kept out new entrants. Removal of these isolating mechanisms in an industry forces a fundamental change in the rules of their markets. Key triggers are deregulation, globalization, a technological discontinuity, and the emergence of a "competency predator" (i.e., innovators who develop a new business model offering large economies of scale).

Since IT enables many of these triggers, it has become a major driver of the mergers we are seeing at present in industries that have not been affected before.

THE OFFSPRING: THE IMPACT OF MERGER STRATEGY ON IT

M&As will have differing impacts on the IT organizations of the two parties depending on what business goal a merger is designed to accomplish. Chatham (1998) suggests that, for IT, there are two critical variables that must be assessed in determining the impact of any merger:

- *The degree of integration of IT desired.* At one end of the scale, very little integration could be required beyond a common, thin layer of applications for administration. At the other, one IT group—people, platforms, and applications—is completely absorbed by another.

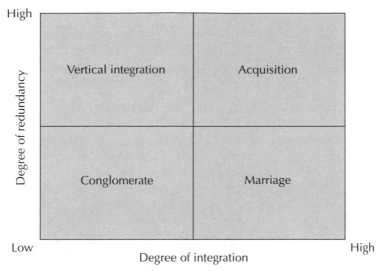

Figure 8.1   *Four types of corporate merger.*

- *The degree of redundancy created.* In some cases, there will be a high degree of overlap in systems and jobs so that software will be replaced and jobs lost. At the other, few redundancies will be created.

This results in four possible types of merger, each with a differing degree of integration required and redundancy expected in IT (see Figure 8.1):

1. *Marriage.* Here, companies of similar size, playing similar roles in the same industry, decide to merge to build market share and take advantage of economies of scale. Although IT must merge work forces, infrastructures, and application portfolios, there is no significant redundancy created.
2. *Acquisition.* When a substantially larger company acquires a smaller one in the same industry, performing a similar role, the business objective is to absorb it. The IT function of the predator company will absorb the valued parts of the target company (e.g., its people and resources), while replacing the other parts (e.g., its infrastructure) with its own ways of doing things.
3. *Vertical integration.* When companies in the same industry merge, but perform different roles, business processes will become more closely linked, but functions will remain complementary. Redundancy will occur in administrative, financial, and human resources (HR) areas, but not in business processes.
4. *Conglomeration.* Here, companies are in different industries, and the acquired company typically becomes a separate division of the resulting conglomerate. Beyond integration of financials at the top levels of the company, some administration, and possible economies of scale in the infrastructure, there is no need for merged IT groups and therefore little redundancy.

The biggest challenges for chief information officers (CIOs) will be in the first three of these types of merger, where organizations and technologies will be required to change significantly. Change will also be more disruptive in an acquisition than in other types of merger.

STEPS TO THE ALTAR: THE MERGER PROCESS

The typical M&A process consists of four stages: target selection, evaluation, transition planning, and merger implementation (explained below). While IT has a role to play in each, its interests are always secondary to the overall business objectives of the merger. Nevertheless, the decisions that are made during this process will have an important impact on the future of IT in the new corporate entity, so it is critical to understand where the company is in the process and what actions, if any, are expected from IT. The most critical stage for IT is the actual merger implementation, and there are increasing suggestions that failure to effectively merge technology and IT during this stage can destroy the overall success of a merger (Pitts, 1998; Gillooly, 1998). Nevertheless, companies are also beginning to realize that compatibility of the two groups is important and that getting IT involved earlier in the M&A process can often prevent more serious problems later on.

SELECTING A MATE: FINDING THE RIGHT TARGET

Prior to the announcement of the marriage, the corporate parents are busy assessing the suitability of potential matches from the financial and strategic points of view. Thus, very little attention is paid to whether their IT offspring are compatible. Although usually critical to the synergies to be gained from a merger, IT issues are considered in less than half of pre-acquisition negotiations (McKiernan and Merali, 1995; Weber and Pliskin, 1996). Fewer than 25% of companies considered IT integration prior to the merger announcement. In short, in a merger, an IT organization is all too often in the position of knowing very little about its proposed spouse prior to the actual engagement.

FIRST MEETINGS: EVALUATING THE RISKS

After a potential mate has been selected, the IT organizations involved will most often be given a chance to meet each other, although only briefly. Time is an important factor at this stage. Pre-nuptial assessments, also known as due diligence, are frequently limited in scope due to the need for speed and secrecy. Often for IT, there will only be a few hours in a hotel room to evaluate do-ability, estimate costs, and to plan for the post-announcement period. There may also be legal restrictions about how much information can be shared prior to the merger's approval.

While there will never be adequate time for mutual appraisal during this period, the earlier the IT shops can be included in negotiations, the better they will be able to do their job. Focus group participants were unanimous that, from the IT point of view, successful mergers were those where IT was fully involved in the merger negotiations. They noted that, while questions about platforms and systems may sound like questions for an IT manager, such decisions fundamentally affect the value and shape of the business and therefore must be addressed as *business* decisions as early as possible in the merger process.

In addition to the obvious risk that the two sets of systems will not work well together, there are several other risks for companies in not getting IT more involved earlier during negotiations. First, there is a risk that the business will miss out on significant benefits if all that is expected of IT is that it keeps the new entity going. "The failure to pay attention to the strategic role of IT in the merged entity precludes some organizations from exploiting it . . . to reshape and reposition the organization in its competitive environment" (McKiernan and Merali, 1995). IT is a business shaper, and a time of change is an opportunity to do things differently. If IT is not involved at early strategy sessions, and is considered simply as a utility, it will have no chance to contribute value to the merger process and will become simply a high cost of effecting the alliance.

A second risk is cost. Merging two IT organizations is frequently underestimated both in effort and time. Frequently, economies of scale are cited as a major business driver of a merger. However, chief executive officers (CEOs) often have little appreciation for the potential costs of merging technologies and their widespread impact on organizations (Dodge, 1998). Francis (1998) suggests that unanticipated IT contingencies have the potential to bring down a modern-day merger, and that the absence of IT planning early enough in the merger process can do substantial damage to a business. One focus group member pointed out that if IT costs are not well understood upfront, it could be a serious embarrassment for the company and its CEO. Another cautioned that it is important to clarify the ownership of all systems involved. In one merger this wasn't done, and it turned out that a critical system was not actually owned by the company being acquired. This added significantly to the cost of the merger.

Finally, there is the risk that IT management will not know the *real* reasons behind the merger. As noted above, there are several different business objectives that can be served by an M&A. For public-relations reasons, executives are frequently deliberately obtuse about a merger's goals. Most mergers are portrayed as marriages, for example, but many are simply acquisitions. This can leave IT managers confused about each IT organization's role in the merger, and can result in them working at cross-purposes with senior management's objectives. Thus, at minimum, IT managers have a responsibility to have the political savvy to recognize the potential of this gap and seek to determine what the true parental expectations for the integration are.

Undoubtedly, in most mergers today IT should be an essential part of business strategy, not a business detail to be worked out later on. IT has both a right and a responsibility to be involved early. Viewing IT as a utility could have significant negative repercussions on the time, cost, and efficacy of any merger. As with other aspects of IT management, IT can play a reactive or a proactive role in a merger. It is reactive when IT is simply asked to accommodate the corporation's plans. It is proactive when it helps create opportunities for competitive advantage, drives organizational change, and facilitates organizational integration, becoming the basis for a single, new, corporate approach to doing business (McKiernan and Merali, 1995).

It is clear that the risks of *not* addressing IT issues at this stage are growing significantly greater for organizations as IT becomes ubiquitous—especially in industries where information is the product (e.g., finance and insurance). Technology will likely be a dominant driver of organizational consolidations and redesign over the next 20 years (Schrage, 1998). One merger was described as "a multibillion dollar bet that technology will guarantee economies of scale . . . and new information infrastructures will creatively bundle cross-selling opportunities . . . at costs that will let them capture market and margin share" (Hoffman, 1998). Clearly, management will lose the bet if the new company cannot swiftly and cost-effectively integrate its disparate systems.

ENGAGEMENT AND THE WEDDING: PLANNING THE TRANSITION

It can be three months to a year from the time of a merger's announcement until the official "wedding day". This engagement period is a time for the partners to get to know each other more fully and to begin planning the official transition to a single entity. A transition team is appointed to study the proposed merger in more detail and then develop an overall plan for the new organization. During this time, IT has two important, but distinct roles.

1   Part of the Transition Team

The transition team develops a bridging strategy for merging the two organizations. Ideally, it will be composed of all key corporate business units, overseen by a steering committee of senior executives, and have a project-manager (Deloitte and Touche, 1997). Focus group members pointed out that it is critical for IT to be represented on this team. If it is not, a strong negative message will be communicated about the importance of IT to the new organization. The transition team plans all aspects of the actual merger in all parts of the business. IT should be involved in two areas (Reed, 1998):

- *General integration planning.* At this level, the business philosophy of the new entity is articulated, and such key issues as its culture, business priorities, and decision-making processes are explored and resolved. These are all vital for IT managers to understand and participate in deciding if they are to be effective in their other integration roles. The team must articulate a compelling vision for the new organization, allocate resources, and impose standards and incentives. The level of cost savings and where they are expected to come from should also be made clear to all parts of the organization.

- *Business integration planning.* IT also has a role in integration planning with individual business processes and business units. As it will be expected to produce the management and support information of the new entity, IT must understand how the business wishes to operate. Furthermore, it has a central role in such things as helping to maintain a "business as usual" image with customers and agents, merging databases, coping with increased volumes, helping to consolidate and move operations, and training staff on whichever systems will be used by the new company.

2   Planning IT Integration

At the same time as IT is participating in planning the overall transition to a new entity, an IT task force must also plan the integration of the two IT organizations. This IT task force should be composed of good people from both IT organizations. People with experience in managing mergers will be extremely valuable on this team. Some companies also add independent transition consultants to this group, but not all focus group members agreed with this approach since it is expensive.

Needless to say, good IT management is essential in planning a successful IT integration. Often, this task force is given a conflicting mandate to implement (Greenberg, 1997); for example, meet *both* layoff and effective operations targets as soon as possible. Some of the activities this team should undertake include:

- *Setting priorities for the transition* (Francis, 1998; Pitts, 1998). Typically, the most important job for IT is to maintain service levels. Most organizations will try to ensure that their customers and sales agents don't feel the pain of the merger. After this, however, the issues get fuzzy and priorities are important to help clarify a confusing and uncertain time.
- *Establishing communication procedures* (Ruotolo, 1997; Pitts, 1998). Clear, consistent communication is essential throughout a transition. The team should set up mechanisms to make sure this happens. Some focus group members have set up hot lines for staff questions, arranged daily videoconferences for long-distance mergers, established a procedure for handling "hot" issues, and prepared materials on the priorities of the new IT organization. One IT manager who has been through three mergers recommended having two or three professional communicators on staff just for IT.

- *Assessing assets* (Francis, 1998). All systems, assets, and resources should be inventoried at this time. Development projects should be assessed and a recommendation to stop or to proceed should be made. New development priorities should be established and existing products and services rationalized.
- *Establishing and managing the critical path* (Pitts, 1998). With so many activities involved in merging IT organizations, it is essential to ensure that time-frames, interdependent activities, and risks are monitored and that problems are dealt with quickly and effectively.

Focus group members noted that the type of merger and the location of the two departments (i.e., how far apart they are geographically) are important factors affecting IT transition plans. Regardless, it will never be business as usual again for either IT group, and it is the transition team's mandate to develop a blueprint for the structure and function of the new IT organization.

THE HONEYMOON PERIOD: IMPLEMENTING A NEW IT ORGANIZATION

While a honeymoon is usually portrayed as a romantic interlude between the wedding and "real life", in an arranged marriage it is often when the spouses get their first hard look at the person they will be spending the rest of their lives with. It is also a time where the ground rules of the marriage are established and where the hard work of building a relationship is begun.

All of this is true of the new merged IT organization, but with the additional elements of significant time pressure and corporate politics. Several researchers have commented on this fact:

> IT departments can expect to work harder and suffer more than other departments during a merger (Greenberg, 1997).

> A merger is long, tense, unrewarding work with tremendous personality conflicts ... especially if you're on the side of the fence that's not going to win (Charles, 1995).

> The importance of speed cannot be overvalued ... a clear 50% of what a manager has to deal with is the issue of time and only 25% is technology (Reed, 1998).

In a merger, therefore, IT must formulate a game plan that takes the fundamental importance of time and human relationships into account.

Focus group participants pointed out that the strains of making the new organization work place an enormous burden on IT management. This may or may not be greater than that facing other parts of the organization (e.g., accounting), but it is certainly perceived to be a significant strain. One manager described it as, "like going to the moon with no disaster recovery plan" (Francis, 1998). Not only are they responsible for maintaining high-quality services, managers must also marry disparate technologies, deal with staff morale and uneasiness, redesign the IT organization and structure, and work to create a new organizational culture for the merged entity. Below, we look at how IT management can contribute to a successful integration of IT departments in each of these areas.

1 The New IT Organization Structure

Ideally, by the time the marriage takes place the key IT management should be appointed. Failure to appoint a CIO and his or her senior management will create a great deal of uncertainty and can lead to problems implementing other portions of the integration plan. Crispness of decision-making is essential in a merger, since delays are deadly. This can only happen if the key decision-makers are appointed right away (Schrage, 1998).

The new IT management must then move to establish the organization structure as quickly as possible. Four weeks is optimal. Structure is needed to help people visualize where they might fit in the new entity. Also, filling it quickly keeps people contributing and helps minimize idle time, while maintaining staff morale and reducing rumors.

2 HR Integration

"While there's never enough talent to go around, often the absolute worst way to solve these problems is through a merger or acquisition" (Greenbaum, 1998). This is because the uncertainty, confusion, and negative synergies that are often associated with mergers (Deloitte and Touche, 1997) can frequently lead to significant numbers of resignations. It is unfortunate but true that, while IT managers are always advised to focus on people first and systems second, in reality technology gets most of the attention in a merger.

Holding on to good people is tough in a tumultuous work environment, so managers must always keep in mind that the effective integration and retention of key personnel is central to performance of the new entity. Recommendations for managers include:

- *Recognize the value of people.* It is important to distinguish between the value of the people and that of the systems being acquired (Hoffman, 1998). People should always be treated with kindness, and no-one should get lost in the shuffle. The transition is a time to encourage people in the two organizations to get to know one another and to treat each other with courtesy and respect. This is particularly important when a merger is clearly an acquisition.
- *Act quickly.* People should be dealt with promptly. In a merger, management's "party line" is almost always initially that no-one's job is in jeopardy, but people typically have no faith in these reassurances. Therefore, ideally, within

a few weeks of the merger, everyone should know where they fit into the new organization. Even if the news is bad, focus group members agreed that it is essential to get it over with as quickly as possible.

- *Do an HR assessment.* Focus group members stressed that IT should do its own assessment of IT staff and go through the hiring and selection process quickly to retain the best staff from both organizations. Staff roles and expectations should be clearly defined. Part of this assessment should include analysis of individual job titles because a systems-analyst in one organization may have quite different responsibilities from an analyst in another. Salary levels must be examined and a commitment made to equalize pay scales for comparable jobs over a reasonable period of time.

- *Let people know where they stand* (Hoffman, 1998; Charles, 1995). The longer uncertainty lasts, the greater the likelihood of losing staff. There are two ways of selecting which staff to retain—all staff can be interviewed and a selection made, or senior IT managers in each organization can be asked to identify their best staff. IT managers should also communicate to their staff the type of skills they are looking for. For example, one organization prepared a recruiting video and information kit for staff to view prior to the selection process. There will usually be three categories of employee: those whose jobs are secure, those who will be essential during the transition but whose jobs will ultimately be eliminated, and those who will be laid off. It is up to management to ensure that people know which category they fall into and that appropriate incentives and supports are provided for each type of staff. For example, transition employees should be given retention bonuses, and laid-off employees should receive assistance in finding a new job.

3   Technology Integration

While technology is usually considered to be a less complex challenge to deal with than people in a merger, it is not a trivial issue. In fact, frequently technology becomes a symbol of the "winners" and the "losers" in an M&A. "For some people," one manager noted, "IT is a religion, and they take rejection of their technology very personally." The key to successful technology integration is to make decisions based on the needs of the new entity and to stick to them. There are three distinct areas of technology that must be addressed at this time:

- *Architecture.* The new entity's technical architecture is of primary importance and must be resolved rapidly because it acts as a framework both for the rest of the integration effort and for any new initiatives that will be undertaken. As part of the architecture, standards should be established and enforced, and the potential growth needs of the new company assessed.

- *Infrastructure.* In an ideal world, the new company should standardize on a single technology platform immediately, but in practice the capital investment involved may preclude a wholesale changeover. However, while it may not be possible to change hardware at once, researchers and practitioners agree that, in spite of the politics that will be involved, it is important to get people using the same software as soon as possible. IT managers should select suites of software to use, not individual applications, because the integration issues involved are too complex and time-consuming to cope with. Even though changing software can be painful, being ruthless at the beginning can prevent a number of problems in the long run.

- *Applications and data.* The integration of applications and data should be influenced by two over-arching elements: the general philosophy of the merger itself (i.e., what type of M&A is it?) and the business strategy of the new entity. IT management will need to consider the new company's position on centralization/decentralization, outsourcing, integration of business processes; and how the company is planning to position itself in the marketplace (Deloitte and Touche, 1997). As with any other type of application development, the needs of the business should be considered first and then the technology that is available assessed (Amy, 1995). One company prepared a technology map to assess areas of overlap and value-added features that each partner's applications could contribute to the new company. Opportunities to better organize information (e.g., to cross-sell products) should also be considered at this time. However, group members warned that this is not a time to go after a 100% solution (which could be too time-consuming), but more a chance to plan an evolution of applications over several stages. It is also a very difficult time to get business direction because, for many business people, IT is not a critical element of the merger.

Technology integration can be an exhausting process for IT staff. Managers should therefore also consider using selective outsourcing as a tool to lessen pressure on them.

4   Cultural Integration

If there is one thing that everyone agrees on in a merger, it is the importance of "cultural fit". "A company must handle cultural issues first if it is ever going to tackle technology integration" (Charles, 1995). "Culture is the single most important thing to get right in a merger" (Reed, 1998). Many misunderstandings can arise due to different approaches to work, corporate values, and even terminology. Focus group members noted that the new culture must be positive and clearly understood because a culture clash can damage cooperation and commitment and increase the likelihood of conflict. While it has become commonplace today to blame a lot of problems on "culture", it is rare to see what people actually mean by the term.

As a result, there is much confusion about how to go about integrating two cultures. Focus group members suggested that, in a merger, the following aspects of the two IT organizations be considered and addressed:

- risk-taking behavior;
- innovation and action orientation;
- degree of top management contact;
- amount of autonomy in decision-making;
- performance orientation;
- reward orientation.

Differences in these behaviors have been shown to lead to poor post-merger effectiveness (Weber and Pliskin, 1996). Other elements of culture that may be important in determining cultural fit include:

- a package versus in-house development orientation;
- professionals as generalists versus specialists;
- IT accountability versus user accountability;
- team versus individual alignment;
- a cost versus value focus;
- bottom-up versus top-down planning;
- direct versus consensus issue resolution.

It is IT management's job to provide leadership in creating a new culture and working relationships for both sets of staff. Here are some of the things that should be done to bring this about:

- *Recognize differences.* By acknowledging what is different between the two organizations and getting things out in the open, management can help staff identify where and why clashes might occur and understand where people may be feeling a sense of loss as well. Understanding differences can make people more sensitive to others and can help guide management in selecting the best aspects of both cultures. It can also emphasize areas of commonality that tend to be overshadowed by differences.
- *Be culturally sensitive.* IT staff must respect each other's territory. Particularly in an acquisition, it is essential to learn the other organization's culture before trying to change it. Little things like wearing ties, deferring to the corporate hierarchy, or understanding the different terminology in use can make a big difference in helping people feel more comfortable and less threatened with the changes that are occurring. One group member suggested "acting like a consultant" when working with the other firm. This means trying to fit in with their culture, backing off from altercation, and not judging their work or their staff.
- *Listen.* At the beginning, give people time to grieve what they have lost, even if they are resentful, before expecting them to get on with things. Listening to people can provide validation of their feelings and reassurance that management cares about their concerns. It can also offer valuable clues as to where fundamental culture clashes might occur and give management an opportunity

to understand people's perceptions (which may be different from reality). Finally, managers should *always* make sure that they heard what was being said accurately. Different cultures have different terms and mannerisms that others may find offensive or confusing. Always confirm what you thought they said.

- *Remove detractors.* In any merger there will be a redistribution of employees. Some will support the changes, but most will adopt a "wait and see" attitude. However, some will clearly never adapt. Rapid integration of IT staff will depend on management being able to skillfully, tactfully, and rapidly identify and remove these detractors from the organization before they can poison the developing new culture.

- *Don't hide behind culture.* Some of the most damaging issues in a merger can be those which never get resolved. Culture should *never* be used as a scapegoat for not coming to terms with an issue. Managers must always aim for complete and positive closure of conflicts. They should never ignore them because conflicts won't go away and *will* cause problems.

As leaders of a significant organization change, IT managers must also recognize that they will be going through change themselves as well as their staff. One focus group manager remarked that it is vital that managers accelerate their own transition process so that they can provide leadership for their IT staff. Thus, special actions should be taken to assist the IT management team to come to terms with the merger and the changes involved as quickly as possible.

CONCLUSION

Managing IT mergers effectively is first and foremost dependent on common sense and the application of good management principles. These are important not only in technology integration, but also in dealing with the people and cultural issues that can undermine a deal that looks good on paper. A successful merger must be more than a financial success. It must look seamless to customers. Employees must feel they have been treated fairly. The new company must retain strategic capabilities and meet growth targets. And the entire organization must feel it is working together for a common goal. Like an arranged marriage, a merger may not be "made in heaven", but it can be happy and fruitful if there is a concerted effort from both parties to make the union work.

REFERENCES

Amy, F. (1995) "When merging, combining technology can be an art," *National Underwriter*, December 11.

Charles, B. (1995) "Big mergers take a human toll," *Network World*, 16 October.

Chatham, B. (1998) "Mergers, acquisitions and saving IT dollars," *Forrester View*, 15 March.

Day, G. (1997) "Surviving a shakeout," *Harvard Business Review*, March–April.

Deloitte and Touche (1997) "Merger integration: The deal's not done yet!" *Chemical Market Reporter*, 22 December.

Dodge, J. (1998) "Can IT sink a merger? We're bound to find out," *PC Week*, 22 June.

Francis, B. (1998) "Merge right," *PC Week*, **15**, 22 June.

Gillooly, B. (1998) "Be ready for the merger monster," *Behind the News*, 1 June.

Greenbaum, J. (1998) "The CA-way works," *Software Magazine*, February.

Greenberg, I. (1997) "Companies are teaming up, leaving IS holding the bag," *InfoWorld*, 28 April.

Hoffman, T. (1998) "How to handle a bank merger," *Computerworld*, 27 April.

McKiernan, P. and Y. Merali (1995) "Integrating information systems after a merger," *Long Range Planning*, **28**, 54–62.

Pitts, G. (1998) "Dash of seasoning eases integration," *The Globe and Mail*, 9 April.

Reed, W. (1998) "Coping with merger-mania: IT's new role," *Health Management Technology*, May.

Ruotolo, F. (1997) "Easing systems integration, post-merger," *Chief Executive*, April.

Schrage, M. (1998) "IT and the Citigroup gamble," *Computerworld*, 27 April.

Weber, Y. and N. Pliskin (1996) "The effects of information systems integration and organizational culture on a firm's effectiveness," *Information & Management*, **30**, 81–90.

9
Leveraging CRM with IT

Just when information technology (IT) organizations thought they had automated everything they could, along came the concept of systems integration—instead of individual systems for individual functions, why not link them all together to get more and better information to enable senior managers to see the big picture? And, why not link these systems to suppliers, and even customers, to get tighter integration, just-in-time (JIT) information, reduce costs and speed up time-to-market? Thus, the enterprise resource planning (ERP) system was born. An ERP handles all those nasty back-office and overhead administrative functions, like human resources (HR), accounting, supply chain management and production, leaving company staff freer to pay attention to where companies actually make money—the customer.

Until recently, customer sales and marketing were perceived as some of the very few areas of the organization that were not amenable to automation. As a result, customer-focused systems have been few and far between. In the past decade, however, companies have realized that they can and should learn more about their customers for many reasons. Today, it is accepted wisdom that new customers are more difficult and expensive to acquire than retaining existing ones. Identifying and working to retain profitable customers and cutting customer turnover have therefore become primary marketing objectives. A recent survey by KPMG Consulting found that 89% of companies consider customer information to be extremely important to the success of their business (King, 2000).

Data-mining was the first initiative many companies took in this area—but it has had only limited results. The same 2000 survey found that only a small percentage of companies were able to obtain even basic customer information (e.g., segmenting their database). As well, with the advent of the Internet, customers are demanding better access to the companies they deal with. Hence, businesses now perceive a need for more complete customer relationship management (CRM) systems. These applications are customer-facing, front-of-the-house systems for customer care and management. Not surprisingly, ERP companies are making a significant investment in CRM systems. A recent casual survey of the Internet revealed literally thousands of websites, most of which are promoting packaged CRM solutions. Like their ERP siblings, CRM systems promise improved results without sacrificing profitability and the smooth flow of information between functional areas. Some of the main functions CRMs are designed to automate include marketing, sales, customer service, and e-commerce (Thompson, 2000). Key benefits cited are 24/7 customer access, the ability to generate high-quality leads, improved understanding of customers' needs, faster resolution of problems, and Web-based transaction processing.

Nevertheless, given the amount of hype about these systems, IT managers can be forgiven if they are somewhat skeptical about the true costs and benefits of CRM. Even before CRM reaches full stride in the hype and frenzy game, there is a strong whiff of danger hanging in the air. Keen (2000) harkens back to the former eras of business re-engineering, total quality management (TQM), and more recently ERP, which he describes as the "technology-as-solution" syndrome—where companies bought software products, hired expensive systems integrators, and discovered that it took three times as long and three times as much money as they had budgeted. Understandably, many IT managers are having a *déjà vu*. But the concept is bullet-proof. Who would argue against managing their customer relationships? This means that CRM cannot be ignored ... leaving only the question of how to "get a handle" on CRM. The situation is particularly critical for IT managers who, at the end of the day, will be called upon to help select and then implement these systems.

In the next section we provide a definition for CRM and describe the role that CRM plays within a larger organizational context. Next, we explore the implications of CRM for IT. Based on the experiences of the focus group, the last section outlines recommended strategies for IT organizations to follow in order to increase their likelihood of successful implementation of CRM.

UNDERSTANDING CRM

When asked to describe CRM, one focus group member claimed that, "CRM is a philosophy about how customers will be treated by this organization." According to Thompson (2000), CRM is the "overall process of marketing, sales, and service within any organization." To IBM Global Services, CRM is "any effort undertaken to improve customer service" (IBM Internal Document, 2000). For others, CRM is software that manages customer interactions with your organization. So, is CRM a mind-set? A set of processes and procedures? Software? None/Some of the above? It became abundantly clear from our focus group that the number of definitions of CRM equaled the number present at the table. At the highest level, it was agreed that CRM focuses on the relationship between an organization and its customers. Beyond that, little agreement was forthcoming.

Subsequent research bore out the diversity of definitions of CRM with the majority tending toward the "all-inclusive" variety; that is, CRM includes marketing, sales, and service. With this state of affairs, it is difficult to know exactly what is/isn't CRM. Even when not explicitly mentioned, there was a predominant sense that "technology" was a key element of CRM—that somehow technology was allowing organizations to manage the relationships with their customers much more effectively than they had previously. Technology, which had not previously been available, was now being applied to the customer interface by enterprising organizations for the betterment of their customer relationships. This was borne out by stories of how technology was allowing organizations to "recognize" customers through caller ID before the first ring of the telephone. It was the technology component that was different.

One focus group member defined CRM and its role in her company as follows:

- CRM focuses on customer relationships from an *enterprise-wide* perspective;
- CRM consists of systems and strategies that enable personal and relevant communications . . . at the right time . . . and through the right channel;
- CRM's goal is to optimize long-term profitable relationships.

The lack of definitional clarity, however, does not diminish the need to improve customer relationships. A study by King (2000) suggests that companies have a long way to go. Results indicated that:

- 12% of companies are unable to say how many customers they have; and
- only 15% of companies are fully exploiting customer information despite the fact that 89% of companies say they consider customer information to be extremely important to the success of their business.

CRM proponents have been able to create a considerable amount of momentum around the idea of catering to your customers more effectively. According to Manasco (2000), the average company now loses half its customers every five years. The fact that selling to new customers can be up to 10 times more expensive than retaining existing customers makes the argument for CRM even more persuasive. Table 9.1 shows the benefits of CRM culled from a sample of various vendors' advertisements.

The breadth of claims for CRM is substantial. Furthermore, the marketing arms of CRM providers are aggressively targeting a number of different parts of the organization at the same time:

1. chief executive officers (CEOs)—to implement CRM;

Table 9.1   *Proposed benefits of CRM.*

- Increase sales effectiveness
- Off self-service websites
- Reduce your sales cycle
- Increase accuracy of sales forcasting and reporting
- Reduce total sales costs
- Integrate legacy and IT systems
- Decrease time-to-market
- Increase marketing effectiveness
- Consolidate customer information
- Improve customer service/support
- Facilitate 1-to-1 marketing

2. sales executives—with solutions that (it is claimed) will vastly increase their sales volume; and
3. chief information officers (CIOs)—with systems to implement (Ingvorsen, 2000).

Faced with what appears to be overwhelming evidence of the effectiveness of CRM and a three-way marketing assault, it is not difficult to understand why CRM has caught everyone's attention. As with other, similar technological developments, IT management's responsibility is now to understand the role of CRM, its value to their organization, and to devise a strategy to reap the advantages that may be forthcoming. The next section examines these issues.

THE ROLE OF CRM

Interestingly, CRM is an old concept—practiced effectively over time by firms small enough to enjoy personal relationships with their customers. It is with the massive growth of companies that the customer relationship has deteriorated. More surprisingly, customers have tolerated this erosion in service. That era, however, is now past. Today's customers have examples of high-quality service and, once experienced, look for similar relationships with other companies. According to Keen (2000), "the customer defines the value chain and decides the relationships, on the basis of quality of interaction, responsiveness, reliability and personalization." The battle cry is "customer-centricity". But what does this mean?

In its broadest terms, customer-centricity is an organizational strategy that focuses on the express needs of customers with a commitment to tailor services/ products in direct response to those needs. It is an "outside-in" approach. It is in direct opposition to a "product-focused" orientation that concentrates on finding markets for existing products/services. According to Reichheld (1996), creating a customer-centric organization requires a radical departure from traditional business thinking. It puts "creating customer value—not maximizing profits and shareholder value—at the centre of business strategy and it demands significant changes in business practice—redefining target customers, revising employment policies, and redesigning incentives." This is not to suggest that you forgo profits to create customer value. On the contrary, Reichheld (1996) estimates that companies can boost profits by almost 100% by retaining just 5% more of their customers. That is an eye-popping claim! If in doubt, try this calculation:

Average sale × Number of sales per year × Years expected to be in business
= Life-time value of a customer

The following example demonstrates the role of CRM. ByeByeNOW.com is a leading clicks-and-bricks provider of vacation travel. In this industry, customers expect businesses to know them—regardless of the channels through which they interact—and personal assistance is taken for granted. This presents challenges for a company that offers customers three ways to purchase vacation travel: via a 24-hour, toll-free customer care center; through its website; and by a national network of franchised travel agencies. Using CRM systems, ByeByeNOW.com can immediately and automatically route online and telephone-based customer inquiries to the correct travel expert, by territory and skill set. When a call comes into the toll-free number, that call is converted to voice-over-Internet Protocol (VOIP). This technology allows the call to be assigned to an agent who is logged in at a franchise location. A caller ID feature looks up the incoming call in the company database to determine if this is an existing customer. If the caller has had previous dealings with a ByeByeNOW.com agent, the call is routed to that agent or agency . . . even before the first ring sounds on the customer's phone. Then, when the agent answers the call, the correct customer's record pops onto the agent's screen. Customers can also reach an agent 24 hours a day through the company's website. Customers communicate in real time with their travel agents via live online chats, VOIP calls, or by face-to-face conversations via PC. Chief technology officer (CTO), Peter Nicoletti, concludes, "we're in the business of enabling travel experts to deliver the perfect trip to their customers by blending their knowledge of their customers and all that the Internet has to offer in the way of online information and travel booking . . . our services are designed to empower the agent with online tools to deliver exactly what their clients want" (http://www.onyxcorp.com/story.asp).

It is apparent from this example that this type of customer management requires a high degree of integration across the business with respect to processes, information, and technology. The process and information, dimensions will be discussed here. The technology dimension will be highlighted in the next section. From a *process* point of view, a comprehensive CRM approach must include elements of market/channel/brand management, leadership, finance and

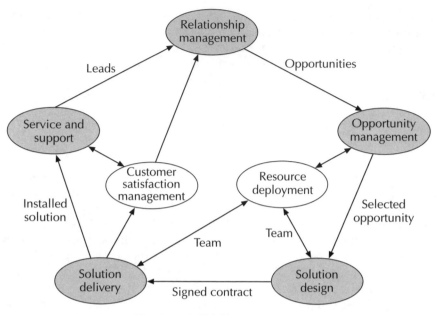

Figure 9.1 *CRM business processes.*

planning, skills management, opportunity management, solution delivery, resource deployment, customer satisfaction management, service and support, as well as partner/supplier management. One focus group member used a flow model to suggest how these processes fit together in her organization (Figure 9.1).

With respect to *information* integration, sales agents must have access to customer data to enable customer identification and customer history. They must also be able to track orders and deliveries, access pricing schedules, expedite high-status orders, and access financing options. Marketing managers must be able to perform customer profiling and marketing segmentation. Account representatives need to "prospect" leads derived internally from customer data and externally from business intelligence sources. Furthermore, this information must be integrated consistently across all channels. According to one focus group member, "you have to integrate all customers' views—CRM has to have a single record of truth plus corporate history." Another focus group member depicted the types of information required by her organization to support their CRM initiative as follows.

1   Information

- One good list of all our customers.
- A specific set of information about our customers.
- One way of capturing linkages among customers (connections).

- One way of linking customers to relationship managers.
- Key information about relationship managers.

2   Opportunity Management

- Identify sales and service opportunities and direct them to the right employee in the right channel.
- Co-ordinate and optimize the number of messages directed to a customer by all channels.
- Store and exchange messages about a client across channels over time.

3   Customer Behavior Triggers

- Understand a customer's "normal" transaction behavior.
- Capture each transaction and interpret it.
- Initiate relevant dialogue with a customer, triggered by an "unusual" transaction.

4   Modeling

- Identify customers who are most likely to buy/accept an offer.
- Identify customers who will most likely make the largest purchase.
- Identify the optimal timing to approach a customer (e.g., life stage/calendar).
- Determine sustainability for customers (e.g., how frequently can an offer be made or an additional product sold?).

CRM: THE IT VIEW

With respect to *technology* integration, CRM is not a "standalone" system. It is built on top of other software much like the hierarchy depicted in Figure 9.2. The engines behind it are data warehouses, data-mining software, and client-profiling systems, which determine an individual customer's exact buying habits and preferences. In most organizations, CRM begins with some form of transaction-based software, much of which is likely legacy software. Data captured at this level must be massaged into more useable forms to support various decision-making activities within the organization. This is accomplished via a mixture of data warehousing, data marts, and data-mining software. Over the last few years, many companies have introduced ERP software to give them the end-to-end integration of information across the organization supplanting much of the older legacy systems at the same time. This provides data in consistent formats to facilitate consolidation of information/reports. CRM software assists the sales/marketing functions, customer-profiling, etc. by interfacing with these other systems to access the required data.

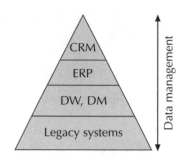

Figure 9.2   *Technology hierarchy of CRM.*

Data management occurs across all levels of the hierarchy. Figure 9.2 depicts how various software layers interact theoretically—in practice it is much more confusing. Lines are blurred between various levels in the architectural hierarchy; there is a mixture of internally developed software and packaged software; and, as always, some level of legacy systems presenting the usual integration challenges.

As stated earlier, CRM is not new. What is new is the availability of data-mining technology that makes CRM possible on a large scale (Madhok, 2000). In the old days, business decisions were constrained by inadequate information extracted from customer databases. Madhok describes this method of querying customer data along single dimensions as:

> . . . passive and inward-looking; the analyst crafts a strategy based on some assumptions on the customers, and queries the data to justify the hypotheses. Such an approach is limited to the analyst's perceptions of the business, and does not necessarily incorporate the customers' viewpoint into strategic planning. Data mining, on the other hand, is an active, discovery-oriented analysis that harvests the data for information consistent with the business objectives. In this respect, the strategy that emerges post-analysis is customer directed.

CRM systems involve a number of components. An examination of the CRM offerings by just two vendors yielded over 200 different technology products. A sampling of these products is reproduced below.

Sales Force Automation

- Product and price configurators.
- Sales opportunity, account, contact, activity/calendar management.
- Incentive/Compensation.
- Field service—shipping, receiving, contract management, service/problem management.
- Territory management, proposal and presentation generators.

Call Centers

- Campaign management (outbound).
- Call center support for the sales force products above.
- Fax and email integration.
- Customer service.

Internet

- Suites of products for Web-based sales, marketing, service.
- Email response systems.
- E-content (product/catalogs).
- Order management, shipping/receiving.
- Plethora of industry-specific applications for hotels, insurance, pharmacy, finance, etc.

The key shared components across these product offerings are the customer information file, the sales force information file, and the product/catalog (with descriptions and pricing). The data management task is to ensure consistency, accuracy, and reliability of these shared components. This, of course, presents a significant and critical task for IT.

Of particular interest is the last shared component—the Internet. Referred to as digital relationship management (DRM) or eCRM by some vendors, it distinguishes CRM activities that transpire over the Web. One focus group member gave an example of his company's eCRM activity as follows: when a customer enters their website, the customer's profile is automatically pulled and an electronic flyer is presented dynamically. This company awards a "CRM score" for each customer and, by merging information from their data warehouse with their CRM systems, offers real-time decision-making to their customers. For instance, a particular customer might be extended extra credit even if their limit had been reached because of their high CRM score. As with other business functions, the Internet allows new and different possibilities for CRM. In the next section, we outline a number of strategies as suggested by the focus group members to ensure the successful implementation of CRM capabilities.

STRATEGIES FOR MANAGING CRM

Members of the focus group were asked to suggest near-term strategies for IT management to facilitate their organization's adoption and ongoing management of CRM. These strategies focused on action items—activities that organizations can begin today in order to ensure their readiness to take full advantage of CRM.

1　Clarify the Value of CRM

Since CRM benefits are often most obvious to senior management, it is the task of senior management charged with overall CRM responsibility to educate everyone with respect to CRM and the role it will play in the organization. One focus group member stated that his executive started with a debate as to whether CRM was "a way to market more effectively" or "a way to provide real value". It was via this debate that they were able to identify and articulate the value that they intended to provide to their customers through CRM. Previous to this discussion, they had implicitly viewed CRM from a "company-centric" point of view—a view which would have ultimately jeopardized the attainment of full benefits from their CRM investment.

2　Create a Single High-level Position to Focus All CRM Activities

Effective CRM involves a clearly articulated vision for the customer experience and commitment starting at the very top. According to Keen (2000), "if CRM isn't important enough for the CIO and a top executive in marketing to take charge, then it is lip service only and will at best limp along." Members of the focus group were unified in their belief in the wisdom of establishing a high-level focal point for all CRM initiatives within their organizations. One member claimed "without silo-busters, you get nowhere." The cross-functional elements of CRM are self-evident—any impediments to intra-organizational flows of customer information short-circuit the attainment of CRM's full benefits. One of the key responsibilities of this CRM office is to clearly articulate a policy of zero tolerance for any department *owning* customer data.

We have argued that this decree is best originating from a high-level, visible office with the full endorsement/enforcement from line management. The only question is: Which office? Historically, CRM has followed a similar path in most companies. That is, CRM started as "sales force automation", moved into "call center management", and is currently tackling the Internet (eCRM as described previously). Because of this history, CRM typically originated as a marketing initiative with IT delivering the systems capability. Because of its strategic importance, group members felt that CRM should probably be located at the very top of the executive ladder residing with the marketing executive working closely with the CIO. One company has created a "President of One-Stop Shopping". Another company has the head of CRM reporting directly to the CEO.

3　Make CRM Part of Everyone's Job

All members of the focus group felt that CRM should be "everyone's job". CRM is not so much a sophisticated system as it is a philosophy. One member stated that CRM starts with ERM (employee relationship management)." In his company, they have three indices of success—earnings per share, customer satisfaction, and employee satisfaction—but, of these, employee satisfaction is key. Satisfied employees drive customer satisfaction, which drives success in the marketplace. For this reason, they believe you cannot just train 1% of employees for CRM—CRM impacts everyone. Another member who described how everything has become global in her company reinforced this—"complaints" systems are global, "leads" systems are global—as they believe that "systematic problems get identified by facing/solving complaints." Another organization uses CRM to identify its best salesperson. Once identified, it captures the skills/techniques employed by this individual to share with others, thus creating a learning organization.

4   Assess Customer Satisfaction

One of the difficulties of attempting to make CRM part of everyone's job is the measurement problem. How do you know if an employee is enhancing the customer's experience? One company created a customer satisfaction index and then used this index as input to employee salary reviews. Typically, customer satisfaction is measured via surveys—in-store, mail-out, or telephone. One of the real advantages of the Internet is the ability to capture customer satisfaction much more easily. For instance, customer satisfaction can be solicited directly from customers while they are shopping on the Internet. Alternatively, customer satisfaction can be inferred indirectly from abandoned shopping carts, analyzing click stream patterns, frequency of visit, duration of stay, etc. Even if the linkage between employees and customers is not direct, having customer satisfaction count in the salary evaluations sends a very clear message to employees that "customers are key".

One of the focus group members outlined her company's seven key customer satisfaction areas (shown in Table 9.2).

5   Establish a CRM Architecture

The CRM landscape is bewildering. With staggering growth projections for the total CRM market, everyone is suddenly rushing to capture market share in the CRM space. Many of these offerings are new products; most are simply re-branded products. That is, yesterday's data management tool is tomorrow's CRM. As major players with significant footprints in organizations, ERP providers are aggressively reinventing their software to provide CRM functionality. According to Webb (2000), these vendors are following one of three paths: buying CRM companies (e.g., PeopleSoft and Vantive Corp.), partnering with CRM companies (e.g., J.D. Edwards & Co. and Siebel Systems Inc.), or building their own CRM functionality (e.g., Oracle Corp. and SAP AG). Unless IT wants to be product-led or vendor-led, members of the focus group argued strongly that IT must work with their business partners to produce a CRM architecture—a

Table 9.2   *Seven customer satisfaction imperatives.*

Cost/Price	Let customers select the service they want to pay for with cost-effective alternatives Tell them the costs upfront
Ease of doing business	Do business in the customer's terms with personalized choices Make our policies and procedures invisible to our customers
Fulfill commitments	Match commitments to the customer's request and deliver on them Coordinate people who promise and those who deliver
Understand the customer	Understand the customer (their industry, business, strategy, processes, organization, and culture) Understand how our solutions fit their needs
Competence	Have the people, products, and services to solve their problems with quality workmanship
Responsiveness and accessibility	Single point of contact (right person, first time) Be available and keep customer informed
Communication	Listen and hear Communicate clearly, honestly, respectfully, and when appropriate

document that (a) identifies the components of the CRM strategy; (b) maps these components into an integrated plan; and (c) orders these components into a priority sequence. This roadmap is then used to drive RFPs (request for proposals) and establish baselines for potential vendors. One of the focus group members used the architectural schemata in Figure 9.3.

6   Plan adoption

A well-defined and clearly articulated architecture guides the integration of CRM capabilities within an organization allowing implementation to proceed in an orderly, planned fashion. One organization formally articulated a strategy "to know, understand, and develop our customer." With this as the guiding principle, they established the following four steps to guide their foray into CRM:

1. Organize different sources of customer data and start producing metrics and analysis from them.
2. Prioritize new application opportunities (like campaign management).
3. Integrate the customer views and strategies with existing customer-facing applications (e.g., call centers, loyalty programs, point of sale [POS] systems, and kiosks).

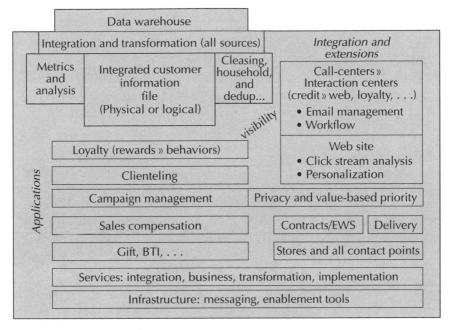

Figure 9.3   *CRM architecture/components.*

4. Eventually move from a supply chain focus ("pushing products") to a demand chain ("delivering what customers want")—a pull strategy.

7   Tie Data-mining to CRM

Building data-mining capabilities into CRM is a huge undertaking. Focus group members all suggested that this task takes a long time and requires significant resources. At one company, they have five people within the corporate architecture group with an annual budget of $20 million to bridge their data-mining effort to facilitate their CRM strategy. The majority of their effort is devoted to meta-data analysis—that is, "data about the data." Calculating such things as "net worth" in large organizations is anything but straightforward. It is this encoding of business rules within the data that requires significant effort. Another company has identified three key roles in managing its corporate data: data engineers (business focus), data architects (technology focus), and data-miners (typically marketing). Through the concerted efforts of these groups of individuals, they are able to maintain all corporate data with overnight update and next day query capability. Without this level of management, the concept of real-time decision-making regarding customers is just that—a concept.

Another focus group member identified their five key priorities for IT with regard to the data side of CRM. They are:

- build and support the corporate data warehouse;
- develop "clean" data feeds from operational systems;
- provide access to and for data-mining;
- find and develop "point" solutions for CRM;
- speed up the CRM learning process.

CONCLUSION

CRM promises huge potential—potential for success and potential for failure. According to Burch (2000) "more than 40 per cent of CRM initiatives/projects will fail during the next two years due to an enterprise's disjointed customer management approaches." Given the forecasted power shift in the direction of the customer, there is a lot to win and a lot to lose. To a large extent, success will depend on an organization's ability to marshal its forces in support of the CRM mandate. This requires high-level executive buy-in from the business and from IT, vision as to what kind of relationship the organization will forge with its customers, and an implementation strategy that involves all major stakeholders effectively. IT can play a leadership role in these activities.

REFERENCES

Burch, C. (2000) "The final word: CRM in a 7×24 world," *Ideas*, p. 22, Microsoft Canada, Toronto.

Ingvorsen, M. (2000) James Martin + co
(http://www.CONSultants-guide.com/00febpc/ooo2a3.htm).

Keen, P.G.W. (2000) "Winning ways", *The CIO Summit*, Toronto, 13–14 November (www. ciosummit.com).

King, S. (2000) KPMG Research Report
(http://www.consultants-guide.com/99marpc/9903a3.htm).

Madhok, V. (2000) "Making CRM pay off," *CIO Canada*, October, 44–50.

Manasco, B. (2000) "Customer relationships that can last a lifetime," 15 September (http://webcom.com/quantera/Empires1097.html).

Reichheld, F. (1996) "Learning from customer defections," *Harvard Business Review*, March–April, 56–69.

Thompson, B. (2000) "What is customer and partner relationship management?" (http://www.frontlinehq.com/crm.htm).

Webb, D. (2000) "CRM: Buy, borrow or build?" *eBusiness Journal*, June, 18–19.

10
ERP Systems: What a Manager Needs to Know

Enterprise resource planning (ERP) systems have become increasingly popular in companies in recent years. But, after listening to the complaints of business and information technology (IT) managers about them, you'd have to wonder why. It seems that, while ERP vendors promise the sun, moon, and stars of complete IT integration and compatibility, what they deliver is considerably less. Yet, in spite of everything, organizations as diverse as Honda Canada, the University of Toronto, and MFP Technologies have decided to adopt them. While initially designed for manufacturing companies, today it seems that a wide variety of businesses are choosing ERPs to help them "leap-frog" over the inadequacies of their home-grown systems.

Yet ERP systems are clearly not silver bullets for companies. While they offer integrated suites of basic applications such as finance, human resources (HR), manufacturing management, and distribution, even their proponents note that they require huge organizational commitment, significant cost, fundamental business process change, and considerable employee angst. And, although the "basics" are provided, it is IT and business managers who need to make the pieces work in their particular companies. Thus, organizations implementing ERPs are faced with innumerable decisions about how they want them to work. Depending on your point of view, this can be seen either as enforcing a valuable discipline on the organization or forcing a square peg to work in a round hole.

This chapter explores the issues surrounding the management and implementation of ERP systems. It has been organized into a series of ten questions about ERPs, which cover the broad spectrum of what a business or IT manager needs to know. It first addresses the nature of ERPs and their benefits and costs. Then, it looks at questions related to their implementation including the amount of effort involved and the problems that can be expected. Next, it examines how ERPs affect organizations and the people who work in them, existing technology, and the IT organization. Finally, it discusses the critical factors that are essential to successful organizational transformation using an ERP.

WHAT IS AN ERP?

Simply put, an ERP is a package of software that claims to provide a total, integrated solution to a company's information processing needs (Markus and Tanis, 2000). But, to understand the controversy these systems have engendered, it is important to understand the central role that they play in any organization where they are installed. ERPs aim to integrate corporate information seamlessly across many business functions and processes, and provide a high-level view of everything that's going on in the company (Slater, 1999a). As Tom Davenport (1998a) explains, "For managers who have struggled, at great expense and with great frustration, with incompatible information systems and inconsistent operating practices, the promise of an off-the-shelf solution to the problem of business integration is enticing."

There are several key differences between an ERP and what we have traditionally come to know as information systems. First, ERPs have an enterprise-wide scope. Whereas other types of systems have typically been limited to one company function, or more recently to a single process, an ERP touches many, if not all business and management functions of an organization. Second, an ERP is a package of generic software, geared to a predetermined, one-size-fits-all method of doing business. In-house-developed systems are designed specifically for a particular company and can incorporate its idiosyncrasies. Other software packages, being more limited in scope, can be more carefully selected to fit with a company's existing business model. Finally, because of these two factors, ERPs represent a commitment by the whole organization for fundamental and continuing transformation. They are more than just another system, they are a "way of life" (Davenport, 1998b), a "corporate ecosystem" and a "strategic computing platform" (Sweat, 1998), and an "IT backbone" (Schottmiller, 1998). As a result, they are forcing businesses to truly step up to the challenge of the information age in ways that piecemeal, home-grown systems have been unable to do.

There are several brands of ERP available in the marketplace each having a slightly different focus and approach. However, they all share several characteristics, including (Markus and Tanis, 2000):

- integrated information;
- purchase or lease from a software vendor and requiring a long-term relationship between the two companies;
- generic best practices;
- configuration and integration required with a company's existing systems;
- continual change both architecturally and functionally.

Currently, the leading ERP systems vendors are SAP, PeopleSoft, Oracle, and J.D. Edwards. Vendors tend to specialize in particular industries and some industries have standardized on a particular vendor. At present, they serve four key industry segments:

- discrete part manufacturing (e.g., PCs, packaged goods);
- process (e.g., chemicals, petroleum, paper, food);
- project (e.g., aerospace, software, construction);
- service (e.g., banking, insurance, healthcare, and retail).

The service sector is the least well penetrated at the present time.

ERPs are designed to overcome the fragmentation of information in businesses. Companies typically collect, generate, and store vast quantities of data spread across hundreds of separate systems in a variety of functions, business units, and regions. While these systems can provide invaluable support for a particular business activity, in combination they are a drag on business productivity and performance. An ERP has at its core a single comprehensive database that collects data from and feeds data into applications supporting most of a company's business activities. Related information is automatically updated. Thus, an ERP streamlines a company's data flow and provides management with real-time operating information (Davenport, 1998a). As one focus group member put it, "A system that effectively does all this is not a nice-to-have but a condition of survival."

But a basic ERP system is just the beginning. Today, ERPs are expanding from their largely traditional back-office domains into other areas of the company. ERP add-ons to improve sales, customer satisfaction, and business decision-making are going to be available in the very near future. E-commerce, customer relationship management (CRM), and advanced planning software are also being added to the basic ERP backbone (Stedman, 1999a). As well, a number of third-party companies have developed enterprise application integration programs (EAI), which are designed to help interface an ERP with a company's legacy applications (Edwards, 1998). And, already, the experts are talking about using ERPs to integrate companies across an entire supply chain or between business partners and stakeholders to shorten sales and design cycles. Ultimately, they believe that this super-company integration will redefine entire industries and speed the development of virtual companies (LaMonica, 1999). In short, what we have come to know as ERPs are changing rapidly and extending to new business functions and processes. Keeping up with ERP evolution as well as application integration promises to be a major job for IT managers in the near future.

WHAT BENEFITS WILL WE GET?

Focus group members and the experts agreed that it takes time to realize the benefits from an ERP. While a company should realize both financial and

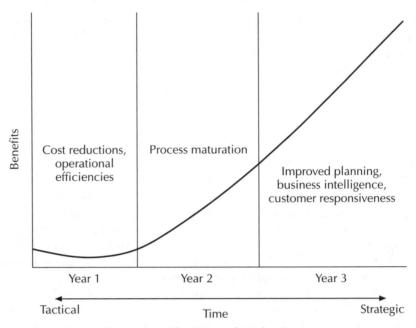

Figure 10.1   *The ERP cumulative benefits curve.*

non-financial benefits, these will come in three phases (see Figure 10.1). In the first phase, benefits come from such things as data clean-up, operational efficiencies, reliability, and salary savings (Connolly, 1999), as well as improved cash management, faster order management, inventory reductions, and reduction in IT costs through the elimination of some legacy systems and their maintenance and support (Stein, 1999). However, these are offset by what has been called the post-ERP slump in business performance, which typically lasts from three to nine months after implementation due to the fact that everything looks and works differently from the way it did before. Increased integration also magnifies mistakes that tend to ripple through the system wreaking havoc before they are detected (Koch, 1999).

Phase 2 begins once the initial resistance to the system has been overcome and people have mastered the use of the system—after about one year. Most companies tend to see very few net benefits in the first 24 months of an ERP's operation. Indeed, the average time before an ERP system shows net benefits is 31 months, according to the Meta Group (Koch, 1999). Another study found that a negative return on investment (ROI) is not unusual for up to five years (Stein, 1999). In this phase, benefits tend to come from process maturation as businesses take advantage of the opportunity for re-engineering by eliminating barriers between functions and reducing duplication of effort. Management decision-making is also improved with access to real-time data. This results in shorter cycle times and the need for fewer resources.

Most focus group members believed that the final phase of benefits will be strategic. They will come from improved planning, increased customer responsiveness, better business intelligence, and potential ERP extensions into e-commerce and supply chain management. ERPs will be especially useful for global organizations since they support multiple languages, platforms, and currencies, thus enabling improved international management. Standard systems also reduce complexity and thus facilitate corporate mergers. Most importantly, companies expect to fundamentally transform their business and reap exponentially improved returns in the long term from the ability to build strategic, high-value systems on the ERP backbone and from being able to more effectively leverage both their data and processes.

Interestingly, however, recent studies have shown that many companies choose to implement an ERP without a clear understanding of its benefits. They believe that ERPs are a necessary investment just to "get in the game" (Stein, 1999). As one focus group member stated: "We didn't do a business case or track savings and benefits. We took a leap of faith." For this company and others, the strategic value of having a corporate "lingua franca", of being able to break down corporate silos, and of implementing standard practices that will enable the development of corporate synergies is most important and does not need to be cost-justified with more immediate tactical returns.

WHAT ARE THE COSTS?

ERPs are not cheap. The average ERP implementation, according to the Meta Group, is $15 million or $53,320 per frequent user. This includes hardware, software, professional services, and internal staff costs for full implementation plus two years' post-implementation costs (Koch, 1999). Another study of 62 companies found that it took 23 months to get an ERP system up and running and cost $10.6 million, with another $2.1 million for maintenance over the next two years (Stein, 1999). These are average costs. Large companies will spend between $50 and $500 million (Davenport, 1998a). One focus group manager stated that the "rule of thumb" he had used for budgeting was that implementation costs should be about twice the cost of purchasing the system. In reality, he found that he spent about 4.5 times the cost of the system.

While most companies plan for some of these costs, few build enough post-implementation costs into their budgets (Koch, 1999). Training is a key expense that is frequently underestimated. Companies should expect to spend at least 10% or more of the overall ERP budget (some believe this figure should be as high as 20%) on end-user training beginning a few months prior to implementation (Stedman, 1999a; Schaaf, 1999). Everyone affected by the system—from executives to clerks—should receive training. Experience has shown that not only do users need to relearn how to do their job using an ERP, they must also have a clear understanding of the bigger picture of how the system operates so that they understand the impact of their work on the system as a whole. This often means radically overhauling training methods.

Additional costs in an ERP implementation can be substantial and need to be factored into a budget. Businesses frequently expect and plan for a reduction in IT costs through the elimination of some legacy systems. However, focus group organizations and other studies (Young, 1999) have found that IT savings are typically negligible. IT people simply moved from one area of need to another. In one medium-sized, focus group IT department, fully 50% of staff are involved in supporting and maintaining its ERP.

Extra people are usually required in the business groups so that others can be freed up to work on the project. There is also considerable time and effort involved in getting buy-in to the business changes that are needed. While this is frequently frustrating, it is critically important to the overall success of the project. In fact, this is a key investment that will shorten the payback period of the project (Johnsen, 1999). Finally, at least initially there will be some negative impact on the corporate bottom line. Not only are they expensive to implement, but ERPs can lead to productivity dips and poor customer service in the short term (Stein, 1999).

HOW MUCH EFFORT IS INVOLVED?

It's no secret that ERPs are a lot of work. The verdict is unanimous that a company cannot overestimate the resources and effort involved in preparing for, implementing, and supporting an ERP. This takes teamwork involving resources from both business and IT at all levels as well as outside support from vendors, consultants, and integrators.

One of the most critical jobs in an ERP project is that of the executive sponsor. Without strong and active support from senior management, the project will fail. The sponsor oversees the ERP implementation from the broad perspective of the organization as a whole and has three key responsibilities. First, he or she must get the project off the ground and ensure support and commitment for it. Second, the sponsor must keep the project on track during implementation and see that it doesn't get derailed. Third, he or she must create an empowered environment and implement the necessary organizational learning so that the ERP's benefits can be leveraged after implementation. Not just anyone can be a sponsor. He or she must possess sufficient authority and skills to gain the support and commitment of the business's divisions and units to the project, and resolve the conflicts which will inevitably occur (Johnsen, 1999). Unfortunately many executives who sponsor ERP projects have no idea what they're getting into. They tend to see an ERP as software, rather than a process, and this leads them to underestimate their role in driving the project forward and leveraging its benefits. Many also underestimate the complexity of the issues and solutions involved, and the scope of the project itself (Ross, 1999; Johnsen, 1999). It is therefore essential that the right executive sponsor be chosen for this project.

Similarly, the quality of the ERP team itself is fundamental to a project's success. Koch (1999) cautions that: "Most companies are still treating their ERP implementations as they would any other software project ... [what they don't realize] is that ERP project teams are not just installing software; they are reinventing how the company does business." An ERP team must have representation from both IT and the business. Ideally, all major business units and/or countries should be involved. Team membership is not a part-time job. Business team members should be assigned full-time and others should be appointed to do their regular work. These members will be instrumental in the change management process and helping business units and employees cope with the fundamental changes involved. IT team members will need different IT skills than in a traditional development project. Focus group members stressed that they will need strong business analysis and relationship management skills. Everyone involved will be working with internal customers, vendors, and consultants. In addition, all team members need excellent conflict resolution skills to be able to deal with the groundswell of objections that will inevitably arise.

A third and important member of the team is the ERP vendor. Companies usually expect their vendors to stand by them through the complexities and difficulties of implementing, maintaining, and integrating their software. Unfortunately, the general consensus is that vendors are not as responsive to company needs as most people would like (Slater, 1999b). One focus group member commented: "The vendors do a good job of selling product 'futures', but, once the deal is closed, they don't really support the implementation."

This supporting job is usually filled by consultants who are charged with the responsibility of making the ERP software work in a particular company. Skilled consultants are expensive and difficult to find, according to the focus group. Therefore, consultant turnover can be an issue with the end result that "consultants are training on your payroll." While most companies employ some consultants on their ERP projects, they make the management job more complex and must be carefully managed. As much as possible, group members stated, consultants should be used to transfer their skills as quickly as possible to internal staff who have a better understanding of the business and who are more likely to be committed to the project over the longer term.

While the effort involved in implementing an ERP is well known, what is often not talked about is the effort involved before the project begins and after installation. Selecting the right ERP package for your business is not a simple process. Focus group members stressed the importance of doing the homework necessary to choose the right package. This involves a clear articulation of the business problems being addressed and examining the underlying business model on which the package is based for its fit with the company's culture. References should be checked, and site evaluations undertaken. A business case should be prepared, and all parts of the company involved in making the final decision.

Similarly, post-implementation is a critical period that is often under-funded and under-resourced (Davenport, 1998b). Constant care from a stable, ongoing support team is essential to delivering an ERP's benefits. Change management, enterprise-wide training, and active and engaged leadership will be needed long after the ERP has gone live. In fact, it is fair to say that an ERP project never really ends. Davenport notes that an ERP is really a way of life and that there will always be new modules and versions to install, and additional value to derive from them. He writes: "Projects for implementing the systems get a lot of resources and attention but I believe that how we live with ERPs will have more to do with the value we receive from them than the quick decisions made during installation" (1998b).

WHAT PROBLEMS CAN WE EXPECT?

Entire forests have died documenting the problems companies have experienced with ERPs, and, indeed, most business and IT people are at least somewhat aware of the pain and challenges in making the changes involved. A recent article described ERP implementation as a "corporate root canal" (Young, 1999). Another noted that "the ERP landscape ... is littered with the walking wounded" (Johnson, 1999). Davenport (1998b) notes that "while these systems offer tremendous rewards, the risks they carry are equally great." A study by the Standish Group concludes that the average cost overrun is 178% for ERP implementations in large companies. The average schedule overrun is 230% (Zuckerman, 1999). Focus group managers identified a number of common problems that seem to recur frequently in implementation after implementation, including:

- *Overblown expectations.* Far too many companies see an ERP as a panacea for their IT problems. Others over-estimate what their ERP will be able to do. Almost all expect that the effort will be easier, cheaper, and faster than it ultimately turns out to be. As a result, most staff are ill-prepared for the impact of the system on how they do their work.
- *System complexity.* ERPs are difficult to master, and this almost always results in a steep learning curve, errors, and delays. Much of this complexity results from the generic nature of the application.
- *Pressures for customization.* One of the biggest problems with an ERP comes when company processes clash with ERP processes. Companies that have tried to modify their ERP to suit their own unique needs have come to regret it. Most experienced ERP managers agree that the business must be modified to suit the system, not the other way around. Make too many changes, they warn, and the company will find it next to impossible to take advantage of new releases.
- *Integration challenges.* Most companies don't replace all their systems with an ERP. As a result, the ERP must be linked with many existing systems.

Furthermore, because an ERP is not a cure-all, companies have to be prepared to invest in developing some additional functionality. Many companies have found that they need third-party applications or middleware that work on top of their ERP in order to get the reports and information they need.

- *Poor problem resolution.* Companies have found that their ERP vendor is less than responsive to them, even when it involves programming errors. Patches and enhancements do not necessarily appear as quickly as most users would like. When gaps or problems are found, it is often not easy to get the vendor to pay attention to the needs of a single customer. As a result, critically needed upgrades may take some time to be incorporated into the software.
- *Not enough training.* Training takes more time than most companies really think. Poorly trained people don't understand the way an ERP works, and will try to work around the system and go back to their old ways of working. Training also needs to be broad-based. One focus group company trained its staff, but not its managers. This was a mistake since managers continued to work with old assumptions about workflow. Another focus group manager commented that the spread of information as a result of their company's ERP has broadened people's job descriptions and their decision-making abilities. This led to a need to train people more broadly and thoroughly than in the past.
- *Poor usability.* ERPs are famous for their unwieldy user interfaces, which frustrate employees and sap productivity. ERPs force everyone to use the same process and do not allow users to skip steps or change workflow. Typically, ERPs are not intuitive applications and are much less tailored to individual needs than home-grown software. Often users complain of unnecessary screen-clicking and window-thrashing, which drives them crazy. Altogether, managers can expect it to take at least six months of live use before users feel comfortable with the system (Stedman, 1999a).
- *User resistance.* It can be extremely difficult to get people to make the changes needed to get the full benefits of the system. Many business units will try to maintain their own islands of automation. Without top management support and full participation of all parts of the company, the value of the ERP will be lost. As one focus group manager pointed out, "the power of an ERP diminishes proportionately with the degree of disintegration."

HOW WILL AN ERP AFFECT OUR ORGANIZATION?

A critical question for executives to answer is whether or not adopting an ERP will give the company a competitive advantage. There is considerable controversy on this point. Some people feel that using an ERP to make a company's information flows and processes essentially similar to those of its competitors will undermine its source of differentiation in the market. Davenport (1998a) suggests that this should not be an issue *if* a company's competitive advantage derives from the distinctiveness of its products. However, if a company competes primarily on cost, a large investment in an ERP may not make strategic sense.

Most focus group members saw an ERP as being a strategic investment for their organization. As one member stated, "the decision to implement an ERP system cannot be considered tactical in a large company since given the enormous resistance to corporate change, the benefits will only be realized over time." Medium and smaller companies feel that their investment in an ERP will enable them to have access to the same type of systems and information as a larger company, thus leveling the playing field between them. "Businesses our size can't develop the processes fast enough," stated another manager. "ERPs allow us to get in the game."

Once implemented, companies can expect to see an ERP's impact in a number of different and often unexpected ways such as:

- *Organization structure.* Universal, real-time access to data enables companies to streamline their management structures and make them flatter and more flexible. Because they involve centralized control of information and processes, they promote more management control. Conversely, they tend to break down hierarchical structures and make greater decentralization and individualization possible without losing coherence. ERPs also enable large global companies to balance commonality and variability by having their business units use different versions of the same system. In short, a great deal of the structural impact of an ERP can be mitigated and managed if a company is clear about what it wants to accomplish with its ERP (Davenport, 1998a).
- *Standardization of data and processes.* Probably the most obvious and desired impact of an ERP is to bring consistency to a company's work flows. Many companies are in the position of having numerous financial reporting systems or multiple order entry systems for different business units, which makes it extremely difficult to derive a clear picture of the company as a whole. "With different parts of the company all working in inconsistent silos, developing their own practices, we believe that implementing standard practices was an important strategic reason for implementing an ERP," explained one manager. Reaction to these changes can range from ecstatic (usually corporate controllers and senior executives) to massive objections from end-users who are expected to change how they work and think. Most companies find the first few months after implementation to be the most painful. Satisfaction with the system improves as people begin to see how the changes are benefiting the larger organization.
- *Growth.* A major reason for implementing an ERP is to handle growth. This is especially important in rapidly growing companies whose current systems are coming to the end of their usefulness and whose needs are becoming more complex. ERPs help position a company for the future by helping it define and understand its processes. The implementation of an ERP often has the biggest impact on processes that were never measured before—things that fell

through the cracks and had a negative impact on cycle time (Ross, 1999). As one focus group manager remarked: "We found processes we didn't even know we had."

- *Decision-making.* ERPs are having a growing influence on both business and technical decision-making. For example, the purchase of third-party packaged applications is likely to be influenced by whether or not they can integrate with a company's ERP. On a broader scale, however, it may also influence a company's choice of a partner (e.g., if a supplier can integrate with the ERP, this may give it an edge over its competition). It can also lock a company in with a single vendor for many years, since it is very difficult to back out of an ERP. On the plus side, there appears to be a consensus that ERPs help companies to make better and faster decisions because they provide better access to information (Sweat, 1998).
- *Perspective.* Because ERPs tear down walls within organizations, they help everyone to understand their impact on an entire operation. Ultimately, companies find their staff adopting an increasingly broad enterprise perspective, rather than a process or departmental one. In fact, one focus group manager felt that his company's ERP had improved user–IT relations by giving them the same perspective on the organization!
- *Extending the organization.* ERPs are beginning to affect cross-enterprise collaboration, as companies connect their ERPs to those of their business partners and customers. While few companies are doing this at present, greater integration across the supply chain is clearly facilitated by an ERP and will not be long in coming for many companies.

HOW WILL AN ERP AFFECT OUR PEOPLE?

A lot of the resistance to an ERP will come from a company's employees who find that their jobs are considerably changed. The post-ERP organization needs a different set of roles and skills from its people, and these will change the daily activities and behaviors of many employees. Using an ERP will not only require training in the "hard skills" of the ERP but also in the "soft skills" of running the business. Schneider (1999) explains, "a warehouse worker managing inventory spreadsheets pre-ERP could be forecasting customer demand and making critical business decisions after ERP." Focus group managers concurred with this observation. "Individuals need more knowledge and have more flexibility to make decisions than in the past," one stated.

It is critically important therefore that companies have the resources to help their employees cope with fundamental job makeovers. This cannot be done without considerable retraining. Training helps to ease anxiety as well. Ultimately, most companies find that, after proper training, ERPs enable employees to have better control of their work and higher job satisfaction. Schneider (1999) suggests the following tips for minimizing cultural problems:

- create a dedicated staff position for change management;
- plan for culture change well before the implementation begins;
- articulate expectations before implementation;
- make sure managers have a clear understanding of the reasons behind the change;
- eliminate non-essential tasks for employees;
- develop incentive programs;
- don't change too much at once; go with minimum functionality to start.

In every affected department, there will also need to be one or more people who are expert users, that is, who know the system and its relationship to departmental processes. Davenport (1998b) suggests that companies should be proactive about clarifying the responsibilities, reporting relationships, compensation, and training of these super-users since they will be ongoing trainers and IT liaisons.

Finally, as the ERP evolves, more and more employees and jobs will be affected. Training, change, and change management will have to be integrated into the ongoing life of the organization. Sweat (1998) points out that, today, only about 20% of an organization's employees are typically affected by an initial ERP implementation. As ERP vendors extend the functionality of their systems, their ultimate goal is to touch at least 80% of staff in the future. Thus, it is critically important for companies to work with their people to address their concerns, develop their skills, and keep them informed.

WHAT IMPACT WILL AN ERP HAVE ON OUR TECHNOLOGY?

While the worst thing you can do is make decisions about an ERP based on technical criteria alone (Davenport, 1998a), it remains true that ERPs are large and enormously complex technologies that will give IT staff a challenging time. Focus group managers all emphasized that the technical infrastructure on which it is built is an important reason for implementing an ERP. One member company had informally surveyed several companies around the world regarding their experiences and recommendations on ERPs. It found that:

> ... all agreed that a significant benefit of an ERP is the solid, scalable architecture on which it is based ... As well, it is critical to have your own technical infrastructure in place and operational prior to implementation, including tuning and performance tools as well as normal support tools ... Response time and performance will also need to be monitored. (Internal focus member document.)

ERPs are usually built on a client/server architecture that is recognized as a solid base for future development and providing a great deal of flexibility for change. This three-tier architecture is a critical platform for most focus group companies.

They view it as a necessity for developing e-business, and see an ERP as the means to jump-start into this new technology.

Markus and Tanis (2000) point out that ERPs are like other kinds of IT in that they are rapidly changing all the time—architecturally, functionally, and in their service arrangements. Focus group members pointed out that this means that contract negotiations that spell out service and support issues are critical. A company will typically have to invest a substantial amount in upgrading its technical hardware and enhancing its help desk to support its ERP. In addition, most companies will want to use data in ways that the ERP won't support, so they must also invest in reporting software and more infrastructure. Thus, middleware and third-party software designed to make an ERP more user-friendly or to help it integrate with an organization's legacy systems is a rapidly growing market.

IT organizations should also be careful to do detailed capacity-planning prior to implementation and continue to monitor traffic after the system is up and running. Many companies under-estimate the surge in traffic that an ERP roll out brings. Weinberg (1998) explains that this is not due to the ERP itself, but to the integration that it brings to business processes:

> Because the whole point of an ERP is to integrate all business processes onto one database, employees who may have been on different systems or on no system at all are now connected. That means an explosion of file transfers and attachment-laden emails in quantities that are virtually impossible to predict.

Altogether, an ERP can be expected to dramatically change an organization's technical environment from the desktop to the computer room. It is therefore essential that a company use its most capable staff to implement it. This will also be the best way of ensuring that a company can maintain business as usual during this critical period.

HOW WILL AN ERP CHANGE OUR IT ORGANIZATION?

IT organizations are not immune from the influence of an ERP. In addition to the fact that it will most likely be the largest, single project ever delivered from the department, there will also be long-lasting changes that will affect IT staffing, development and maintenance, and competencies. IT managers need to anticipate and plan for these changes to make the transition as smooth as possible.

IT Staffing

From the beginning, an ERP will impact IT's human resources. Focus group managers stressed that only the "best and the brightest" should be put on the ERP team. These people should be full-time project members. Surveys of ERP implementations strongly suggested that: "Part-time assignments just did not work" (Internal focus group member document). Thus, other parts of an IT organization will be strained by the staffing of the ERP.

Furthermore, IT managers should plan to be invaded by a large number of highly paid consultants. About 30% of an ERP team will be made up of consultants brought in to supplement (relatively) inexperienced internal staff. Theoretically, consultants have better knowledge and skills in the ERP itself, which can smooth the process of implementation. In reality, skilled consultants are in such demand that companies often find themselves paying market rates for people with only a few months' experience under their belts. Focus group members warned that IT managers should actively and closely manage their consultants to ensure that they are actually getting what they are paying for.

Consultants can also affect an IT organization in another important way. It is not uncommon for internal team members to feel that they can capitalize on their ERP skills by becoming consultants themselves. Therefore, IT shops often find that their turnover increases significantly during and after an implementation. IT managers who wish to retain these skills in-house should be prepared to compensate team members appropriately and to implement a retention strategy (e.g., bonuses) to make it worth their while to stay on the team.

Development and Maintenance

An ERP changes the traditional development process of build, test, interface, and train. With code development representing a small portion of the project, there is considerably less emphasis on this aspect of development. Markus and Tanis (2000) suggest that an enterprise systems experience cycle is more appropriate than a traditional, systems development life cycle for these projects. This consists of four phases:

1. *Chartering.* This phase consists of all activities leading up to the funding of the ERP, including building a business case, selecting an ERP software strategy, identifying the key management and sponsors, and the approval of a budget and schedule. It is at this stage that the company's approach to an ERP is identified. While many companies decide to go with a single software package, some use a "best of breed" approach where the best modules from differing ERPs are selected. Finally, some brave firms decide to build their own ERP.
2. *Project.* This phase includes all the activities needed to get the system up and running in the business, such as software configuration, system integration, testing, data conversion, training, and roll-out.
3. *Shakedown.* During this phase the company actually adjusts to the ERP and "normal operations" are finally achieved. Activities include bug-fixing, performance-tuning, re-engineering, and transfer from the project team to operational personnel.
4. *Evolution.* In this phase, upgrade packages are implemented and continuous

business improvement is undertaken. The system can be extended to other modules, usability and reporting problems addressed, and bugs identified and fixed. Ideally, companies should monitor their business case to track the system's benefits.

IT Competencies

Probably the most significant change an ERP will have on an IT organization, however, will be on its competencies. Focus group members agreed that managers will need to place a strong emphasis on the development of business, analysis, and information engineering skills since IT staff must have a strong understanding of how the business operates and the skills to map business models against the functionality of the ERP. Planning skills are also essential. Staff must understand the information flows in the company and be able to identify areas where the ERP will need to be supplemented. Davenport (1998b) suggests that knowledge management be used to leverage human support of the ERP. He notes that it is extremely important to capture both system and process knowledge so that others can benefit from it. These skills changes, in addition to specific ERP training, need to be cultivated over time. A smart IT manager will start early and build in incentives for staff who develop them.

WHAT ARE THE CRITICAL FACTORS FOR ERP SUCCESS?

This chapter has shown that there are a huge number of factors that can affect an ERP's success. Markus and Tanis (2000) point out that some of them, such as competitive position, industry, financial position, prior experience, and management systems are all *starting conditions* that are external to an organization's control and that may predispose it to success or failure. However, there are other critical success factors that are under management's control, including:

- *Keeping goals realistic.* Focus group members recommended keeping plans as simple and straightforward as possible. Many companies opt to implement only a single module (e.g., finance or HR) to begin with and to gain experience. Goals should be set in relation to the starting conditions of the organization. In other words, some companies should set more modest goals than others. Goals should also be tailored to the problems the business is trying to solve. As one manager stated: "An ERP is often sold as a panacea. It rarely is. You've got to know what problems you're trying to solve . . . and not try to fix twenty disparate problems all at once" (Martell, 1999).
- *Making an ERP a business project.* While technically complex, experts and focus group members are agreed that an ERP project must primarily be seen as a fundamental shift in how an organization will do business. Because of this, the

business community should own and lead the project *and* be responsible for its benefits. A business case should be developed and the expected strategic and tangible benefits documented.

- *Planning carefully.* Plans should be linked to a company's starting position and its goals. Planning and program management practices should be applied throughout the project. Detailed work plans, milestones, and deadlines should be carefully spelled out (Young, 1999).
- *Insisting on management attention.* Management involvement and support is essential for ERP success, everyone agreed. Care must be taken to ensure that senior managers remain focused on what the organization is trying to do and do not get distracted by minor problems.
- *Executing effectively.* A methodology is not a substitute for good execution. Davenport (1998a) suggests implementing an ERP one business unit at a time. This not only ensures the effort is manageable, but helps the team refine the system and processes as it goes along. A broadly representative implementation team also ensures that the decisions about the system's configuration can be made with the widest possible understanding of the business.
- *Resolving problems.* Unforeseen problems *will* arise. Successful companies deal with these by changing their goals, plans, and outcomes to achieve a favorable outcome.
- *Defining metrics and measuring them.* A business case is an excellent management tool for monitoring ERP success. This should be a dynamic document with clear performance targets and budgets that can be tracked post-implementation. Failure to meet targets should be a trigger to management to focus on problems in a particular area.

CONCLUSION

An ERP is business software that is designed to fundamentally transform an organization—its processes, its data, its jobs, and its structures. As such, it is not a project to be undertaken lightly, and cannot be left to IT alone to install. A successful ERP implementation requires an enterprise-wide effort from both IT and the business units of a company. An ERP's cost and scope alone should be enough to convince top company executives to lead the decision-making and maintain a careful watch on its implementation. However, unless the entire executive team understands the costs and implications of an ERP, as well as its expected benefits, it is likely not to have the intended results. Choosing to implement an ERP has long-term consequences for an organization that need to be carefully articulated and properly managed. More than any other software application, an ERP is ample demonstration of the widespread and strategic impact of IT on business today.

REFERENCES

Connolly, J. (1999) "ERP: corporate cleanup," *Computerworld*, **33**(9), 1 March, 74–78.

Davenport, T. (1998a) "Putting the enterprise into the enterprise system," *Harvard Business Review*, **76**(4), July/August, 121–131.

Davenport, T. (1998b) "Living with ERP," *CIO Magazine*, 1 December.

Edwards, J. (1998) "Expanding the boundaries of ERP," *CIO Magazine*, 1 July.

Johnsen, C. (1999) "And now a word for our sponsor," *CIO Canada Magazine*, **7**(5), May, 25–32.

Johnson, M. (1999) "ERP trauma ward," *Computerworld*, **33**(30), 26 July, 32.

Koch, C. (1999) "The most important team in history," *CIO Magazine*, 15 October.

LaMonica, M. (1999) "Life after ERP," *InfoWorld*, **21**(33), 16 August, 34–35.

Markus, M.L. and C. Tanis (2000) "The enterprise systems experience—from adoption to success," in R.W. Zmud (ed.), *Framing the Domains of IT Research: Glimpsing the Future through the Past*, Pinnaflex Educational Resources, Cincinnati, OH.

Martell, T. (1999) "Scaling the ERP Mountain," *CIO Canada*, **7**(5), May.

Ross, J. (1999) "Clueless execs still keep ERP from delivering value," *Computerworld*, **33**(38), 20 September, 30.

Schaaf, R. (1999) "What trainers need to know about ERP," *Training*, **36**(5), May, ET4–ET12.

Schneider, P. (1999) "Wanted: ER people skills," *CIO Magazine*, 1 March.

Schottmiller, P. (1998) "Your new risk—an unresponsive IT infrastructure," *Bobbin*, **40**(1), September, 57–58.

Slater, D. (1999a) "An ERP package for you … and you … and you … and even you," *CIO Magazine*, 15 February.

Slater, D. (1999b) "Promises, promises," *CIO Magazine*, 1 December.

Stedman, C. (1999a) "ERP user interfaces drive workers nuts," *Computerworld*, **32**(44), 1–24.

Stein, T. (1999) "ROI: Making ERP add up," *Informationweek*, **735**, 24 May, 59–68.

Sweat, J. (1998) "ERP: The corporate ecosystem," *Informationweek*, **704**, 12 October, 42–52.

Weinberg, N. (1998) "Preparing for ERP," *Network World*, **15**(44), 2 November, 47–51.

Young, L. (1999) "Step two: Consultants say it's time for ERP's second wave," *Merchandise Management and Distribution*, May, 35–37.

Zuckerman, A. (1999) "Part 1 ERP: Pathway to the future or yesterday's buzz?" *Transportation and Distribution*, August, **40**(8), 37–44.

11
Estimating the Benefits of IT

Estimating information technology (IT) benefits is the process of determining and representing the likely outcomes of pursuing a specific course of action (with respect to IT) and evaluating the consequences in terms of a value proposition— usually a financial rate of return. It is understood that the flip side of benefits is costs, and both must be taken into consideration in order to arrive at value. The process of estimating IT benefits is considered a cornerstone of virtually every-thing that is accomplished within IT. It is on the basis of these estimates that key decisions are made regarding resource allocation among IT projects, and it is on the basis of these decisions that business opportunities are exercised or forgone (Kulatilaka and Venkatramen, 1999).

Thus, estimating IT benefits plays a key role in organizations. As a recognized activity, it has been under the spotlight for some time due to its central role. Evidence would suggest that, despite its importance, our skills with respect to estimating benefits leave room for improvement (Tallon et al., 2000). This same evidence suggests that our ability to accurately estimate benefits from extremely large IT projects is suspect at best. As a result, most organizations have adopted a strategy of breaking large IT projects into smaller ones with deliverable "chunks" (most often not exceeding six-month developments). Whether or not this strat-egy is followed, the need to improve our ability to estimate IT benefits accurately and completely is vital.

Estimation is a universal prerequisite for project initiation. Based on early-stage estimates, resources are (or are not) committed to various IT projects. When estimation is done effectively, project prioritization and selection results in sig-nificant value creation. When done less effectively, opportunities are squandered. Because of its recognized importance, it is the rare organization that does not have well-established procedures for estimating IT benefits. Typically these organizations follow some method of return on investment (ROI), payback, internal rate of return (IRR), return on investment base, or other similar strategy.

In this chapter, we discuss the nature of IT benefits, review current practice with respect to assessing these benefits, explore the need to explicitly incorporate risk into benefit estimation, present relevant frameworks and models, and conclude with a number of strategies to follow in the interest of improving current practice.

ESTIMATING IT BENEFITS

A study by Ryan and Harrison (2000) indicates that our current approaches for estimating IT value leave room for improvement. They discovered that formal quantitative methods are used in approximately 31% of IT investments. Of these methods, by far the most popular were ROI, IRR, and net present value (NPV) calculations. These techniques were found to be useful for estimating tangible benefits, but much less so for quasi-tangible benefits (e.g., individual productivity improvements) and intangible benefits (e.g., better decision-making ability). They found that these quasi-tangible and intangible benefits were sometimes recognized and considered in the IT investment decision process, but typically without the benefit of a rigorous, formalized process. According to the authors, the greatest shortcoming is the demonstrated failure to identify "hidden" or seldom-considered costs and benefits—which they termed the "social subsystem costs and benefits" that stem from employees' expertise, judgments, decisions, and task interdependencies (Ryan and Harrison, 2000, p. 12). Further, they speculate that this failure explains the fact that over 50% of IT projects cost more than twice their original estimates (Webb, 1997).

Assessing IT benefits is not an easy task. According to Devaraj and Kohli (2000, p. 41):

> ... the difficulty in identifying impacts from technology has been the isolation of benefits of IT from other factors that may also contribute to organizational performance. Furthermore, benefits from technology investments may be realized over an extended period of time. Finally, IT benefits may accrue when they are done in concert with other organizational initiatives such as business process reengineering.

Adding to the difficulties mentioned above is the complication that this assessment must be done *jointly* by IT and the business. Typically, the business assumes responsibility for delineating the benefits of the IT project while IT assumes responsibility for identifying and assessing the costs of delivery. The difficulty arises due to the different orientation of IT and the business with respect to performance measures—what Fisher (2000) refers to as the "cultural divide". This is explained as follows:

> When traditional IT managers consider ROI milestones, they are likely comparing the performance of software and hardware against the budget they have received

to buy, make, and implement the solution. When sales and marketing managers contemplate ROI, they are thinking about revenue growth and market share.

Given the cultural divide between IT and the business, it is easy to see how the "social subsystem costs and benefits" can fall through the cracks. Responsibility for the assessment of these benefits (e.g., productivity improvement, quality, improved decision-making ability, and labor savings) and costs (e.g., training costs, change management, and on-the-job learning-curve costs) must be delineated jointly. Until the business gains a full understanding of the technology's potential and until IT acquires an appreciation of the business strategy, the full benefits of an IT investment cannot be estimated with any degree of confidence.

The formulaic understanding of IT benefits is seductively simple—revenue less cost nets profit. This leaves two levers of control—the increase in revenue and/or the decrease in cost—all other factors being held constant. The benefits associated with some IT systems are clearly aimed at cost reduction (or avoidance); with others the goal is clearly revenue growth. The majority of IT projects have some healthy mix of both goals. Benefits (as well as costs) can be categorized along many other dimensions as well. Common among these classifications are the following: tangible versus intangible, short-term versus long-term, internal versus external, hard savings versus soft savings, direct versus indirect, and strategic versus tactical. These classifications are useful for organizing the different types of benefit as well as providing a template to encourage organizations to explore the various types of benefit as completely as possible. It is by means of the complete delineation of benefits that forceful and compelling project proposals are tabled.

In Figure 11.1, IT benefits are jointly classified along three dimensions. Along the horizontal axis, they are identified as being direct, indirect, or inferred. The vertical axis differentiates benefits with respect to their difficulty of implementation. The third dimension is time. The chart suggests that IT projects that promote competitive gains leading to survival occur over longer time-frames. In contrast, cost-focused IT projects often deliver shorter term gains. Figure 11.1 also suggests another aspect of IT benefit estimation—the fixation on financial returns. Arguably all benefits are reducible to a single monetary value, but with varying degrees of difficulty/accuracy. A cost displacement benefit where five employees are made redundant, for example, results in a straightforward calculation. In contrast, the dollar value of an "enhanced customer experience" is less easily determined. As a result, organizations tend to exhibit a predilection for projects with "hard" benefits.

Table 11.1 presents a classification of IT benefits using three categories: (1) expanded services/products delivered internally and/or externally; (2) cost savings/avoidance; and (3) enhance work environment. This table, which is used by one of the focus group firms, demonstrates the range of benefits attributed to IT and is useful for estimating their impacts.

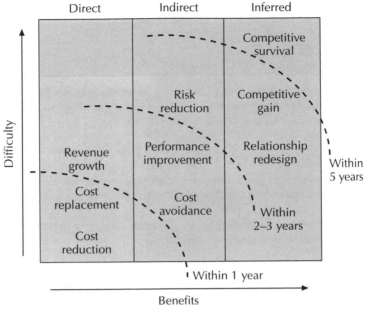

Figure 11.1 *Types of IT benefit.*

THE NEED TO ASSESS RISK

Standard practice in estimating IT benefits suffers from a major flaw—the omission of an explicit assessment of risk/uncertainty. To understand this, we need to differentiate between deterministic models and probabilistic models. All the models described (e.g., ROI, payback, IRR, breakeven analysis) are typically used deterministically as opposed to probabilistically. With a *deterministic* model, best estimates of benefits are represented by a stream of numbers over the planning horizon of the anticipated IT project. These numbers are then further reduced to a single number (such as an NPV) arrived at by discounting the future stream of benefits/costs using a fixed discount rate. With a *probabilistic* model, each of the annual estimates of benefits is surrounded by a probability distribution. While the application of a deterministic model might result in a forecasted IRR of 15% for a proposed project, an equivalent probabilistic model would result in a forecasted IRR of 15% *with a likelihood of no greater than 65%*. Probabilistic models have the benefit of capturing the inherent risk/uncertainty surrounding the development of an IT project, but, unfortunately, require some additional effort as well as mathematical sophistication. For these reasons, they are not in widespread use.

The difficulty with our preoccupation with deterministic models is manifest in a number of ways. *First*, we delude ourselves into thinking that we can "deliver the benefits on a project" simply by bringing it in on time. The benefits (and to a

Table 11.1   *Types of IT benefit and their roles.*

---

(1) EXPANDED SERVICES/PRODUCTS DELIVERED INTERNALLY AND/OR
EXTERNALLY

- *Improves ability to deliver*—provides employees wtih access to information via desktop to allow them to respond to customer enquiries more accurately and quickly.
- *Improves access to services*—increases the number of people who can be reached. Customers are provided multiple points of access to the organization—telephone, email, Internet—in addition to existing mail services.
- *Improves access to information*—employees gain direct access to resources or information enabling them to perform daily tasks more efficiently.
- *Improves accuracy*—improves accuracy by reducing the need for manual data entry or reducing the number of data entry errors, thereby improving integrity of data. This may improve productivity and reduce operating costs by reducing time spent on error correction.
- *Improves compatibility*—solution is compatible with existing facilities or procedures, requires less training of personnel or less new equipment and software; solutions meet IT architecture requirements.
- *Improves effectiveness and impact of information delivered*—on-line interactive training provides opportunities to improve skills, increase participation in training, and improves retention of new information. May increase productivity, reduce turnover, etc.
- *Provides options or flexibility for capturing future opportunities*—investments that provide the ability to capture additional gains in the future. This approach can be helpful in garnering support for investments in infrastructure or pilot projects.
- *Improves security*—system improves security in terms of fraud prevention, protection of confidential information, or enhances data security.
- *Reduces risk*—back-up systems that reduce the risk of data loss or applications that improve timely delivery of critical information.

(2) COST/SAVINGS/AVOIDANCE

- *Improves the ability to maintain a system*—investments for which maintenance resources are more readily available. Ease of maintenance is relevant to both software and hardware.
- *Eliminates duplicate assets*—investments that replace multiple, non-compatible, or stand-alone systems.
- *Improves reliability*—system has better performance record (less down time). Reductions in down time inversely impact productivity and may also reduce labor costs.
- *Accommodates increases in workload or demand without additional costs*—systems that will avoid hiring additional personnel to handle increased workload or responsibilities in the future.
- *Reduces manual operations*—systems that automate manual processes freeing staff to perform other functions, reducing or eliminating staff. Lower salary level staff may perform functions.
- *Improve efficiency*—improved access to information or tools decreases time required to perform daily functions.

(3) ENHANCE WORK ENVIRONMENT

- *Facilitates ease of use*—generally thought of in terms of increased efficiency or productivity, can also improve the social and physical environment for employees.
- *Improves physical environment*—systems that reduce paper clutter in a work area, noise, or eyestrain.
- *Improves response rates*—assets that reduce stress by improving employees' ability to respond to customer enquiries.

---

lesser extent, the costs) of a project are subject to a number of forces well beyond our control (e.g., a competitor's action, business model changes, legislation, new products/services offerings, a vendor's service level, interest rates). As a result, realized benefits may vary dramatically from anticipated benefits—in either direction. *Second*, any risk/uncertainty assessment carried out by IT tends to focus on the technology associated with a project since this is the part for which IT assumes responsibility. As a result, few projects are undertaken without assurances from IT that they are "technically feasible". Armed with such assurances, we proceed in the belief that we have accounted for (or worse yet, eliminated) the risk. The preoccupation with technical feasibility can diminish the importance of assessing "operational", "financial", as well as "organizational" risk. *Third*, without an explicit assessment of the risk/uncertainty side of the equation to balance the "return" side, we are left with no ability to differentiate among competing project proposals having identical ROIs.

In the next session, we identify some strategies for estimating the benefits of IT investments taking risk into account.

STRATEGIES FOR ESTIMATING IT BENEFITS

Estimating IT benefits should be viewed within the larger scope of *IT value management*—the art of assessing, measuring, and communicating the value of information technology beyond just dollars and cents (Meta Group quote in Fisher, 2000). While the bottom line is the ultimate test, companies are realizing that flexibility, leverage, and speed to market represent IT-enabled areas that generate significant value to the organization. Value management implies tight linkages between technology and business strategy; it implies a level of shared understanding and effective communication between business and IT; it implies a clearly articulated role for IT within the organization; and it implies mutual trust—where the business trusts IT to introduce appropriate technology solutions and IT trusts the business to deploy the technology opportunistically. As one focus group member stated: "IT used to look at 'IT things'; now IT has to look at total business value." The following strategies adopt this more encompassing "IT value management" perspective.

1   Establish IT's Role in Creating Benefits.

IT must have a clearly articulated role within the organization in terms of delivering IT benefits. This was expressed by one focus group member by claiming that: "what you find depends on where you look". She was referring to the "service" role that was cast for IT within her organization. In this role, IT was limited to providing systems as (and when) specified by the business. IT was not a full partner of the business and was not canvassed when designing the strategy to be pursued. A new chief executive officer (CEO) soon discovered that parts of the organization had not been upgrading their technology to the detriment of the overall organization. As a result, IT was recast into the role of full partnership with the business and, in this new role, became the driver for a new CRM initiative. This was not a case of estimating benefits more effectively. It was a situation where IT brought different ideas/solutions to the table that might not otherwise have been considered. She stated that they discovered that: "the real value of IT was in the strategic/integration area all the while IT was perceived as being in the service business."

Tallon et al. (2000) argue that there are a number of important differences among organizations with respect to the role that is cast for IT. Specifically, they suggest that in order to understand executives' perceptions of IT benefits/impacts, one must first consider these impacts within the context of the firm's goals for IT. They suggest that it is the balance that an organization strikes between the two IT goals of operational effectiveness and strategic positioning that determines the types of benefit that will actually transpire (see Figure 11.2), and hence the value that will be created. By using such a model, it is possible to clearly articulate a role for IT in creating organizational value. Relating this to the

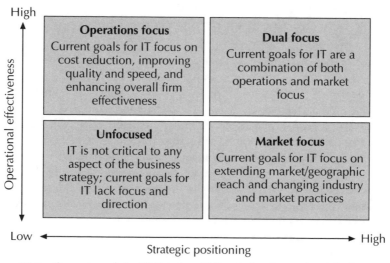

Figure 11.2   *Corporate goals for IT (data from Tallon et al., 2000, used with kind permission).*

focus member's story above, her organization had shifted its IT goals from the "unfocussed" quadrant (or the "operations focus" quadrant) to the "market focus" quadrant. This had resulted in rather sweeping changes to the benefits and overall value that IT created within the organization.

2   Classify Benefits within Your IT Portfolio.

Weill and Broadbent (1996) classify IT projects into the following types:

- strategic—alters the basis of competition;
- informational—increases control, provides better information and better integration;
- transactional—cuts costs, increases throughput of business transactions;
- infrastructure—enables business integration, flexibility, and reduces IT costs;
- research and design (R&D)—explores emerging technologies for potential value to the business.

It can be seen that each of these types of system delivers different types of benefit and therefore should be considered separately—perhaps using a different approach to estimating IT benefits. Infrastructure projects, for instance, often create value by enabling new, unforeseen benefits within transactional, informational, or strategic systems. Strategic systems, unlike transactional systems, have a high failure rate (50%), but also have some spectacular successes. They can take two or three years to bring to the market, but can command premium-pricing once there. Organizations should not estimate the benefits of all projects, regardless of type, on a strict ROI basis. In fact, it was pointed out by one focus group member that, because all IT projects are forced through the same financial review at her organization, "some of the really valuable systems had to be done under the radar."

According to focus group members, much of the existing R&D work is "skunk works"—that is, work that is not charged back to a particular line of business and, for all intents and purposes, does not officially exist. The R&D investment is essential, and there are no benefits in treating it as anything less than what it is. The time and effort spent investing in an emerging technology should be considered as "taking an option", to adopt a term from finance. Furthermore, this option should be made transparent to the organization. This demonstrates to the organization that IT is ensuring the continuity of the technology investment and, as such, represents a highly desirable and rational pursuit—not something to be hidden.

3   Map IT Benefits onto Business Strategy

One focus group member mapped IT benefits directly onto the critical success factors (CSFs) identified by his organization. This forced alignment between IT and the "business value model". Estimation of IT benefits became a two-step model; the first step was to link the IT project directly to the CSFs, and the second step was to map these CSFs to measurable bottom-line numbers. By separating the estimation of IT benefits into two separate steps, all IT projects were business-focused first. It resulted in some projects, despite attractive ROIs, failing during the first step.

Another focus group member developed a template used by his organization to bridge the "cultural divide" (mentioned earlier). This template (see Table 11.2) is used to rate the benefits of all proposed IT investments along the following key business drivers:

- maximize the utilization of company assets and resources;
- improve information management;
- retain and attract customers for the company;
- improve relationship with business partners;
- attract, develop, motivate, and retain high-performing employees;
- grow the distribution business;
- optimize the technical infrastructure investment;
- accommodate regulatory requirement;
- add financial value.

For each key business driver, a description is required of the solution's potential *impact* on the organization as well as a *performance indicator* to measure each impact. The benefit of this approach is its ability to force alignment between IT and business strategy, to ferret out the "hidden social subsystem costs and benefits", and its requirement to identify performance indicators in advance. This is a comprehensive scheme that facilitates benefit estimation due to its requirement of advance identification of system impacts and indicators of success.

Table 11.3 depicts a process-oriented model developed by Tallon et al. (2000) to assess the impacts of IT on critical business activities within the value chain. By identifying the six major steps along the value chain and by determining how IT impacts each of these steps, it is possible to tie IT benefits directly into the value chain. This process also demonstrates how proposed IT changes will deliver value and identifies who will take ownership of (and responsibility for) achieving the promised benefits. Based on a clear understanding of how/when/where value will be created, a significant part of estimating benefits involves managing the process (see the next section).

4   Build IT Benefits into Project Development.

One of the focus group members pointed out that: "estimation and benefits are not disassociated ... we *engineer* the benefits ... it's a process." This insight demonstrates how the whole activity of estimating IT benefits should be approached. It is a proactive approach rather than a reactive approach. An ERP

Table 11.2 *Benefit rating template:* ● *represents "solution impact";* □ *represents "sample performance indicator".*

| | Rating scale benefits | | | | |
	-2	Neutral	1	2	3
Maximize the utilization of company assets and resources	● The functionality will add work to the existing process	● No change in staff productivity	● Ability to take on more workload without hiring more staff	● Improves productivity within a single or multiple departments	● Can take on work from other companies
	□ Requires increase in staff	□ 0% change in staff	□ Maintain productivity with increased workload	□ Reduce staff by y%	□ Reduce staff by greater than y%
Improve information management	● No additional information will be made available as a result of this project	● Project contributes to standardized corporate reporting	● Project contributes to the ability to generate *ad hoc* reports from the desktop	● Project contributes to generating information for strategic planning	
	□ Incremental tool to support	□ Elimination of duplicate reporting solutions	□ Reduced report requests	□ Timely information to prepare for strategic planning	
Retain and attract customers for the company family	● Project will be perceived as negative by company customers	● No impact on existing customers	● Improves communication with company customers	● Streamlines/Refines existing processes between the company and customers	● Adds new customers or reduces customer transfer to alternate fuel source

continued

Table 11.2 (cont.)

	Rating scale benefits				
	−2	Neutral	1	2	3
	□ x% of customers change to alternate fuel source	□ No change in number of customers	□ Number of company-initiated customer contacts increase—upselling	□ Increase in x sector by y%. Decrease of y% in transfers	□ Increase in x sector by y%. Decrease of y% in transfers
Improve relationship with business partners	● Project will be perceived as negative by company business partners	● No direct impact on business partners	● Improves communication with business partners	● Streamlines an existing process between company and business partners	● On-line and interactive communication methods for staff and business partners
	□ Increases work effort of company or business partners	□ Processes remain unchanged	□ Increases the points of access to company	□ Reduces work effort for company or business partners	□ Reduces cycle times and increases productivity
Attract, develop, motivate, and retain high-performing employees	● Staff will perceive the project as reducing efficiency or impacting productivity	● Staff do not perceive any value to workflow or processes	● Staff looking forward to change	● Staff perceive the project as being critical to their growth/personal job satisfaction	
	□ Definite resistance to change or acceptance of project	□ Staff indifferent to change	□ Improved work morale	□ New processes developed for added services	

Grow the distribution business	• Puts barriers in place to acquisition of other businesses	• No impact on strategic plan to grow the distribution business	• Supports performance measurement and balanced scorecard reporting ☐ Increase customer additions by 5%	• Contributes to the branding of the company	• Facilitates the acquisition of other businesses
Optimize the technical infrastructure investment	• Adds incremental technology to the infrastructure	• No impact on existing technical infrastructure	• Will replace and/or enhance system and improve consistency ☐ Reduces reliance on legacy systems	• Will replace existing computer system to allow compatibility with other components of the system ☐ Removes the dependency on legacy infrastructure	• Will replace existing manual system
Accommodate regulatory requirements	• Conflicts with or inconsistent with regulatory approach ☐ Creates additional work to meet regulatory obligation	• No regulatory implications	• Enhances relationship with regulator ☐ Prepares systems for potential regulatory change	• Mandatory regulatory requirements ☐ Complies with regulatory requirements	
Add financial value	☐ Increase operating costs	☐ No impact	☐ Cost avoidance up to $0.5 million	☐ Cost reduction up to $0.5 million	☐ Cost reduction over $0.5 million. Potential revenue generator greater than $1.0 million
Estimated financial	$	$	$	$	$

Table 11.3 *Mapping IT benefits onto the value chain (Tallon et al., 2000).*

DOES INFORMATION TECHNOLOGY . . .

Process planning and support
- Improve internal communication and co-ordination?
- Strengthen strategic planning?
- Enable your company to adopt new organizational structures?
- Improve management decision-making?
- Streamline business processes?

Supplier relations (inbound logistics)
- Help your corporation gain leverage over its suppliers?
- Help reduce variance in supplier lead times?
- Help develop close relationships with suppliers?
- Improve monitoring of the quality of products/services from suppliers?
- Enable electronic transactions with suppliers?

Production and operations
- Improve production throughput or service volumes?
- Enhance operating flexibility?
- Improve the productivity of labor?
- Enhance utilization of equipment?
- Reduce cost of tailoring products or services?

Product and service enhancement
- Enhance the value of products/services by embedding IT in them?
- Decrease the cost of designing new products/services?
- Reduce the time to market for new products/services?
- Enhance product/service quality?
- Support product/service innovation?

Sales and marketing support
- Enable the identification of market trends?
- Increase the ability to anticipate customer needs?
- Enable sales people to increase sales per customer?
- Improve the accuracy of sales forecasts?
- Help track market response to pricing strategies?

Customer relations (outbound logistics)
- Enhance the ability to provide after-sales service and support?
- Enhance the flexibility and responsiveness to customer needs?
- Improve the distribution of goods and services?
- Enhance the ability to attract and retain customers?
- Enable you to support customers during the sales process?

system will not produce benefits *all by itself*; it is only through the thoughtful reorganization of the business that allows people to perform much more effectively that will allow an ERP system (or any other for that matter) to create significant benefits.

Benefits don't just fall out of project development, they must be built in. Responsibility for this resides with the project-leader. Working directly with key business users, the project-leader must ensure that the system is both usable and useful. Developing a system that fails either test jeopardizes the ultimate realization of anticipated benefits. Some of the critical project management areas follow:

- Project development involves "gating"; that is, making certain that well-specified deliverables have been attained at certain checkpoints. At each gate, it is necessary that all estimated benefits be revised in light of any/all new information that has arisen. Armed with these new estimates, every project must pass through a "go/no-go" test. Failure to kill projects at these gates due to organizational inertia or personal attachment is injurious to the health of the organization. Realizing IT benefits starts with denying projects where benefits are uncertain.
- In the words of a focus group member: "IT brings discipline to projects . . . this allows benefits to be realized." She cited an example where IT "blew the whistle" on a project that was seen to be misaligned with the business model. Another member organization actually "gives marks" for killing projects. They did not want any stigma attached to ending a project where the benefits had changed significantly. Far better to cut one's losses than persevere with a doomed project. Of course, where IT assumes a service role in the organization, this type of activity is less frequent and may be impossible.
- The old habit of making IT responsible for costs and the business responsible for the benefits is simplistic. Focus group members cited many examples where shared responsibility was the best alternative. Engineering benefits is a partnership. Business processes have to change to reap the benefits of new technology solutions just as technology solutions must have usability designed in. It begins with a business need, follows with a technology strategy, and where the two meet benefits result.

5 Use Risk to Discount IT Benefits

Given an indeterminate future, risk is a fact of life. It is not to be denied or ignored. It must be explicitly accounted for within our planning frameworks when estimating the benefits of IT projects. It is neither good nor bad—it only reflects the existence of uncertain future states. Unfortunately, for most individuals risk has a negative connotation—risk of failure, risk of harm, risk of loss. When viewed this way, the desire is to *minimize* risk. But there also exists risk of reward, risk of success, and risk of growth. According to Kulatilaka and Venkatramen (1999, p. 7), a strategy of minimizing risk can constrain the "bandwidth of opportunity", inadvertently limiting the range of possible options that an organization can exercise.

The strategy for making risk an integral part of the process of estimating IT benefits consists of three steps:

- measure risk;
- discount IT benefits based on risk;
- select your comfort zone for risk (i.e., a point somewhere along the risk-aversion–risk-proclivity continuum).

Risk measurement need not be overly complex or overly accurate ... as long as it is done. For reasons presented earlier in this chapter, there is greater danger in not assessing risk than in a poor assessment of risk. One focus group member described her firm's approach as simply categorizing a project's overall risk into three groups: high, medium, or low. Another firm identified the key risk factors for each IT project (e.g., size of project, task complexity, technical complexity, and readiness of organization for change) and evaluated each factor on a scale from 1 to 10. These individual numbers were then combined to produce an overall risk assessment for the project.

Discounting benefits can be accomplished equally simply. One firm mapped all potential IT projects onto a 2×2 grid with ROI on the horizontal axis and risk on the vertical axis. In general, one would normally expect a higher return to compensate for higher risk—that is, placement along the diagonal. "Off-diagonal" systems are special cases being either high return and low risk, or low return and high risk. The latter are to be avoided and the former are "low-hanging fruit". Once plotted on this risk-return grid, selections among potential projects are made with full considerations of the tradeoffs.

Finally, firms must explicitly *select* their risk comfort zone. A risk-aversion strategy may forgo potentially rewarding IT opportunities while a high-risk approach may jeopardize a firm's viability. Most focus group members felt that organizations should balance the overall risk within their IT portfolio rather than adopting a steady diet of either high- or low-risk projects. It was felt that taking on some high-risk (and potentially high-return) projects to offset the lower risk projects results in a healthier mix within the IT portfolio. These approaches are not highly mathematical or scientific. Nonetheless, they are useful for focusing the discussion of senior executives on the balance of potential lucrative and potentially risky endeavors. At the very least, the inherent riskiness of IT projects is made overt.

6   Put Post-implementation Reviews (PIRs) to Work

When asked, virtually every IT organization acknowledges the merits and necessity of conducting PIRs. When asked how frequently PIRs are conducted, these same organizations typically respond with one of the following answers:

- "for some systems";
- "not always";

- "should be doing it more regularly and conscientiously"; and/or
- "maybe next year we'll embed PIRs into our normal practice".

So, why are PIRs, while universally acclaimed to be beneficial, not universally deployed? In most cases, it is due to two factors. First, as soon as projects are completed, everyone is immediately reassigned to a new project and dispersed. Three to six months later, they can barely remember the project let alone the details, decision points, discussions, etc. The second reason for not conducting PIRs has to do with committing the required resources. After the project is implemented, it can appear to be a waste of effort to revisit the project. Many organizations would prefer to have their scarce IT resources working productively on new projects . . . not reviewing what is now considered to be "water under the bridge".

PIRs serve the vital purpose of learning by "closing the loop". At the outset of a project, estimates of benefits are made, perhaps altered along the way, and, finally, based on these estimates, decisions are taken to develop/acquire some new IT capability. If a PIR is not conducted, it will never be possible to learn and hopefully improve your ability to estimate benefits. Some organizations, in an attempt to revitalize this important step, refer to PIRs as "benefit-harvesting". Tallon et al. (2000, pp. 165–166) examined PIR techniques and found that: "firms that use post-implementation reviews are in an ideal position to bring 'best practice' or lessons learned from these reviews to bear on future IT investment decisions."

Table 11.4 contains a PIR guide used by one of the focus group members. This guide is completed prior to beginning the interviews as a vehicle for communicating the scope of the PIR to interested parties. This is quite extensive in its coverage of the issues under examination during a PIR and could be adapted easily to fit other organizations.

CONCLUSIONS

The importance of estimating IT benefits is widely acknowledged. It is on the basis of these estimates that decisions to implement (or forgo) new technologies within organizations are established. It is also on the basis of these estimates that, via a PIR, we learn how/where/why benefits were realized. In both these activities, it is understood that benefits are actually engineered. One of the focus group members summed up our discussion nicely as follows:

- IT must approach the business with business needs and processes (not technology);
- the business needs to be "driving for" and "accountable for" benefits;
- IT needs to meet process and functional commitments; and finally
- IT needs to understand the CSFs or, beyond that, must measure up to the metrics.

Table 11.4   *Post-implementation review (PIR). This PIR guide is completed prior to beginning the interviews as a vehicle for communicating the scope of the PIR.*

PROJECT X: CLEARLY STATE THE SCOPE OF THE PROJECT (WHAT WAS IMPLEMENTED, WHEN, IN WHICH DEPARTMENTS)

PIR: scope and purpose of review

- Conduct a review of [Project X] to assess what has changed as a result of the system implementation:
  - Determine if there is initial evidence of benefits to the implementation area.
  - Identify any areas of risk to further implementations.
  - Identify opportunities to streamline processes and enhance efficiencies.
  - Identify strategies to achieve additional benefits and to enhance end-user satisfaction.

Proposed methodology

- Present intent to conduct a PIR to project sponsor for approval.
- Identify the staff to be interviewed/observed. Arrange meetings.
- Provide communications to the staff about the review.
- Collect data through a combination of observations and interviews.
- After data-gathering, compile the analysis into a draft report.
- Review findings with project sponsor.
- Present report to steering committee.

Interviews (approximately one hour in duration)

- Project-sponsor.
- Manager of the department(s) affected.
- Project-manager.
- Vendor.
- Trainer.

Combination of observations and interviews (approximately two hours in duration)

- Representative sample of staff of the departments affected.
- Demonstration of the new system.

Documents required

- Project definition.
  - Documents that describe the new business model (including work flows, roles).
  - Departmental performance indicators.
  - Revised policies and procedures.
  - Value proposition.

Sample interview/observation questions

- In your opinion, why was this project implemented? What problems was the implementation to address?
- How has the new system improved the business? Can you give some examples of how this business has improved (e.g., improved accuracy and timeliness of information, improved communication between members of the organization, improved productivity)?
- How does the new system impact your daily routine? Do you have a clear definition of your roles and responsibilities? Have changes to work flows been documented? Were you trained adequately on the new system and changes to your work?
- What were the challenges in the implementation of this project?

- What strategies would you suggest to facilitate achieving benefits?
- What advice would you give on implementation?

PROJECT X: PIR—ADDITIONAL SAMPLE QUESTIONS

Requirements

- Determine if the results of the new system met the original objectives as stated in the business proposal.
- Determine at the project's conclusion whether the project met the success criteria as defined in the project definition.
- Were the expected benefits of the new system realized?
- Does the system perform as expected?
- If there were differences found in expectations and actual results, were they investigated and dispositions noted?
- If there were inefficiencies noted, were they documented and the dispositions noted?
- How has the system changed the way in which operations are performed?
- How has the system changed the accuracy of information that users receive?
- How has the system changed the timeliness of information that users receive?
- How has the system changed the completeness of information?
- How has the system changed the interactions between members of the organization?
- How has the system changed productivity?

Cost/Benefit

- Determine if the cost/benefit analysis was correct.
- Compare the actual versus budgeted costs and benefits.
- Evaluate the reasons for the differences in actual versus budgeted costs and benefits.
- Do the reasons for the variances appear valid?

User satisfaction

- Determine if the user is satisfied with the new system and evaluate what points should be considered in another project.
- Determine if the user is satisfied with the operations of the new system.
- Are there problems or inefficiencies in the new system that can be corrected?
- Is there a need for ongoing training?
- Have all problems been corrected?
- Does the system meet the user requirements?
- Does the system provide all the required information?
- Conduct a survey of the users (a sample is acceptable) to determine if training was sufficient, the system is operating as expected, reports are providing the required information, problems are being resolved.

Application controls

- Determine that the application was adequately designed to meet the financial business requirements.
- Review any changes to the application during all phases of the project to determine if they significantly changed the projects's original goal.
- Are all changes documented?
- Are all changes reviewed and approved by the project team?
- Does upper management approve all changes that affect the project scope?
- For any significant changes, is the project re-evaluated to determine the feasibility/cost/benefits?

REFERENCES

Devaraj, S. and R. Kohli (2000) "Information technology payoff in the health-care industry: A longitudinal study," *Journal of Management Information Systems*, **16**(4), Spring, 41–67.

Fisher, S. (2000) "Metrics for e-success," *CTO FirstMover*, 15 May, 27–30 (www. infoworld.com).

Kulatilaka, N. and N. Venkatramen (1999) *Measuring Information Technology Investment Payoff*, Idea Group Publishing, Hershey, PA.

Ryan, S. and D. Harrison (2000) "Considering social subsystem costs and benefits in information technology investment decisions: A view from the field on anticipated payoffs," *Journal of Management Information Systems*, **16**(4), Spring, 11–40.

Tallon, P., K. Kraemer, and V. Gurbaxani (2000) "Executives' perceptions of the business value of information technology: A process-oriented approach," *Journal of Management Information Systems*, **16**(4), Spring, 145–173.

Webb, G. (1997) "Make IT work," *Airfinance Journal*, **197**, 52–53.

Weill, P. and M. Broadbent (1996) *Leveraging the New Infrastructure: How Market Leaders Capitalize on Information Technology*, Harvard Business School Press, Boston.

12
IT Project Prioritization

When most people think of project prioritization, they think of the annual budgeting/planning cycle when information technology (IT) works with the business to identify projects that will go "on the books for the next year" ... meaning that resources can be marshaled to support them. Of course, in preparation for this activity, projects must be identified, described, evaluated, and placed in the queue according to some order of urgency. It is the process of placing projects in order of urgency that represents the essence of project prioritization. And contrary to popular myth, it is a continual process as projects arise throughout the year.

This chapter seeks to investigate project prioritization by mapping the process that governs projects from their inception (an idea) through to project launch (i.e., assigned resources ready to start). The first two sections define project prioritization and position it with respect to related organizational processes (project life cycle management, project selection, capital appropriation decisions, and project-budgeting). The next section positions project prioritization within the larger framework of portfolio management. The final section of the chapter outlines a number of strategies for effective prioritization that emerged from our discussions during the meeting.

IT PROJECT PRIORITIZATION: WHAT IT IS AND WHAT IT ISN'T

IT project prioritization can be defined as the management exercise of assigning priorities to IT projects where the output is a list rank-ordered by implementation preference. In order to fully understand IT project prioritization, we need to position it within the broader organizational context of creating a portfolio of projects that collectively maximizes the IT-derived competitive advantage for the

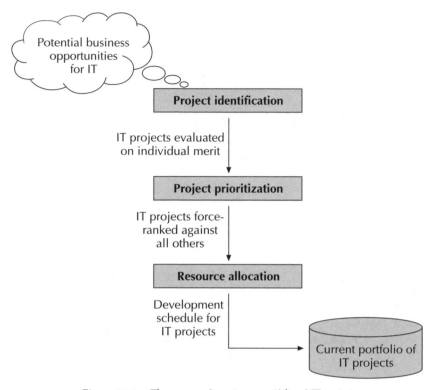

Figure 12.1   *The process of creating a portfolio of IT projects.*

firm (see Figure 12.1). To do so, we will examine four elements that frequently obscure how the process of IT project prioritization actually works.

1   Project Identification

Often the processes of project identification and prioritization are jointly described as project selection, but this term mixes up two very distinct activities. *Identification* is the process that is used to discover and present potential IT applications to the business. Although this process differs from organization to organization, its key role is to screen potential projects. Where project identification is ineffective, organizations can find their ability to match technology with business opportunity severely jeopardized. Improper identification arises from inappropriate screening. With a porous screen, a glut of potential projects is presented for prioritization, and unnecessarily overburdens this downstream activity. A screen that is too restrictive results in the organization forgoing potentially rewarding business applications of IT.

2 Resource Allocation

Resource allocation can also be confused with project prioritization. The input to resource allocation (i.e., the output of prioritization) is a list of IT projects rank-ordered by preference. As such (see Figure 12.1), IT project prioritization logically precedes resource allocation. *Resource allocation*[1] is the process of committing resources to projects (starting with the highest ranking projects) until the available resources are fully depleted. This is typically done in less than ideal conditions—too many potential projects competing for too few dollars coupled with too few development people working under time schedules that are too stringent.

Where the confusion occurs is during the actual process of resource allocation. Frequently an organization finds itself in the position where the top three IT projects consume most of the available resources such that the fourth-ranked project (if it is large) cannot fit within the development plan. However, the fifth- or sixth-ranked projects, being smaller, can fit. In this case, perhaps one (or both) of these lower ranked projects are included as part of the development plan for the upcoming fiscal year. Because of this out-of-priority sequencing, the boundaries and distinctions between prioritization and resource allocation become fuzzy. Nevertheless, the difference is significant, and it is important to keep these two management processes separate if for no other reason than to remove affordability as a decision criterion when establishing priorities.

3 Capital Appropriation

The commitment of resources to the development of IT projects is a capital appropriation decision—one of many made throughout organizations. These decisions (e.g., a new product launch, a building expansion, a major equipment purchase, or the generation of a marketing campaign) have three features in common: (1) a commitment of capital and resources to the proposed venture; (2) a decision *not* to pursue a competing project (or projects) at least at this time; and (3) a belief that this appropriation will result in a favorable impact on the business. Most companies make IT projects compete against other IT projects for resources drawn from a pre-allocated IT budget. In contrast, some companies place IT projects into a general competition against business (i.e., non-IT) projects. With this approach, an IT project is judged against all other possible capital projects (e.g., a new marketing campaign). The philosophy is that both proposed projects consume capital resources, both affect the business (hopefully) favorably, and, more importantly, funds should not be earmarked for various functions within the organization as this may not necessarily lead to an optimal allocation of the organization's limited capital resources.

---

[1] We prefer to use the more descriptive term "resource allocation" to the term "budgeting", which is also commonly used.

4   Project Life cycle

Most companies adhere to a life cycle model for IT projects—a series of well-defined stages delineated by decision points that collectively characterize the life of a project from birth to death. Once triggered by the submission of a "service request" by a business manager, the typical life cycle of an IT project might consist of the following stages: preliminary investigation; detailed investigation; development testing, and validation; full production/implementation; and a post-implementation review. Cooper et al. (2000) introduce the term "stage-gating" to highlight the need for each IT project to successfully pass through a "gate" at the end of each stage in order to proceed to the next stage. They argue that stage-gate processes are instrumental in improving the quality of information generated during project development by: (1) defining the tasks, activities, and account-abilities within each stage; (2) defining the deliverables required for the gate decision—a list of information items that senior management needs in order to make effective "go/kill" decisions at each gate; and (3) specifying the criteria against which each project is evaluated (Cooper et al., 2000, p. 24).

Formal prioritization typically occurs at the completion of the detailed inves-tigation stage. At this point, the project has successfully passed the preliminary investigation and has received a "go" at the completion of the detailed investiga-tion. The go/kill decision determines whether or not the project will proceed; the prioritization process determines the project's ranking—the higher the impor-tance, the greater the ranking. Organizational resources are committed to the highest ranking projects first. At any point in time, it is typical to have a number of approved projects (those that have received a "go") sitting in the queue awaiting resources ... more or less "on hold". These projects remain in the queue until there are sufficient resources to commit to their development. Because of the volatility of business, however, the rankings of IT projects resting in the queue are subject to change with the result that some projects will never come to fruition ... always being supplanted by the promotion of others in the priority sequence.

PROCEDURES AND TECHNIQUES

As illustrated in Figure 12.1, the output from project identification is a list of projects judged to have high potential for the organization based on individual merit. Each project would have a business sponsor to serve as its organizational advocate/champion. These projects then enter the IT project prioritization process—typically a straightforward[2] procedure as follows:

---

[2] Difficulties in prioritization arise when politics become involved. In these cases, the process can be anything but "straightforward". Influential players can dominate during decision-making and other organizational levers such as lobbying, coalitions, and side payments can exist as part of the overall process. A full discussion of the nature of these interactions, however, goes beyond the scope of this chapter.

- Projects are divided into two groups (large versus small projects) based on their expected development costs. The difference between "large" versus "small" depends on the size of the organization[3].
- *Small projects* are presented to a department/division level prioritization committee. Small project prioritization committees meet frequently (at least monthly). These projects typically result in minor impacts to the business such as new reports, upgrades, or minor production changes. In these cases, these decisions are the prerogative of departmental management and are funded by a department IT budget. The remainder of the chapter will focus on "large" IT project prioritization.
- *Large projects* are presented to a corporate level committee. These corporate level committees include executives from different areas of the business and are charged with the task of ranking large IT projects based on their potential business value. These committees typically meet quarterly, but may meet on an *ad hoc* basis to take advantage of a unique business opportunity.
- The results of these deliberations are a list of IT projects ranked from highest priority to lowest from all parts of the enterprise. This can be a very dynamic process—as corporate priorities change, new projects may supplant existing projects pushing others down in the hierarchy. The saying "always a bridesmaid never a bride" applies to some projects.

A key part of the prioritization process is ascertaining a project's potential business value. A number of specific techniques are commonly used by organizations. These techniques are usually *template-driven* to ensure that all projects undergo a review based on a uniform set of criteria. Sometimes these techniques are quite elaborate and sometimes they are "one-pagers". Some of the more popular techniques are:

- *Net Present Value (NPV)—deterministic version.* Using a set rate (typically equal to the cost of capital), all project costs and benefits are placed on a time line and mathematically reduced to a single monetary value expressed in current dollars. Given the assumption that the rate is not expected to change, this single monetary value (NPV) is mathematically equivalent to the stream of the project's projected costs/benefits. This is a deterministic version since all costs and benefits are single numbers.
- *NPV—stochastic version.* A "stochastic" version takes probabilities into consideration. This means that the projected costs and benefits are not single numbers on a time line, but probability distributions. The project is estimated as having a certain likelihood of returning a range of values.
- *Derivative rates of return.* Different rates of return are easily derived from the NPV calculations. For instance, it is possible to calculate the rate at which the

---

[3] Some organizations consider any project whose expected development time exceeds six months to be large.

projected stream of benefits is equal to the estimated costs of the project. This rate is sometimes referred to as the internal rate of return (IRR). Another derivative reflects the minimum cost for a project to break even and the breakeven horizon. Other manipulations of the NPV formula can be used to explore the effects of the timing of the benefit stream, the effects of front-loading costs versus offsetting costs, etc.

- *Checklists.* These are generic devices to ensure that potential projects pass certain predetermined checkpoints. These are typically "yes/no" questions. Examples of such questions are:

  o Has the project been reviewed by direct line management?
  o Does the project directly address (at least) one of the strategic mandates?
  o Are all affected departments aware of this proposed project?
  o Has IT approved the project's viability? Time-frame?

  These check lists are typically used as screening mechanisms; they are less frequently used to assign priorities.
- *Simple scoring models.* Individual attributes of projects are rated on scales (typically low/medium/high or 1–5-type scales). This allows projects to be rated on a number of aspects beyond financial considerations. For instance, it is common for projects to be rated on features such as the following:

  o Alignment with business strategy.
  o Agreement with customer-focused initiatives.
  o Quality of service provisioning.
  o Impact on market channel partners.

  It is common practice to simply add up the scores for each attribute to produce an overall evaluation. This ability to produce an overall evaluation based on multi-factor ratings (and not just financials) is undoubtedly the greatest asset of scoring models, making them a popular choice for management for ranking proposed IT projects. Interestingly, this ability to combine disparate evaluations to reach an overall assessment is also the troublesome part of simple scoring models. To overcome some of the limitations of simple scoring models, weighted scoring methods can be used.
- *Weighted scoring models.* This is an adaptation of the simple scoring model. Realizing that not all attributes of projects are equally important, a "weight" (which could be a number from 1 to 5) is assigned to each attribute to reflect the relative importance of this attribute. The score for each attribute is now multiplied by its associated weight and these are added together to produce a final evaluation for each project (see Table 12.1 for an example of such a weighted scoring scheme).

Based on feedback from the focus group managers, valuation technique preferences appear to be firm-specific; that is, some companies favor quantitative techniques while others favor qualitative techniques.

Table 12.1 Sample weighted scoring model (from Larsen and Luecke, 1993). Saint Alexis Hospital Medical Center Project Prioritization Worksheet. Project: Laboratory Instrument Interface (reproduced by permission of Nelson Publishing Inc.).

Criteria	Weight	A	B	C	D	Extension
Return on investment	4	>$10,000 0.50	>$3,000 0.33	>$0 0.17	No return 0.0	2.0
Medical staff impact	4	Attracts new physicians 0.57	Retains current physicians 0.33	Retains specific physicians 0.10	No medical staff impact 0.0	1.32
Matches hospital goals	3	Very helpful, short term 0.60	Very helpful, long term 0.30	Somewhat helpful, short or long term 0.10	No impact, long or short term 0.0	1.8
Promotes CQI process	3	Very helpful, hospital-wide 0.60	Somewhat helpful, hospital-wide 0.30	Very helpful, individual team 0.10	Somewhat helpful, individual team 0.0	0.3
Meets external reporting	3	Meets legal requirements 0.50	Meets corporate or external requirements 0.33	Helpful in serving external requirements 0.17	No external requirements 0.0	0
Meets departmental plans	2	Very helpful, short term 0.60	Very helpful, long term 0.30	Somewhat helpful, short or long term 0.10	No impact, long or short term 0.0	1.2
Ease of completion	1	< 8 hours 0.70	< 24 hours 0.20	< 40 hours 0.10	> 40 hours 0.0	0
					Project evaluation rating	6.62

IT PROJECT PRIORITIZATION AND PORTFOLIO MANAGEMENT

It is advantageous to view IT prioritization within the overall goal of effective IT portfolio management. Cooper et al. (2000) suggest that portfolio management entails: (1) *resource allocation*—how your business spends its capital and people resources, and which development projects it invests in; (2) *project selection*—ensuring that you have a steady stream of big new-product winners; and (3) *strategy*—it is one method by which you operationalize your business's strategy. Portfolio management is therefore:

> . . . a dynamic decision process whereby a business's list of active new . . . projects is constantly up-dated and revised; new projects are evaluated, selected and prioritized; existing projects may be accelerated, killed or de-prioritized; and resources are allocated and re-allocated to the active projects (Cooper et al., 1998).

Thus, portfolio management demands that new projects be force-ranked against *all* projects in the "auction"[4]. This forces two dramatic changes in prioritization: first, a different comparison set (i.e., individual projects are evaluated against all potential projects), and, second, a different set of criteria (i.e., individual projects are evaluated against established portfolio goals . . . and not just individual project merits). Therefore, a project may have solid credentials on its own yet not receive a high-priority ranking simply because of the existence of other projects of greater individual merit. In both cases, there is no absolute measure of a project's worth—there is only *a relative assessment of the strength of its business case measured against all other projects in the auction at a point in time.*

When using a portfolio management perspective, project prioritization decisions tend to focus on one or more of the following three broad goals (Cooper et al., 2000):

- *Value maximization.* This seeks to allocate resources to maximize the value of the portfolio in terms of a particular business objective (e.g., profitability). For organizations adopting a value maximization goal, project prioritization guidelines are established based on financial returns—such as payback or NPV—with established minimums (e.g., all projects must yield at least a 14% return on investment and/or a one-year payback).
- *Balance.* This seeks to achieve a desired balance of projects in terms of a number of parameters: long-term projects versus short-term projects; high-risk versus low-risk projects; across various markets, technologies, and project types. Organizations adopting this goal might establish guidelines based on percentages of the portfolio earmarked for new development versus maintenance, web-based applications, enterprise-level applications, or development under six months.

---

[4] Cooper et al. (2000) refer to all projects at or beyond the detailed investigation stage as being in the "auction".

- *Strategic direction.* This attempts to ensure that the final portfolio of projects reflects the business strategy. Here, organizations establish selection criteria that reflect their strategy (e.g., to develop new marketing channels, a revised customer retention strategy, or an expanded product/service offering).

The effect of these approaches is to direct project prioritization by pre-allocating portions of the available budget. If the goal is *strategic*, you might earmark portions of the budget in alignment with your strategy (e.g., 60% of the IT development budget is directed to new business projects). If the goal is *value-maximizing*, you will use financial yardsticks to apportion the budget (e.g., only those projects with a payback of less than one year). If the goal is *balanced*, the budget will be allocated among different buckets to achieve the desired allocation (e.g., 30% of all projects must be high-risk). Finally, these goals are not mutually exclusive. The selection of a particular goal does not preclude others. Typically these goals are structured hierarchically. For instance, an organization might adopt a "strategic direction" goal first and "maximize value" second.

STRATEGIES FOR IMPROVING IT PROJECT PRIORITIZATION

Members of the focus group were asked to suggest strategies for information systems (IS) management to improve the practice of IT project prioritization based on their experiences. These strategies represent activities that can be undertaken immediately (in the "near-term") to position the organization for the future.

1   Improve the Project Identification Process

Because project prioritization is "downstream" from project identification, it is therefore impacted directly. Where project identification is ineffective, project prioritization also suffers. In most organizations, project identification begins with a request for an IT-supported initiative typically submitted by a business manager. From there, the request is fleshed out, sized, and led through various channels of approval until it is a project complete with a business case/abstract—or it dies. While this process is understood well enough, a well-articulated strategy for project identification is often lacking. As a result, appropriate reward structures may not exist to encourage individuals to submit their ideas for IT projects. Worse yet, individuals may not see project identification as being a part of their job. As a result, project identification may be transparent but not particularly well aligned with overall business strategy.

One member of the focus group outlined the procedures that transformed project identification into a highly successful process within his organization:

> Anyone in the organization can submit a Business Opportunity Proposal (BOP). For anyone lacking the skills to accurately articulate their own BOP, full support is

provided. Decisions regarding BOPs are made within 30 days. BOPs are template-driven, web-enabled, and managed by workflow software. Responsibilities for each component of a BOP are specified. The progress of each BOP is tracked and made available to virtually anyone thus ensuring transparency. It is everyone's responsibility to see that a BOP meets its 30-day mandate. Penalties apply to anyone identified as the person who causes a BOP to be delayed.

The implementation of this procedure resulted in some dramatic changes in the number and type of new IT project proposals. First, a host of new ideas from unconventional sources emerged. Second, decisions were made quickly by senior executives enabling good ideas to move with exceptional speed. Third, the overall quality of business proposals increased significantly. Fourth, individuals felt personally gratified when their BOP received a "thumbs-up" further encouraging them to contribute their ideas.

2   Remove Cost as a Decision Criterion during Prioritization

The difference between IT project prioritization and resource allocation has a significant impact on how decisions are made. It basically reduces to whether or not to use "cost" as a criterion in the IT project prioritization decision. Project cost is an appropriate criterion for the resource allocation stage, but is inappropriate for the project prioritization stage. Introducing project costs during this stage blankets the inherent merits of the project with affordability issues. Affordability, falling subject to a number of different forces, may fluctuate at the whims of a "bad budget" year versus a "good budget" year—while the merits of a project are significantly more immutable. According to Brenner (1994, p. 40):

> . . . project cost should be appropriate for the project benefits. The objective should be to allocate the necessary resources for the best projects and to spend the appropriate amount for the expected benefit. In other words, cost is NOT a selection criterion, but is used to determine how many of the best projects can be afforded.

One organization represented within the focus group established the following explicit priority for ranking projects:

- Priority 1—Security of infrastructure.
- Priority 2—Potential stoppage of existing service.
- Priority 3a—Revenue generation.
- Priority 3b—Cost savings/avoidance.
- Priority 4—Productivity improvement.

By making rankings explicit and by eliminating cost as a criterion, projects are evaluated on a uniform scale and stand on their inherent merits. Affordability issues are explicitly avoided.

3 Make IT Project Prioritization a Part of Portfolio Management

With the adoption of a portfolio management perspective, an organization is no longer satisfied with ranking projects based solely on their individual merits. Instead, the goal is to rank projects based on their ability to maximize the overall value of the current (and future) portfolio of projects. This further clarifies the need for differentiating project identification from project prioritization. During project identification projects should be evaluated individually. During project prioritization projects should be ranked in terms of their support for the overall portfolio of projects according to the goals established by the organization (i.e., value maximization, balance, and/or strategic direction).

When considering *proposed* projects, priorities should therefore be determined based on the project's ability to address the following three key concerns:

- Does the project improve the balance of projects within the portfolio?
- Does the project readjust the mix of projects to address gaps?
- Does the project enhance the alignment of the overall portfolio?

It is interesting to note that with this approach a project's high individual merit does not guarantee high overall ranking. This may, of course, be due to the existence of many other high-ranking projects, but, more likely, the project may simply fail to address the above three questions despite its individual merits (e.g., a high return on investment [ROI]). Stated differently, the greatest sin in portfolio management is to ignore *the effect to which an investment in one project will affect the profitability of other ongoing or potential projects.*

4 Appoint a Joint Business–IT Prioritization Team

A portfolio management perspective necessitates the assessment of the interplay of proposed projects on the existing/future portfolio during project prioritization. This assessment has both *technical* considerations and *business* considerations. One organization went so far as to create a new role that they called "business architect", reflecting the reality that business and technology opportunities are best envisioned jointly.

The technical considerations derive from the fact that IT projects are tightly interrelated. They have a logical structure. Some systems simply do not operate without other systems being in place. An enterprise resource planning (ERP) system, for example, will have significant impact on virtually all other systems (e.g., financials, customer relationship management [CRM], and supply chain management [SCM]). Infrastructure systems may have little business value all by themselves, but enable others that do provide direct functional capability.

For this reason, IT management must have a strong voice during project prioritization decisions.

The need for business management to have significant input to all project prioritization decisions is equally vital. Decisions regarding projects must be aligned with the overall business strategy. Despite a promised quick payback, a project to develop an Internet product offering may be delayed (or denied) by business management when viewed in the context of the overall portfolio. There may be a wish to put a sales support initiative in place first. Or, other projects may address the imbalance within the portfolio more effectively. Even though the proposed project passes the technical and financial requirements, it may fail to pass the business requirements as based on the portfolio decision criteria.

Given the nature of portfolio deliberations, it is clear that the individuals charged with the task of project prioritization must bring both an IT and a business focus to the decision. It follows that a joint business–IT team should be appointed and meet frequently so as not to delay the process. Focus group members suggested that this committee should include senior-level management from IT and senior management from all business areas. It should have two primary responsibilities. First, it must establish the decision criteria to be used during project prioritization and, second, it should rank all IT projects on an ongoing basis. The process to be followed when ranking projects should ensure that:

- projects are force-ranked against *all* projects in the auction (i.e., at or beyond the detailed investigation stage);
- all rankings are dynamic and subject to review;
- new projects are "merged", which results in bumping others in the queue.

5   Make IT Portfolio Management an Ongoing, Continuous Process, Not a One-time Decision

We have argued that portfolio management consists of three stages (see Figure 12.1). The output of project identification is a list of projects that have been evaluated on the basis of their individual merits; the output of project prioritization is a rank-ordered list of projects; and the output of the resource allocation stage is a balanced list of development projects. The final outcome of portfolio management (i.e., the list of development projects) can be depicted as in Table 12.2. With this example, Projects 1 through 4 have been authorized to receive full funding through completion. Projects 8 through 10 will not be funded. Projects 5 through 7 are the difficult ones. The funding and resources for these should be focused on alleviating their weaknesses and attempting to elevate them into the next category. If they cannot be salvaged, they should be eliminated.

It is evident from Table 12.2 that, as time rolls forward, projects are resourced, put into development, and eventually removed from the list. At the same time,

Table 12.2 IT project ratings (adapted from Brenner, 1994).

Project	Rating	Decision
1	90	Commit development funding
2	87	
3	81	
4	75	
5	64	Redefine and/or refocus
6	57	
7	48	
8	37	Do not fund
9	35	
10	30	

new projects will be identified, evaluated on an individual basis, and submitted to the prioritization process. These new projects will then be force-ranked against all others in the list and merged into the list. It is not uncommon for new projects to be merged at the very top of the list thereby pushing all others down the queue. It is this process that makes portfolio management so dynamic.

The danger is to treat portfolio management as a one-time decision—where projects are reviewed at a point in time and final decisions are made. Instead, it should be viewed as a dynamic process—where projects are mobile and malleable over time. Allowing for this dynamism creates flexibility and experimentation and actually *is a risk-reducing strategy*. According to one member of the focus group, "decisions are made based on the best information available at the time . . . which presents a risk factor in managing the project portfolio." When projects are allowed to "reappear" before the review team (after being reworked), the risk of missing an opportunity (or heading in the wrong direction) is reduced.

In the end, the creation of a much more flexible structure and approach to project prioritization—both a blessing (it insures that IT projects are responsive to the ever-changing nature of business) and a curse (it makes long-term planning more difficult for IT)—provides significant benefits to organizations over time.

CONCLUSION

Project prioritization is a critical linkage mechanism between IT and the business. When done effectively, it ensures that the IT investment is focused on high-potential applications. When done within the context of portfolio management, it ensures a goal-oriented and synergistic set of IT applications in support of the business. As with many other business processes, a deliberate strategy for managing IT project prioritization is needed. This chapter has outlined a set of steps that should be taken in order to move an organization closer to realizing the full benefits of project prioritization ... toward making its project portfolio a competitive reality.

REFERENCES

Brenner, M.S. (1994) "Practical R&D project prioritization," *Research & Technology Management*, September–October, 38–42.

Cooper, R.G., S.J. Edgett, and E.J. Kleinschmidt (1998) *Portfolio Management for New Products*, Perseus Books, Reading, MA.

Cooper, R.G., S.J. Edgett, and E.J. Kleinschmidt (2000) "New problems, new solutions: Making portfolio management more effective," *Research & Technology Management*, March–April, 18–33.

Larsen, T. and R.W. Luecke (1993) "Priority worksheet brings order to information systems projects," *Computers in Healthcare*, February, 44–46.

Part C
Managing Technology

Managing technology is a three part challenge: new technologies must be introduced to the organization; existing technologies must be maintained; and old technologies must be retired as their ability to support the business wanes. These, of course, must all be accomplished while the organization continues to operate. It's a bit like changing the planks on the hull of the ship while sailing. Unfortunately, with today's businesses, there is no analogous "dry dock" option available.

This section of the book examines what the focus group members considered to be the key issues with regard to managing technology. Chapter 13, "Managing the Technology Portfolio", espouses an approach to technology acquisition where individual technology decisions are based on their impact on the balance and structure of the overall technology portfolio—and, to a lesser degree, their individual merits. Chapter 14, "Emerging Technologies and the Surfer Syndrome", recognizes the gatekeeper role that information technology (IT) plays with respect to the introduction of new technology. This role, which involves R&D, experimentation, and venturing with emerging technologies, must be managed carefully to ensure effective technological support for the business. When done well, the introduction of new technologies within the workplace can be orchestrated almost seamlessly to the point of being unnoticed.

The remaining chapters collectively map out a blueprint for an organization's technological platform. Chapter 15, "IT-sourcing: Build, Buy, or Market", describes new sourcing opportunities within the emerging marketplace for IT services. In order to reap the benefits of such a marketplace, however, organizations must implement a flexible architecture as described in Chapter 16, "IT Architecture for Enterprise Flexibility"; they must adopt strategies to enable integration across existing applications as suggested in Chapter 17, "Enterprise Application Integration"; and they must implement successful reusability practices in order to leverage their investment in technology.

13
Managing the Technology Portfolio*

In today's information technology (IT) world, technology is changing with ever-increasing rapidity. As a result, organizations are continually adding new technology just to keep up. Hardware, software, languages, development tools, communications linkages, and methodologies are all substantially different today than just five years ago. But, new technologies don't always replace old ones. Applications dependent on old technologies may need to be kept running without significant rewrites. Unfortunately, older technology often doesn't work well with newer technology leading to extra work for IT staff who often have to jury-rig connections to keep everything running smoothly. As a result, an organization's technology stockpile simply grows. Most IT organizations would therefore like to "sunset" older technologies (i.e., set a date to get rid of them permanently). However, for many practical reasons (e.g., cost, politics), this is not easily accomplished and not always possible. And, so, the problem becomes bigger each year. The management challenge is thus to develop a strategy, not just for retiring older technology, but for managing new *and* old technology effectively—to ensure that a business's technology portfolio remains cost-effective.

Before such a strategy can be developed, however, it is first necessary to understand technology and the attendant problems it presents. In the next section we examine the nature of information technology and the concepts of age and obsolescence. We then highlight examples of some of the technical and organizational issues encountered when attempting to manage a technology portfolio. Based on this understanding, the chapter concludes by suggesting

* McKeen, J.D. and H.A. Smith (2002) "Managing the technology portfolio," *Communications of the Association of Information Systems* (CAIS), August, **9**(5), 64–76 (reproduced by permission of the Association for Information Systems).

strategies for managing technology based on the collective insights and experiences of the focus group of senior IT managers.

WHAT IS "OLD" TECHNOLOGY?

Information technology is considered "old" (or at least "dated") when it is superseded by a newer version; it is considered obsolete when it ceases to be supported by the vendor and/or user community; and it atrophies only if it is physical/mechanical. When managing IT, the concept of age is actually irrelevant. The process of atrophying and the stage of obsolescence are important only to the extent that they contribute to the costs and risks of technology. Let's examine why this is so.

Information technology includes both hardware and software, which tend to be treated differently due to the physical nature of hardware. Physical things (e.g., cell phones, data lines, monitors, servers, PCs, and storage devices) atrophy and therefore require ongoing maintenance and eventually replacement. Realizing this, most companies adopt an "ever-greening" approach for hardware replacement (i.e., a strategy for the planned replacement of technology on a fixed schedule). One focus group company, for example, renews its desktop computers every 3.5 years, its laptops every 2.5 years, and its desktop software every quarter. However, this same company runs its primary operations on the back of a system written in the 1960s! Why is it not surprising to find 40-year-old application systems?

The answer is because software, unlike hardware, does not atrophy. If it runs once, it will do so for ever. It matters not that a currency conversion function is written in some long-forgotten language. As long as a need for currency conversion exists, this code will do the job. Not surprisingly, IT professionals have taken full advantage of this by encapsulating older code within newer applications. Indeed, it makes little business sense to rewrite code in a newer language only to provide the identical functionality. At some point, however, it may not be possible to add new functionality to old software, or it may be too expensive to do so. When this happens, the software should be renewed.

When managing the IT portfolio, however, hardware and software *should be treated identically* because both exist to serve the organization's needs. When the cost of providing this service becomes excessive, the technology (either hardware or software) should be replaced. The fact that hardware may fail outright (unlike software) is important only to the extent that this possibility of failure is correctly reflected within the total cost structure of the hardware (i.e., the costs of backups, redundant operations, spare parts, and/or service contracts). Stated differently, information technology should be renewed when it fails to provide adequate functionality to support the business in a cost-effective manner. This is when it should be considered obsolete.

DEALING WITH OBSOLESCENCE

Every organization has obsolete technology. As one focus group member stated, "It's IT's dirty little secret"! This comment is revealing. First, why should the status of an organization's information technology be "secret"? And second, why suggest that it is "little"? When asked to *size* the problem of obsolete technologies, no-one in the focus group had a confident answer because none of their organizations had undertaken to assess it. However, anecdotally, the following quotes by members of the focus group collectively reveal the significance of the problem:

- The one-time cost to replace our old technology is easily tens of millions of dollars.
- The maintenance costs associated with testing new releases, not to mention the delays, are enormous ... do all 600 products work on the new operating system?
- Because we do not actively manage our licenses, we do not know the full costs of licensing obsolete technology.
- We have twice the technology we actually need.
- The skill base to maintain obsolete technology is rapidly declining and training is expensive.
- We have built over 700 medium to large applications over the last 30–40 years. They are heavily customized, running on multiple technologies, without any common architecture. Even "code ports" to accommodate hardware updates are challenging.

Sinur (2002) argues that the problem will only get worse and in fact will likely accelerate. He anticipates that *core* applications (i.e., those that have an impact on the stock price or value proposition) will become *commodity* applications (i.e., those that are available readily through multiple sources) in much shorter time-frames—a process he refers to as entropy. When members of the focus group were asked about the *urgency* of the problem, they expressed a general feeling that the time to address this problem is *at hand* ... but no organization placed it in the critical zone. Some of the justifications given for inaction were as follows:

- the problem with obsolete technology has always existed;
- obsolete applications continue to function *adequately*;
- it is easier to interface systems than to understand and address the underlying problem;
- if it ain't broke, don't fix it;
- we are waiting (hoping) for better vendor solutions.

In response to the question, "What is your worst case scenario regarding obsolete technology?", one senior IT manager reported that his organization has eight major databases to support. The oldest of them, written in an obscure language, supports a single customer-facing application developed in the 1960s. Worldwide expertise for this system is virtually non-existent ... actually "one guy on a beeper"! Some of the other seven databases are now totally unsupported. Another organization cited its worst case scenario as a large 16-bit application currently supporting a key line of business. The huge replacement cost, estimated at $5–7 million, is due to the labor-intensive effort required. There are no available conversion tools to assist with the task. Action must be taken soon. Arguments for replacing the system are not based on a return on investment (ROI) calculation, but rather on the risk of unrecoverable failure and the attendant loss of face with the customer base. Despite this, line-of-business management is reluctant to spend their IT resources on this initiative, which "does nothing to facilitate new business".

These examples highlight the *technical* aspects of managing a technology portfolio; for example, contracting vendor support for technologies, finding/retaining people with the necessary skills/expertise to work with technologies, tools for bridging/migrating between technologies, and succession-planning. Unfortunately the difficulty with managing technology is not limited to these aspects. The following three cases highlight some of the *organizational* aspects of managing technology.

Case 1   The mainframe email system

In the late 1970s, the company purchased an email system. The fact that it ran on the company's mainframe computer made it easy to control access, perform backups, and ensure continuous 24/7 availability for worldwide operations. Over the years, this system was extensively modified to add new features (such as mass-mailing and calendaring). Much of the added functionality, however, came at a high price as the original mainframe system was not designed to accommodate these new features. The system became filled with clever "workarounds"; for example, to make text terminals "more GUI-like". The ability to add features eventually came to a screeching halt in the late 1990s when the IT department tried unsuccessfully to enable attachments to emails with the mainframe system. It was now clear that the system had to be replaced. When the IT department suggested moving to a client–server package with all the desired features, there was an open rebellion by the thousands of devoted business-users worldwide.

This case illustrates an application system that became so engrained within the workday lives of the business community that users actively resisted all efforts to have it replaced. As a result, the system continued well beyond its normal (and productive) life expectation. One focus group member cited another version of this phenomenon. It happens when a new system replaces an old system, but users keep demanding their arcane "OD-35 report". In order to supply this report, the previous application must be kept running, which postpones the benefits to be achieved by switching to the new system ... and the previous system, in some cases, *is never retired.*

Case 2   The divisionalized company

The company was structured into semi-autonomous and geographically dispersed divisions. Divisional management assumed profit and loss responsibility and full control over all expenditures including IT. Divisions currently ran on OS/2 servers with "green screen" applications and no IP capability. As it became obvious that this platform could not take advantage of new functionality/opportunities, corporate management strongly encouraged divisional management to update their technology base. Divisional management, with their eyes on the bottom line, felt that IT expenditures should compete with other possible investments. While some managers could see the return of a technology upgrade, others remained unconvinced. Corporate management realized that the full advantages of an upgrade would be severely limited if some divisions did not buy in. What began as a technology issue soon devolved into a political hot potato.

This case demonstrates how technology decisions play out within the larger organizational arena. What appears to be a straightforward technology issue quickly becomes politicized as it rubs against the fabric of the organization—in fact challenging its strategy, structure, and goals. The situation is not uncommon.

Case 3   The "M&A" (mergers and applications) company

Over the years, the company grew on the basis of a number of mergers and acquisitions. In order to keep a "business as usual" facade, the company absorbed the hardware, software, people, and systems unique to each of the newly acquired companies. Not surprisingly, the IT staff became very creative in "bridging" these systems to provide a high-level "look and feel" of cross-business integration. Underneath, it was a legacy nightmare! Any decision to retire old technology (and rationalize the IT portfolio) was exacerbated by the duplication and proliferation of systems (as well as the cross-platform bridging). Interestingly, business managers were largely shielded from (and hence, unaware of) this reality and were caught surprised by the chief information officer's (CIO) warnings of the consequences of their continued corporate growth strategy.

Organizations experience chronic difficulty when meshing various technologies. When organizations merge with (or acquire) another organization, this particular issue becomes acute. Sometimes such an event can serve to coalesce management decision-making resulting in dramatic consolidation with respect to technology. Other times, as in this case, the problem is paved over.

It can be seen from these examples that the key factor in the management of obsolete technology is the assessment of the technology's ability to continue to support the organization and meet its future needs. While technical considerations underlie such assessments, decisions regarding technology renewal must be judged against other possible demands for resources within the organization. As a result, these decisions must first and foremost be business decisions. In the next section, we outline a business approach to managing a technology portfolio.

STRATEGIES FOR MANAGING A TECHNOLOGY PORTFOLIO

Due to the realities of competitive pressure, customer demand, and the drive for increased efficiency, organizations have few options but to follow the path of innovation. Within IT, the innovation challenge is to manage a technology portfolio so that it continues to support the needs of the business in a cost-effective manner. Faced with a relentless parade of innovative technologies and the ongoing need to be responsive to new business initiatives, this balancing act can be daunting. The solution is to manage the technology portfolio exactly the same as if it were any other valuable corporate asset.

Technology (either hardware or software) is deployed to provide valuable functionality to support the business. When more cost-effective technology becomes available, a *business* decision must be made regarding the replacement of the existing technology based on knowledge of the true costs of the technology. Unfortunately, IT management usually fails to make these costs known. In fact, one focus group manager declared that, "IT does a good job of *masking* the problem." When business managers do not fully understand the status of their application systems and the attendant full costs of modifying them, the organization can be led into less than optimal (or poorly timed) technology decisions. When IT initiatives compete openly with other potential initiatives for the same limited pool of resources, it becomes immediately clear that technology management must be a shared responsibility between IT and the business.

Information technology, like any other asset, must be maintained in good working order for it to be a continually producing asset for the organization. In short, it must be managed. This requires all the following activities:

- an ongoing inventory process;
- a technology life cycle model to enable management strategies to be tailored to individual lifecycle stages;
- the development of governing policies to outline what, how, and when technology will be used;
- the appointment of technology stewards who assume management responsibilities for overseeing individual technologies;
- skills development to parallel the evolution of technology; and
- a viable funding model for technology renewal.

With these activities in place, organizations should have the means to ensure that their technology continues to serve the purposes of the organization in a cost-effective and efficient manner. Each of the activities is described in more detail below.

1 Inventory Your Technology Portfolio

Part of the Year 2000 (Y2K) exercise of locating and identifying all instances that might prove troublesome upon entering the new millennium was to create a detailed inventory of all existing applications and technology. This inventory has become one of the unexpected side-benefits of undergoing the Y2K challenge. For many organizations, this inventory, once started, has been maintained allowing them to identify the status of their technology assets at any point in time. As a result, many organizations now have accurate and detailed reporting capabilities for their technology including licensing and contracting information. This is the first vital step in managing a technology portfolio.

One focus group company maintains records for the following:

- release and version;
- description;
- vendor;
- licensing/contracts;
- product steward (see Management Strategy #3);
- status (lifecycle stage);
- deployment (primary uses of product as a cross-reference).

A database provides a single-source location for information on all technology products. One person within IT has the job of maintaining the database to ensure that all information is current and accurate. It is structured to provide valuable information for the active management of all technology in the firm. For instance, it can be used to locate all licenses with a particular vendor, determine the age of current contracts, identify all uses of a specific technology, and list all complementary technology products to ensure that they reflect similar life cycle classifications.

2 Adopt a Technology Life Cycle Model

Technologies follow predictable life cycles—that is, sets of progressive stages that technologies pass through during their useful life. These life cycles can be based on a specific aspect of the technology (e.g., its operational efficiency) or on a specific management strategy (e.g., acquire, manage, retire) related to the technology. Although the *time* dimension is typically employed by these life cycles (see example of a cost life cycle in Figure 13.1), as we have pointed out, the age of a technology is less important than its current stage. Since the primary benefit of a life cycle model is its ability to explicitly represent the

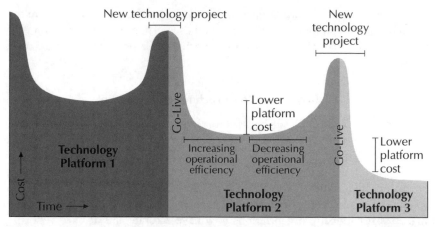

Figure 13.1   *Cost life cycle of a technology platform. This figure (McLean Report, 2002) demonstrates the cost life cycle of a technology platform. This particular model separates the cost characteristics into two stages: increasing operational efficiency and decreasing operational efficiency. This model is particularly important when it is recognized that the majority of the lifetime costs of a technology (e.g., a business application) are consumed in ongoing support and maintenance often dwarfing the original acquisition costs (termed "new technology project"). While it is apparent that with successive platforms the average costs decrease overall, it is more important to focus on the width and depth of the U-shaped cost curve for each particular technology platform. This, of course, requires accurate costing of the particular technology platform, but the benefits of such a costing model are significant. This information provides a basis for deciding when to move to a new technology platform. That is, an organization could determine how expensive the existing technology would have to become for it to automatically decide to replace it, and how cheap new applications would have to become in order to migrate to them. It is suspected that few organizations currently have costing models with sufficient detail to support this type of analysis (reproduced by permission of Info Tech Research Group).*

"status" of a particular technology other dimensions are more important to consider.

Duggan (2002) has developed a life cycle model for software consisting of four stages of deterioration: adult, mature, aging, and elderly. In addition, they identify eight indicators that allow an assessment of the stage of a given technology and provide actions to be taken at each stage to manage the stage transitions. One of the focus group companies bases its technology decisions on a life cycle model determined by the expected longevity of a particular technology and its anticipated/projected strategic value to the organization. Using these two dimensions, managers position the firm's technologies on a 2 × 2 matrix (see Figure 13.2). Expected progression within this matrix is counter-clockwise beginning with the "Watch" quadrant and ending with the "Eliminate" quadrant. This matrix (internally referred to as the "WISE" grid) is used to reflect the status of all technologies—hardware (i.e., computing, storage, and communications), operating systems, business applications, languages, and methodologies. On a regular

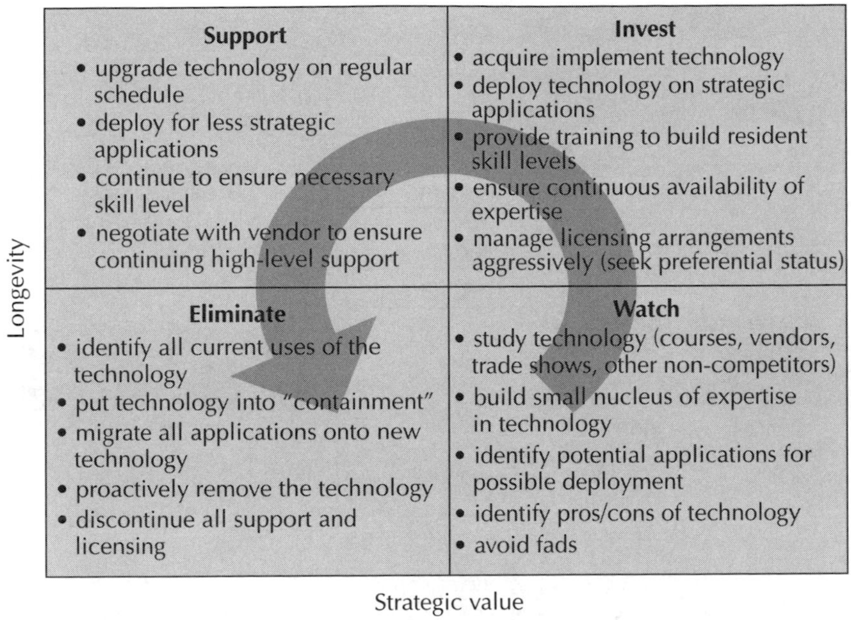
Support
• upgrade technology on regular schedule
• deploy for less strategic applications
• continue to ensure necessary skill level
• negotiate with vendor to ensure continuing high-level support
Invest
• acquire implement technology
• deploy technology on strategic applications
• provide training to build resident skill levels
• ensure continuous availability of expertise
• manage licensing arrangements aggressively (seek preferential status)
Eliminate
• identify all current uses of the technology
• put technology into "containment"
• migrate all applications onto new technology
• proactively remove the technology
• discontinue all support and licensing
Watch
• study technology (courses, vendors, trade shows, other non-competitors)
• build small nucleus of expertise in technology
• identify potential applications for possible deployment
• identify pros/cons of technology
• avoid fads
Longevity
Strategic value

Figure 13.2 *A "WISE" grid for managing technologies.*

basis (at least annually), all technologies are assessed and migrated to the appropriate quadrants.

Quadrant classifications on the WISE grid have ramifications for how a technology is to be managed. As strategic applications are assigned priorities, technologies from the "Invest" quadrant are identified to be deployed for their development and implementation. Technologies from the "Support" quadrant would tend not to be used for these strategic applications if there was a similar technology already within the "Invest" quadrant. Many of the oldest applications within the organization are based on technologies relegated to the "Eliminate" quadrant. Additional functionality for these systems is implemented with newer technologies wherever possible. The WISE grid has proven to be an effective tool not only for classification but also for signaling to the organization (both business and IT) the status of its application portfolio. Knowing that your key business applications are built on technologies relegated to the "Support–Eliminate" side of the grid provides strong incentive to upgrade their health. The WISE grid can also be used as a basis for risk assessment calculations for these key systems.

3 Create Policies to Govern the Usage of Technology

An inventory lists the technology that is currently available. In contrast, a technology usage policy specifies which technology should be used and how

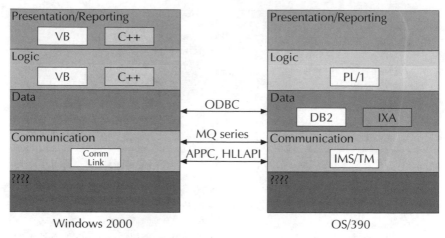

Figure 13.3   *Sample technology blueprint.*

it should be used. One focus group company has developed a unique policy (which they refer to as a "blueprint") for each major type of development (e.g., client–server, mainframe, Web-based). Each blueprint specifies the appropriate technologies and how they are to be used by separating the development functions into the following five categories:

- presentation/reporting;
- logic;
- data;
- communication;
- control.

These functions are highlighted in the sample blueprint in Figure 13.3. Technologies in the grey boxes are "in containment"; those in the white boxes are "mainstream". The information within a blueprint can be used in conjunction with the WISE grid mentioned earlier. That is, the graduation of technologies from stage to stage determines blueprint status. A technology within the "Watch" category would not appear within a blueprint. Within the "Invest" category, however, it would be represented within a blueprint. As this particular technology enters the "Support" category, its blueprint status would likely change again. Finally, as the technology enters the "Eliminate" stage, it disappears from any existing blueprints.

A technology blueprint is a convenient way to establish the preferred usage of a given technology for a given type of development. It is recommended that information be cross-referenced in the inventory so that, for every technology, it is easy to find all blueprints where it applies. Finally, blueprints are useful in that they send an important signal to system-developers—*there are sanctioned technologies and their usage is expected*. Any deviance from the prescribed technology requires special permission to be determined on a case-by-case basis.

4   Create a Technology Stewardship Role and Appoint Stewards

Each type of technology should have someone responsible for its management (i.e., a steward). Since it is difficult, if not impossible, to identify someone who is expert (or even familiar) with multiple technologies, the role of stewardship is typically assigned to various individuals. This role is not typically full-time. In most organizations, the individuals who introduce a new technology and usher it through its early stages tend to take on its stewardship role at least initially. As the technology matures within the organization, the role can (and does) change hands.

Some of the duties assigned to a steward include:

- monitoring new technology releases/upgrades;
- communicating important information concerning the technology (changes, new functionality, linkages with related technologies);
- keeping abreast with the vendor community (e.g., new developments, partnerships);
- exploring possible uses/applications of the technology within the organization;
- working with technology vendors (e.g., beta tests);
- joining and becoming active within industry user groups;
- educating others within the organization (e.g., centre of excellence, community of practice);
- building resident skill levels with the technology (see next section).

5   Evolve Skills to Parallel Your Technology Life Cycle

As a technology evolves, so too must the skills of the IT staff. One of the focus group companies developed a model to guide the path of evolving skills within his organization. The stages are identified in Figure 13.4. It can be seen how skills first enter and then disperse throughout the organization over time. As the skills are made redundant by advances in the related technology and their need declines, the skill must be recentralized to ensure that the organization retains adequate (albeit minimum) skills to support its waning technology.

There is a direct and parallel relationship between skills and technology. As a new technology enters an organization, resident skill levels must by created to ensure that the technology is deployed effectively (i.e., the features and capabilities of the technology are understood and fully deployed by the members of the organization—both business and IT). As a management aid, it is possible to combine the WISE grid (Figure 13.2) with the Skills Evolution chart

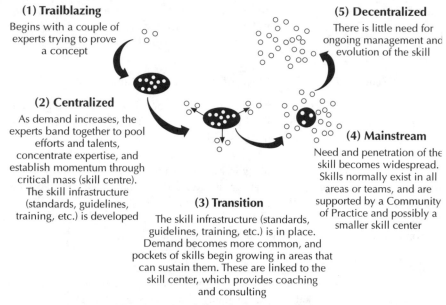

(1) Trailblazing

Begins with a couple of experts trying to prove a concept

(5) Decentralized

There is little need for ongoing management and evolution of the skill

(2) Centralized

As demand increases, the experts band together to pool efforts and talents, concentrate expertise, and establish momentum through critical mass (skill centre). The skill infrastructure (standards, guidelines, training, etc.) is developed

(3) Transition

The skill infrastructure (standards, guidelines, training, etc.) is in place. Demand becomes more common, and pockets of skills begin growing in areas that can sustain them. These are linked to the skill center, which provides coaching and consulting

(4) Mainstream

Need and penetration of the skill becomes widespread. Skills normally exist in all areas or teams, and are supported by a Community of Practice and possibly a smaller skill center

Figure 13.4   *Skills evolution for a technology.*

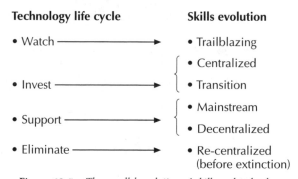

Technology life cycle	Skills evolution
• Watch ⟶	• Trailblazing
• Invest ⟶	{ • Centralized { • Transition
• Support ⟶	{ • Mainstream { • Decentralized
• Eliminate ⟶	• Re-centralized (before extinction)

Figure 13.5   *The parallel evolution of skills and technology.*

(Figure 13.4) to demonstrate how skills development must parallel the technology life cycle (Figure 13.5). A technology–skills life cycle model enables the co-management of both elements. It can be used *reactively* to identify existing technology–skills gaps and to highlight where the organization is inadequately prepared for the introduction of a new technology. There are costs associated with these gaps. For instance, developing skills too far in advance of the arrival of the technology and/or taking possession of the technology without ensuring an adequate skills base handicaps the organization and results in postponing the promised benefit stream resulting from the new technology. Technology–skills gaps may occur at the end of a technology's useful life as well. One organization was chagrined to discover that they were still sponsoring courses for their IT staff in a skill that had been put into "containment"!

This same model can be used *proactively* with equal benefit. For instance, the graduation of a technology from one stage into the next can be used to trigger the associated skills development activity. By linking a technology directly with its associated skill base, an organization can articulate a migration plan to guarantee a successful (and uneventful) technology transition. In addition, the formal identification of technologies and skills within a life cycle model allows IT professionals to reflect on their careers in terms of the skills they possess and the technologies they have mastered. As technologies move into the "containment" stage, for instance, individuals whose skill base is based largely on this particular technology may wish to explore some emerging technologies. Where organizations have managed the evolution of skills and technologies by effectively deploying models such as these, they have enabled smooth transitions to new technologies and kept resident skills current. Where organizations have failed to actively manage their technologies, skills gaps can proliferate, technology transitions can be disastrous, careers can be dead-ended, and costs can skyrocket.

6   Create a Funding Model for Technology Renewal

The final technology management activity is funding. The effort required to manage technology effectively from the "watch" through "eliminate" stages is large and ongoing and therefore expensive. Nevertheless, the risks of letting technology age to the point of inadequacy—when it ceases to be a healthy, productive asset—are significant. As one focus group member commented, "risks are unrealized costs." Such risks include the loss of efficient support to internal business processes (e.g., sales reports delayed), the inability to provide effective customer service (e.g., Web transactions unavailable), the outright failure of a key business function (e.g., a communications network collapse), and/or exorbitantly high costs to the business due to a technology platform being within the "decreasing operational efficiency" stage of its productive life. These are *business* risks based on technology and must be assessed by senior management in light of other business risks. If there has been a consistent shortcoming across organizations, the focus group agreed, it has been their failure to *make technology a business decision.*

If technology represents a business risk, how should it be financed? The focus group felt that the most important part of any technology funding was that it should be articulated using the same accounting procedures used for other organizational assets and should be made visible to the business. It should definitely *not* be hidden within the IT department's budget and should be clearly identified as a "technology renewal" fund to be administered by senior management. Members of the focus group suggested that the selection of a funding strategy should be in alignment with the organization's current governance model. For instance, if IT is treated as a corporate overhead, then a technology renewal fund should probably be established similarly. On the other hand, if all IT expenses are charged back to the business units, then a technology renewal fund should be part of these charges. The key point is that the technology renewal funding be visible, recognized by general management as a true cost of doing business and mitigating risk, debated, and costed as accurately as possible.

Within the focus group, two different approaches to the creation (and administration) of a technology renewal fund were described. They provide examples of how organizations can adopt different yet equally effective strategies for achieving the same goal (i.e., funding technology renewal). One organization described the origins and functioning of their technology renewal fund as follows. In a presentation to senior management, the CIO argued the wisdom of continually investing in the technology that basically "ran their business". On the basis of this, a designated technology renewal budget was created, and the CIO was awarded full discretionary powers over the usage of these monies for technology upgrades. Technology renewal decisions are based on the recommendations presented to the CIO by members of the corporate architectural council. These recommendations are then presented by the CIO to the senior capital committee. The majority of technology upgrade decisions are determined on the basis of "cost to support". The amount devoted to technology renewal is not a fixed percentage, but differs year by year depending on factors such as business performance, timing of vendor offerings, competing business needs, and extraordinary one-time technology upgrades.

Another focus group member described his organization's approach to funding technology renewal. In his words, a fund was created to upgrade the "hard core technology that you can't get the business to fund directly." The following set of guidelines was created to create and administer this fund:

1. The technology renewal fund was established strictly for upgrading technology. It was *not* to be used for application development, maintenance, or infrastructure, nor was it to be used for research and development (R&D). It was to be used to replace technology that is: "impeding the ability to deliver solutions—to get rid of something or to improve something—to facilitate projects to enable the effective delivery of business solutions."
2. Business units are "taxed" at a fixed percentage of the total IT services used by each unit. IT is accountable for how it spends the fund and all expenditures are reported to the business units. Each business unit is responsible for scheduling technology renewal projects within their annual IT planning.
3. IT is responsible for administering the fund. All applications for technology renewal must be accompanied by a business case prepared with assistance from a project management office. Decisions are made by a process review board whose membership is drawn from IT and the business.

This approach to funding technology renewal has achieved a significant measure of success. One benefit is that the business units now recognize the need for technology renewal and see its direct linkage with attaining their business objectives. Due to the joint business and IT membership on the review board, decisions tend to be readily accepted and technology renewal is seen as a shared partnership between IT and the business. Although no-one likes a "tax", there is no doubt that it sends a tangible signal to the organization indicating that, in this case, technology renewal is vital to the health of the business.

CONCLUSION

With the dependence of business operations on technology comes the need to ensure that this technology not only continues to function effectively but also provides the capability to support the future needs of the business. To do this requires a management strategy that treats IT as any other valuable corporate asset. This can best be accomplished by an effective partnership between IT and the business. This chapter set out to describe the difficulties in dealing with the ever-changing worlds of business and technology in order to understand how technology can be managed to provide continuing support to the business in a cost-effective manner. Based on the experiences of a group of senior IT managers from leading-edge organizations, a number of successful strategies were outlined. It is anticipated that following these will enable organizations to ensure the vitality of their technology portfolio.

REFERENCES

Duggan, J. (2002) *Assessing the Stage of Software Systems*, Research Note DF-15-4788, February 13, GartnerGroup, Stamford, CT.

McLean Report (2002) *Retiring Old Applications*
(http://www.mcleanreport.com/current_issue.asp#1).

Sinur, J. (2002) *Portfolio Entropy: The Hidden IT Disease*, Research Note SPA-15-2509, February 11, GartnerGroup, Stamford, CT.

14

Emerging Technologies and the Surfer Syndrome

It has happened in almost every company. The chief executive officer (CEO) goes on a business trip and happens to glance at a copy of the airline magazine. In it he sees an article extolling the virtues of the latest whiz-bang technology and how it has literally saved another firm *millions* while providing infinitely better information and service than in the past. The article usually concludes that whiz-bang is *definitely* a new paradigm for technology that will *fundamentally* change how all businesses operate. Failure to catch this wave *immediately* will mean that your company will be left out in the cold and probably be playing catch-up for many years to come. The CEO then decides that he knew all along that his information technology (IT) organization didn't know what it was doing and returns with a glint in his eye to confront the chief information officer (CIO) about why they aren't using whiz-bang. And the next thing you know, there are several senior-level IT personnel pulled off critical projects to hurriedly prepare reports on the technology, priorities are changed, and the IT organization is left looking hopelessly inept.

Within IT, catching "surfer syndrome" has traditionally been seen as a relatively minor business ailment, somewhat akin to the flu. It's troublesome, it takes time to get over it, but essentially nothing is changed. In the past, it was fairly easy to address non-technical executives' concerns with the IT equivalent of two aspirins and a "we know what we're doing attitude." Thus, today, many executives see IT as a patronizing establishment department that acts as a barrier to improved organizational information, technology, and health. As a result, they often feel they must research and implement alternative technology options on their own.

There are significant dangers to this approach. First, many consultants and vendors are getting rich by giving executives what they want, rather than what they really need. Second, it can disrupt IT strategy creating standalone, non-standard islands of technology that are impossible to maintain and difficult to integrate. Third, with technology changing so rapidly and becoming so important to businesses, it is growing increasingly critical to get it right. Fourth, the IT function can lose significant credibility, and this can lead to more serious cases of "surfer syndrome." Thus, CIOs are concluding that their organizations have to do a better job of dealing with this phenomenon before it becomes an epidemic and/ or before their company makes some ill-informed technology decision, which can have much more serious repercussions for the firm.

This chapter looks at how IT organizations research, evaluate, integrate, and manage emerging technologies both as a preventative of the "surfer syndrome" and as a means of taking advantage of what these technologies have to offer. It first situates the challenges facing IT managers regarding emerging technology in the context of the rapidly changing business and technical environment with which most enterprises are dealing today. It then explains the need for a systematic process to assess the business opportunities that are continually arising as new technologies and new uses for technology develop. Finally, it examines the three steps in this process: keeping current; assessing new technologies for your enterprise; and integrating new technology into the organization, and provides some practical strategies for managers on how to implement them.

THE CHALLENGES OF THE CURRENT BUSINESS AND TECHNICAL ENVIRONMENTS

Today, a business is no longer a passive responder to its environment; it also interacts with and helps shape it. As a result, there is now a need for firms to continually assess all aspects of their environments so that they can reposition themselves appropriately externally and rearrange their internal infrastructure accordingly (Henderson, 1994). Increasingly, the need to thoroughly understand and interact with the environment is becoming a critical piece of any organization's design. In a world of continuous change, therefore, a key management skill is the ability to understand what is going on in the broader world of business and technology and to determine its relevance to the firm in order to be able to develop a coherent response. This ongoing "conversation" between the organization and its environment suggests that it is not the environment that "causes" organizational change, but a set of interactions between firms and their environments that lead to cycles of change as a normal part of organizational growth and development (Applegate, 1994). Because of this, modern firms must see exploration of their environment as both an important way to gain insight and direction and a way to help shape the environment in which they operate.

In the past, this type of assessment occurred in patches throughout the middle and lower parts of the organization. Today, it is a key function of senior management and the leadership of the firm to continually learn and evolve and to actively manage how change, complexity and uncertainty will affect their organization (Applegate, 1994). Thus, while different parts of an organization may assess different aspects of the business and technical environment separately, senior management must be prepared to absorb and integrate what is learned in each area in order to both design an effective response and to assess the impact of that response.

By now, all managers know that change is an ongoing facet of business life due to rapid technological improvements and a host of social and organizational factors. Change is more dramatic in some industries than in others and the degree and dimensions of change in any particular one will affect the nature of a firm's response to its environment. Nevertheless, it is not wise to be complacent about change. Too many businesses have had a crisis thrust upon them because they weren't prepared. Change often occurs in the form of strategic discontinuities. These are the big changes in technology, deregulation, or logistics that change what is possible in an industry. Today, many firms are facing multiple strategic discontinuities where "the competitive landscape . . . changes unexpectedly and has many hills, mountains and valleys" (Hitt et al., 1998).

There are three different ways that organizations deal with environmental change (Applegate, 1994):

- *Anticipate.* Firms can continually scan their environment, identify disruptive patterns, and take action to deal with them.
- *Drive.* Leaders on their own can shake up their organizations by restructuring and establishing "stretch" goals for them.
- *React.* Organizations can wait until a crisis hits and then deal with it.

The first two responses assume that an organization (or at least its leader) is proactively assessing how changes in all parts of the environment might affect its business. As Bradley and Clemons (1998) point out, "the safest and least painful way to prepare for an uncertain future is to invest to enable a rapid response to multiple contingencies and to monitor the environment for clues to emerging scenarios." Similarly, Hitt et al. (1998) explain that, "while random events cannot be forecasted . . . top managers may use vision and foresight . . . to allow firms to reduce periods of instability by making rapid and effective changes." Assessing the amount and type of change an organization faces is therefore the first step involved in being able to cope effectively with it as an organization.

In today's business environment as well, companies cannot afford to overlook new sources of competitive advantage. They must learn to recognize new competitive positions as they open up and become more aware of how such changes could affect them and their competition. New ways of competing could come from new customer groups, new needs, new technologies, new materials, or a combination of these. Often, because such positions are not obvious, long-standing competitors do not do this well, leaving themselves vulnerable to new entrants in a marketplace (Porter, 1996).

Just as organizations must function in an external business environment that will affect their strategies, so they must also function in an external IT environment. Today, there is a fundamental change in the role of IT in organizations because it can provide the strategic differentiation that firms are continually seeking. Senior executives are now realizing that there are specific technologies that could shape new strategic initiatives for the firm. As with other aspects of the business environment, continuous assessment of information technologies and practices is therefore essential to enable the firm to position itself appropriately and to structure itself effectively (Henderson and Venkatramen, 1999). With the potential impact of IT being so much higher than in the past, it can no longer be assumed that business strategy will drive IT strategy (although this may be the case). Instead, organizations must be open to all possibilities and must be prepared to make adaptations on an as-needed basis. It is thus essential to continuously scan the technology environment to regularly identify the newest and most effective technologies relevant to a business and to understand the skills required to use them (Hitt et al., 1998).

DESIGNING A PROCESS TO MANAGE NEW TECHNOLOGIES

Clearly, which technologies an organization chooses to look at, and how it goes about determining how and where they should be integrated within the enterprise, is a significant aspect of how a firm responds to its environment. Research comparing many different companies in the same industry shows that even given common, competitive access to common resources and technical savvy, some companies do a much better job of selecting and integrating new technologies into their business strategy than others. This research also shows that these differences occur long before companies have to choose to make a major investment – in other words, they occur during the critical process of determining which technologies are important and how they should be used (Iansiti, 1997). A further distinguishing factor between successful and unsuccessful companies in this area is not how much money a firm spends on new technology, but how rapidly and efficiently it can translate its new technology research into products that meet market needs (Iansiti and West, 1997).

Until recently, most IT organizations have had only very limited and highly informal mechanisms for doing this. A survey in 1992 identified no best practices in researching new technologies and found that few companies were actively engaged in scanning, evaluating, developing, or experimenting with new forms of technology. A second survey in 2001 found that there was much more interest among IT managers in doing this, but still no recognized best practices in how to do it well (Bresnahan, 1996). In spite of this, a recent *CIO Magazine* poll found that a majority of CIOs said that keeping up with new technology was the most difficult aspect of their job and that they spent about 30% of their time on it (Bresnahan, 1996). Some of the reasons they gave for this include:

- it's important to have your thoughts in order and have a strategy you can articulate with confidence;
- CIOs who value their jobs must also be prepared to discuss the supposed miracle technologies their bosses discover in airline magazines;
- you must be vigilant to spot new trends and applications.

When it has been formally handled at all, new technology research in IT has typically been handled by a small internal group that explore new technologies and choose which ones will be used. Then a small development group creates a prototype and, eventually, the technology is integrated into the organization via a full-scale development project (Iansiti and West, 1997). More likely, the process is *ad hoc*. As one focus group participant described it:

> We have two methods of identifying new technologies in our firm. Either the business pushes a solution based on the latest "hot button" and IT reacts, or IT selects a technology and pushes it on the business.

Today, we are beginning to learn that dealing effectively with emerging technologies as a business is a "unique managerial competency" (Henderson, 1994), and that turning new technologies into organizational opportunities requires both intuition and discipline (Hoenig, 2001). Commitment to systematic practices is therefore critical to success in this area (Drucker, 1998). There are three key steps to doing this well in IT (Henderson, 1994):

1. Keeping abreast of changes in technology.
2. Generating diverse options and cross-fertilizing ideas for how a business can take advantage of new technology.
3. Successfully integrating new technology into the existing organization.

Focus group participants added that, to do this well, IT must also keep current in where the business is going, reinforcing that dealing with emerging technologies can never be addressed in isolation from the business context.

KEEPING CURRENT ON NEW TECHNOLOGIES

With over 2,000 new hardware, software, and information-related products being produced *each month*, tracking new trends, applications, and opportunities for IT has become an impossible task for most organizations (Bresnahan, 1996). Therefore, the first thing that managers must accept is that no company can research every relevant discipline on its own (Iansiti and West, 1997). Typically, companies have tended to focus on their immediate competition and rely on a limited number of channels for collecting information. However, increasingly the number and variety of new technologies is leading companies to improve and broaden their intelligence-gathering in both formal and informal ways (Kodama, 1992). Identifying what technologies a firm should take an interest in requires: "a conscious, purposeful search within the company and the industry as well as the larger social and intellectual environment . . . The key is to know where to look." (Drucker, 1998). Systematic looking should take a number of forms:

- *Listening and asking.* IT should be listening to its users to identify opportunities for new uses of technology. These opportunities will usually be framed in business terms (e.g., emerging markets, unexpected occurrences, demographic changes, or what the competition is doing), and will need insights from IT to determine how changes in technology can help take advantage of these opportunities (Drucker, 1998). Other sources of opportunities will be the firm's customers, particularly early adopters of new technologies. Some firms have created councils of technologically savvy customers to help them pinpoint latent, unarticulated customer needs. Speaking with customer service staff is often another way of determining these needs (Hemp, 2001). One focus group company has created a formal process whereby anyone in the company can communicate with its technology group about new technologies and their potential. Sometimes people simply want to be reassured that their firm understands and knows about a particular technology, but many useful technology opportunities have grown out of this process. This company also actively monitors its help desk, and works with individuals who think they have identified a new opportunity to determine what its business potential might be.
- *Networking.* More and more, IT organizations are also looking beyond their own boundaries to generate technological possibilities. They are building a network of partners, vendors, consultants, and universities to keep them up to date on what technologies are available and how they might be effectively used. Frequently, senior IT managers share their business strategies with their key partners, who in turn share their technological insights with them. Creating a rich network of allies can help companies to leverage value for their research dollars and to focus internal efforts more effectively on the next two steps of the managing-new-technologies process, which are highly company-specific (Iansiti and West, 1997).
- *Scanning.* Many technologies "emerge" in an industry after a period of evolution and growth in narrow niches. Thus, it is critical that organizations develop the capability to look beyond the boundaries of their own industry and to cultivate openness to new ideas. Group participants noted that frequently their business customers are so focused on current business needs that they tend to have difficulty seeing the potential of technologies for which there is no immediate demand. It is therefore incumbent on the IT organization to pay attention to unfamiliar technologies and other industries, to see what can be adapted from them. One CIO explained how he had "adopted" the concepts embedded in American Airline's SABRE (airline reservation)

Table 14.1   *"Tech Brief" template.*

SAMPLE TECHNOLOGY:

What is it?
- Description of technology (in point form)
- Clarify positioning of technology within enterprise and/or potential applicability

What can it do for our company?
- Business focus (not technical)
- Key functionality and business benefits (not features)

What are the business opportunities?
- Impacts on customer satisfaction, employee satisfaction
- Potential for increased revenue, decreased expense

What are the business risks?
- Potential negative impacts, suggested mitigation

Availability?
- What is marketplace availability?
- What is company availability?

What are related marketplace trends?
- Competitor positioning, emerging technology adoption
- Industry news/trends

system for his own life insurance company a few years ago, and how this led to a considerable and sustained business advantage for his company.

- *Researching.* The most commonly used method of identifying interesting new technologies is through reading the business press and attending conferences. In some organizations, there is a small group dedicated to doing this; in others everyone is expected to participate. However, only three organizations in the focus group had a formal procedure for capturing what is learned in this way. One firm makes extensive use of email and leads technical "chats" about various new technologies until the technology is either considered ready to implement or is no longer of interest. A manager monitors, participates in, and documents these conversations, and everyone in the organization is encouraged to contribute to them. Another firm uses its research group to write "Tech Briefs" on emerging technologies. It has created a template document, that can be easily completed or updated, to outline potential applications, risks, and trends for a particular technology. These are distributed to senior IT managers and are available on the company's intranet site for anyone who is interested (a sample template is included in Table 14.1). A third organization has created an intellectual capital database open to everyone in the firm that includes both formal research documents and informal updates from staff who attend conferences or meetings and find something interesting of note.

ASSESSING NEW TECHNOLOGIES

In addition to knowing *what* types of technology are available and how they *might* be used, IT managers must make choices based on educated guesses about their businesses and the technology market to narrow the focus of any research effort. This is not always easy to do. While most companies are well equipped to identify technologies that will provide incremental rates of improvement to their products and services, they have a strong tendency to reject radical or disruptive technologies as not having enough value. The following quotes illustrate this very real dilemma:

- With over fifty foreign cars already on sale here, the Japanese auto industry isn't likely to carve out a big slice of the U.S. market for itself (*Business Week*, 2 August 1968).
- "I think there is a world market for about five computers" (Thomas Watson, Chairman IBM, 1943).
- "There is no reason for any individual to have a computer in their home" (Ken Olson, President, Digital Equipment Corporation, 1977, cited in Cerf and Navsky, 1984).

Time and again, research has found that companies do not have the processes in place to deal with disruptive technologies (Bower and Christensen, 1994; Friar and Balachandra, 1999; Day and Schoemaker, 2000). Typically, marketing and financial managers will not support disruptive technologies because they tend to have different attributes that are not yet valued by the firm's customers or that don't initially appear to perform as well as existing technologies. For example, in an informal survey in 1996, the authors found many IT managers didn't recognize the need or the value of being able to communicate electronically outside their organizations, even though email was well established internally. Thus, it may be necessary to have separate processes to manage those technologies that will improve or sustain existing business models and those that are potentially disruptive (Bower and Christensen, 1994).

With sustaining innovations, determining what areas to focus on is a decision that can be made jointly with the business and then periodically re-evaluated. Many companies have established technology councils or architecture boards to evaluate potential technologies for the firm. One focus group member's council is composed of key IT groups that categorize interesting, emerging (as well as existing) technologies by their potential "strategic-ness" and estimated longevity. The result is a 2 × 2 matrix that helps determine what IT should be doing vis-à-vis each technology (see Figure 14.1). "Using this matrix has proven very useful for 'fit' discussions with our business partners," our participant commented. "We use the 'watch' quadrant for those technologies which appear to be of interest to our company but which we are not yet ready to invest in."

Disruptive technologies may require more creativity and subterfuge on the part of IT. As a start, they need to be identified as disruptive. A telltale sign of

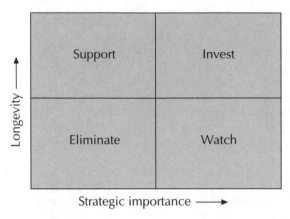

Figure 14.1   *The technology watch matrix.*

such a technology is when IT people think a technology is important, but business people do not (Bower and Christensen, 1994). One focus group member told the story of how IT wanted to install debit technology in his company's retail stores only to have his users reject it because, "it will never catch on". Naturally, the following year these same users were all screaming to have the technology immediately! Furthermore, disruptive technologies are rarely one-to-one replacements of existing technologies. They usually generate new ideas and new concepts, not only for existing customers but also for new ones. Therefore, traditional techniques for determining customers' needs may not work for these technologies since the needs these technologies will serve are still latent (Friar and Balachandra, 1999). As Bower and Christensen (1994) write: "Our behavior changes in a new context. It doesn't transform from the old context. That's a key way to visualize how new technology gets deployed in new markets." One focus group member described how pagers were initially rejected by his business management because they tried to use them like notebook computers. It was only when they changed how they were using these devices that the adoption rate in the company soared. "Now we're buying these things by the carton—everybody wants one," he says.

While improving technologies can usually be cost-justified in traditional ways, disruptive technologies may require a different type of assessment. Focus members agreed that it might be necessary to experiment "under the radar" with some technologies in order to be able to demonstrate value to the business. Experimentation is a good way to figure out the strategic significance of disruptive technologies and to be able to predict their impact. Sometimes, a group of users and/or external customers will be willing to work with IT on this, but the experts caution that these people should be the more flexible and leading-edge ones, not necessarily your "best" customers (Bower and Christensen, 1994). In other cases, established companies let start-up firms experiment and monitor what they are doing. Finally, simulation and prototyping can go a long way toward helping IT and business understand the potential of a disruptive technology and its applicability for a particular company (Thomke, 2001).

To know when to capitalize on a particular emerging technology, one high-tech focus group firm has revamped its assessment processes to make sure that it doesn't miss a technology opportunity. Anyone in the firm can create a "business opportunity proposal" (BOP) if he or she has a good idea for how to use a new technology. A BOP is a short document created from a template that helps senior managers separate hype from reality while ensuring that technologies that make sense for the organization are identified. It identifies the benefits of the technology, the competitors using it, the adoption rate, and maturity of the technology as well as the benefits of using it. "This process makes it easy to make a case to the company to move ahead with a particular technology," our member explained. "If it fits with our critical success factors and makes sense for our organization, we will base our business strategy around a BOP. An ROI [return on investment] is not necessary." To level the playing field between senior and junior staff, executives are required to create their own BOPs, while the office of the chief technology officer will help more junior staff to develop their proposals. This firm receives over 20 suggestions each week and generates about two BOPs from them. This process is particularly effective, our participant stated, because it helps the organization to truly listen to every idea and provides an easy means of speeding up the justification process.

Often, not enough is known about either the potential market or what the technology can do to warrant a full-scale investment, yet IT may wish to do more than a low-level experiment. In this case, an options approach can be used to justify further investments in emerging technologies (Day and Schoemaker, 2000). This approach suggests that, in addition to their "big bets", companies maintain portfolios of investments in a variety of technologies, somewhat like insurance. By viewing these investments as a series of steps, not as a "go–no go" decision, managers can nurture a wide variety of opportunities for their organizations. Such options are seen as a "hedge" against certain future scenarios and are held until it becomes apparent which direction the technology and the market will take. Thus, assessing an emerging technology becomes an iterative process of research, development, and implementation that can be modified, abandoned, revamped, expanded, or delayed as key uncertainties are resolved (Johnson et al., 2001). Technology investments become part of a portfolio of choices available to the company until one or more are mature enough to be integrated into the business in some way. For example, using this approach, in the company discussed earlier in this section, IT could have made some preliminary investments in debit technology when it was first identified. These would have provided an invaluable base for a rapid scale-up in the following year when the business recognized its value. These types of strategic experiments are a very effective way to overcome the challenges of potentially disruptive technologies because they can help companies explore their potential to the business at relatively low risk.

INTEGRATING NEW TECHNOLOGIES

As noted above, the ability to rapidly and effectively integrate new technologies into the business is a key distinguishing factor of competitive organizations. Researchers have found that this factor is more important in explaining performance than differences in project management methods, leadership qualities, and organizational structure (Iansiti and West, 1997). Thus, business management plays a crucial role in the innovation process, and it is essential that organizations have the ability to overcome their "deeply engrained mindsets, information filters and problem solving strategies" to enable them to accommodate new technologies (Henderson, 1994). Some of the challenges companies face in this area include:

- viewing new technologies solely in terms of cost-cutting and overlooking their potential for innovation and revenue growth (Thomke, 2001);
- failure to distribute information on new approaches and technologies to the front line and failure to listen to them (Abramson, 1999);
- Inability to see a wider range of possible futures (Schoemaker, 1995);
- investing in technologies to retain current customers, but not making investments for the customers of the future;
- sticking with the familiar (Day and Schoemaker, 2000).

Focus group members agreed. As one noted, "communication about new technology is a challenge; many business people don't understand its relevance." Another pointed out, "it's very frustrating when the business doesn't see the value of a technology. Our challenge is to build mindshare." It is therefore essential for IT to put the value of new technology into business terms. This must be an ongoing effort that occurs at several levels in the organization and approaches the subject in several different ways. One focus group organization uses a picture of the "IT house" to illustrate to the business how infrastructure investments help support the work of the business (see Figure 14.2). It couples this concept with real business examples of how each aspect of the "house" can affect business; for example, narrow bandwidth only enables simple graphics such as a series of green "Xs" on a screen; broader bandwidth enables full graphics, which are much more attractive to a customer. In this firm, the CIO introduces new technology and responds to business ideas from a strategic point of view at the executive level while account managers gather ideas from mid-level managers and help prepare the business to receive new technologies. An architecture group work to ensure that the house has a good foundation.

One way to help business managers break out of their current mindsets is with scenario-planning. This is a disciplined process that helps them to imagine a variety of possible futures and how the business might deal with them. Typically,

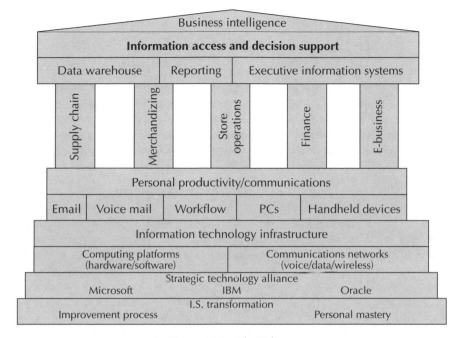

Figure 14.2   *The IT house.*

organizational strategies tend to be static and linear. Scenario-planning en-courages managers to identify the variable elements of a variety of future states and the joint impact of a number of uncertainties. By changing several variables at one time, the method tries to capture new states that will develop after major changes and helps prepare managers for a number of different futures. Schoemaker (1995) lists a number of companies that have successfully used this method to help them anticipate change and adapt to new ways of operating. (This article also identifies the steps that are involved in doing scenario-planning.)

Another way to approach changing company thinking about new technology is to establish a beachhead (Smith, 2001). Business and technology guru Peter Keen suggests that this should be viewed as a landing party for invading a competitive environment with a well-orchestrated initiative. More than a pilot, but less than an enterprise-wide venture, a beachhead is a business venture first— designed to help a company mobilize its thinking around technology *and* strategy. A good beachhead is therefore a specific campaign plan *within* an overall business strategy. It must not be viewed as a project or a prototype, but rather as a venture that is value-driven. A project approach is appropriate for traditional IT initiatives where there are known benefits to a company (e.g., increased revenues, services, or cost savings). However, a beachhead is essentially an experiment. Unlike traditional IT projects, which are designed to eliminate uncertainty and surprise, a properly designed beachhead should be able to embrace calculated uncertainties because these can lead to new sources of value and business effectiveness. The key to a good beachhead is to closely link it to business strategy and design. Only a clear understanding of how an enterprise derives its value will enable the difficult, but necessary design decisions and business tradeoffs to be made. Keen notes:

> Our problem with e-business up to now is that we have tried to work from the bottom up. We have had good IT people trying to make up business strategy and usually copying what others have done. Unfortunately, the guys at the top have a visualization problem. They're not stupid, but they will need help from IT to do this (Smith, 2001).

Fully integrating disruptive new technologies can take time, and approaches need to be tailored to the culture of each organization and the character of the technology (Day and Schoemaker, 2000). In some cases, a separate business unit may need to be set up that can leverage the parent's strengths while avoiding absorption into the mainstream business. In other cases, complete integration of the technology into every aspect of the business is more effective because it enables the organization to learn from and better shape the technology to business needs (Smith, 2001). The key is to keep strategically important disruptive technologies in a context that is small enough to develop proof of concept. In addition to sticking with the familiar, one of the most common pitfalls in integrating emerging technologies is a lack of persistence. Many firms have little patience for failures or adverse results in spite of the significant learning that can result about customer needs or behaviors. Frequently, they underestimate the potential for further improvements in the technology or how customer behavior will change over time. Successful integration of truly radical technology will therefore need aggressive customer service to get insights into latent customer needs and diagnostic software to get information on product use and potential glitches. Altogether, a business's goal at this level should be to methodically test product requirements, test the validity of concepts, and create a climate of collaborative innovation.

In integrating new technologies into a business, IT's challenge is to find an appropriate balance between leveraging its existing strengths and identifying new technology opportunities. Typically, forum members pointed out, calls for new technology vary from wild over-enthusiasm ("gotta have it yesterday") to serious skepticism ("it'll never work"). IT needs mechanisms for walking the line between these two perspectives and ensuring that, while technology doesn't get too far ahead of the customer, the company is able to catch and ride new technology waves effectively (Hemp, 2001). For this reason, many focus group member firms are reviewing their technology investments monthly. They find an iterative discussion helps both business and IT people to find common ground on technology integration. Changes to budgeting and goal-setting processes from annual to a rolling quarterly assessment also help firms to make adjustments in rapidly changing technology conditions (Hemp, 2001).

CONCLUSION

The increasing emphasis on dealing with new technologies heralds a changing role for IT. Now that significant amounts of development and maintenance are being outsourced, this role is becoming more and more apparent. More than ever before, the choices that IT makes are affecting a corporation's bottom line and its competitive position (Stephen, 2001). As a result, IT managers are stepping up their efforts to improve how they identify, assess, and integrate new technologies into their organizations. Unfortunately, there are no "silver bullets" for ensuring an organization makes the right choices in technology. As the number of technologies is growing exponentially and whole industries are being shaken up by non-traditional competitors using radically different business models, an ongoing "healthy paranoia" is justified and probably desirable to keep both business and IT on its toes. It is essential, therefore, to adjust internal IT and company processes for evaluating and investing in new technologies to maximize flexibility for as long as possible. Modified investment practices, creating an open-minded learning environment about technology potentials and designing collaborative processes to effectively integrate new technologies, will each help to ensure that organizations are well positioned to catch and ride successive new technology waves without falling prey to the dreaded "surfer syndrome".

REFERENCES

Abramson, G. (1999) "All along the watchtower," *CIO Enterprise Magazine*, 15 July.

Applegate, L.M. (1994) "Managing in an information age: Transforming the organization for the 1990s," in R. Baskerville, S. Smithson, O. Ngwenyama, and J.I. DeGross, (eds), *Transforming Organisations with Information Technologies*, North Holland, Amsterdam.

Bower, J. and C. Christensen (1994) "Disruptive technologies: Catching the wave," *Harvard Business Review*, January–February, 43–53.

Bresnahan, J. (1996) "Mission possible," *CIO Magazine*, 15 October.

Cerf, C. and V. Navasky. (1984) *The Experts Speak*, Pantheon Books, New York.

Day, G.S. and P. Schoemaker. (2000) "Avoiding the pitfalls of emerging technologies," *California Management Review*, Winter, 42(2), 8–33.

Drucker, P. (1998) "The discipline of innovation," *Harvard Business Review*, November–December, 3–8.

Friar, J. and R. Balachandra (1999) "Spotting the customer for emerging technologies," *Research Technology Management*, July–August, 42(4), 37–43.

Hemp, P. (2001) "Managing for the next big thing: An interview with EMC's Michael Ruettgers," *Harvard Management Review*, January, 131–139.

Henderson, J.C. and N. Venkatramen (1999) "Strategic alignment: Leveraging information technology for transforming organizations," *IBM Systems Journal*, 32(1).

Henderson, R. (1994) "Managing innovation in the information age," *Harvard Business Review*, January–February, 101–105.

Hitt, M.A., B.W. Keats, and S.M. DeMarie (1998) "Navigating in the new competitive landscape: Building strategic flexibility and competitive advantage in the 21st century," *Academy of Management Executive*, **12**(4), 22–42.

Hoenig, C. (2001) "A disciplined sixth sense," *CIO Magazine*, 15 December 2000–1 January 2001.

Iansiti, M. (1997) *The R&D Challenge of the 1990's*, Note 9-697-048, 15 August, Harvard Business School Press, Boston.

Iansiti, M. and J. West (1997) "Technology integration: Turning great research into great products," *Harvard Business Review*, May–June, 69–79.

Johnson, L.D., E.H. Neave, and B. Pazderka (2001) *Knowledge, Innovation and Share Value*, Framework Paper 01-11, July, Queen's Centre for Knowledge-Based Enterprises, Queen's School of Business, Kingston, Canada.

Kodama, F. (1992) "Technology fusion and the new R&D," *Harvard Business Review*, July–August, 70–77.

Porter, M.E. (1996) "What is strategy?" *Harvard Business Review*, November–December.

Schoemaker, P. (1995) "Scenario planning: A tool for strategic thinking," *Sloan Management Review*, Winter, 25–46.

Smith, H. (2001) "Business: Strategy and structure," *CIO Canada Magazine*, May.

Stephen, S. (2001) "Eye on the prize," *CIO Canada*, April.

Thomke, S. (2001) "Enlightened experimentation: The new imperative for innovation," *Harvard Business Review*, February, 67–75.

15
IT-sourcing: Build, Buy, or Market*

Information technology (IT) sourcing—that is, the locus of IT service provisioning—advanced through successive eras. In the beginning, IT-sourcing was focused on the "build" versus "buy" decision. Over time, outsourcing gained currency as a means to "lease" IT services effectively from external providers. Soon came the "rent" era ushered in by the application service providers (ASPs). For the first time, it was possible to use only what you wanted and pay for only what you used. Today, we stand on the threshold of the "market" era where IT managers will buy *and* sell services on the open market as the distinction between buyer and seller disappears. Welcome to the "brave new world" of IT-sourcing.

The motivation behind all IT-sourcing decisions is the opportunity to save significant amounts of time and money by trading off the management of IT services—internally versus externally. The prospect of letting someone else take on the headaches of managing a large portion of traditional IT services is appealing to many established companies. Smaller and newer enterprises are attracted to renting because of the opportunity to access expensive software on a time-sharing basis and to deliver full service IT to their customers without the typical start-up time and expenses. Regardless of the era, the driving factors behind IT-sourcing decisions remain time-to-market, economies of scale, competitive differentiation, critical mass, possession of expertise, competitive necessity, the "not-invented-here" syndrome and, of course, technology itself. As the "market" era emerges, we are likely to deploy the same (or similar) decision factors, but played out within the framework of a market strategy.

* McKeen, J.D., H.A. Smith, N. Joglekar, and P.R. Balasubramanian (2002) "IT sourcing: Build, buy or market?" *Communications of the Association of Information Systems (CAIS)*, September, **9**(8), 120–135 (reproduced by permission of the Association for Information Systems).

In 2002, a large number of service providers are taking positions in this rapidly evolving arena. Some are hardware/software vendors; others are integrated services providers (ISPs) and telecommunication providers; still others are Web hosts, service aggregators, and full service providers. This provider diversity creates a considerable degree of confusion concerning:

- the overall value model;
- the identity of key providers (not to mention their viability); and
- appropriate strategies for benefiting from a new provisioning model.

Some aspects, however, are certain.

- First, the service market is clearly immature and in a state of flux (facing numerous growing pains, shakeouts, and takeovers). While still in their infancy, ASPs are already being supplanted by yet more expansive service offerings (e.g., business systems providers [BSPs]) that are becoming known as xSPs (i.e., generic service providers).
- Second, a value model is not yet articulated.
- Third, support is not reliable.

These aspects leave IT managers facing some key questions. Can they afford to ignore this emergent (and potentially disruptive) technology-driven opportunity? Should they make investments now as a hedging strategy? What are the key factors that will assist their decision-making? What steps should they take to best position their organizations for the future, when the market era becomes a reality?

This chapter provides a review of the current literature to provide some perspectives on how various service provisioning models are changing the IT environment for organizations. Starting with the "rent" era (Section 1), the chapter provides an overview of the ASP phenomenon, explaining ASPs and how they work. Section 2 introduces the concept of an IT marketplace for services—that is, market-based sourcing. Then, the elements of a market-based sourcing strategy are outlined (Section 3). The chapter concludes (Section 4) by outlining some of the implications of the emerging marketplace of IT service provisioning for IT management.

1   ASPS: THE "RENT" ERA

Scholars in the strategy and the IT community have studied sourcing for some time (Lacity and Hirschheim, 1993; Hirschheim and Lacity, 2000; Lacity and Willcocks, 1998; Venkatramen, 1997). One recent development that attracted considerable attention in this regard is the emergence of the ASP model. ASPs led to the "pay as you go" era. In its simplest form, an ASP is:

> ... a third party service firm, which deploys, manages and remotely hosts a pre-packaged software application through centrally located servers in a rental or lease arrangement (Weller, 1999).

In concept, an ASP is similar to the service bureaus of the 1970s. Back then, however, there was no cheap, non-proprietary means for a desktop computer to communicate with an off-site application and no standard environment in which they could interact (McKie, 1999). Today, the Internet enables services to be delivered to companies from a central site using network infrastructure. This advance in technology gave the shared-service concept a new lease on life.

The ASP business model differs from traditional outsourcing in a number of key ways:

- first, it offers shared operations and delivery over the network;
- second, it provides full life cycle services for applications, rather than operations and maintenance only;
- third, it is based on simplified pricing and billing and limited customization of applications;
- finally, it offers rapid implementation of applications and attempts to hide some of the complexity of operations from the business (Terdiman, 2000b; Terdiman and Berg, 2000).

ASPs offer their customers access to a complete application environment. They make the necessary investments in application licenses, servers, people, and other resources. Typically, an ASP either owns the software involved or has a contractual arrangement with one or more software vendors. The ASP performs the initial application implementation and integration, provides ongoing data center management, and continuous uninterrupted connectivity and support. It is also responsible for regular hardware and software upgrades. While more than one partner may be involved in delivering services, the ASP maintains the customer relationship and is responsible for ensuring that services are provided as promised. As shown in Figure 15.1, an ASP offers its customers a complete end-to-end solution for one or more applications (Gillan et al., 1999).

In return for these services for one or more applications, customers pay a usage fee and forgo software customization—in effect, trading customization for speed. Because customization is not offered, an ASP can provide the same services to many other customers and can therefore leverage its investments in hardware and software many times over (Leong, 2000). Common applications offered by ASPs include:

- enterprise resource planning (ERP);
- customer relationship management (CRM);
- e-commerce;
- e-procurement;
- data warehousing; and
- email.

These applications are considered to be ideal for the ASP model because they are enterprise-wide and require large capital outlays and technical resources to implement and manage. They also typically take a long time to implement.

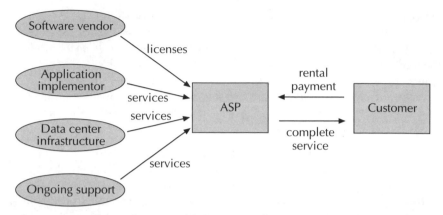

Figure 15.1   *The ASP business model (data from Weller, 1999, used with kind permission).*

Pricing of ASP services currently comes in two flavors:

- *Fixed pricing.* This model is dominant in 2002. Customers are charged a fixed fee per user per month based on the number of services required (e.g., number of servers, number of applications).
- *Usage pricing.* Here, the customer pays for the actual time or resources used.

The pricing models are based on the premise that an ASP can offer a more predictable cost model and a faster return on investment (Leong, 2000). However, it is also possible that an ASP's greater economies of scale will reduce the significant costs of implementing and operating enterprise-wide applications. One estimate suggests that ASPs can reduce project installation and set-up costs and time by between 50% and 75% (Anonymous, 2000a). Thus, while speed of procurement and style of cost management are seen as the major incentives for businesses to use ASPs, some experts suggest that the ability to lower the total cost of ownership is also becoming a significant driver (Terdiman et al., 2000).

The "rental" market is in a state of flux. As quickly as some players leave, others enter (Terdiman, 2000a), and their presence further clouds the ASP market-place. Players within this market include (Leong, 2000):

- *Web software vendors.* Software companies (e.g., Oracle, Siebel) that are repositioning themselves to provide ASP capabilities. Typically, they partner with a data center and network providers to handle the back end of their services. Through their ASP offering, they hope to provide an alternate distribution channel for their software.
- *Service aggregators.* These firms aggregate the individual pieces of an ASP service (e.g., software, integration and data center, and applications) from

other companies. They usually provide a variety of applications (e.g., ERP, CRM, e-commerce). Systems integrators, consulting firms, and traditional outsourcers fit into this category (e.g., EDS).

- *Full service providers.* These companies make a significant investment in infrastructure. They run their own data centers with a high level of security and reliability. Typically, they have strong technical expertise. Hardware vendors fall into this category (e.g., IBM Global Services).

- *Telecommunication providers.* These firms specialize in deploying and managing telecommunication and data centers. They may also offer strengths in Web-hosting. With large customer bases and a global reach, they are in a good position to become ASPs even though they do not have core competencies in application-hosting and management. ISPs, telephone companies, and Web-hosting firms fall into this category (e.g., AT&T, Qwest).

In 2000, the ASP marketplace was at a crossroads. The good news was that the marketplace was experiencing significant growth. Estimates anticipate an industry of $22.7 billion by 2003 (Terdiman, 2000a; Terdiman et al., 2000). GartnerGroup predicted that, by 2003, over 30% of enterprise application software will be sold through ASP channels (Terdiman et al., 2000). The bad news was that the industry was clearly in the throes of turmoil. In 2000, GartnerGroup predicted that, by the end of 2002, 50% of that year's ASPs would be out of business[1] "due to poorly thought-out business models, choice of partners, inability to execute and consolidation in the ASP marketplace" (Terdiman et al., 2000). Most ASPs, whose business models were based on economies of scale to be achieved through rapid growth, still had a negative cash flow leaving their long-term viability in question. Mergers were also starting to occur and were predicted to continue through 2003 and perhaps 2005 (Terdiman et al., 2000). Given their unproven credibility, customers were expressing legitimate concerns about the reliability and quality of service, as well as security and vendor stability. As best we can tell the assessment in 2000 still holds true.

At present, ASPs are attracting mainly small- to medium-sized firms, rapidly growing companies who need to scale up their systems quickly without a huge upfront investment. For firms in this category, the benefits of ASPs can possibly outweigh the risks. However, for companies with substantial IT assets, there is little to lose and more to gain by waiting until the ASP market settles down or evolves. In most cases, ASPs fail to offer a compelling value proposition to their customers at present. Furthermore, while offering sourcing flexibility at the application level, the ASP model does not alleviate the critical issue of integrating solutions across different generations of technology based on disparate software.

---

[1] For example, in July 2000, Pandesic (a relatively large ASP established by SAP and Intel) shut down its operations. The company cited "lower-than-expected demand in the B-to-C market and said that it could not foresee a timely road to profitability" (Kontzer, 2000).

To address these issues, attention needs to be focused on the development of infrastructure, common platforms, and architectural standards. Furthermore, it requires universal access through Internet-based delivery. Collectively, solving these issues would permit a much more robust approach to IT service provisioning. Enter the next generation—the "market" era.

2   xSPs: THE "MARKET" ERA

This era rests upon the key assumption that companies will "buy their information technologies as services provided over the Internet rather than owning and maintaining all their own hardware and software" (Hagel and Brown, 2001). Just as ASPs ushered in the "rent" era, xSPs pave the way for the "market" era. xSPs (where the "x" denotes a generic service) are in the business of providing technology, systems, and processes, not just applications. The key players this time are those with significant influence in the marketplace (e.g., Microsoft) who are willing to make (and capable of making) sizeable investments to create the infrastructure necessary to sustain a viable Internet-based services network. In this era, controlling and setting architectural standards is seen as more important than which application a firm uses.

Figure 15.2 shows how different types of xSPs could all work together within a services marketplace to provide a wide variety of technology services to customers. This particular rendering of xSP architecture is based on Microsoft's view of the marketplace (Cornfield, 2001). Organizations such as Microsoft see their role as the application *infrastructure* providers (AIPs)—those who will build the large computing ecosystem within which other types of xSP will operate. In this system, ASPs (i.e., those that survive) play a key role, but represent only one

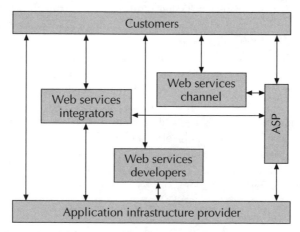

Figure 15.2   *Market-based architecture for xSP services (reproduced by permission of the Solution Provider Institute [www.spinstitute.com] and Rick Juarez, Robertson Stephens).*

Table 15.1 *Web services platforms ranked by early adopter preference (from Gilpin, 2001).*

IBM WebSphere	33%
Microsoft.NET	22%
J2EE with Web services add-ons	19%
Oracle 9i applications server	7%
BEA WebLogic	6%
SunONE iPlanet	4%
Other J2EE application servers	9%
	Sample size = 120

component within a much larger services market—a market that includes Web services integrators, a Web services channel, and Web services development.

Such an ecosystem requires an enabling architecture such as the one proposed by Hagel and Brown (2001). Theirs is a three-layer non-proprietary architecture whose top layer consists of business-specific application services (such as credit-checking); a middle layer provides inter-firm brokerage utilities to handle buyer–seller transactions (such as payments); and a bottom layer of standards and protocols to allow application-to-application communication. Such architecture permits the free exchange of services among suppliers and providers. Further-more, it allows for easy access to services, mobility among service providers, and a blurring of the distinction between suppliers and providers. In short, if and when such a model gains acceptance, it would provide a dynamic market mechanism for services.

This brave new world of IT market-based sourcing is given significant cre-dence as major players declare their interests. Results of a recent market research study (Table 15.1) identify the preferences of early adopters regarding key Web services platforms (Gilpin, 2001). The commonality of these platforms is limited as the battle over architectural standards has yet to declare a victor. IBM launched "WebSphere" services, which build on the MQSeries architecture; Microsoft unveiled the ".Net" strategy; and Sun advocates the Java™ 2 Platform Enterprise Edition (J2EE), which defines the standard for developing multi-tier enterprise applications (Sun, 2002).

It is interesting to speculate how such a services market will function. Each platform provider is gambling on the premise that most revenues will be gener-ated from infrastructure services. It is unlikely that certain forms of software (e.g., personal productivity tools) will become a service. Enterprise support, core processes, and distributed applications are also unlikely targets. In industries where there are shared standards (e.g., healthcare), however, shared applications services may be provided. The most probable targets for the market era are well-defined business processes (components of, rather than, whole applications) with universal appeal such as credit-checking, reconciliation, customer validation, encryption and security, forecasting, materials-planning, and accounting. Processes such as these provide basic building blocks that can be coupled together to form whole (and unique) applications. Given the highly decoupled computing environment made possible by the proposed three-layer architecture, organizations can go to the services market for "best of breed" processes (i.e., components), which can then be cobbled together dynamically with others to collectively provide the necessary functionality—tailored to any degree desired. Because of this ability to provide a Lego^{TM}-like[2] variety of systems, organizations can avoid one of the major pitfalls of the ASP model—the limitations of generic software.

Hagel and Brown (2001) assert that the xSP model promises significant benefits. As with rental, the xSP model allows IT managers to buy only the functionality that they need, when they need it. This characteristic substantially reduces investments in IT assets, thus freeing up significant capital resources. As responsibilities for maintaining systems shift to outside providers, the argument for keeping IT specialists on payroll declines. Furthermore, the need to keep at or near the leading edge of technology is also transferred to the providers since they now "own" the requirement to provide up-to-date technology. Standard "plug-and-play" architecture makes it easy for companies to outsource activities and processes in response to changing economics. Outsourcing, in turn, makes it easier for companies to shift operations and partnerships in response to market conditions. Hagel and Brown (2001) claim that IT managers can "integrate the extraordinarily diverse set of applications and databases residing within most enterprises while at the same time making these resources available to business partners."

With claimed benefits this substantial, one wonders about the down side. Certainly there are a host of questions concerning the security of a "utility-based" IT services market and its ability to protect sensitive customer data. Another question involves the ability to deliver mission-critical applications over the Web in a guaranteed manner. Still other questions involve the portability of the software, the interoperability of its components, and the substitutability of competing providers. These concerns, and others, make decision-making regarding IT problematic. To alleviate this situation, the elements of a market-based sourcing strategy are developed in the next section.

3   A MARKET-BASED SOURCING STRATEGY

The IT-sourcing decision really comes down to *what* and *how*; that is, what services to provide internally versus externally and how to provide these services. The different eras (i.e., build, lease/rent, and market) provide options

---

[2] All Lego^{TM} building blocks conform to a set of standards that allows individuals to create unique structures from generic blocks where interoperability is guaranteed.

regarding how external services are provided. This section presents a decision framework to tackle the what question.[3] It views an xSP as an intermediary means of sourcing, lying between complete outsourcing to a single platform/ infrastructure provider and complete insourcing (Joglekar and Balasubramanian, 2002). It suggests that there will be times when companies need to reserve the right to bring outsourced capabilities in-house and vice versa, or to switch providers for the component services. Furthermore, with market-based sourcing, opportunities exist for "selling" as well as "buying". Where organizations feel that they have a "best of breed" capability, they can explore the possibility of making it available to the market. This dual approach represents a significant change for IT managers. The other (perhaps even more) significant change is the focus (or granularity) of the sourcing decision, which involves components as opposed to whole applications or functions. In a very real sense, IT managers will be responsible for re-architecting the external boundaries of the firm, insofar as IT-sourcing is concerned. They will need a structure, architecture, and contracts that will facilitate this flexibility.

The ease with which a particular company can adopt a market approach will depend on the industry and on the standards being used. The first step for a company is to design its technical platforms to enable flexible sourcing to occur. One initiative already under way in many organizations is enterprise application integration (EAI) (Bove, 2001; Linthicum, 2000). Within the EAI initiative, it is possible to "web-ify" the existing applications and deploy "hub and spoke" communication technology (e.g., middleware software) to manage the complexity of exchanges among the many applications within a portfolio. In addition, applications can be re-architected by modularizing them into functional components. The decoupling of these components, the adoption of standard communication protocols, and the application of interface (translation) mechanisms make it possible not only to integrate across these enterprise systems but also make them "xSP-ready". When the IT services marketplace become a reality, an organization that is xSP-ready will be in a strategic position to reap significant benefits because its applications are IP-enabled thus facilitating interconnection with other applications available on the Web.

An IT-sourcing strategy should be built on decision criteria established by identifying the factors that favor external sourcing as well as articulating the potential adverse affects. Senior IT managers can use this list of advantages/ disadvantages as a starting point to assess external IT-sourcing opportunities. For example, organizations could use the list of advantages as a checklist to help articulate their reasons (and justification) for investigating external providers as

---

[3] We build on earlier work by Lacity and Willcocks (1998) that addresses partial or selective outsourcing of IT services. However, our focus is not on the degree of outsourcing. Regardless of the degree of outsourcing, market-based sourcing refers to a relatively long-term commitment to a particular platform architecture that allows switching components and/or integration suppliers on a more frequent basis.

well as a means of establishing goals. The list of disadvantages provides the basis for establishing threshold conditions to be met (or overcome) for external provisioning to become an attractive (or viable) option. Because each organization has unique needs regarding IT, faces varying pressures, and starts with a different legacy platform, their sourcing strategy needs to be custom-tailored. At a minimum, IT managers must identify candidate services for external sourcing and set out a decision framework to guide the timing of their foray into external provisioning.

Some of the potential advantages (and concerns) of external IT-sourcing are described next.

Advantages of (and Opportunities for) Market-based Sourcing

Options. External sourcing enables companies to take advantage of new technologies, for a minimal cost, at times when the business and technology environment are unclear. Companies can "buy time" while their in-house organizations do a more thorough assessment of the service and its long-term potential for their organization. External sourcing also provides an easy exit strategy. Companies can walk away from a technology or move successful applications in-house relatively easily. Due to the increased granularity of components as opposed to whole business functions (as with outsourcing in the past), the challenge and complications of insourcing (Hirschheim and Lacity, 2000; Lacity and Willcocks, 1998) are greatly reduced.

Funding Flexibility. External sourcing, basically a rent-not-buy approach, avoids capital investments in favor of variable pricing. This choice frees financial assets to be directed into other areas. The advantages result in predictable monthly fees, lower capital costs, and improved total cost of ownership (Jaruzelski et al., 2000).

Quick Starts. Several companies use external IT-sourcing to address new business needs quickly in generic mode (Jaruzelski et al., 2000). Where external providers have strong application-specific expertise, they provide companies with a way to take advantage of new business opportunities very quickly. Businesses then have more time to evaluate a service's value and decide on whether to bring the application in-house for more attention and customization.

Low-priority Applications. External sourcing is also a way for a business unit with low-priority needs to gain advantages from technology. For example, if a business unit can live with a standard, non-customized application, an ASP's monthly fees and implementation expertise mean that the application can be installed with no capital costs. Typically, the business case for such a project curries favor with management due to the decreased investment level, the reduction in time-to-market, and the desire to reduce multiple software platforms across the enterprise. Human resources systems are a typical candidate for scenarios where this strategy can be used effectively. British Petroleum's deal with Exult provides an example of this approach (E. Inc., 2002).

Revenue Generation. With the "market" era comes the opportunity for companies to become a source of business components—that is, to become a supplier as well as a buyer of external IT services. Where companies developed "best of breed" components, these components can be advertized and made available to other companies. To do so, of course, depends on the effective implementation of the "service grid" (i.e., top layer within the three-layer model proposed by Hagel and Brown, 2001, as described earlier). Best-of-breed components could be developed by a single company (e.g., an auto manufacturer), a consortium of companies within an industry (e.g., an airline alliance group), or by alliances of software vendors and companies (e.g., IBM plus a major financial organization). This is an age-old practice for vendors of whole systems.

Rollouts and Upgrades. Some external providers have developed substantial expertise in particular types of complex application (e.g., ERP, CRM). This expertise enables them to ensure that the latest versions of applications are always available to a business, wherever they are needed. Furthermore, because software is delivered via a browser, this service helps in-house IT staff avoid lengthy and expensive site-by-site implementations and management. Hiring this knowledge can be particularly attractive in geographically dispersed organizations.

Potential Dangers with Market-based Sourcing

The potential dangers listed here work in two directions. We discuss the dangers from the point of view of a component buyer. However, if a firm is also a component seller, then its clients will expect the firm to mitigate the risks or at least be cognizant of the risks that the people that buy from them face.

Data Ownership. When an application is sourced externally, the question of who owns the data arises. This problem is especially acute if the company database is also located externally. Risks increase further when an external provider goes out of business. At that time, ownership of data may be unclear. "There is an urgent need for some ethical rules concerning the exchange of business-critical IT information between the ASP and its customers" (Slavid, 2000).

Service Delivery. It is unclear whether external IT providers can deliver services when and where they are needed with the reliability and quality businesses expect. When services are delivered over the Internet or when processors are shared, slow response times can occur that are beyond the control of the external provider. Furthermore, when providers themselves are composed of a network of third parties, the risk is even greater that all the components will not always operate seamlessly.

Security and Privacy. A company is dependent on its external IT provider to maintain back-ups, firewalls, data redundancy, disaster recovery, and quality assurance checks. The risks of a security breach increase when business services are delivered over the Internet. Regardless of who manages an external service, however, businesses are extremely vulnerable if problems occur because the credibility of their operations is at risk. These risks grow greater with an external provider since a company has even less control over how its services are managed.

Customization. When an entire application is being sourced externally, it is difficult for the provider to customize the application for specific needs. This problem is critical for ASP providers whose model is based on a "one size fits all" version of software. Not all customers are willing or able to accept standard solutions. As one commentator points out (Anonymous, 2000b), most of the aggravation of implementing applications in-house revolves either around the challenges of adapting the application to fit users' requirements or in converting the data, modifying the internal processes, training the users, and migrating to the new package. Even when the external IT service is able to deliver components (as opposed to complete applications), this problem will remain for any/all companies who need whole applications and are not interested in building applications themselves out of components.

Business Expertise. Many remain skeptical about the ability of external providers to deliver business expertise and processes to companies. Even within an industry, everyone is different enough to make standardized processes unlikely. Furthermore, the difficulty of providing business expertise in combination with technical expertise makes business service provisioning difficult in the near term. The "componentization" of IT services, however, promises to alleviate much of this problem.

Unanswered Questions

Beyond these advantages/disadvantages, a significant number of unanswered questions remain. At the beginning of 2002, much of the promise of the "market era" of IT-sourcing is just that—a promise. Until the infrastructure is further advanced, it is difficult to respond to these questions with any authority. With huge investments being made in the infrastructure by players with demonstrated staying power, it is safe to assume that the "market" era of IT-sourcing will be fully funded and exercised thoroughly. It is also likely that the computing environment will be changed for ever because of this development. In the next section, we explore some of the implications of the "market era" for today's technology managers.

4 IMPLICATIONS FOR IT MANAGEMENT

The developments that are under way within the external services marketplace undoubtedly will impact the internal functioning of IT departments. We can expect that, with a growth in external provisioning, the organization of the IT department will change to become much more "market-facing". New roles are likely to emerge as different skill sets become important. The number of people within IT may decline over time, as delivery of IT capability becomes more "assembly" and less "development". It is also apparent that in-house IT skills, albeit altered, will remain critically important because the use of an external provider does not absolve IT of any responsibility whatsoever! IT managers will be called upon to revisit their IT strategy to determine when (and how) it should be recast to take advantage of the market era. At the very least, internal capabilities will be developed for dealing with a dynamic services marketplace.

IT managers will continue to be responsible for understanding the implications of changing delivery models and for identifying the opportunities that they represent. They will be expected to develop a "plug and play" architecture that crosses the boundaries of the firm to facilitate the flexibility of the business model. As the IT function begins to play a much more active role within the services market, it will need to enhance its resident IT skills base in a number of key areas including the following:

- identifying candidate capabilities (i.e., applications, processes, and/or technologies) to be market sourced;
- the evaluation/selection of service providers;
- crafting service level agreements (SLAs) and other contractual terms;
- contract monitoring and management;
- environmental scanning.

The evolution of the external IT services market provides many more provisioning possibilities for IT managers. In the past, applications tended to be developed in-house, operated on resident computers, linked over dedicated leased lines, and updated on company databases. This relatively self-contained environment involved few transactions with the external market. Even if the application were purchased/leased/outsourced, it resulted in a limited number of interactions with the market (likely single purchase/lease/outsourcing agreements) that typically were in force over extended periods of time. As the possibility of Web delivery approaches operability, this same "application" might consist of a loosely coupled set of disjoint processes provided by separate vendors that collectively yielded the identical functionality as the previous in-house application. Given a standard

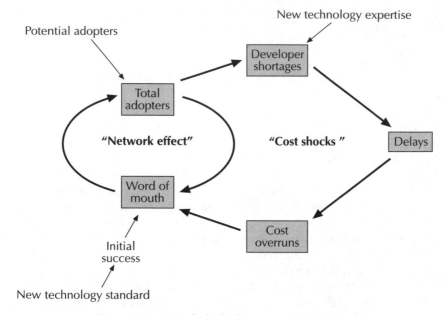

Figure 15.3   *Cost shocks develop as network effects grow.*

infrastructure platform, processes within the overall application (i.e., "components") would be easily (and readily) replaced by superior components as they became available on the market. Thus, market transactions will occur at the component level rather than at the application level, and these transactions can be expected to occur with much greater frequency. Furthermore, the incentive to play the market actively would be significant as anyone not doing so could subject their firm to suboptimal delivery of IT solutions.

This scenario, assuming that the appropriate infrastructure and guarantees are established, demonstrates the dynamic characteristics of such a services market (Figure 15.3). Furthermore, the implications for IT departments enmeshed within such a market are significant because of network effects[4] and cost shocks.[5] IT services would be subject to any (and all) network effects present within the market. Disruption could come at any point and new service providers could be added into (or removed from) the market with little warning. Wherever disruptions and integration gaps arise, shocks will occur—such as higher costs and labor shortages. These shocks will likely lead to delays and interruptions of service. In a network economy, cost shocks occur when more and more firms

---

[4] "Network effects" allude to markets when the value of a product to one user depends on the number of other users (Shapiro and Varian, 1999). Dutta (2001) provides a useful discussion of network effects in an IS context.

[5] "Cost shock" is a term coined to capture the steep increase in the wages/expenses associated with the labor pool due to shortage supply for their particular skill set.

begin to use a particular technology (e.g., client–server, ERP), causing developer shortages to occur and prices to rise. The size of the shock is dependent on the size of the network involved (Figure 15.2). However, it is also possible that an accelerator effect[6] could occur if a service provider invests in this technology. In this case, the cost shocks could be even greater. Further shocks in the marketplace could come from the increasing functionality (and hence the capability to compete) of small- and medium-sized enterprises (SMEs) as a result of their use of xSPs.

To anticipate cost shocks and accelerator effects, IT managers will need to model the dynamics of the markets involved, much as they already model such factors as capacity and job flow. Modeling is essential because the non-linearity of the marketplace prevents extrapolation from the past. Managers must learn to recognize where the key decision points are in this model, where to put their money and time, and what the risks are. In short, companies will need to model the whole market to understand who the players are and what the likelihood of cost shocks and accelerator effects will be. For example, if cost shocks are anticipated prior to an ERP decision, an xSP contract can be written as a hedge against developer shortages. The specific model depends on the category of technology to be delivered through the xSP market environment. To be useful, these models should provide insights that help managers develop robust strategies for dealing with the tensions created by this marketplace. They should try to document what the costs of service will be in both the near and long term and how contracts should be written to cover the risks involved. Modeling represents no small challenge, but, as with most initiatives, the rewards are substantial for those IT managers who outperform the competition.

CONCLUSION

The emerging, external IT services marketplace offers rich opportunities and many possibilities for IT organizations to become more cost-effective. This chapter presents a picture of how IT services may be delivered in the future. We believe that strategic business applications development and management for

---

[6] The multiplier and acceleration effects allude to concepts from classical economics theory (Harrod, 1961). The following explanation is available (HET, 2001): "if investment increases, there will be an increase in output as a result of a 'multiplier' relationship between equilibrium output and the autonomous components of spending." The principle of accelerator suggests that investment decisions on the part of firms are at least in part dependent upon expectations of future increases in demand, which may, in turn, be extrapolated from any current or past increases in aggregate demand or output. Thus, the multiplier principle implies that investment increases output whereas the acceleration principle implies that increases in output will themselves induce increases in investment.

mission-critical applications will be in-house, but delivery for standard and meta-industry applications, processes, and technology will be off-site. Thus, for most companies, it is likely that external IT providers will form part of their future service delivery package and that some will become both consumers and sellers of components. However, as is so often the case in the IT industry, today's reality falls far short of what the industry promises. Companies wishing to take advantage now of what the external IT services marketplace can offer must evaluate the market carefully and must proceed in full awareness of the risks involved. It is recommended that organizations articulate a sourcing strategy that balances internal versus external capabilities to take advantage of the IT services marketplace. The framework presented in this chapter outlines the choices available for IT-sourcing decisions within such a market.

REFERENCES

Anonymous (2000a) "Emerging technology: Software development application service providers," *dotcomadvisor* (http://www.mcleanreport.com/), 20 September.

Anonymous (2000b) "The same old mouse trap," *CIO* (http://www.cio.com/archive/101500/confidential).

Bove, T. (2001) *EAI: Providing Stability in the Whirlwind of e-Commerce* (http://eai.ebizq.net/str/bove_1.html).

Cornfield, E. (2001) *The Next Wave of Opportunity for Service Providers and Their Partners*, Keynote Address at the xSP-World Conference, The Solution Provider Institute, Boston.

Dutta A. (2001) "Business planning for network services: A systems thinking approach," *Information Systems Research*, **12**(3), September, 260–283.

E. Inc. (2002) *Press Release* (www.exult.net/Press_Events/exult_pressrelease_120999.htm).

Gillan, C.S., G.M. Levitt, J. McArthur, S. Murray, V. Turner, R. Villars, and M. Whalen (1999) *The ASPs' Impact on the IT Industry: An IDC-wide Opinion*, International Data Corporation, Boston, MA.

Gilpin, M. (2001) *Giga ETS Polling Results: Web Servicers Early Adopters*, Report RPA 122001-00013, Giga Information Services, Cambridge, MA.

Hagel III, J. and J.S. Brown (2001) "Your next IT strategy," *Harvard Business Review*, Article # R0109G, October, 105–113.

Harrod, R.F. (1936) *The Trade Cycle: An Essay*, 1961 reprint, Augustus M. Kelley, New York.

HET (2001) *History of Economic Thought*, New School of Social Research, New York (http://homepage.newschool.edu/het/).

Hirschheim, R. and M. Lacity (2000) "The myths and realities of information technology insourcing," *Communications of the ACM*, **43**(2), 99–108.

Jaruzelski, B., F. Ribeiro, and R. Lake (2000) *ASP101: Understanding the Application Service Provider Model*, Booz, Allen & Hamilton, New York.

Joglekar, N. and P. Balasubramanian (2002) *Dynamics Sourcing of Information Services*, Boston University, Boston.

Kontzer, T. (2000) "Pandesic calls it quits," *InformationWeek*, July.

Lacity, M. and R. Hirschheim (1993) *Information Systems Outsourcing: Myths, Metaphors and Realities*, John Wiley & Sons, Chichester, UK.

Lacity, M. and L. Willcocks (1998) "An empirical investigation of information technology sourcing practices: Lessons from experience," *MIS Quarterly*, **22**(3), 363–409.

Leong, N. (2000) *Application Service Providers: A Market Overview*, Internet Research Group, Los Altos, CA.

Linthicum, D. (2000) *Enterprise Application Integration*, Addison-Wesley, Upper Saddle River, NJ.

McKie, S. (1999) "Outsourcing with ASPs in the internet age," *Business Finance* (http://www.businessfinancemag.com/archives/appfiles/Article.cfm?IssueID = 304& ArticleID = 13186).

Shapiro, C. and H.R. Varian (1999) *Information Rules: A Strategic Guide to the Network Economy*, Harvard Business School Press, Boston.

Slavid, P. (2000) "It's time for an ASP reality check" http://www.aspnews.com/analysis/analyst_cols/article/0,2350,4431_391851,00.html).

Sun Microsystems Website (2002) www.sun.com/products-n-solutions/software/oe-platforms/java2ee.html

Terdiman, R. (2000a) *ASPs: What Are the Current Marketplace Trends?*, Research Note, 11 January, GartnerGroup, Stamford, CT.

Terdiman, R. (2000b) *What Is a 'True' ASP?*, Research Note, 30 June, GartnerGroup, Stamford, CT.

Terdiman, R., A.E. Paulak, L. Stone, and T. Berg (2000) *Application Service Providers: 2000 and Beyond*, Strategic Analysis Report, 19 June, GartnerGroup, Stamford, CT.

Terdiman, R. and T. Berg (2000) *Application Sourcing: Application Service Providers, Legacy Systems and More*, Strategic Analysis Report, 20 October, Stamford, CT; GartnerGroup.

Venkatramen, N. (1997) "Beyond outsourcing: Managing IT resources as a value center," *Sloan Management Review*, **38**, Spring.

Weller, T. (1999) *Application Hosting Market*, 2 August, Legg Mason Equity Research, Baltimore, MD.

16
IT Architecture for Enterprise Flexibility

Companies today are placing increasing demands on their information technology (IT) organizations to deliver technology that can help them keep up with and react to rapidly changing market conditions. "Flexibility" is the new buzzword for guaranteeing business success and competitive advantage. But creating and delivering flexible IT—which is generally understood to include hardware, software, applications, data, and communications (among others)—to support organizational change is easier said than done.

In the not-too-distant past, the role of the IT function was to create and manage structures of technology that would meet the needs of a stable, static organization. Cycles of change averaged five to seven years (Meta Group, 1997) and could be responded to *after* the change had occurred. More recently, IT has been asked to partner with senior executives to capture business changes *as they occur* and to match the IT strategy to them. Now, the changes in business are practically continual, and IT is being asked to understand the *future* business environment and to *predict* the infrastructures that will support it.

The pace of technological change has paralleled and even driven rapid business change. Whereas technologies used to be limited to a small number of vendors and have a useful life that could be measured in years, today the number of vendors and possible technologies has simply exploded and change is measured in "Web years" (i.e., three months). Thus, the IT options available to an organization today are almost unlimited and changing all the time.

It is clear to everyone that traditional approaches to designing the form and type of technology an organization uses, commonly known as its IT architecture, will not meet present and future conditions of change. Yet it is also clear that some structures and principles must be in place to direct the choices a company makes about its IT. IT managers are thus wrestling with two seemingly conflicting concepts: the need for concrete structure and direction, and the need to be flexible and constantly changing. The challenge for today's IT executives is therefore to develop an IT architecture that will guide but not limit IT choices, anticipate likely IT needs but not restrict the future, and accelerate the implementation of new technology without taking unacceptable risks (MacSweeney, 2001).

This chapter looks at whether it is possible for such a flexible IT architecture to be developed. It first examines the concepts of IT architecture and flexibility individually in more detail. Then it explores the linkages between the two, with particular emphasis on identifying the principles and best practices that make them work. Finally, a number of guidelines for managers have been identified to help them move their organizations forward toward a flexible architecture for IT.

WHAT IS AN ARCHITECTURE FOR IT?

To some people, the term *architecture* is an inappropriate one for today's business needs because it implies a design that is cast in concrete that cannot be altered or changed. Others, however, point out that, properly applied, architecture can mean just the opposite. By anticipating future uses, well-architected structures are easier to adapt because they have the tolerances and the features built into them that allow for growth and change. Focus group members pointed out that architecture becomes increasingly important as demands on a structure grow. Thus, a rope bridge in a jungle that supports occasional foot traffic does not need a complex architecture and would probably work without one. However, a major international airport with high volumes of traffic and high expectations of public safety must be highly designed to ensure that all aspects of its development meet present and future needs.

Organizations are often stuck in a quagmire of incompatible technologies resulting from "various internal and external groups operating independently of each other" (Koch, 1997). Business and technology pressures to adapt quickly have led to a variety of technology decisions and infrastructure investments, which in many cases have led to a "complex and fragile computing environment that is intolerant of change" (Meta Group, 1997). As new layers of technology of all types—from hardware to systems—have been added, organizations have actually become *more* intolerant to change because modifications are harder and more cumbersome to make. This problem has been compounded with the addition of the Internet and e-commerce to the mix (Silver, 2001; Sambamurthy and Zmud, 2000). Thus, there is a pressing need to develop a coherent strategy for managing all aspects of an organization's technology investment.

In construction, nothing of any size gets built without a blueprint. An architect, drawing on established industry principles and the needs of the building's owners, first provides a sketch, then drawings, and finally blueprints for a building's development. These act as tools to communicate the building's specifications to city authorities, owners, contractors, trades people, and interior designers. Similarly, an *IT architecture* can be defined as a blueprint for a company's IT. It follows a set of principles, standards, guidelines, and technologies that describe and direct an organization's technology design for the future. It also describes to executives, business managers, IT managers, technical specialists, and vendors, in increasing levels of detail, what needs to be built.

The term *IT architecture* is often thought of as referring to technical design issues only and therefore not being of much interest outside IT. In fact, an architecture for IT must reflect both the needs of business and the current potentialities of IT. Thus, there is a growing trend to reframe IT architecture into *enterprise architecture* (EA) to ensure that the joint influences of *both* business and technology are represented in it (Strassman, 1996; Herman, 2001). This term will be used throughout the rest of this chapter to preclude any confusion between the more inclusive and the narrower interpretations of an architecture for IT.

Business Influences on Enterprise Architecture

The type of business, its geographic layout, its management style, and the nature of its products and services will all affect the type of architecture a business needs, just as the type of function and location of a building dictates the architecture needed in construction. Furthermore, financial considerations, the business's stability, and its relationship to its customers and suppliers will influence the breadth and depth of technology needed. Each of these factors needs to be made explicit so that IT will be able to properly design the type of technical architecture needed to support the business.

There are six views of architecture that are necessary to generate the desired business results, only one of which is technical. The other five include:

- *The business view*—a model of the future enterprise showing it as a series of logical services linking internal and external clients (Herman, 2001; Anonymous, 2000).
- *The work view*—showing who will do what, where, when, and with what tools (Tapscott, 1993).
- *The information view*—describing the information requirements of the future organization (White, 2002).
- *The application view*—identifying what applications will support the work of the organization (Cubine, 2001).
- *The external view*—the technology, applications, and information needed to support an organization's external interactions with customers, suppliers, and partners (MacSweeney, 2001).

This is why focus group members commented that business people have an important role to play in developing an enterprise architecture and in influencing technical architecture. Strassman (1996) is particularly vehement on this point:

Enterprise design is unique ... adopting an EA is therefore one of the most urgent tasks for top executive management ... Never delegate creating the enterprise master design plan for information systems to computer experts for they will judge it only on its technical merits.

The Technology View of an Enterprise Architecture

Technology naturally plays an important role in developing an EA. A technical architecture has three conceptual layers:

1. *Application environments.* This is where the work of the business is done. This layer consists of procedure groups to which IT can be applied, which are naturally linked and common across several parts of an organization (e.g., customer interaction, document storage and retrieval, and desktop toolkit). These groupings provide a critical link for connecting the business views of architecture and technology (i.e., they integrate what is desirable with what is possible technically).
2. *Technology environments.* Each application environment will require certain technology services to support it, such as user interface management, information management, desktop management, Internet/intranet management, transaction management, operating systems, and communications management. Technology environments are implemented using a variety of system software and a variety of sourcing strategies (McKeen et al., 2002). Ideally, they should be based on industry standards.
3. *Technology platforms.* Hardware is also needed to support an application environment. Platforms are closely linked to particular technology environments and include processors and servers, local and wide area networks, switching systems, and, more recently, peer-to-peer and mobile technologies (Smith et. al. 2002).

An enterprise architecture thus provides the context for how technology will be used in a business. From a business point of view, it supports and facilitates business strategy by ensuring that the information, tools, and applications needed to create information for the running of the business are identified and available as necessary. From an IT point of view, it is a means of selecting appropriate technologies and applications and of ensuring that individual projects are conforming to larger organizational and industry directions. In short, an EA is the best means of identifying what technology needs to be in place for a business and when.

WHAT IS FLEXIBILITY?

Flexibility in IT is something executives have been demanding for years, but it took on new imperatives in the lean, mean 1990s. Flexibility is generally used to refer to the ability or the potential of an organization to adapt or change. But how this ability is interpreted by managers varies widely. Upton (1995) notes that, at minimum, it involves three things:

- the ability to respond to customers (users) quickly;
- the ability to introduce new products or services quickly;
- the ability to provide a broad range of existing products and services.

The increasing need for flexibility is being driven by shrinking product cycles. In the past 10 years, cycle times have shrunk from around 5 to 7 years to between 12 to 24 months (Meta Group, 1997; MacSweeney, 2001). Thus, business processes are having to change more rapidly too.

In fact, according to Prager (1996), in a world of continuous change, flexibility is becoming equivalent to stability:

> ... in a rapidly changing market, stability really means long-term, healthy survival ... Flexible employees also create a sense of stability because they feel more secure knowing their organization can readily adapt to change.

But why are product cycles shrinking? Baldwin and Clark (1997) explain that increasingly complex products and processes are being developed in a *modular* fashion. That is, they are being built from smaller components that are designed independently, but which function as a whole because their interfaces are clearly specified. The adoption of modularity in product/service development is driving a number of important changes in organizations:

- *innovation* is increasing;
- the *rate of change* is increasing;
- *complexity* is increasing, as is the organization's ability to deal with complex products/services;
- *relationships between companies* are changing as individual companies become responsible for designing products or producing individual modules;
- *flexibility* is increasing.

The key to being flexible in any part of the organization is therefore to develop strategies based on *modularity* (Baldwin and Clark, 1997). Modularity emphasizes loose linkages or intentional independence between individual components. Changes in one component therefore do not affect other components. This increases adaptability. At a design level, modularity emphasizes standard interfaces between components enabling individual components to be substituted without completely redesigning the overall product. This enables mixing and matching of components to create a large number of variations, again increasing flexibility and adaptability (Sanchez and Mahoney, 1996).

Interestingly, the converse of flexibility is integration. Koch (1997) writes: "As business pushes IT to integrate more and more systems and information, IT is unable to respond quickly and spends an increasing amount of time customizing and maintaining system[s]." Similarly, Upton (1995) found that, where technology is primarily designed to deliver information or improve quality, "the additional complexity resulting from computer integration has been a competitive millstone around companies' necks."

Thus, what may appear to be a cohesive, integrated solution now may look like a tangled mess in the future. In the focus group's opinion, today's companies are still focusing too much on dealing with inter-application chaos, rather than planning for it. Again, what's needed is a coherent strategy for managing technology flexibility at a corporate level (Brown et al., 2000). This is where architecture comes in.

DEVELOPING A FLEXIBLE ARCHITECTURE

If the key to flexibility is modularity, then a flexible architecture must be modular. While IT has practiced modular design in its systems for some time, these same principles are only recently being systematically applied to the overall organizational and technical framework of the organization (Brown et al., 2000). A flexible architecture establishes an overall structure of modules, functions, interfaces, and standards, within which business and technical teams can operate independently. By specifying the *outputs* required, each component can be partitioned into tasks that can occur autonomously and concurrently. The information provided in a modular architecture thus provides the embedded coordination needed for simultaneous development on a number of fronts.

Organizations need to have three things in order to develop a flexible enterprise architecture:

- *principles*—basic precepts that must be agreed on in order for the architecture's development to be effective;
- *practices*—actions that should be followed to establish the architecture;
- *implementation guidelines*—ideas to make the introduction of an architecture easier.

Principles

Several over-arching principles must guide any flexible EA initiative. First, in order for an architecture to be effective in achieving flexibility, its primary goal must be adaptability. Other considerations, such as cost, performance, user-friendliness, risk, and response time, while important, must be secondary. Companies have to be prepared to accept these tradeoffs to achieve competitive advantage when short cycle times are the driving force behind organizational success (DeBoever and Buchanan, 1997). Upton (1995) notes that flexibility is rarely achieved unless it is a specifically stated goal and unless managers give up their focus on other factors that have nothing to do with flexibility.

Architecture principles

- Flexibility must be the *primary* goal.

- People must be integral to its development.

- Each enterprise architecture is unique.

- An enterprise architecture is never finished.

- Knowledge is critical to both flexibility and an effective architecture.

- Standardization is essential.

- A flexible architecture takes effort and investment.

Second, as we have noted, there is a symbiotic relationship between technical and non-technical factors in an EA. This integration is essential at all levels and in all parts of an architecture's development. People make decisions about architecture. All too often, both business and technical decisions can be made for reasons other than flexibility. In addition, people skills such as effective business communications, and social skills are essential to developing the necessary partnerships to anticipate change. IT staff must be able to do such things as: educate users about technology; continuously seek input from the business; tactfully question the need for applications or technology; and understand the change cycle. Finally, people make the process work. It is critical to get a buy-in to the overall strategy from both IT staff and users at all levels. Without it, any architectural effort will fail, regardless of the quality of the design.

A third principle is that each organization must develop its own architecture and make the tough underlying decisions required to make it work in their business. Architectural development is not something that can be done *for* a company. Strassman (1996) points out that there is no such thing as a standard IT architecture (although generic architectures may be a good starting point for some companies). Each is unique because each company functions differently.

Fourth, an enterprise architecture is never finished. DeBoever and Buchanan (1997) note that "architecture efforts are so agonizing that no one wants to undergo them twice." Nevertheless, it is a fundamental principle of a flexible architecture that it must be approached in an ongoing and iterative fashion. Without this evolutionary dimension, it will become a static, concrete entity that will either lose its relevance or become a barrier to change. They suggest having an ongoing architectural advisory board that regularly feeds new requirements, criticism, and breakthrough ideas to those responsible for the architecture. Many focus group companies have a central architecture committee composed of users as well as IT managers to continually review new trends and technologies from both the business and IT points of view.

Fifth, knowledge is a necessary precondition to flexibility because it enables the making of predictions, causal associations, and prescriptive decisions (Bohn, 1994). An effective architecture requires a high level of knowledge about how its components function and interact (Olin, 1999). Knowledge about different components of an architecture can be highly variable. Ideally, we want to maximize our knowledge before decisions are made, but, in practice, we usually have to work with incomplete information. Nevertheless, knowledge acquisition (learning) can be managed to make it faster and more effective. Baldwin and Clark (1997) recommend undertaking deliberate activities to promote learning, especially in those areas that will have significant economic implications for a company. These in turn will have a direct impact on improved organizational knowledge and thus better decisions.

Sixth, standardization is essential. Standardized interfaces are the most important way to achieve both increased flexibility and inter-organizational connectivity (Sanchez and Mahoney, 1996). Selecting hardware and software that follow industry standards is the ideal because these enable complete connectivity and vendor independence, both of which are essential to flexibility. While architecture is more than standards, standards are essential to both portability (i.e., the ability to transfer hardware or software from one environment to another) and to interoperability (i.e., the ability to exchange information with other hardware and software).

Finally, a flexible architecture takes effort and investment. Focus group members emphasized that flexible architectures must be something in which companies are prepared to invest time and money. Without resources from both IT and business, an EA will not happen. All too frequently, architecture can get sidelined in the struggle to deal with more immediate day-to-day problems. There is a perceived conflict between architecture and short-term operational goals, which must be overcome if a company is going to make the necessary investment in architecture. It is therefore incumbent on IT managers to communicate the reasons for building an EA and its value to the company. To engage executives' attention, this value must be communicated in business rather than technical terms and should focus on the strategic advantages an architecture can deliver to the organization as a whole.

Practices

The lack of a process whereby organizations can design an effective architecture has been a fundamental barrier to the adoption of architecture in organizations (Brown et al., 2000). Ideally, an EA should follow a process including conceptualization, analysis, design, implementation, and optimization steps. At present, few members of the focus group are following a formal EA development process. There are five basic steps that should be covered:

1. *Determine the preferred direction.* The first step in getting anything done is to know where you are going. This starts with a series of fundamental beliefs about the architecture that are understandable to both IT and business managers; for example, "Our architecture should utilize standard, shareable, and reusable components across the enterprise." Then, these high-level fundamentals are used to further develop an architectural direction from the five different, but linked, perspectives outlined above.

2. *Describe the current (baseline) architecture.* Once you know where you are going, it is also important to know where you are beginning. Most organizations are coping with a hodgepodge of applications and technologies. Very few have the luxury of a "green field" approach to architecture. Legacy systems, practices, and technologies therefore must be identified and understood as collectively forming the *de facto* enterprise architecture of the organization. All efforts to develop a future EA must start from this base.

3. *Identify gaps and develop standards, guidelines and interfaces.* This step refines the preferred direction by adding more detail to the architectural framework outlined in Step 1. Models of the target architecture are developed to describe its benefits and capabilities to both business and technical audiences. This step is key, stressed focus group members. Unless the business value of an architecture can be communicated, something else of higher priority will always come before it. Benefits could include: tangible savings from minimizing duplication; enabling reusable code, data, and processes; improved ability to adapt to change; disaster avoidance; and the speed with which the organization can respond to change. More detailed standards and guidelines should then be developed to further describe the target architecture. These should emphasize such things as how interfaces are controlled, creating a loosely-coupled design, and presenting a single image to the user (DeBoever and Buchanan, 1997). The locations of knowledge in the company should also be understood and carefully designed (White, 2002).

4. *Develop a migration plan.* This step outlines a plan to close the gap between the current and the target architectures. Typically, it involves a series of stages that allow benefits and costs to be gradually realized. Priority should be given to external processing and information in implementation because it is this part of the architecture that concerns the revenue of the organization (Strassman, 1996; Silver, 2001). The focus group recommended balancing control of applications programs and software in several layers in the organization in ways that reflect human working relationships. As the plan is implemented, it is important to continually assess it to accommodate experience and ongoing business and technology changes (Brown et al., 2000; Laartz et al., 2000).

5. *Manage the evolution of the architecture.* Because change is occurring continually, an organization's architecture must also evolve, and its evolution must be carefully managed. Procedures must be put in place to identify new tools, technologies, practices, and products that may affect the organization and how to integrate them appropriately. These should include special advisory groups

(see above) whose responsibility it is to look for and identify changes that could affect the organization.

Finally, measurements must be established to evaluate whether the architecture is doing its job. The most important measure is flexibility. Focus group members felt that the speed with which an organization can respond to change should be the key measure of effectiveness. This can be measured by such things as the speed with which applications can be delivered once requested or by assessing the number of function points delivered per person-month.

Implementation Guidelines

Focus group managers came up with a number of dos and don'ts, which, from their experience, made an enormous difference in the effectiveness of the architectural effort:

- *DO communicate value.* Without a real understanding of what an architecture is doing for the organization, investment in architecture will always have a tendency to lose out to more immediate needs in both business and IT.
- *DO build trust.* Users who cannot trust architects to understand their needs will not support an architecture effort. Building this relationship is central to an effective architecture initiative.
- *DO focus on coordination.* This is the means by which individual teams developing parts of the architecture are kept on track. This is also how hidden requirements or information are revealed.
- *DO learn carefully and systematically.* Try things out. Learn what works and what doesn't. Establish a means where learning about business and learning about technology is formalized and communicated. Some ways this can be done are through prototyping, simulation, and learning from other organizations with similar situations.
- *DO change attitudes about how technology should be controlled.* Any EA design will probably never be fully achieved before it will need to be changed. As technical expertise becomes more widespread in organizations, complete control of IT is unrealistic. Instead, IT staff should recognize user-developed applications and user-implemented technology as the road signs of change that tell IT what's really going on in the organization.
- *DO seek continuous input.* Formal architecture-monitoring groups are important, but informal observation can often frequently be an effective means of predicting change. Without an ongoing effort in this area, it is easy for IT to become misaligned with business.
- *DO deliver.* Doing what is promised is a key means of building trust and credibility. Many organizations start small with architecture projects to develop the mutual commitment it will take to undertake an enterprise

architecture project. Once success has been demonstrated in a small way, it will be much easier to move to a more encompassing effort.

- *DON'T attach architecture to a single project.* Focus group members were adamant that trying to grow a complete architecture on the back of a single project would result in an inadequate and inappropriate architecture. While it is tempting to try to get architectural work done in the context of a project because of the business's skepticism about its value, the imperatives of a single project will likely drive the results. Architecture does play an important role in guiding how individual projects develop, however, and architectural reviews should be part of every project.

- *DON'T forget about legacy systems.* While it is difficult to apply architecture to legacy systems, they form an important part of most organizations' existing technology. Migration paths must be planned for these systems.

- *DON'T turn architecture into a list of approved products.* While product lists are important, DeBoever and Buchanan (1997) note that different development teams can use the same products radically differently. Architecture must also provide guidance about how to use these products to achieve the goals of the enterprise.

- *DON'T fail to do ongoing planning.* As has been shown, enterprise architecture is not a monolithic concrete structure. A flexible architecture, by definition, is always changing, and organizations need mechanisms to identify and capture new ideas and criticisms.

THE ROLE OF THE ARCHITECT

Who actually designs and implements an organization's EA? This is a question that many companies in the focus group are wrestling with. While the standard answer is that an IT architect is the key player in this process, few people are sure of what an architect should do and what skills he or she should have. As a result, there was a lot of disagreement among focus group members on this question. One company is trying to define exactly what an architect delivers and how he should effectively contribute to ongoing projects. Others have yet to create this role, preferring to split it between a number of technology specialists and managers. Still others have created full architecture groups, which they are trying to integrate more closely into the realities of their business. In the absence of a clearly defined role, it is up to each individual organization to make proactive decisions about how the architectural function should evolve.

The position of the architect is a very powerful one because he or she is the creator of the visible design rules (i.e., those decisions that affect all subsequent design decisions: Baldwin and Clark, 1997), and the architect must know a great deal about the inner workings of the overall organization or process he or she is designing. As a result, it is a very personalized role. Both the characteristics of the individual and the organization must be taken into consideration. There are three fundamental aspects of an architect's job:

1. The architect is first of all a catalyst or facilitator. He or she must work at the highest levels in the organization to interpret and document the overall business context in which the architecture will be developed. At this stage, the architect must be business-oriented, be able to communicate clearly, and be able to establish good working relationships with senior management.
2. At the same time, the architect must work within IT to explore the overall technical context within which the organization will function. Not only must the architect understand the technical issues involved, he or she must also be able to communicate them and their implications clearly to business managers. In this aspect of the job, the architect needs both technical knowledge and communication skills. Because both aspects of the architecture must be developed synchronously, the architect plays a key interpretive role translating business needs into technical principles, standards and guidelines, and technology issues to business people.
3. Like a building architect, the IT architect must understand both form and function at increasing levels of detail and be able to work with a team to turn vision into reality. The architect must provide packaged technical environments within which applications-developers can work. This involves matching appropriate technology to the work, applications, and information users need. It also involves ensuring that the basic principles of flexibility are adhered to in business and technical decisions and in projects. Finally, following the development of an architecture, it is the architect's job to monitor and refine it, paying particular attention to signs of change—both technically and in the business—that will affect the architecture.

CONCLUSION

An enterprise architecture is an essential precondition to attaining the kind of flexibility that business requires. However, most focus group members feel that implementing it is still a "leap of faith" because there are so many unknowns and challenges involved. Without a true understanding of the role, value, and deliverables of an EA at all levels in the organization, it is easy to see how architecture could be perceived as just another "flaky, IT ivory tower activity" with no real benefit to the organization. IT management's first job therefore is to educate both itself and business managers about enterprise architecture and what it can do for the organization. Its second job is to demonstrate in some small, but tangible ways the value that architecture can bring to a company. It is only after these two steps have been taken that it is likely that business will be prepared to invest the time and effort to make a full enterprise-wide architecture work.

REFERENCES

Anonymous (2000) "Information architecture practice: An interview with Seth Gordon Zefer," *Bulletin of the American Society for Information Science*, August–September, **26**(6).

Baldwin, C. and K. Clark (1997) "Managing in an age of modularity," *Harvard Business Review*, September–October.

Bohn, R. (1994) "Measuring and managing technological knowledge," *Sloan Management Review*, Fall.

Brown, G., M. Fisher, N. Stoll, and D. Deeksma (2000) "Using the lessons of Y2K to improve information systems architecture," *Communications of the ACM*, October, **43**(10).

Cubine, M. (2001) "Paper industry IT architectures: Putting the software pieces together," *Pulp and Paper*, April, **75**(4).

DeBoever, L. and R. Buchanan (1997) "Three architectural sins," *CIO*, 1 May.

Herman, J. (2001) "Creating a business architecture," *Business Communications Review*, December, **31**(12).

Koch, C. (1997) "Sounding the alarm," *CIO*, 15 November.

Laartz, J., A. Scherdin, D. Cafarelli, and K. Hjatar (2000) "Evolve your architecture," *CIO*, 15 September, **13**(25).

MacSweeney, G. (2001) "Building IT for the customer economy," *Insurance and Technology*, 15 November, **26**(13).

McKeen, J., H. Smith, N. Joglekar, and P. Balasubramanian (2002) "IT sourcing: Make, buy or build?" *Communications of the Association of Information Systems (CAIS)*, September, **9**(8), 120–135.

Meta Group (1997) *Enterprise Architecture Strategies: An IT Foundation for Rapid Change*, Meta Group, Stamford, CT.

Olin, J. (1999) "Knowledge management across multi-tier enterprises: The promise of intelligent software in the auto industry," *European Management Journal*, August, **17**(4).

Prager, K. (1996) "Managing for flexibility: The new role of the aligned IT organization," *Information Systems Management*, Fall.

Sambamurthy, V. and B. Zmud (2000) "The organizing logic for an enterprise's IT activities in the digital era—a prognosis of practice and a call for research," *Information Systems Research*, June, **11**(2).

Sanchez, R. and J. Mahoney (1996) "Modularity, flexibility and knowledge management in product and organization design," *Strategic Management Journal*, **17**, Winter.

Silver, B. (2001) "Process automation meets the e-business era," *Bank Systems and Technology*, **38**(5), May.

Smith, H., N. Kulatilaka, and N. Venkatramen (2002) "New developments in practice III: Riding the wave—extracting value from mobile technology," *Communications of the Association for Information Systems*, **8**.

Strassman, P. (1996) *The Politics of Information Management*, Information Economics Press, New Canaan, CT.

Tapscott, D. (1993) *Paradigm Shift: The New Promise of Technology*, McGraw-Hill, New York.

Upton, D. (1995) "What really makes factories flexible?" *Harvard Business Review*, July–August.

White, M. (2002) "Information architecture and usability," *Econtent*, April, **25**(4).

17
Enterprise Application Integration*

Enterprise application integration (EAI)—the plans, methods, and tools aimed at modernizing, consolidating, and coordinating the computer applications within an enterprise—has suddenly become a hot topic. Given that the need to integrate across applications is an age-old challenge, one might wonder why EAI suddenly finds itself under the spotlight. For the answer, you need only to look at yourself—and your behavior and expectations—in your role as a customer of any company. Your relationship with your bank, for instance, is most likely via a *browser* where you *expect* to be provided access to the full range of banking services conveniently *integrated* on a single screen ("mybank.com") allowing you to query the status of your checking/savings/investment accounts, reconfigure your mortgage, buy/sell stocks/bonds/funds directly, transfer money to other accounts (not necessarily at your branch *or even your bank*), enact payments (automatically and/or electronically), take advantage of bill consolidation and presentation ... and expect this to be done *instantaneously*. The fact that these transactions cross multiple business lines, require coordination among many applications/databases resident on different technology platforms with different architectures and must be done perfectly (consider how delighted you would be as a customer if your bank reported your account balances correctly *most of the time!*) is of very little concern to you. As a customer, you have come to expect this level of service. There is little doubt that the impetus behind EAI is the business need to respond to customer demand.

EAI, however, is not an easy problem to solve. Maybe that is why it has been an ongoing, continuous struggle. Paul Margolis, past Chairman of the Open

* McKeen, J.D. and H.A. Smith (2002) "Enterprise application integration," *Communications of the Association of Information Systems (CAIS)*, June, **8**(31), 451–466 (reproduced by permission of the Association for Information Systems).

Applications Group (OAG, Inc.—a consortium of major enterprise resource planning (ERP) vendors formed to create open interface standards so that all the member companies' products can talk to one another), draws the following analogy:

> Imagine if you didn't have common electric outlets and plugs in your house and every time you bought a new appliance, you had to wire up the appliance to the wires in your wall. And everybody's wires in everybody's walls were different. And everybody's appliance wiring was different. That's really the way it works today with trying to integrate business software applications (Koch, 1996).

Unfortunately, this analogy is not so far-fetched. It is common in most organizations to have multiple applications (custom, legacy, and packaged), multiple platforms, multiple databases, multiple transaction processors, multiple data entry points, multiple versions of the same data, and incompatible business data. This state has evolved over time as waves of new technology have swept over the landscape. Different groups operating independently of each other have built application systems at different times. Early programs in areas such as inventory control, human resources, sales automation, and management were designed to run independently, with no interaction between the systems. They were custom-built in the technology of the day for a specific need and were often proprietary systems. As a result, organizations are stuck with incompatible architectures and hard-to-maintain, but even harder to eliminate, legacy applications. In addition, organizations have embraced a "buy before build" strategy that favors purchased application packages over internal development—a practice that is vulnerable to the proliferation of different standards. The problem is severe. One focus group company discovered that:

> 70% of their code consists of interfaces, protocols, and other procedures to link applications. They also found that 30–40% of their development time is spent building interfaces rather than increasing functionality.

The first section of this chapter describes the integration problem and its genesis. The second section describes the four levels of integration where EAI can be focused. Following that is a presentation and categorization of the EAI technology. The final section of the chapter outlines a number of strategies for managing the EAI effort.

UNDERSTANDING EAI

According to Bove (2001), the driving factor behind the push to achieve EAI is the need to redirect systems:

> In the 1950s and early 1960s, systems were used to reduce costs and headcount by automating rote tasks as part of a predominantly static and structured approach to corporate growth. During the 1980s and 1990s, business practices shifted toward

the concepts of stability, repeatability, return on long-term investments and economies of scale . . . In today's digital economy, these dynamics are passé. Existing and emerging Internet technology enables—and capital markets reward—innovation, decisiveness, rapid response and (over the long haul) excellence in execution. The ability of companies to completely infuse and develop these Internet-ready characteristics into information systems used by all their employees—across the board and in every department, from the loading dock to marketing and sales and to customer service—will separate the winners from the losers.

What is needed is 24/7 availability, instantaneous scalability, personalized easy-to-use self-service systems, and fast and unerring transaction-processing that customers demand. This can only be achieved when applications within the organization work together to route and transform information in response to service requests originating from customers, suppliers, and/or employees. This redirection of systems will be possible only by integrating the disparate, disconnected applications that are used within organizations to automate business processes.

But how did we get to the point of having disparate, disconnected applications? Was this the result of poor technology choices? Was it a planning failure? Was it a lack of standards? Doesn't EAI represent just another layer of software that in time will contribute to the problem? And, while we are on the topic, whose fault is it anyway? According to the focus group, business managers often ask these very questions. Finding answers to them is necessary in order to gain an understanding of the problems associated with integrating business applications within an enterprise. What is readily apparent is that the "problem" did not suddenly appear. It has been in existence since the start of information technology (IT). It just worsens in direct proportion to the number and size of business applications. And, with IT enabling (if not driving) most organizational initiatives, application portfolios have grown dramatically over the years, sharply increasing the need for (and challenge posed by) integration. It should be pointed out that EAI exists because it embraces the diversity ("heterogeneity") that will always be part of businesses, considers it an inevitable part of large-scale systems design and development, and serves as the connection/broker/translator linking autonomously designed applications into a cohesive whole.

Every year organizations launch new applications. New technology (hardware, software, methodology) replaces old technology. New standards replace old standards. Yet, it is impossible to upgrade all applications continuously. In fact, it would be imprudent to attempt to do so. As a result, the typical applications portfolio consists of a blend of old and new technology. Superimposed on this situation is the imperative that businesses must continually change to meet the evolving needs of customers, suppliers, and employees. To do so sometimes requires new applications but more often requires integration across existing databases, applications, technology platforms, and lines of business. Applications are almost never autonomous; data and transactions are constantly transferred among different systems within an enterprise and outside to its trading partners.

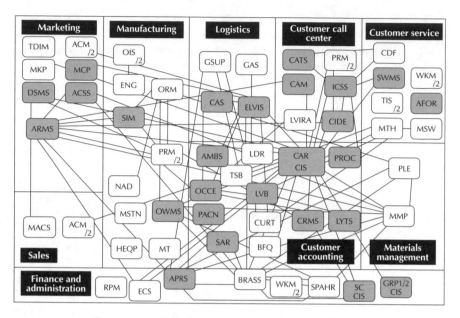

Figure 17.1   *Typical interactions among business applications.*

The application integration challenge, arguably the most critical challenge facing IT today, will continue into the foreseeable future. The bright side is that, for those organizations that manage to integrate applications effectively, financial rewards will result from their ability to effectively leverage their investment in IT.

Standards play an important role in application integration. Without standards, the ability to integrate across applications is reduced to unique, handcrafted solutions. With standards in place (and rigorously imposed), the costs of integration in terms of expended effort and time-to-market are drastically reduced. The adoption of standards (pertaining to programming techniques, languages, hardware, software, or methodologies) is therefore crucial to the ability to integrate applications, but it does not obviate the need for application integration[1]. The real integration problem facing IT managers derives less from the *standardization* of communications than from the *volume* of communications. Figure 17.1 depicts a typical (*and much simplified*) application portfolio. As the number of applications increases, the number of possible interconnections increases *exponentially*! Until recently, these inter-application connections have been handled on a one-to-one basis, often hard-coded within applications. The result has driven up the level of

---

[1] According to GartnerGroup (2001), "standards are powerful tools for system architects and vendors to use, where practical. Some of the standards are well on their way to making a difference in how we build systems; others will make a difference in how we connect systems. To claim that a standard will make application integration moot or easy is to take a good thing and perhaps take it too far."

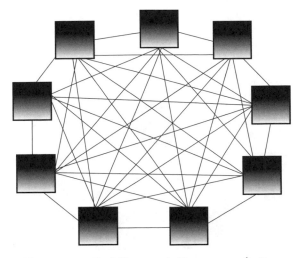

Figure 17.2   *Pre-EAI communication among applications.*

complexity within the application portfolio to the point that changes to a single application can wreak unforeseen havoc on other applications connected through a vast web of interrelationships.

Theoretically, the solution to this complexity rests with componentization, decoupling, and standardized interfaces. Applications-developers have known (and deployed) these techniques for years within applications. It is now accepted practice to invoke standardized routines/objects, calls to databases, and GUI front-ends from within applications. With EAI, the same strategy is applied only at a different level—where some of the process (and translation, workflow, and communication) logic is removed from individual applications and reconstituted centrally. This effectively decouples individual applications and orchestrates communication through legitimate channels. This difference is depicted as a "before EAI" picture in Figure 17.2 and a "with EAI" picture in Figure 17.3.

It is evident that new software (called middleware, discussed later) plays a key role in the struggle to integrate across existing applications. As with any software product, it too ages and becomes "legacy". As such, the question is legitimately raised that this additional layer of software is really just paving over the problem and not eliminating it (or even fixing it), and, in time, will become part of the problem instead of the solution. The response by the focus group members was unanimous. First, they quickly acknowledged the fact that today's software is tomorrow's legacy. This was accepted as fact. There was little interest, however, in the search for universal and timeless solutions. Second, they pointed out that the middleware software offerings comprise some very powerful tools, which enable the integration of a number of otherwise disparate systems with relative ease. As a result, the return on this investment is both substantial and evident. Third, the middleware itself imposes development standards that applications

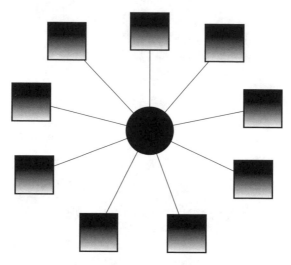

Figure 17.3   *Communications among applications using EAI.*

must adhere to in order for integration to be realized. Fourth, as has been argued, middleware attacks complexity directly by offering tools to manage inter-application communication (and translation and workflow) by decoupling individual applications. Finally, they argued that, because the need for application integration represented such an enormous challenge for virtually every organization in existence, there is a huge incentive for software vendors to continue to develop products to address it. In fact, GartnerGroup (2001) estimates the worldwide market size for middleware in 2005 will be $11.1 billion. As such, middleware tools, as good as they are today, will only improve.

THE FOUR TARGETS OF EAI

An analysis of the four possible targets of integration (data, application, process, and inter-organizational) is useful for managers to help them to understand their greatest needs and subsequently to better focus their EAI initiatives. Experience has shown that comprehensive EAI strategies need to focus on more than a single target. For instance, application integration without data integration would provide only part of the solution; and application integration without process integration would fall far short of the goals of EAI. With full recognition of the interrelationships among these different foci, vendors are beginning to develop tools that span these areas. The categorization that follows, partially based on work by Linthicum (2001), outlines each of the four main focal points for EAI:

- *Data-level integration.* Historically, applications were designed with their own unique data structures making it difficult to share data with other applications (e.g., purchasing uses different product codes than inventory). This problem was solved in the past by hard-coding data format translation programs or by writing file transfer programs to replicate and reconcile data from each application's database in order to build a single "logical" database that all the integrated applications could access. Data warehousing tools soon appeared that facilitated *replication* (the moving of data between two or more databases while honoring schematic/model differences) and *federation* (the integration of multiple databases and database models into a single unified view of the databases). Today, advanced data integration products not only perform required transformations and normalization of data from different applications but often can dynamically route and distribute data based on a set of pre-configured rules. Data-level integration is not just limited to data and databases but also includes distributed objects (i.e., the combination of data, logic, and communications within a single entity). By means of a distributed architecture, objects can be combined to execute whole business functions producing an elegant (some would argue the ultimate) integration approach.

- *Application-level integration.* Beyond the data-level integration, there is a need to link diverse applications in order to accomplish specific business processes (e.g., opening a new account might involve credit-checking, billing, work-processing, etc.). In the 1980s, application integration was achieved by the two-tier, client–server computing paradigm that amalgamated the user interfaces of multiple server applications into a single client-based interface, allowing users to interact with the multiple applications from a single screen. Another approach was simply to write hard-coded, point-to-point interfaces that allowed the business logic in one application to call the business logic of another application as if that logic were part of the calling application. This has come to be known as A2A integration.[2] Today, A2A integration is facilitated by means of *infrastructure software* and application adapters. The most popular type of infrastructure software is referred to as messaging-oriented middleware (MOM). These message brokers transport information ("messages") between applications by identifying, transforming, and routing messages to the appropriate applications on an event-driven, asynchronous basis. They tend to be focused on the back-end operations and process-oriented applications within firms. As organizations attempt to meet the online, 24/7 requirements of Internet customers and partners by adopting zero-latency, straight-through processing, MOM unfortunately often proves inadequate (Bove, 2001). Instead, enhanced capability is required to manage distribution, back-up, load-balancing, and system capacity to deal effectively with inter-application communication. Application-specific *adapters* enable the

---

[2] The key advantage of A2A EAI is its focus on surfacing and integrating the application logic that implements business processes within an organization—the same business processes that e-commerce partners and customers need to interact with over the Web (Bove, 2001).

conversion between different types of application based on different technologies. Intra-vendor connections (e.g., linking a SAP R/3 application to a Baan application) are relatively straightforward with available adapters. Their advantage is to allow application independence and transparency while facilitating integration. Another integration tool—*screen scrapers*—allows input data captured in one application to be shared with other applications, thus effectively connecting many custom or packaged applications. Many of these tools are capable of accounting for differences among schema, content, and application semantics by translating the information moving between the systems in real time.

- *Process-level integration.* The next level of integration is to coordinate the flow of logic among the integrated applications. According to Bove (2001), "this is often achieved by writing a new program that calls the business logic of the integrated applications through their adapters. When this new application is executed, it calls each of the integrated applications in a sequence that corresponds with the flow of an enterprise-wide business process." Some writers refer to process-level integration as "event-oriented" or "transaction-oriented" integration where transactions/events provide the linkage among various applications. Examples of tools used to effect transaction integration include transaction processing (TP) monitors and application servers. This approach enables organizations to create common methods (e.g., transactions) and share those methods among many connected applications.

  Recognizing a universal need, software vendors have developed a new set of products to specifically address process-level integration. These offerings—business process automation products and application servers—are based on workflow technology. *Application servers* access the business logic exposed by adapters to be tied together into a cohesive, end-to-end transaction flow. They are focused on application development (i.e., the front-end) and are particularly good at supporting portal-oriented integration. The *business process automation products* provide useful management capabilities including tools for IT architects to model the flow of business logic using point-and-click techniques (rather than programming) to create a new enterprise-wide business process from the logic contained in a set of integrated applications (Bove, 2001).

- *Inter-organizational-level integration.* Process-level integration typically focuses on bringing together relevant processes found *within* an organization to obtain maximum value while supporting the flow of information and logic between these processes. To do this, a set of easily defined and centrally managed processes is layered on top of existing processes within a set of enterprise applications. The next step is to link processes *beyond* the organization to include trading partners—both suppliers and customers. Many organizations are already involved with business-to-business (B2B) initiatives that share/combine business logic. While this is a simple extension of the process-level integration, it represents another level of coordination, negotiation, and complexity and is therefore fraught with management challenges.

According to Linthicum (2001), "the ultimate goal is to bind all trading community systems together in such a way that any application can access any method or any piece of data without delay to support any business process."

THE EAI TOOLKIT

Like any clichéd buzzword, the term EAI has come to mean many different things to many different people. Nowhere is this more apparent than within vendor software offerings—typically referred to as "middleware". According to the GartnerGroup (2001), EAI middleware is runtime system software that directly enables interactions among independently designed applications in a distributed computing environment. For the sake of common definitions, the EAI market space as a whole is separated into four primary categories of software services/products (see below). This categorization is taken from Allen (2001), who notes that products in all these classes of software also include a variety of *adapters* that provide connectivity to leading applications, databases, and middleware. It should be noted that data-modeling technology and data-warehousing are vital parts of an EAI toolkit particularly for the data-integration level. They are not discussed here as they have been well described elsewhere:

- *Asynchronous event/message transport.* Typically referred to as MOM, these products enable asynchronous routing of business events between applications ... meaning that they can defer delivery of business events until applications are available. This facilitates loosely coupled relationships among applications—a fundamental design principle of EAI solutions.
- *Transformation engines.* These tools convert data and business events from one format to another. For example, a transformation engine could convert customer records from an ERP system into formats required by a "home-grown" customer service application. These are typically batch-oriented and operate at the database table or file level.
- *Integration brokers.* Also known as message brokers, these tools provide the ability to intelligently route and manipulate business events between multiple applications and data stores. For example, an integration broker could receive order requests from a Web-based application and route those requests to one or more target applications based on information in the order. The source event would be transformed into the format expected by the destination applications. Therefore, by definition, integration brokers also include data transformation services. Integration brokers support an event paradigm and deal with individual records, rows, or autonomous business events.
- *Business process management frameworks.* These tools, which enable business logic to be separated from process flow logic, consist of two distinct categories: process automation and workflow. *Process automation* products provide a framework that allows multiple, disparate software components to

participate in an integrated business process flow. *Workflow products* support a similar paradigm, but focus on process steps performed by human interactions with the system. As business events move through a process flow, they require routing and transformation services. Therefore, by definition, process automation/workflow frameworks also include either their own integration broker services or the ability to use the services of an external integration broker. Most of these products also contain *management* tools that monitor application processing and assist in identifying bottlenecks.

It should be noted that the ability of EAI tools to manage business processes is as much a business issue as a technology issue. According to one focus group member, "EAI software can help to automate task delivery/process control. This being the case, process and business knowledge *and* business influence is critical to the success of efforts that leverage EAI process capabilities. Choosing not to leverage process capabilities (like business ware) could point to the fact that organizations are not exploiting the full functionality/potential of EAI technology."

MANAGEMENT STRATEGIES FOR EAI

The following strategies for managing EAI were suggested by focus group members based on their experiences. All strategies are designed to be "near-term" ... meaning that they can all be started immediately with the expectation of yielding results within months.

1   Craft a Corporate Integration Strategy

EAI does/will not happen by itself. Nor does it stand much of a chance if left to one or two courageous individuals within the firm. Focus group members suggested that someone within IT has to first recognize the need for a concerted effort to approach EAI. They also suggested that this individual often resides within the IT architecture group (although not necessarily so). Once identified, this individual becomes the EAI *champion*. His or her first task is to gain the support of the senior IT executive team for the EAI initiative to begin. The next order of business is to craft an EAI strategy. According to focus group members, such a strategy has (at a minimum) the following parts performed in roughly the same order as they appear below:

- *Target strategic applications*. Identify the applications that require integration. Of these, decide which are strategic. For the strategic applications, conduct interviews with IT leaders and determine the specific integration needs for these applications. Non-strategic applications will benefit from EAI efforts eventually.

- *Do your homework.* Based on an analysis of these applications, identify the most appropriate levels to focus the integration effort and EAI toolkit best suited to meeting those needs. This step requires the champion to learn about EAI vendors, products, services, and the experiences of other organizations already investing in EAI. Someone has to become the in-house EAI expert.
- *Identify the "status quo" costs.* Based on these strategic applications, conduct scenario-planning to assess the costs of the "status quo"—let's keep on building applications the same way—approach. These costs should represent rough estimates of additional development, maintenance, and time-to-market costs associated with this approach.
- *Build the business case for EAI.* Again based on these strategic applications, map out the advantages of the planned EAI toolkit. Focus group members pointed out that vendors can (and should) play a role in this exercise. Be specific in terms of the exact functionality that EAI products can provide, and express these deliverables in business terms. Omit the "this will increase our productivity" arguments. Instead, base your arguments on things like, "this will enable our customer service reps to query the status of customers' orders, payments, and delivery schedules online."
- *Estimate resources.* An EAI initiative will require people, tools, new skills, education, and procedural and structural changes (more on this later) within IT. First, identify the individuals who will be directly involved with the EAI implementation effort. Then estimate the acquisition costs for the EAI toolkit (more on the EAI toolkit selection later), training costs, and effort needed to bring everyone in IT up to speed working with new EAI tools, the necessary architectural changes to the technical platforms, and the system installation and configuration.
- *Create a plan.* Identify the necessary tasks to integrate the previously identified strategic applications. Combine these tasks into a workable plan specifying the logical order of the work, a realistic time-frame for these changes to be achieved, and a preliminary benefits delivery schedule.
- *Sell the EAI strategy to management.* An EAI strategy will require senior IT management's full endorsement. As with other major initiatives within IT, EAI must be presented convincingly to senior management. This presentation should be based on a thoroughly prepared business case—deploying whatever pro-forma analyses are customarily used by your organization. EAI business cases are typically derived from the ability to integrate disparate business applications to provide new functionality. Interestingly, as one group member pointed out, EAI can also "accelerate the business by reducing the time it takes to deliver meaningful functionality to the business." He claimed that, in his company, EAI software release cycles approach (if they are well planned) the same speed with which Web solutions are deployed (i.e., 3–4 month increments). So, time-to-market should definitely be a part of the business case presented to senior management.

2   Assemble Your EAI Toolkit

The assembly[3] of an EAI toolkit requires a deliberate strategy. It begins with an analysis of the firm's strategic applications to suggest the key focus of the integration effort (i.e., data, application, process, or inter-organizational). This, in turn, suggests the most appropriate categories of EAI tools. This understanding enables you to categorize the various EAI software vendors and helps you to discuss their respective product offerings more intelligently. According to Allen (2001), "understanding the various categories of EAI services will help you refine the EAI requirements specific to your enterprise, which will keep you from buying the whole house when all you need is a kitchen sink." Allen (2001) provides an excellent checklist for dealing with vendors complete with questions to ask and tests to be undertaken covering vendor negotiations from needs determination through vendor "bake-offs" to implementation.

Focus group members agreed that no single vendor provides a complete package, so IT managers are left to select the best offering and augment it with other products/services. This puts you in the "general contractor" mode. The group felt that the following criteria (McLean Report, 2002) provide a good starting point for evaluating EAI systems:

- *Internal and/or external integration.* Depending on your specific needs, some EAI projects need to integrate internal systems, while others require integration with customer or supplier systems.
- *Business process management.* EAI software must support this feature to manage changes to business processes when they happen (which can be very frequent). Without this functionality, it will take a long time to re-map databases and data flows to applications when business processes change.
- *Security.* This is especially important if you're dealing with entities outside your organization. Data encryption and user authentication (and program authentication for automatic data exchanges) are both necessary features.
- *Ease of use.* This criterion is especially important if your business-users will be maintaining business process or workflow information and must use the EAI toolkit frequently.
- *Technology management functionality.* No matter how good the rest of the package is, the application will be useless if you can't quickly tell if all available network bandwidth is being used or the application is in an endless loop that will fill up all your storage. The EAI toolkit must tell you in detail what it's doing with your infrastructure and notify you when there are problems.

---

[3] We use the word "assembly" instead of "selection" since no single vendor supplies all the necessary products/services for end-to-end EAI, covering all four levels of integration.

3   Deploy "hub and spoke" design

Figure 17.3 depicts a classic "hub and spoke" design. With this design, there are three organizing principles:

- don't connect anything directly to anything;
- design applications should be autonomous, and don't allow them to share any databases directly;
- all knowledge of interconnections is removed from the source (and target) and placed within the hub.

A number of the focus members indicated that they had adopted the hub-and-spoke architectural model. They described its operation as follows:

> Applications are empowered to create messages encapsulating additions (and/or changes and/or deletions) to their business objects. A broker then routes and distributes these messages to the various integrated applications. At this point, the broker transforms the data into the appropriate representation for the destination. It is the broker that contains the logic to assist in the execution of the business process workflow.

Adopting hub-and-spoke architecture greatly reduces the complexity of one-to-one integration by organizing all the communication, transformation, and process workflow within the hub where it can be managed effectively. This achieves operational simplification and facilitates change. Individual applications can be replaced with relative ease since much of their logic, communication, and translation functions have been removed. The final advantage of this architecture is its ability to leverage reusability.

4   Create an Integration Core Competency Team

The adoption of hub-and-spoke architecture represents new challenges for application development. Because many of the functions normally resident within applications are now physically removed to the hub, application development is affected in significant ways. One focus group member suggested that application developers must undergo a mindset change from that of "developer" to that of "integrator".

With this new architecture, the hub is recognized not just as a sophisticated messenger, but as a full-functioning organizational asset complete with hardware and software. As such, it has to be scaled and must operate within a release-controlled environment much the same as other computing environments. Two member organizations have created central groups (called integration core competency teams[4]) for each hub. These groups manage the business functions as

---

[4] In one of these organizations, these individuals are called the "hub" people!

well as the software and hardware associated with the hub. They take responsibility for the following activities:

- maintaining all integration documentation;
- performing (and assuming ownership for) the detailed design of each interface;
- constructing the middle pieces of the interface;
- establishing best practices;
- performing broker marketplace evaluations; and
- administering all middleware software products.

Each hub should have its own team. In addition, a small team of architects should be appointed to manage across hubs. One member organization has appointed an enterprise IT architectural council charged with the responsibility to develop standards, preferred architecture(s), and policies to govern their implementation and use. These standards and policies are then pushed down to the system architects and deployed on an enterprise-wide basis. In this organization, it is mandatory for all application development teams to use hub people for all interfaces. Also, they have placed responsibility for the delivery of all cross-platform projects with the hub people. In essence, the hub people are the project-managers for these projects.

It is interesting to note how the adoption of a different architectural design affects the structure of the IT department. In a way, the structure of IT mirrors the technology. As soon as the hub-and-spoke architecture model is adopted, we see differences being drawn between "hub" people (with interface and integration responsibilities) and "spoke" people (with more traditional application development responsibilities). There are good reasons for this. As already mentioned, the role of application development is changing from that of "developer" to that of "integrator". In addition, EAI tools are special-purpose tools and IT professionals need to be trained in the use of these tools. Hub people also need to develop "process" skills. In one member organization, they have created "business process" analysts to reflect these skills. At the moment, individuals with "hub" skills are rare, as IT organizations have yet to commit significant staff to these roles. As the deployment of EAI spreads, this is likely to change dramatically.

5   Reintegrate Your Legacy Applications

A key part of EAI involves legacy systems for no better reason than the fact that legacy systems predominate. With legacy systems, anything less than wholescale replacement involves deconstruction—dismembering the application into its three main components/layers of *presentation* (the user interface), *business logic* (the rule-based reasoning), and *communications* (the data and inter-application linkage). Within typical legacy systems, these three components are inextricably bound together, making it complex, time-consuming, and even impossible to separate and/or distribute the layers for integration purposes. Decoupling each

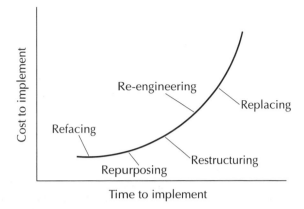

Figure 17.4   *Cost—Time tradeoffs for "five Rs" (2001).*

of these components/layers enables the application to be reconfigured into a series of common, shareable tasks that paves the way toward integration. When reintegrating these legacy applications, there is a continuum of approaches based on the degree of application invasiveness. Dubbed the "five R's" (2001), these strategies are refacing, repurposing, restructuring, re-engineering, and re-placing (Figure 17.4):

- *Refacing*. Standard terminal emulation screens are replaced with a graphical user interface (GUI) for each application. The approach is non-invasive and the underlying legacy application is not modified. Overall functionality has not been altered, but, due to the refacing, integration among enterprise applications is facilitated by the usage of common front-ends.
- *Repurposing*. Like refacing, repurposing uses a GUI for the presentation layer. Unlike refacing, repurposing integrates the screen-based business logic of many legacy applications and allows changes to the workflow of legacy applications to better facilitate the underlying business processes. Even though the underlying applications remain unchanged, repurposing can build in new business logic for various purposes such as updating data sources, performing calculations, triggering events, and otherwise automating tasks that can result in significant process-streamlining and enhanced productivity.
- *Restructuring*. This is the process of separating the presentation and business logic components within an application. Once separated, these components can be wrapped with new interfaces and integrated into any number of new refacing or repurposing types of application. This allows an organization to leverage an application procedure whose logic is proven to work while preserving data integrity in the communication layer. Only through restructuring can you invoke the desired application procedure directly.

- *Re-engineering*. This entails rebuilding the entire application. Built to exact specifications, this approach provides the organization with a chance to build in the integration necessary for it to meet its business and technology needs.
- *Replacing*. Sometimes it is best to procure an off-the-shelf solution to replace the host application. This approach allows the organization to choose what operating platform the application will run on, as opposed to being bound by the original.

The first two approaches are non-invasive, requiring no modification to host applications, and hence provide the quickest remedy. For this reason, and if possible, refacing and repurposing are preferred solutions. By contrast, the last three approaches are invasive, requiring modification, and even replacement of host applications. As can be seen from Figure 17.1, each of the approaches requires greater time to implement and greater costs. What is not apparent from Figure 17.1 is the fact that restructuring, re-engineering, and replacing often provide enhanced benefits not possible with refacing, for example. Decisions regarding the integration of legacy systems should be based on a cost–benefit analysis in alignment with the organization's overall integration strategy. One-off decisions regarding individual legacy applications provide short-term solutions at best. Applications should be mapped onto an integration strategy as part of overall application portfolio management.

6   Next Steps . . . the "Collaborative Enterprise"

Technology is enabling organizations to become intricately connected in a host of ways. By linking systems with trading partners, an organization can check a supplier's inventory directly, check the status of in-process orders, preview pricing structures, choose delivery options, and interface ordering systems directly with a supplier's fulfillment systems. As these "electronic fingers" bond organizations in myriad ways, they create significant value by enabling the "instantaneous" movement of data, products, and services thus eliminating the "float" between an action (e.g., the placement of an order) and its realization (e.g., the processing of that order). To do this requires collaboration between trading partners, hence the term "collaborative enterprise". Customers are demanding it, competitors are doing it, the business needs it, executives are asking for it, and the burden of delivery rests on the shoulders of IT.

The technological challenge presented by the collaborative enterprise is enormous. It requires the integration of application systems across firms thus elevating the integration challenge to a new level. Even within organizations, integration presents a daunting task and *here they have control over the technology*. Beyond their boundaries, organizations have little control over the technology of partner organizations[5]. Furthermore, current software solutions deployed on the

---

[5] This sort of struggle was played out in the EDI arena a few years ago.

edges of enterprises are expensive, do not scale, and are complex to implement across enterprises (Donato et al., 2001). They argue that inter-organization integration will require a new technology architecture that makes integration much less difficult, expensive, and time-consuming. That technology is "Web services"—an emerging technology architecture that could make integration as easy as plugging an appliance into the electrical grid. It is based on the notion of building applications by discovering and collaborating with network-available services—the just-in-time integration of applications:

> Collaborating enterprises will be able to plug applications and business processes into a service grid that is ubiquitously accessible and affordable to most companies. Web services are designed to enable a collaborative environment that is decentralized, dynamic and diverse. This emerging architecture will enable companies to reap unprecedented productivity rewards from a more focused and integrated set of business processes and partners. Indeed, machine-to-machine execution of loosely coupled business processes by enterprises and their partners will touch every company, customer and employee. It will redefine enterprises, and even industries, by facilitating agility (Donato et al., 2001).

While it is difficult to know when Web services will become a reality,[6] it is easy to see the transitions that would be required. Web services will revolutionize the definition of enterprise architecture, changing the enterprise from a self-contained set of applications into a nexus of services, data flows, and business process interfaces shared by other enterprises. According to Hagel and Brown (2001), Web services would create a market economy for services operating much like an electricity grid, where organizations draw from (or supply to) the grid. With such a marketplace, EAI represents the "table stakes". Firms not advanced in terms of EAI would simply not be ready to "plug and play" and would lose opportunities to competitors who were more advanced with regard to EAI development. The advantages of collaborative enterprises are such that it is likely that every effort will be made to make Web services a reality. Regardless, focus group members felt that now is the time to take significant action in terms of integrating enterprise applications. This effort provides immediate benefits to the firm while paving the way toward the web services where integration transcends organizational boundaries. For this reason, organizations should view their EAI efforts in light of the broader goal of enabling the collaborative enterprise—that

---

[6] Donato et al. (2001) are optimistic about the chances of Web services becoming a reality. They claim, ". . . this is not a utopian vision based on vaporware. Web services are becoming available and can be piloted by companies with relatively little incremental investment in time, money or new information technology. Many of the key elements of the architecture are quickly coming to market through application platforms from IBM, BEA, Sun and Microsoft. In addition, the industry is coalescing around standards such as XML, SOAP, UDDI and WSDL. However, a shared integration infrastructure is also required to cost-effectively manage complexity."

is, integrating their organization's technology within a web of partner organizations to facilitate the free flow of data and functionality. Specifically, they should do the following:

- Craft an EAI strategy that explicitly recognizes the eventuality of an inter-organizational architecture (e.g., Web services).
- Use this strategy to guide internal EAI efforts. For instance, opt for industry standards over in-house standards where possible. This will increase your chances of being inter-organizationally integrated.
- Join industry associations involved in establishing architectural standards. The "best case" scenario is that this involvement provides an opportunity for you to influence the selection/adoption of standards; the "worst case scenario" is that you receive early notification of industrywide decisions regarding the adoption of standards. These are "no-lose" options.
- Assess your key business processes to identify any/all that might provide value to other organizations (i.e., best-in-class processes). Investigate the potential market for these processes both within and beyond your industry.
- Investigate the market for best-in-class offerings that might complement (or replace) your current business processes.
- Pilot Web services as early as possible with non-critical processes. When Web services become a reality, you should be ready to move.

CONCLUSION

The need to integrate applications across the enterprise has reached a crucial stage. Due to customer/supplier demands for instant access and 24/7 service, EAI has changed from a "nice to have" to a "do or die" situation. This chapter has described the dimensions of the integration problem, outlined the challenges it presents for IT, and presented a number of strategies for dealing with EAI effectively (based on the cumulative insights of our focus group of senior IT managers). As with many organizational challenges, EAI can be seen as a problem or as an opportunity. Given the impact that EAI will have on the marketplace, it is arguably best to approach EAI as an opportunity to create enhanced value for both customers and suppliers.

REFERENCES

Allen, D. (2001) "Assembling your EAI toolkit" (http://eai.ebizq.net/str/allen_1.html).
Bove, T. (2001) "EAI: Providing stability in the whirlwind of e-commerce" (http://eai.ebizq.net/str/bove_1.html), August.
Donato, C., S. Durchslag, and J. Hagel III (2001) "Web services: Enabling the collaborative enterprise" (http://e-serv.ebizq.net/wbs/donato_1a.html).

Five R's (2001) "Approaches to enterprise application integration involving legacy host applications: The five R's" (http://www.attachmate.com/article/0,1012,3163_1_3858.00.html).

GartnerGroup (2001) *Gartner Dataquest*, June, GartnerGroup, Stamford, CT.

Hagel III, J. and J.S. Brown (2001) "Your next IT strategy," *Harvard Business Review*, October, 105–113.

Koch, C. (1996) "The integration nightmare: Sounding the alarm," *CIO Magazine*, 15 November (http://www.cio.com/archive/111596_alarm_content.html).

Linthicum, D. (2001) "Chasing the tail of the beast," *Software Magazine*, February–March (Wiesner Publishing, New York).

McLean Report (2002) "Enterprise application integration (EAI): Software buyer's guide," McLean Report (http://www.mcleanreport.com/current_issue.asp#2), January.

Part D
People and Productivity

Information technology (IT), in and of itself, does not create value—value is created by people. It is our belief that IT, when deployed effectively, leverages people's skills and abilities thus allowing them to be more productive. The key words are *when deployed effectively*. The challenge is to match people with technology to create organizations that are efficient (in operational aspects), effective (in the creation of products and services), and responsive to customers/suppliers within the marketplace. Thus, effective IT deployment results from focusing on people and productivity first and technology second. Nowhere is this more apparent than within the IT organization.

This part of the book highlights the four key aspects of people and productivity—that is, recruitment, development, proven practices, and the measurement of results. *Recruitment* issues are explored in Chapter 18, "Recruiting and Retaining the Best in IT". This chapter outlines the critical roles of selection, recruitment, and retention when it comes to securing top candidates within the ranks of IT. The two most critical skills within IT are undoubtedly project management and leadership. The *development* of these skills is discussed in Chapter 19, "Developing Effective IT Project-managers", and in Chapter 20, "Developing Effective IT Leaders", respectively. Skilled individuals must be organized into highly functioning units within organizations in order to maximize their contribution to (and support of) the business. Chapter 21, "Best Practices in IT", outlines the rationale behind effective organization and identifies a number of *proven practices* that contribute to IT success. Chapter 22, "Managing the Virtual Workforce", focuses on an emerging organizational form to highlight the key management issues for IT and for organizations in general. The final chapter, "The IT Measurement Matrix", explores the ways and means to assess the organizational contribution of IT. The old adage that "if it can't be measured, it can't be managed" applies. Strategies to implement procedures for recruitment, development, and proven practices will be unproven (perhaps ineffectual) until the *measurement of results* is made possible.

18
Recruiting and Retaining the Best in IT

Recruiting and retaining outstanding people is tantamount to survival. The information technology (IT) organization is no exception. Talented project-managers and skilled programmers are worth their weight in gold. The difference in productivity between the best and the poorest programmer within a single organization can be a factor of ten or greater (DeMarco and Lister, 1987). As a result, IT organizations with superior personnel out-produce their competitors significantly. With the growing reliance on IT to produce strategic products and services, long-term organizational vitality will increasingly be determined by the prowess of the IT organization. It is already possible to identify many organizations whose economic value resides with its IT competencies. The removal of the development teams, for example, from any software organization would leave little net worth.

The realization of the value of employees is not new to organizations or to IT departments. What is new, however, is a changing landscape faced by today's organizations. There appears to be both a *growth in demand* for IT skills and a *demand for growth* in IT skills combining to produce a critical shortage of skilled IT professionals. Faced with an over-heated market for IT professionals and the constant organizational demand for new IT applications, IT managers are struggling to find solutions to their staffing problems in order to meet the needs of business. The situation is nearing crisis in many organizations.

This chapter describes the forces at work within the industry from the point of view of the hiring organizations as well as individual IT personnel. It argues that, although the need for good people has unchanged, effective strategies for hiring and retaining IT personnel must reflect the underlying forces at work within the marketplace in order to take full advantage of the opportunities to build a top IT organization.

The chapter lists a number of proven strategies suggested by the focus groups of senior IT managers.

UNDERLYING FACTORS

It is important to understand the forces that are causing the present situation in order to separate the causes from the symptoms. This allows solutions to address root causes. Some of the causes are certainly market effects and, to a large degree, beyond the influence of individual organizations. Added to these market effects, however, are certain organizational factors, which, in some circumstances, magnify the market effects. Many of these are certainly within management's prerogative. Finally, people's needs are changing, and this plays importantly into the equation of acquiring and retaining top performers in IT.

Market Effects

There continues to be a shortage of qualified IT people in the marketplace. Industry statistics demonstrate a persistent inability for the supply of trained IT professionals to keep pace with the demand (ITAC, 2002; McGee, 1996; Williamson, 1997). Many, who have seen gaps in the market before, believe this situation to be different in a number of significant ways. As pointed out earlier, there is both a growth in demand for IT skills and a demand for growth in IT skills due to the changing skill set. What explains this growth? The focus group outlined a number of possible explanations.

First, every company seems to have discovered that IT has the ability to enhance productivity. Until recently, the really heavy use of IT was concentrated within a small number of industry sectors—particularly the financial industry. Now, organizations regardless of industry see IT as the facilitator of productivity improvements, the means to link buyers and suppliers end-to-end, the way to get "intimate" with customers, and the means of satisfying the customer demand for self-service (i.e., Web-servicing). Flush with this new religion, these organizations have entered the market for IT skills in force creating a virtual bidding war for scarce resources. It is estimated that one-quarter of new IT jobs will go unfilled (ITAC, 2002).

Second, there has been a significant shift toward the services market, which has undoubtedly heightened the stress within the marketplace and resulted in increased levels of competition. Faced with dwindling profitability in hardware and software markets, vendors such as IBM have realigned themselves so that a much greater share of their revenue is derived from services such as consulting and services management. In order to address the demands of this service industry, they have had to recruit many new IT people—people who would otherwise be working for their clients. According to McGee (1996), competition for IT resources now comes from computer vendors, systems integrators, out-sourcers, and consulting firms who raid each other's workforce—a practice typically unheard of previously.

Third, changing technologies and customer expectations continue to pressure IT skill sets. The widespread adoption of Web services has resulted in heightened demands for IT professionals with related experience including Internet-based languages (e.g., JAVA), middleware (to bridge legacy systems with Internet front-ends), and large enterprise systems (e.g., enterprise resource planning [ERP] systems). The study commissioned by ITAC (2002) identified the top five IT skills as SQL Server/SQL Windows, security skills, Windows NT Server, Micro-soft Exchange, and wide area networks (WAN). Where you can find these skills, you can expect to pay a premium to acquire them.

Fourth, at the same time as new skills are emerging, most organizations are faced with declining expertise in older mainframe skills (such as COBOL and MVS). These skills have suddenly become in short supply since many of the individuals with these skills are reaching (or have reached) retirement age and are leaving the workplace. Despite plans to simply replace legacy systems with newer systems, many organizations have found new life for their legacy systems by interfacing them with Internet applications. Rather than replacing them, they are now retrofitting them. By extending their working lives, these organizations have also committed themselves to continuing a least some level of expertise in older technologies. These skill demands co-exist with mainstream skills such as project-manager, IT business analyst/consultant, and database administrator—skills that have the greatest forecast shortages in the IT market-place (ITAC, 2002).

Finally, many point their fingers to colleges and universities for their failure to meet the demand for more graduates trained in IT. The failure, however, is the inability to interest students in IT careers, and this is not the sole responsibility of colleges and universities. Furthermore, as recently as a few years ago, there was a surplus of IT professionals on the market. There is a larger issue here, which we will return to later in this chapter.

For all the above reasons (and perhaps others), it is apparent that the supply of IT professionals falls significantly short of the demand, and there is no evidence that this trend will be short-lived. As a pessimist, one could argue that this shortage is a market effect about which individual organizations appear to be able to do little. As an optimist, however, one can see opportunities for proactive strategies to counter some of these effects effectively.

Organizational Factors

Within the constraints of these market forces, there are a number of organiza-tional factors that also affect our ability to hire and retain top people in IT. For example, not all organizations are equally attractive to IT professionals. Some people in IT may not find the packaging firm as appealing as an investment house. Geography plays a role too. Some may not find a large urban center as inviting as a more attractive setting.

Another organizational factor cited by the focus group is the inseparability of IT and the business. While there are still demands for pure technology expertise, more often the top IT professionals are those who are able to combine technical skills with an understanding of the business. Bridging the gap between the business and IT enhances the ability to recognize solutions that otherwise might elude the organization. This need suggests there should be strategies for balancing business training with technical training, which would enhance employee skills, benefit the organization, and engender employee loyalty.

The final organizational factor that appears to impact the hiring and retention of valued IT employees is the policies of the human resource (HR) department. For example, it is not uncommon for compensation policies to be in place that make it very difficult to hire/retain the IT people an organization needs. In some cases, pay scales are tied to promotion, the company is unable to offer attractive investment options, childcare facilities are non-existent, and/or flexible work arrangements are unavailable, etc. Certainly, strategies for hiring/retaining the best people in IT will involve a level of cooperation between HR and IT.

Personal Factors

In addition to the market and organizational factors cited above, there appear to be a number of individual factors that affect hiring/retaining strategies. The reasons why IT people seek employment are as varied as these individuals. This suggests that organizations need to invest in their employees, to understand them and their desires, and to be in tune with their needs.

Over the past few years, organizations have removed themselves from the business of assuming responsibility for managing the careers of their employees. This duty has now been passed over to the employee. "Lifetime" jobs are not offered by organizations today. This has a direct impact on employee loyalty. After a round of downsizing, organizations have difficulty impressing employees with slogans such as "our people are our most precious asset." Not surprisingly, employees feel decreasing levels of loyalty and, by assuming ownership of their careers, take on a renewed interest in their own well-being above and beyond that offered by their employer. A proponent of equity theory would suggest that employees are simply balancing the loyalty equation—as the organization lowers its loyalty to the employee, the employee lowers his or her loyalty to the organization. "Making the hard choices" and "looking out for oneself" appear to be the mottos of today's employers and employees, respectively.

With the "lifetime employment guarantee" gone, it is now expected that the majority of people will experience multiple career changes throughout their working lives. With these career changes, employees seek to balance personal aspects of their lives with working aspects. With two working parents the rule rather than the exception, family life often takes precedent over working life, and tradeoff decisions are made to maximize career and home life. Recently, an organization decided to relocate part of its IT operations and found that no employees were willing to make the move! This suggests that the most successful hiring/retaining strategies will be those sensitive to the unique needs of the individuals employed by the organization. This can only be accomplished with a thorough understanding of these employees' motivations—what brings them to the workplace and what keeps them in the workplace.

Considering the market, organizational and individual factors together, a composite picture emerges. Where we have had a buyer's market in the past, we now see a super-heated supplier's market especially in the high-demand skills segment. Coupled with a rebalanced loyalty equation, we see the tensions of a free market working; that is, employee mobility, short-term inequalities, organizational restructure, and information disequilibrium. In addition, job-hopping, price wars, staff raids, and salary inequities can be expected.

SUCCESSFUL STRATEGIES

In this section, we present a number of strategies that were suggested by the focus group to address the hiring and retaining of IT personnel. These suggestions are based on their insights, their experiences (both positive and negative), and their ability to speculate about the future.

1 Identify Critical Skills

It is surprising how many organizations still do not undertake a thorough skills needs assessment. Without this, it is extremely difficult to establish an effective strategy for hiring and retaining staff within IT. The group suggested that an organization should evaluate (a) its technical environment, (b) its business environment, and (c) the work environment in order to assess these critical skills:

- *Assess the technical environment.* The first step is to analyze your *current* technical environment. The next step is to analyze your *future* technical environment. These assessments need to be done concurrently since the migration path from your current to your future environment will indicate the need for "hold-over" skills, the need for new technical skills, as well as the transition timing, which is the key factor. One group member, for example, described his organization's current environment as one with host MVS transaction processors, host VM applications, many departmental local area networks (LANs), some mid-range equipment, and an emerging enterprise LAN service. This was in contrast to their future environment which used the mainframe primarily as a data server, VM applications on Lotus Notes, transaction processors on AIX, and application integration on the workstation. Moving from the current technical environment to its desired future environment will drive a shift in the types of skill needed as well as the quantity of skills needed.
- *Assess the business environment.* It is important to assess the business environment since it will dictate many of the critical skills needed for the future. Failure to do so can result in some nasty surprises. In one company, the

business was planning some extensive process re-engineering to move them into a highly matrixed environment with cross-functional clients. This could only be supported with highly integrated data, and the capability to provide this was not currently available. The IT group was not aware of this situation in time to build the necessary resources and, as a result, forced the plans to be delayed. What is the partnership between IT and the business? Is the business looking to IT for technical leadership or workable options? Will there be significant change in the nature of the relationship between IT and the business? What sort of change is anticipated? In most organizations, the relationship between IT and the business is becoming more complex. This drives the demand for additional leadership and relationship skills. Making these assessments, apart from the technological considerations, will highlight the need for skills to be acquired by IT.

- *Assess the work environment.* Because most organizations already perform an annual budgeting exercise for IT expenditures, an assessment of the actual systems to be delivered over the next two years can be created with reasonable accuracy. This assessment should be adjusted in light of the assessments of the technical and business environments (as described above). The analysis must classify the work by technical environment (i.e., different platforms), estimate the amount of work, and identify the necessary roles (project-managers, programmers, business analysts, etc.) and the numbers required for each role. This will outline the skills base necessary in the near term. A second aspect of work assessment is creating an inventory of resident skills. For *each position* within the IT organization, a skills profile can be established. In addition, for *each person* within the organization, a skills proficiency appraisal should be performed. There are many packages to facilitate this type of skills management. Finally, perform a *gap analysis*; that is, compare the necessary skills base to the inventory of resident skills. Two situations should be highlighted—areas where there are an abundance of skills and areas where there are skill shortages. All the following strategies can be applied selectively to these two situations. It is important to stress that the needs assessment must be done carefully since all hiring/retaining strategies will be based on these results. It is recommended that IT organizations make these activities a mandatory part of their personnel evaluations with a minimum six-month update.

2   Make Developing Skills within the Organization a Top Priority

According to Gaylen Duncan, chief executive officer (CEO) of ITAC, "the IT industry likes to think of itself as an exemplary promoter of life long learning and continuous improvement. And while that may be true, we're not meeting the expectations of many of our employees" (ITAC, 2002). This needs to be addressed. It is well known that the cost of retaining an employee is a fraction of the total cost of acquiring a new employee. For this reason alone, it is in an organization's interest to develop the necessary skills in its existing IT personnel if at all possible. Using the two-year window of the "skills needs assessment" process, organizations should design a systematic process to develop the requisite skills.

The key to the success of such a process is for the organization to establish the framework while leaving ownership of the process with the individual employee. This approach, if done effectively, leads to a "win–win" situation. The organization, having done a thorough skills needs assessment, knows what skill sets it needs to build over the near future. The individual needs to know this information so that he or she can master these necessary skills. In essence, the organization creates a process that enables its employees to author their own future within the organization. According to Waterman et al. (1994), there is a new covenant wherein "the employer and the employee share responsibility for maintaining— even enhancing—the individual's employability inside *and outside* the company."

How does the process work? To begin with, the skill needs assessment must be made public. This permits each employee to compare the organization's skill needs with their own skills based on their annual skills proficiency appraisal (described above). Using this comparison, each employee develops (and takes ownership of) their *individual skills plan*. Each plan should contain personalized education and training targets, business exposure through work rotations, skill mastery (and certification), opportunities to gain experience to reinforce new skills, and a statement of career objectives and milestones within the organization. Some organizations include metrics to measure accomplishment and success. Others tie this to the annual performance appraisal activities.

With the individual assuming ownership, the organization must take responsibility for providing the requisite support. One organization has instituted a mentoring program. This is a formal, but voluntary program for mentors and "mentorees". Time spent mentoring is rewarded as billable hours. This program assists each employee in building his or her individual skills plan. Another organization has adopted a resource center approach, which assists employees in the development and management of their individual skills plan and ensures that the employee skills inventory matches the organization's needed skills both now and in the future. If assigning the responsibility solely to individual employees is at one end of the continuum and developing a resource center approach is at the other end, an interesting mid-way approach is the development of employee-managed skills teams. With this approach, teams assume the responsibility for developing critical skills plans to facilitate and support the employee skills inventory. Teams could be organized around technology platforms or along business lines. With each of these various approaches, the common thread is the formalization of skill set-planning; the differences are attributable to the specific methods used to force the alignment between individual skills sets and the organization's necessary skill sets.

It is also important not to restrict skills development to current IT personnel. In most organizations, there is a cadre of "expert users"—people who work on the business side, but possess advanced systems skills. This combination of business understanding and vision with IT skills makes them prime candidates for a move into IT. These people are often extremely effective at bridging the gap between IT and the business, primarily because of the credibility they bring. Effort should be expended in identifying these people and encouraging their ties with IT.

3   Be Creative in Your Approach to Hiring

IT organizations will always need to hire new recruits if for no other reason than to fill vacancies due to retirements. Hiring will also be necessary to respond to needs that arise due to urgent business opportunities, unforeseen problems, or through unexpected turnover. Hiring presents an opportunity to welcome new people with varied backgrounds who bring novel ideas and different viewpoints into the organization. Prudent management should be able to harness this influx of talent and energy to the benefit of the organization.

Given the market situation as depicted earlier in this chapter, it is clear that new approaches to hiring are necessary. This observation is based on the fact that those organizations fairing the best in terms of hiring are using some very creative approaches. Some of the advice offered by members of the group follows:

- Maximize your hiring channels—jobs should be advertized in newspapers, on the Internet, on campuses, and in professional/trade journals. Examine media such as television and radio that are pervasive in society, but rarely used for recruiting. Participate in job fairs. Use head-hunter agencies and search firms. There does not appear to be one best solution. Casting the widest possible net is recommended. One organization found that their municipal government, whose mandate was to encourage new business development in their geographic area, was willing to work with them on joint marketing campaigns to attract new employees.
- Attract your temporary help—most IT departments augment their regular staff with part-time personnel. Part-time help typically accounts for about 15–20% of the total headcount. These individuals, who may be contractors, outsourcers, programmers, work-term students, or consultants, are potential recruits for permanent IT positions. The advantage is that the organization has had the opportunity to assess their work and they have had the opportunity to assess the organization. Hence, both parties are much better informed than in a typical recruiting situation. If these people possess the necessary skills, make every effort to pursue them (provided this is not in contempt of any contractual specifications).
- Begin an employee referral system—undoubtedly your employees are aware

of others in the profession either through professional or casual connections. Offer them a finder's fee if they bring a new recruit to your organization. This can be a one-time reward, awarded if you actually hire the individual, or it can be a graduated system where the reward increases in proportion to how far the recruit makes it through the hiring process.

- Increase your presence on campuses—colleges and universities are still the main supplier of IT professionals. Recruiting on campus provides a certain level of visibility for organizations, but there are lots of other ways to increase exposure. A classroom appearance as a guest lecturer provides an opportunity to present your organization to the student population. Sponsoring an internship program is another way to gain exposure and, in addition, gives you first bargaining rights on the intern. Participate in career days. Sponsor events. Provide speakers for campus forums and panel sessions. Partnering with colleges and universities on any number of projects can lead to significant long-term gains.

A few organizations have been very creative in their approach to hiring students and deserve mention. For example, EDS offers an annual competition among the top business schools in North America. A team of students from each school is selected to visit EDS to analyze a real-world company situation. Basically, EDS has discovered a way of getting the top students from the best universities to voluntarily spend two or three days at their headquarters. During their visit, EDS has an exclusive opportunity to impress these students and is usually successful in hiring a number of them. The cost of this weekend extravaganza pales in comparison to the cost of having EDS's personnel visit all the top schools in North America. Aside from the cost, there is little chance that any EDS campus visit would be able to attract the very best students to their recruiting venue. It is a clever way of attracting the best recruits to their organization.

4   Manage the Acclimatization Process for New Recruits Carefully

The acclimatization process begins when the new recruit arrives and usually lasts about three months. This probationary period, referred to as "shake and bake", is critical because it sets the tone for the employee's tenure at your organization. First impressions, for employer or employee, can be lasting. One of the group members claimed that "hiring is the easy part—cultural integration and orientation are much more difficult." For these reasons, IT organizations should make every effort to integrate their new recruits.

During orientation and integration, most organizations issue a guide for new staff. One organization offered a "survival kit". This document included advice, candid tips, dos and don'ts, how to's, where to find's, organizational road maps, and other assorted hints and suggestions to make the assimilation process as smooth as possible. Some organizations have implemented a buddy system where new recruits are teamed up with another junior member of the IT staff—someone to show them the ropes, particularly during the early phases of employment. This eliminates the need for new recruits to always be asking "dumb" questions of their supervisors or fellow workers. By having an assigned buddy, the new recruit does not feel as if he or she is bothering other workers.

Many, if not most, organizations today are using mentoring programs. Unlike the buddy system, the organizational mentor is responsible for advising the employee regarding career decisions by assuming a coaching role. Since the mentor is not the supervisor, he or she can carry out the role as a third-party confidant(e) with no vested interest in the mentoree other than seeing that his or her best interests are served by the organization. Another successful idea is to arrange "executive interviews" where new recruits meet with senior executives to gain the big picture of the organization and to create feelings of being part of a larger team than their own work department. One organization installed a program called "breakfasts for new hires" where new recruits attended a series of breakfasts where they are exposed to various organizational issues. The agenda can be extremely varied, but the intent is always to integrate the candidate successfully. These ideas are simple, but extremely important. Unfortunately, in our hectic schedules, we often forget some of the easiest yet most effective strategies to acclimatize the newest additions to our most valued resource pool.

5   Create an Exciting Work Environment

There is belief that "people start looking for employment elsewhere when they are dissatisfied." Whether or not this is true, it is in every organization's best interests to create an exciting work environment to increase the chances that employees are not dissatisfied. Group members agreed with this premise, and many ideas for creating a challenging, exciting, and productive work environment emerged; many of these are described below:

- *Develop recognition programs.* We frequently hear about projects that miss deadlines. On the other hand, many projects meet their deadlines. When they do, they should not go unrecognized or unrewarded. The celebration of accomplishments creates a positive attitude and builds cohesion among employees—everyone likes to be on a winning team. Organizations have been known to hand out T-shirts advertizing the fact that certain accomplishments were attained. One organization took an entire team white river-rafting. Recognition awards can be as small as coffee and donuts.
- *Showcase your technology initiatives.* In many cases, organizations fail to showcase their technology and their exciting new ventures. It never hurts to demonstrate your accomplishments. Since everyone in IT is a technologist, a technology fair can be very effective. In addition, providing up-to-date

equipment is a clear signal to employees expressing the organization's desire to support its workers. If you are at or near the leading edge of technology, advertize it. If you were one of the first in your industry to implement a particularly successful business application, share this with your employees. If there is any part of your deployed technology that is innovative, make it known. The effects of showcasing your technology initiatives can have demonstrative effects on employee morale—everyone is proud to be part of successful ventures.

- *Offer challenges.* It is well known that IT workers are high-need achievers who are motivated more by challenges than other common rewards. Yet, it is surprising how often IT organizations fail to provide significant challenges for their employees. Offer promising employees a fast-track program within the organization. Provide expanded organizational responsibilities to see how effectively employees rise to the challenge. Put employees on special assignments that are time-boxed. Solicit new ideas and, when promising ideas are presented, challenge the originator to follow through.

- *Link training, challenges, and performance.* Most organizations are adopting a just-in-time approach to training provided in an e-learning environment. An extension to this thinking is to link training to new challenges/responsibilities with established performance deliverables. A member of the group gave an example of this approach. His organization offered to let IT employees bid for a project to build an intranet to provide business users access to existing legacy systems. This project involved training (e.g., RDBMS software, JAVA) and was given well-defined deliverables and deadlines. This was a competitive bid and employees were free to choose their own teams. The employees saw the project as exciting, challenging, and as an opportunity to enhance their skill set. This approach works for less exciting projects as well. The organization described above had such success with the intranet project that it established a special "changeover" project to introduce a new development methodology. The successful team was given training, extra money, and firm deliverables. The team saw themselves as reaping rewards, receiving recognition, and even attaining new skills. The same approach works for legacy systems—the classic back-water of IT. In one organization, the word "legacy" is never mentioned. Instead, the organization speaks of "service leadership" in recognition of the fact that work on legacy systems provides essential functionality to the organization.

- *Provide opportunities for learning.* One member suggested that people should be allowed to take risks and not get "punished for mistakes". Mistakes are useful when they are learning experiences and as long as they are not too frequent. Part of creating a challenging work environment is to build in some opportunity for risky ventures. Success lies in managing the level of risk. One member boiled down his organization's approach to three elements: *excellence, excitement,* and *empathy*.

6   Develop Retention Programs

Despite the very best efforts at creating an exciting place to work, there are always situations where retention efforts are necessary. These are deliberate activities that organizations undertake to keep valued employees. These activities go beyond the normal organizational benefits (e.g. health, vacation, insurance). It is important for organizations to identify those valued employees who are at risk of leaving and use strategies to retain them. Given the current market situation, retention programs have become even more important.

There are myriad forms of retention programs. Some of the more prevalent forms are mentioned here. Organizations should think creatively about available options to retain their employees:

- *Special awards.* One organization allocates stocks in the company—called "Blue Chip" awards. These awards, which can be up to an additional 20% of the employee's salary, are payable in Years 2 and 3 from the time of the award. Unlike other types of award, the recipient must stay with the organization for an extended period of time in order to collect his or her award.
- *Service awards.* These awards are given in recognition of outstanding service to clients. They are typically based on a process that provides formal feedback from clients. The form of the award can be financial, but need not be (e.g., "employee of the month" designation).
- *Bonuses.* These are one-time bonuses usually awarded for achievement or recognition of "hot" skills. These are typically financial (5–10% of salary), but could be offered in other forms.
- *Increased salaries.* These are increases to base salary and, as such, will benefit the employee this year as well as all subsequent years. These increases can, in some cases, far exceed typical bonuses. One member gave an example of awarding a salary increase of over 30% for a particular valued individual. Sometimes the flexibility to make these types of award is hampered by existing HR policies, but that is another problem.
- *Promotions.* We are not suggesting that organizations promote employees just to retain them, but, as one member declared, if the employee at risk is in line for promotion anyway why not accelerate the process? It demonstrates that the organization recognizes the employee's potential and is willing to entrust the employee with additional responsibilities. Promotions offer the employee new challenges, are accompanied by a commensurate salary hike, and, as such, are considered part of the retention arsenal.

7   Revisit Your Compensation Package

It is critical that organizations maintain a compensation package (i.e., salary plus benefits) that parallels market realities. Retaining employees whose salaries are 10–20% lower than the market is a difficult battle to win. Employees know the job market as well as their employers. The difficulty for organizations is to be responsive to a market that can take sharp turns. There is no solution other than to keep abreast of the market by understanding its causal pressures.

Salaries, however, are only part of the compensation package. Many organizations are discovering that non-salary benefits can provide real competitive advantage. Organizations should consider their interest in (and ability to offer) flex-time programs, telecommuting arrangements, wellness and fitness programs, childcare programs, financial services, casual dress programs, educational support programs, exceptional attendance programs, long-service awards, employee safeguards, and social programs. These benefits can be used in combination to create attractive packages, which build switching costs into the employee–employer relationship. Not only must organizations offer these types of package, but they should market them to their employees—both current and future. One organization developed a "Did You Know" brochure that outlined all the employee benefits to demonstrate how their offerings surpassed the competition's. Effective communication goes a long way.

CONCLUSION

Hiring and retaining top personnel is a continuing challenge for IT organizations. Some of the factors that affect the market for IT professionals are within organizational control and others not. This chapter has sought out those areas where management has the ability to respond and has suggested a number of possible strategies. By tailoring these strategies to fit their organizations, IT management has the means to ensure the continuation of a base of skilled IT professionals.

REFERENCES

DeMarco, T. and T. Lister (1987) *Peopleware: Productive Projects and Teams*, Dorset House Publishing, New York.

ITAC (2002) "IT skilled labour shortage returning in 2002," News Release, 6 May, Information Technology Association of Canada (http://www.itac.ca).

McGee, M.K. (1996) "Stretched to the limit—the market for talented IT staffers is tighter than ever. Once you find them, good luck holding on," *Information Week*, 2 December.

Waterman Jr, R., J. Waterman, and B. Collard (1994) "Toward a career-resilient workforce," *Harvard Business Review*, July–August, 87–95.

Williamson, M. (1997) "No quick fixes for IT skills shortage," *Computing Canada*, **23**(3), 3 February.

19
Developing Effective IT Project-managers

Although information technology (IT) professionals possess myriad skills, their truly unique talent is their ability to design and build systems. In the past, they have been routinely called upon to produce systems to handle the operations of business, to report on the functioning of business, and to support the decision-making activities of management. More recently, as information systems have become *product* technologies in addition to *process* technologies, they have been charged with the responsibility of creating the entities with which their organizations compete. While this has not changed the role that IT professionals play, it has certainly increased their visibility within the management ranks. Never before has there been so much attention paid to the successful delivery of systems and never before has the role of the IT project-manager been so critical.

Developing systems is not (and never has been) the problem. The problem is (and always has been) *managing* the projects . . . to design and build systems . . . *successfully*. There is little doubt that IT professionals are good programmers, designers, data flow diagrammers, testers, trouble-shooters, and technicians. The questions are: Are they good project-managers? What does it take to become a good IT project-manager? To answer these questions, we need to understand the nature of IT projects. We also need to understand the organizational dynamics that surround their development. Through this understanding, we can identify which employees are potentially good IT project-managers as well as the types of training that will assist them in becoming effective in this role.

This chapter examines the practice of systems development and investigates project management as it relates to the development of systems. Then, a set of three key questions are posed: make versus buy; nature versus nurture; and certification. Finally, a list of management strategies for developing successful IT project-managers is presented.

THE NATURE OF SYSTEMS DEVELOPMENT

As long ago as 1979, Marvin Zelkowitz reflected on the lamentable state of systems development by drawing the following analogy:

> When the Verrazano Narrows Bridge in New York City was started in 1959, officials estimated that it would cost $325 million and be completed by 1965. It was the largest suspension bridge ever built, yet it was completed in November 1964, on target and within budget ... No similar pattern has been observed when we build software systems larger than those ... built previously. Software is often delivered late. It is frequently unreliable and usually expensive to maintain ... Why is bridge engineering so exact while software engineering flounders so?

This raises an important question: Is software-engineering similar to bridge-building? If so, then we should be able to apply the same project management rigor to software projects as we do to bridge-building. If not, then the IT profession must define its own best strategies for managing projects. Let's examine the analogy. What is quickly discovered is that bridge-building and systems development are both similar and dissimilar. They are similar because (1) they are complex undertakings depending on multiple, interdependent stages; (2) they depend on close, often iterative, interactions between design and construction; and (3) they require coordination among a number of skilled trades people (developers).

They are also dissimilar. A bridge is a physical object. A program—the product of systems development—is entirely logical. The engineering of a program differs from that of a physical device (such as a bridge) in the following ways: (1) there are no natural laws limiting the tolerance to which a program can be manufactured—it can be built exactly as specified and, once built, it will behave exactly as prescribed; (2) there is no friction or wear—the correctness and performance of a program will not decay with time; and (3) it can be reproduced at relatively zero cost. It is only our human frailties that limit the quality of systems—a fact that differentiates its development from that of a physical product and limits the analogy with bridge-building.

This suggests that the practice of developing systems is unique. Limited only by their imaginations and without the boundaries imposed by natural laws, IT professionals are often led down blind alleys. They are guided by possibilities. It has frequently been said, "if you can imagine it, then you can probably get a computer to do it," and this has been a beacon for development. Few would refrain from attempting to build a system just because nothing like it has ever been developed before. If asked for a "marketing intelligence system to anticipate customer response to new product launches," IT cannot dismiss the request out-of-hand. However, if an entrepreneur asked a contractor to build a "bridge to the moon", little time would be wasted on determining the feasibility of this proposal. Physical laws, such as the tensile strength of steel and the compression characteristics of poured concrete, would dictate futility. IT project management must account for the absence of similar physical laws.

THE NATURE OF IT PROJECT MANAGEMENT

The goal of a good IT project-manager is to develop, test, install, and implement a system (on time and within budget) that meets (or exceeds) established specifications. A number of these points need explanation. First, "development" may entail the writing of a series of programs, or external contracting for the writing of these programs, or the acquisition of these programs through lease or purchase. Second, full system specifications are developed as part of IT project management and, as such, represent an active component to be derived jointly with the business partner through the process of project management. Finally, implementing a system, once written, represents an enormous amount of activity in and of itself. Successful implementation includes documentation, training, conversion, and a host of follow-up activities to ensure that the new system is used correctly by the business.

The challenge of IT project management is attributable to its nature. As such, each IT project-manager must cope with two significant and interdependent realities:

1   IT Project Management Carries a Significant Risk of Failure

According to the Standish Group (Johnson et al., 2001), 23% of IT projects are canceled before they ever get completed; 49% of IT projects are over-budget; and the cost of these failures and over-runs are just the tip of the iceberg since the opportunity costs are simply not measurable. The same group estimates that only 28% of software projects are completed on time and on budget.

One of the reasons for such a high failure rate is that each IT project is unique. The operative phrase today is "if you can buy it, don't build it." If the system has been built elsewhere, then why would you want to build it again? Organizations rarely build general ledger systems or payroll systems. What they do build are those systems that are not immediately available, those that are unique to their particular organization, those that have not been built before, or those that enable them to differentiate themselves from their competitors. Therefore, each IT project is a venture into uncharted waters.

Another reason for the high failure rate is because IT projects tend to be large. While it is true that many IT projects represent only minor enhancements to existing systems to provide additional functionality, organizations do not thrive on a diet of this type of project. In order to realize significant value from IT and reap competitive advantage, organizations are encouraged to undertake large projects. Even the current practice of "staging" IT projects (i.e., breaking projects into smaller deliverable pieces) does not negate the fact that most projects, in their logical entirety, are large. History suggests that we can manage small projects, it is the large ones that represent IT management's greatest challenges.

Another explanation for the high failure rate is the complexity of IT projects. Complexity is a function of many factors including size and originality. But complexity also arises because of the need to work with new hardware, new software, new people, and/or even new methodologies. As well, complexity increases directly with the amount of interaction among systems. The nature and number of these interactions result in a substantial degree of complexity and make the development and testing of new systems (and therefore their management) extremely difficult. Complexity is company-specific and individual-specific; that is, what is complex for one project-manager may not be complex for another because of different experiential backgrounds. However, as complexity increases, the ability to guarantee the reliability and quality of the resultant system is severely hampered and the effort to do so increases logarithmically.

2   Business Requirements Are Elusive

The first task of an IT project-manager is to elicit a set of complete and accurate business requirements. Given complete requirements, IT project management becomes software-engineering. Unfortunately, ascertaining business requirements is arguably the most difficult task faced by IT project-managers. The difficulty is attributable to three factors. *First*, business managers rarely have the skills, training, or fortitude to establish their business requirements at the level of detail necessary for IT project development. Furthermore, attempts to keep users at the table long enough to achieve the necessary level of detail regarding business requirements can lead to stressful situations. Many IT project-managers are prematurely dismissed by business managers with instructions to fill in the blanks.

The *second* factor making business requirements problematic is the lack of mutual understanding between IT and business managers. Stated simply, business managers must first develop an appreciation of the capabilities of IT before they can identify potential business applications involving IT. Similarly, IT project-managers must develop an understanding of the business if they are to assist management in the beneficial deployment of information technology. There is usually a strong correlation between business requirement specification and IT–business partnership—the stronger the partnership, the better the project specification.

Finally, business requirements are typically in continual flux as organizations attempt to react to their environments. If business didn't change, ascertaining correct and complete requirements for IT projects would now be a science, not an art. Unfortunately, organizations need to react to external pressures, and if IT is to continue to support the business it too will need to be responsive to ever-evolving requirements. Delaying project development to achieve a set of perfect requirements leads to inaction and is unacceptable to the organization. At some point, business requirements must be deemed complete in order for development to proceed.

These realities, which surround IT project management, are for the most part beyond the reach of management and must be accepted as existing limitations to the development of information systems. As a result, IT project-managers must come to terms with managing projects that (1) may lack the guarantee of complete business specifications, (2) may lack some of the necessary technical skills at the outset of development, (3) promise unforeseen setbacks and detours, and (4) depend entirely on the marshaling of human resources to collectively overcome all the above difficulties. These challenges, magnified by the fact that IT projects are often deemed mission-critical by their organizations, render IT project management as one of the most difficult (and occasionally rewarding) organizational activities. The value to today's organizations of effective IT project management is enormous—top IT project-managers are simply "worth their weight in gold."

THREE KEY QUESTIONS

There appear to be three key questions regarding IT project management. How an organization chooses to answer these questions determines their overall orientation toward the development of IT project-managers. The questions relate to specific decisions: make versus buy; nature versus nurture; and certification. Each is discussed below.

1   Make versus Buy

The question posed to the focus group was: Should organizations "make or buy" IT project-managers? The answer was "both"—with qualifications. They felt that organizations should keep a foot in the market so that they are in a position to buy when excellent prospects become available, but they should place most of their effort into developing effective IT project-managers internally as this is the most reliable source of building material. In addition, since a significant part of project management involves marshaling organizational resources, effective IT project-managers need to have credibility within the business as well as awareness of the political machinations of the organization. Both of these attributes take time to master. The dangers of stepping over informal organizational boundaries and/or violating cultural taboos can be injurious to the health of aspiring IT project-managers.

2   Nature versus Nurture

Some managers would argue that the most effective IT project-managers are born, not developed. They would argue that charisma is genetic, as is the ability to lead. Others would argue that, to be an effective IT project-manager, one must acquire a skill base that takes time and practice and certainly is not acquired at birth. The focus group, while not resolving the issue, felt that there were elements of truth to both arguments with neither dominating. They felt that, for IT project-managers, it was an issue of "nurturing" those gifts that were given by "nature". Most in the focus group could cite examples of individuals who developed into outstanding IT project-managers after appropriate experience and training—each adapting skills to complement their unique personal style.

3   Certification

This is undoubtedly the most contentious of the three questions. Certification of IT project-mangers involves the development of a professional body to establish industry standards for IT project-managers. This body (the Project Management Institute is one such professional organization) determines the requisite skills and knowledge base and, based on mastery of these attributes, ascertains who qualifies as an IT project-manager.

In theory, the primary advantage of certification is professionalism. IT project-managers are recognized as a body of practicing professionals complete with standards, codes of conduct, and prescribed ethical behaviors. Skills are recognized, accepted, and transferable. IT project-managers are accredited—indicating mastery of project management and the attainment of certain standards of achievement. Furthermore, the body of practicing IT project-managers works to develop, enhance, and defend their professional ranks. According to proponents, certification does more to guarantee a continued source of IT project-managers than any other approach.

In practice, however, certification of IT project-managers falls short of its lofty goals. Within the focus group, there were strongly held, mixed feelings about the certification of IT project-managers. Many remained unconvinced that the benefits of certification would actually outweigh their costs (which are significant). In addition, they were not comfortable with what attainment of official status as "IS project-manager" really represented, pointing to the fact that different professional bodies awarded different certificates. Furthermore, they worried that, like carpentry, knowing how to use every tool in the box does not guarantee that one is a skilled craftsperson!

Because the majority of the members of the focus group believed that the internal development of IT project-managers was of the greatest importance, the next section concerns itself exclusively with this issue; that is, what strategies should organizations follow if they are interested in developing successful IT project-managers internally?

MANAGEMENT STRATEGIES

The task facing organizations is to determine how to improve their IT project management skills. To do so requires the development of a set of strategies for defining the roles of IT project-managers, developing appropriate training programs to facilitate the teaching/learning of the appropriate skills, measuring skill attainment and performance, creating appropriate structures to recognize and reward project management skill acquisition, and, finally, building a culture of success regarding IT project management. Focus group members had many ideas for how best to achieve these goals. Their ideas are presented below as management strategies.

1 · Establish a *Job Profile* for an Effective IT Project-manager

An effective IT project-manager can mean very different things to different organizations. Even within an organization, it is possible for two individuals to view themselves as successful project-managers despite the fact that they perform different types of function. Therefore, it is important to define the role of an IT project-manager as clearly as possible. One organization uses the following definition:

> A project manager is responsible for the coordination of the development, delivery, and implementation of customer-focused new products and services requiring technology support. This encompasses the coordination of business case preparation, negotiating and issuing project plans which specify the product, schedules, budgets, controls, resources, accountabilities, and the resolution of issues.

This general definition of an IT project-manager's responsibilities is then further subdivided into three major activities: project initiation, project execution, and project success (see Table 19.1 for a complete description of each of these activities). The careful delineation of the project-manager's job profile provides identifiable benefits to organizations. First, it allows project-managers to resolve any questions about their role. Second, it allows aspiring IT project-managers the opportunity to review the activities that will be asked of them should they pursue project management as a career. Based on this review, they can perform a self-assessment of their abilities to determine their potential to become an IT project-manager. Finally, accurate job profiles provide the basis for annual performance evaluations.

The evaluation of IT project-managers is an essential organizational task. The job profile (as described above) identifies the activities that must be performed. Once identified, it is possible for organizations to assess a project-manager's accomplishment of each of these tasks. As well, it is important for organizations to assess those individuals with aspirations of becoming IT project-managers.

Table 19.1   *Description of major activities for successful IT project management.*

(A) PROJECT INITIATION

The successful initiation of a project requires the project-manager to:

- support the creation of the business case to establish the project's scope, budget, time lines, cost–benefits, and contribution to the business;
- translate the business needs into technical specifications and the technical outcomes into business terms;
- initiate the work orders (or plans) directed toward the development of a product concept;
- negotiate for staff support;
- develop the product concept in collaboration with the business sponsor;
- coordinate and issue the project charter and plans;
- formulate the funding requirements;
- ensure that all the appropriate disciplines and stakeholders are represented on the project team;
- prepare the work plans;
- manage the budget/approvals/research;
- work with the business partner(s) to determine the best solutions, directions, time lines, and costs to meet objectives.

(B) PROJECT EXECUTION

The successful execution of the project plan ensures the product integrity, cost control, and achievement according to the schedule. The project manager must:

- enforce alignment with the plan and authorized changes only;
- coordinate activities and resources;
- conduct all communication requirements (meetings, status reports, etc.);
- manage the interactions with the project team;
- maneuver the project against a background of changing and conflicting priorities, and escalate issues where appropriate to meet business objectives;
- communicate status with business partners to ensure continued buy-in and understanding, and to manage expectations;
- assess risks to determine alternatives and remove roadblocks.

(C) PROJECT SUCCESS

In order to ensure success, the project manager should perform the following activities:

- control all changes/contingencies to the project plan;
- audit the items to be delivered under the project scope;
- manage vendors (if applicable) to contin costs, negotiate and select appropriate tools;
- ensure that the business partner provides appropriate input and buy-in;
- advise appropriate senior levels on problem issues and make recommendations to resolve them;
- direct the project team to alternatives when problems are encountered;

continued

Table 19.1   (cont.)

- ensure that senior management approvals for milestones are obtained in a timely manner;
- ensure that all project issues are quickly resolved;
- coach the project team members on appropriate development and efficient delivery of tasks;
- motivate, recognize the need for, and provide feedback to project team members as required.

---

2   Define the *Key Competencies* of a Successful IT Project-manager

The assessment of key competencies helps to explain why some project-managers are more successful than others and, at the same time, helps organizations to identify those individuals with the greatest promise of becoming successful IT project-managers. To do so, organizations must first identify the key competencies of successful project-managers (i.e., the set of proven skills) that allow them to succeed at their jobs. Unlike a job profile that identifies the things project-managers do, key competencies identify the skills they possess. By assessing an individual's mastery of these competencies, organizations are able to determine that individual's potential for IT project management.

The group members were asked to list the competencies that differentiated outstanding IT project-managers from mediocre performers. In total, they identified the 16 competencies listed below. Fuller descriptions of each competency are included in Table 19.2. Even top IT project-managers would not be expected to excel at all these competencies. Instead, most organizations look for a good balance:

- integrity and trust;
- interpersonal savvy;
- organizational ability;
- sizing up people;
- negotiating;
- priority-setting;
- process management;
- total quality management;
- customer focus;
- building team spirit;
- learning on the fly;
- managerial courage;
- dealing with ambiguity;
- innovation management;
- business knowledge;
- technical knowledge.

Table 19.2 *Key competencies for IT project management.*

Competency	Definition
1. Integrity and trust	Is widely trusted; is seen as a direct, truthful individual; can present the unvarnished truth in an appropriate and helpful manner; keeps confidences; doesn't blame others for his or her own mistakes or misrepresents himself or herself for personal gain or protection.
2. Interpersonal savvy	Relates well to all kinds of people, up, down, and sideways, inside and outside the organization; builds appropriate rapport; listens; builds constructive and effective relationships; uses diplomacy and tact; truly values people; can diffuse even high-tension situations comfortably.
3. Organizational ability	Knowledgeable about how organizations function; knows how to get things done both through formal channels and the informal network; understands the origin and reasoning behind key policies, practices, and procedures.
4. Sizing up people	Is a good judge of talent; after reasonable exposure, can clearly articulate the strengths and limitations of people inside or outside the organization; can accurately predict what various people are likely to do across a variety of situations.
5. Negotiating	Can negotiate skillfully in tough situations with both internal and external groups; can settle differences with minimum noise; can win concessions without damaging relationships; can be both direct and forceful as well as diplomatic; gains trust quickly of other parties to the negotiations; has a good sense of timing.
6. Priority-setting	Spends his or her time and the time of others on what's important; quickly zeros in on the critical few and puts the trivial many aside; can quickly sense what will help or hinder accomplishing a goal; eliminates roadblocks; creates focus.
7. Process management	Good at figuring out the processes necessary to get things done; knows how to organize people and activities; understands how to separate and combine tasks into efficient work flow; knows what to measure and how to measure it; can see opportunities for synergy and integration where others can't; can simplify complex processes; gets more out of fewer resources;

continued

Table 19.2   *(cont.)*

Competency	Definition
	is able to perform risk analysis to determine appropriate direction for project and can formulate contingency plans to remove roadblocks impacting the completion of projects and meeting of deadlines.
8. Total quality management	Is dedicated to providing the highest quality products and services that meet the needs and requirements of internal and external customers; is committed to continuous improvement through empowerment and management by data; is open to suggestions and experimentation; creates a learning environment leading to the most efficient and effective work processes.
9. Customer focus	Is dedicated to meeting the expectations and requirements of internal and external customers; gets first-hand customer information and uses it for improvements in products and services; talks and acts with customers in mind; establishes and maintains effective relationships with customers and gains their trust and respect.
10. Building team spirit	Creates strong morale and spirit in his or her team; shares wins and successes; fosters open dialogue; lets people finish and be responsible for their work; lets subordinates present to senior management; acts as if real success is the success of the whole team; creates a feeling of belonging in the team.
11. Learning on the fly	Learns quickly when facing new problems; a relentless and versatile learner; open to change; analyzes both successes and failures for clues to improvement; experiments and will try anything to find solutions; enjoys the challenge of unfamiliar tasks; quickly grasps the essence and the underlying structure.
12. Managerial courage	Provides current, direct, complete, and "actionable" positive and corrective feedback to others; doesn't hold back anything that needs to be said; always lets people know where they stand; faces up to people problems quickly and directly; is not afraid to take negative action (e.g., put on probation, fire, demote, etc.) when necessary.
13. Dealing wich ambiguity	Can effectively cope with change; can shift gears comfortably; can decide and act without having the total picture; isn't upset when things are up in the air;

	doesn't have to finish things before moving on; can comfortably handle risk and uncertainty.
14. Innovation management	Has good judgment about which creative ideas and suggestions will work; has a sense about managing the creative process of others; can facilitate effective brainstorming; can predict how potential ideas may play out in the marketplace; is good at bringing the creative ideas of others to the market.
15. Business knowledge	Has an excellent understanding of the business; makes the business priorities his or her priorities; suggests creative solutions (not always "technology" solutions) to business situations thus enhancing credibility with the business.
16. Technical knowledge	Understands the technology well enough to identify opportunities to match technology with business strategies; can anticipate the problems with new (bleeding-edge) technologies; can differentiate potential technologies based on an assessment of the balance between promise and performance.

This list provides a good foundation. Organizations should augment this list to reflect their own particular culture and environment. Once established, the list can be used to assess the potential of IT staff members. Those staff displaying high aptitude for (or mastery of) these competencies should be actively encouraged to pursue IT project management as a career. It also can be used as a guide (or signal) to direct the personal development of potential project-managers.

3   Establish a *Program* to Develop IT Project-managers

IT project-managers represent a critical organizational resource. Truly outstanding IT project-managers are in very short supply. As a result, losing a top IT project-manager to another organization can be extremely detrimental to an organization's health. This situation means organizations are exposed to serious risks should anything happen to their senior IT project-managers. Therefore, IT project-management resources must be managed proactively and effectively.

One organization instituted an orchestrated *program* to develop IT project-managers. This program, dedicated to the advancement of IT project-managers within the organization, is based on the following six fundamentals:

1. *Assessment.* This represents mechanisms that allow the organization to model, measure and assess, train, and certify project management skills and skill attainment.

2. *Tools*. This represents the collection of tools and information to assist project management. It contains techniques to facilitate planning management, risk management, cost management, communications management, people management, quality management, time management, procurement management, and scope management.
3. *Methods*. This represents the collection of all project management methods and procedures used within the organization.
4. *Guidance*. This outlines those functions to be used to mentor junior project-managers in their development.
5. *Direction*. This represents a guide to the project management processes followed by the organization.
6. *Compensation*. This represents the organization's documented approach to the remuneration, rewards, and recognition for project-managers.

The benefits of instituting such a program are significant. This organization in particular claims that their program has (a) increased the supply of IT project-managers, (b) instilled a new culture of professionalism and excellence within the organization, (c) increased the satisfaction of business partners as well as IT staff, (d) created a framework for continuous improvement for IT project management competencies, (e) resulted in senior management's promise to make a strategic long-term investment in IT management competencies and skills, and (f) resulted in significant annual cost savings due to the increased success rate of all IT projects. The realizable long-term benefits of such a program should not be ignored. It is strongly recommended that IT organizations take a similar approach toward the management of this critical resource. The only question is whether to build or buy such a program. The focus group could see benefits in both, so perhaps the best approach is a combination of "build and buy"; that is, acquire methodologies from other organizations, but tailor them significantly to accommodate the culture of your organization.

4   Professionalize IT Project Management

The approach taken to development of IT project-managers by the majority of IT organizations is based on two beliefs; first, project-managers are best developed internally; and, second, project-managers "learn the trade by doing". While these beliefs are not stated explicitly, adherence to them is practiced dutifully. The preference for developing IT project-managers internally follows the argument that this ensures that they will know the business as well as the art of project management. Certainly, few would argue that effective IT project-managers need to understand both worlds. Furthermore, those IT project-managers developed internally will understand the nuances of how project management works in their own organization. The "learn the trade by doing" approach is also based on learned wisdom and is well accepted and difficult to refute. Unfortunately, approaching IT project management from this internal, experiential viewpoint can be contrary to the view of IT project-managers as true professionals.

Organizations need to "professionalize" their IT project-managers. Certainly, certification is one way to professionalize your IT project-managers, but there are many other approaches. For instance, organizations can delineate various levels of project management. One organization defined job titles of "junior" and "senior". Another organization developed a three-tier classification. As an IT project-manager becomes more proficient, he or she is given projects with greater scope. For instance, a Tier-I project-manager would not be assigned a project with a budget exceeding $500,000.

Each of these classifications dictates the required skill level, demonstrated accomplishment, and competency base. This reinforces the notion of IT project management as a career and a profession where advancement through the ranks leads to a highly-sought-after prize. Furthermore, it builds on the "learn the trade by doing" philosophy with the development of a "cumulative experience effect" where an effective development program specifically takes junior project-managers and exposes them to different levels of complexity and challenge while simultaneously testing their ability to deliver. Finally, this approach avoids the progression of good project-managers into general management as their only career/growth option.

Other organizations have implemented mentoring and training programs. With these programs, senior IT project-managers are responsible for mentoring, coaching, and training more junior project-managers. They are rewarded for this activity and their annual reviews assess the quality of the training provided. These activities instill the notion that one owes something to the profession. In this case, one owes the training of those more junior. Sending project-managers for courses offered by outside agencies also signals that professionals need continual updating.

One member of the group described how her organization has attempted to professionalize project management by establishing a three-pronged approach. This approach focuses on the:

- project-manager;
- project management environment; and
- broader project environment.

With respect to the *project-manager*, skills and behaviors were established that are used in annual reviews to focus on any gaps that an individual reveals. This identifies deficiencies and shows prospective project-managers exactly where to focus their energies to master the requisite skills. Regarding the *project management environment*, a project consulting office was established to provide metrics, a project history database, a project management network structure, courses, training, simulation, certification, and competency models. Finally, with respect to the *broader project environment*, there is recognition that other factors impact project success. As a result, all projects are assessed with respect to the degree they affect (or are affected by) the organizational architecture (e.g., business and technology blueprints), methodology, culture (e.g., sense of urgency, ownership), and alignment. This structure creates a facilitating and supportive environment for the conduct of IT project management.

CONCLUSIONS

IT project management is both a science and an art. As a science, every effort should be made to clarify, classify, structure, and measure those elements of the practice of project management that can so benefit. This will assist the profession to learn from its mistakes and advance successful practice. As an art, every effort should be made to preserve the human components of what is a very creative, exciting, and rewarding profession. Because of the critical role that IT project management plays in organizations, steps should be taken to ensure its continual development and advancement.

REFERENCES

Johnson, J., K.D. Boucher, K. Connors, and J. Robinson (2001) *Collaborating on Project Success*, The Standish Group International, Dennis, MA (http://www.softwaremag. com/archive/2001feb/CollaborativeMgt.html)

Zelkowitz, M. (1979) "Perspectives on software engineering," *Computing Surveys*, **10**(2), June, 197–216.

Project Management Institute, Newtown Square, PA (http://www.pmi.org).

20
Developing Effective IT Leaders

A lot has changed in our thinking about leadership. It used to be that leaders were considered to be those few senior executives at the top of the organization. Now, it is accepted that leadership is no longer the exclusive purview of senior management. Everyone in the organization has the potential to display leadership behavior, and, furthermore, organizations benefit from effective leadership at all levels. Information technology (IT) organizations are no exception—in fact, it could be argued that IT leadership has become much more important over time as IT has taken on expanded responsibilities for effecting change within the organization. To the extent that we can build effective leadership within the IT function, we can infuse our organizations with vigor, optimism, enthusiasm, and creative energy resulting in much more productive organizations than otherwise possible.

To do this, however, requires an understanding of leadership. We need to identify the techniques of effective leaders and how they decide which technique is most applicable in a given situation. We need to understand what motivates an effective leader. We need to examine our personal experiences—when we have witnessed effective leadership and when we have assumed positions of leadership ourselves. We all experience leadership on a daily basis at play as well as at work. We see leadership displayed by pre-school children as well as by senior citizens. We see leadership displayed under situations of stress and relaxation. The challenge is to gain insight by examining these experiences. In thinking about leadership, we need to consider subordinates and colleagues as well as supervisors. In addition to thinking about what it was that these effective leaders did, we also need to examine our reactions to their actions. Finally, we need to examine the world of IT to see if it places unique challenges on the leadership role.

The next section covers some definitional attributes of leadership. This is followed by a discussion of the nature of leadership. The final section presents a number of strategies that IT organizations can adopt in order to foster a climate that encourages and rewards effective leadership within IT.

THE NATURE OF LEADERSHIP

There is little agreement on the definition of leadership. This fact, however, has not prevented us from forming opinions regarding leadership. Below are a number of definitions listed chronologically by Yukl (1998):

1. Leadership is "the behavior of an individual ... directing the activities of a group toward a shared goal" (Hemphill and Coons, 1957, p. 7).
2. Leadership is "the influential increment over and above mechanical compliance with the routine directives of the organization" (Katz and Kahn, 1978, p. 528).
3. Leadership is "the process of influencing the activities of an organized group toward goal achievement" (Rauch and Behling, 1984, p. 46).
4. Leaders are those who consistently make effective contributions to social order and who are expected and perceived to do so (Hosking, 1988, p. 153).
5. Leadership is a process of giving purpose (meaningful direction) to collective effort, and causing willing effort to be expended to achieve purpose (Jacobs and Jaques, 1990, p. 281).
6. Leadership ... is the ability to step outside the culture ... to start evolutionary change processes that are more adaptive (Schein, 1992, p. 2).
7. Leadership is the process of making sense of what people are doing together so that people will understand and be committed (Drath and Palus, 1994, p. 4).
8. Leadership is about articulating visions, embodying values, and creating the environment within which things can be accomplished (Richards and Engle, 1986, p. 206).

It is difficult to select the best definition; each of the above definitions of leadership is arguably correct. Their differences arise from the fact that each chooses to reflect a different aspect of leadership. If we concentrate on the similarities (as opposed to the differences), it is evident from the above definitions that leadership involves the conscious *influence* of one person over a group of other people; that this influence is a *process* as opposed to an event; that this influence is *purposeful* even goal-directed; that this influence is *motivational* and thus encourages others to accomplish things that otherwise would not be accomplished; and that this influence arises from *social* interaction. Leadership is a complex, multifaceted phenomenon. It is like defining beauty—we don't know what it is ... but we know it when we see it. Drawing on the similarities of the above definitions, Yukl (1998) defines leadership as:

> ... the process wherein an individual member of a group or organization influences the interpretation of events, the choice of objectives and strategies, the organiza-

tion of work activities, the motivation of people to achieve the objectives, the maintenance of co-operative relationships, the development of skills and confidence by members, and the enlistment of support and co-operation from people outside the group or organization.

This definition has a certain appeal. First, it treats leadership as a specialized role. As such, it is tangible and can be experienced. Most people can identify specific situations where they have experienced effective leadership. Second, leadership is defined as a social influence process. No-one can be an effective leader without someone else to lead. Leadership has no meaning without a social context. Finally, this definition treats both rational and emotional processes as essential aspects of leadership. These are the elements of motivation. Our capacity to influence others will, in most cases, depend on our ability to relate to them on an emotional level. It is this ability to touch our hearts and souls that results in extraordinary leadership.

It is common to distinguish two types of leadership: transactional and transformational. *Transactional leaders* exert influence by setting goals, clarifying desired outcomes, providing feedback, and exchanging rewards and recognition for accomplishments (Bass, 1985). *Transformational leaders* exert influence by broadening and elevating followers' goals and providing them with the confidence to go beyond minimally acceptable expectations specified in the exchange. Transformational leaders exhibit four behaviors: (a) individualized consideration, understanding and appreciating different needs and viewpoints within the group; (b) intellectual stimulation, questioning of assumptions, reframing of problems, and thinking about concepts using novel paradigms; (c) inspirational motivation, energizing group members' desire to work co-operatively to contribute toward the collective mission, and (d) idealized influence, broader consideration of perspectives, moral issues, and implications of one's actions (Bass and Avolio, 1990). Both types of leadership are valued within organizations.

Now that we have a working definition of leadership, there are a number of refinements that must be discussed:

- *Type of influence.* Should the definition of leadership be limited to the exercise of influence resulting in enthusiastic commitment by followers, as opposed to indifferent compliance or reluctant obedience? One might argue that a person who uses control over rewards and punishments to manipulate or coerce followers is not really "leading" them. The opposing view is that this definition is too restrictive because it excludes some influence processes that are important for understanding why a manager is effective or ineffective in a given situation (Yukl, 1998).
- *Purpose of influence.* Should the definition of leadership be limited to the exercise of influence for the purpose of task objectives or group maintenance, or should it include influence for the purpose of unethical behaviors or

personal aggrandizement? Acts of leadership often have multiple motives, and it is seldom possible to determine the extent to which they are selfless rather than selfish (Yukl, 1998).

- *Leadership versus management.* Should leadership be differentiated from management? It is possible to be a leader without being a manager, and it is certainly possible to be a manager without being a leader. Bennis and Nanus (1985) suggest that "managers are people who do things right and leaders are people who do the right thing." For the purposes of this chapter, we will concentrate on transformational leadership and equate transactional leadership with management.
- *Leadership effectiveness.* How do you measure leadership effectiveness? Should leadership be limited to the successful attainment of task objectives? Or, should leadership effectiveness include the attitudes of subordinates toward the leader, and the ability of the leader to contribute to the quality of the group's processes and cohesiveness? Should the leader be evaluated in terms of the short-term realization of immediate goals or the long-term benefit of enhanced profits?

These issues are not raised here for solution, but rather for clarification. When discussing leadership, we must be aware of these different frames of reference. One's description of an effective leader may presume goal attainment as the criterion while another's description of an effective leader may presume social cohesiveness as the valued outcome. Without clarification, we might not be able to reach agreement as to the identification of an effective leader and much less agreement regarding the attributes of such a person.

THE STUDY OF LEADERSHIP

Although the purpose of this chapter is not to conduct a study of leadership, it is instructive to understand the various approaches to the study of leadership. It is through this understanding that we are able to clarify our own perceptions of leadership activities and arrive at insightful conclusions.

Leadership research can be classified into five different approaches and four different levels of analysis (Yukl, 1998). The five approaches are described briefly below:

1. *Trait.* This approach studies the individual characteristics of leaders based on the assumption that some people are natural leaders endowed with certain traits not possessed by others. One such trait might be charisma.
2. *Behavior.* This approach studies the individual behaviors of leaders in an attempt to understand *what they do* (as opposed to the trait approach that attempts to understand *what they have*).
3. *Power-influence.* This approach studies the ways in which leaders can exert

power over co-workers. Here interest focuses on power-sharing, empowerment, and participative leadership techniques. While this research draws on both the trait and behavior approaches, it differs in its focus on the single attribute of power—its nature, origins, and uses.

4. *Situational*. This approach emphasizes the importance of contextual factors such as the nature of the work, the type of employees, or the external environment. This research attempts to determine the extent to which leadership is universal. That is, would an effective leader be equally effective in all situations? A number of contingency models emerge from this research that attempt to suggest which types of leadership are indicated for a variety of different organizational settings.

5. *Integrative*. This approach extends the situational approach by focusing on the leader–follower effects. This research searches for explanations for the fact that leaders can have very differential effects on different followers. In order to understand this, much attention is directed to understanding the leader–follower interaction.

According to Yukl (1998), leadership can be analyzed at four levels:

1. *Intra-individual*—because most conceptions of leadership involve interactions between individuals, this focus, which examines the processes within a single individual, is less popular. Nevertheless, research has shown that motivation, decision-making, and cognition can help to explain certain aspects of leadership behavior. Understanding how we are motivated individually, for example, suggests leadership strategies for motivating others.

2. *Dyadic*—the relationship between a leader and another individual, typically the follower. Key issues are how to develop a cooperative, trusting relationship with a follower, and how to influence a follower to be more motivated and committed.

3. *Group*—focuses on the nature of the leadership role within a task group and how a leader contributes to group effectiveness.

4. *Organizational*—looks at leadership in the larger context of the whole organization where groups are all subordinate to the larger social system. Differences among the leadership roles within groups, for instance, may be explained when seen in the light of the social rewards system of the organization.

The important point is that the study of leadership is informed by research at *all levels of analysis* using *every approach*. Most would agree that leadership is not simply an inherited trait, nor is it the result of exercising certain behaviors. By examining the unique needs of individuals in task groups within organizations, we will come closer to understanding the requirements of those who will be called on to lead. There is no escaping the fact that some individuals are more richly blessed genetically than others. Indeed, some are predisposed to be more effective as leaders than others, but the important point is that *we can all improve our capabilities and mastery of leadership skills and techniques*. Furthermore, individuals should be encouraged to enhance their leadership abilities as there is little doubt as to the benefit that accrues to organizations that nurture effective leaders.

THE NEED FOR LEADERSHIP WITHIN IT

Leadership used to be the exclusive purview of senior management. It was their duty to create the vision for the organization, to motivate employees to achieve objectives, to organize work activities, to maintain cooperative relationships, to ensure development of the skills and confidence of employees, and to marshal support and coordination from people outside the immediate group or organization. Today, after successive rounds of delayering organizational ranks, the leadership task is too large (and too important) to remain the exclusive mandate of senior management. As a result, leadership has become part of everyone's task. No longer do you find designated "leaders" any more than you find designated "followers".

This phenomenon is especially true within IT now that IT is expected, as a full partner of the business, to create new organizational value. Because of this, IT leaders are as valued by the business as by the IT function. To understand this, we need to examine the organizational role that IT plays.

IT is charged with the task of implementing technology-based change. To do this, IT professionals must examine organizational processes with an eye to redesigning business operations. The difficulty, however, lies not with the analysis, but with the implementation of change and stems directly from the fact that the IT organization has no formal power over business units in realizing this change. Without formal organizational authority, the IT organization must rely on their ability to persuade and influence others—that is, their integrative leadership capabilities to lead others toward change. This ability is based on their technical prowess, business knowledge, proven track record, and credibility with the business units. With effective leadership, IT can fulfill key roles in helping to transform their parent organizations.

This leadership role is critical within IT as well. Succumbing to the same re-engineering impetus, the IT organization has pushed responsibility and authority down the hierarchy and empowered lower level employees to take risks and make decisions in partnership with business units on behalf of the organization. This is an "individual leadership" model as opposed to a "hierarchical leadership" model. In some organizations, account executives within IT have the ability to commit resources to new business ventures in collaboration with their business partners following a model of risk–reward sharing. It can be shown that, through such empowerment, the effort of management is greatly reduced. No longer must

Table 20.1   *The changing values and behaviors of IT leaders.*

Previously valued attributes	Preferred attributes
Supervisors, coordinators	Leaders, coaches, mentors
Focused on customer	Focused on all stakeholders
Information distributor	Information marketer
Directive	Participative
Equality, sameness for everyone	Fair, but recognizes individuality
Controlling, limited scope of authority	Empowering and empowered
Cautious	Risk-taking, accepting of failure
Supportive of business	Passionate for the business
Structured	Flexible, able to deal with ambiguity
Environment of authority	Environment of trust
Accountable for driving work	Accountable for ensuring roadblocks to success are removed; results-oriented

management look over everyone's shoulder on a regular basis. This model, however, can only work if everyone within IT assumes a situational leadership role—that is, everyone takes on the leadership role for a given situation. On a development project, for example, someone will lead the architecture-planning while someone else takes the lead on auditability requirements or the management of the system-testing environment. "Taking the lead" means assuming responsibility for the delivery of the particular activity, motivating others to work in a coordinated fashion, removing the roadblocks, and building the relationships necessary for the successful completion of the task. The "leader" will take "ownership" of the given task. Because a project consists of many tasks, each project will have many leaders. Individuals could have a small leadership role or a large leadership role. It is in this sense that "everyone is a leader".

The benefits of an "individual leadership" model over a "hierarchical leadership" model are significant. In the individual model, it is expected that everyone will practice leadership. As such, leadership is a continual activity and the nurturing of leaders is accomplished gradually over time. Leaders are recognized early in their organizational development—not just on promotion. These changes in leadership models, however, are subtle. One group member outlined the new leadership values and behaviors that his organization rewards in Table 20.1.

In the next section, we outline the role of leadership and the behaviors and learned practices that enhance leadership. Building on this, we identify a basic set of skills that constitutes effective leadership within IT. In developing these, we argue that the mastery of certain skills is *necessary, but not sufficient*. Skill mastery must be complemented with the ability to know when and where particular behaviors/skills are required and to know how they should be deployed.

MANAGEMENT STRATEGIES

The task facing organizations is to determine how to improve their IT leadership skills. To do so requires the development of a set of strategies for defining the roles of IT leaders, developing appropriate training programs to facilitate the teaching/learning of the appropriate skills, measuring skill attainment and performance, creating appropriate structures to recognize and reward leadership skill acquisition, and, finally, building a culture of success regarding IT leaders. Focus group members had many ideas for how best to achieve these goals. Their ideas are presented below as management strategies.

1   Define the Role of Leadership within IT

Senior IT management must articulate a clear vision of the nature and role of leadership within IT—a vision that should be communicated to all members of IT. At a minimum, this vision should delineate what makes an effective leader, and how effective leadership is expected to impact the organization. This enables IT personnel to understand the leadership requirements and the expected results of leadership activities. It is necessary for everyone to be able to distinguish the specific leadership requirements for each task. In addition, they should understand what leadership attributes they now possess and what attributes they would need to acquire in order to qualify for any position within IT. This makes leadership an integral part of each employee's development to be managed as part of regular career advancement.

One organization depicted leadership as one of the three vital attributes for success in IT (see Figure 20.1).

It is in the heart of these three concentric circles where the challenges lie for IT and where success will be gained. Some individuals will need to have more technical knowledge, others more business knowledge, but everyone will need

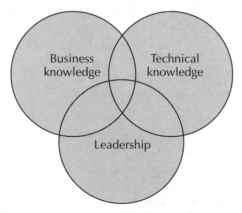

Figure 20.1   *Three critical knowledge/skill areas for IT.*

Table 20.2 *Differences between managers and leaders.*

Manager	Leader
Administers	Innovates
A copy	An original
Maintains	Develops
Focuses on systems and structure	Focuses on people
Relies on control	Inspires trust
Short-range view	Long-range perspective
Asks "how" and "when"	Asks "what" and "why"
Has an eye on the bottom line	Has an eye on the horizon
Imitates	Originates
Accepts the status quo	Challenges the status quo
A classic good soldier	His or her own person
Does things right	Does the right things

leadership to augment their specialized capabilities in order to function effectively within IT. It is through their leadership abilities that IT will be able to promote the successful marriage of technology solutions with business opportunities.

Defining the role of leadership also entails differentiating leadership from management. As pointed out earlier in this chapter, management is equated with *transactional leadership* and defined as *doing things right* while leadership is defined as *doing the right things*. Other differences are suggested by Bennis (1989) in Table 20.2.

The distinction between a leader and a manager is important. Organizations need both. Furthermore, as explained earlier, they are no longer different people. Individuals must assume leadership roles as well as management roles—both are necessary. The debate as to whether you can be an effective leader without being an effective manager (or vice versa) is generally futile.

2   Make Leadership a Priority within IT

Leadership must be established as a top priority within IT. Without a recognizable and concerted effort to build, enhance, and reward leadership, it will be left to happenstance—some natural leaders will emerge while others will remain undetected and undeveloped (or underdeveloped). The worst situation involves individuals who are placed in positions of leadership despite woeful inadequacy. This can have devastating effects on employee morale, motivation, and performance.

Campaign slogans, while necessary, are insufficient. Making leadership a priority involves clearly articulating:

- the need for leadership within IT;
- the requisite leadership skills;

- the process for attaining these skills;
- the personal rewards to be realized through mastery of these new skills; and
- the measurable benefits to the organization that result from enhanced leadership.

The reason for clearly articulating these elements within the IT organization are to convince individuals of three things: (1) that they *can improve* their leadership skills, (2) that they *will benefit* from doing so, and (3) that it is *expected* for their career advancement. To the degree that this is done convincingly, employees will find the motivation to seek those very skills that have been identified as necessary to benefit the organization.

3 Define the Key Competencies of Successful IT Leaders

The term *competency*, as we have chosen to use it, may refer to a trait, a behavior, the exercise of power or influence, or the situation-specific application of a behavior. When group members were asked to reflect on their personal experiences with effective leaders, they identified a number of competencies that were used to create a composite picture of an effective leader (Table 20.3).

When asked to compare effective leaders with ineffective leaders, the group cited many differences. In some cases, the differences were simply due to omission; that is, good leaders had certain competencies and ineffective leaders lacked

Table 20.3 *Profile of an effective leader.*

Visionary	Creates a clear vision; uses vision to inspire and/or motivate; maintains the large picture to help orchestrate the details
Communicator	Knows when/how to communicate effectively; communicates more than on a "need to know" basis; makes sense of events; engages/involves others
High expectations	Encourages others to accomplish more than they thought they could; always expects the best in people; uncompromising in excellence
Confidence builder	Shows confidence in others' ability to do things not done before; allows others to fail by letting them try; fosters learning by providing leadership opportunities
Trustworthy	Honest; unwilling to promise anything that cannot be delivered; no hidden agendas
Creditable	Knows the business; knows the technology; has track record to prove it; digs deep enough to be an expert
Supportive	Offers encouragement; shows flexibility when it matters; encourages others to take initiative

Table 20.4   *Eleven key leadership competencies.*

---

(1) FOCUS TO WIN

- *Customer insight*—developing a clear understanding of the value proposition
- *Breakthrough thinking*—developing the ability to take some risk
- *Drive to achieve*—developing the ability to challenge the process for opportunity

(2) MOBILIZE TO EXECUTIVE

- *Team leadership*—developing the ability to lead the team
- *Straight talk*—developing honesty and integrity
- *Teamwork*—developing the ability to be an effective part of the team
- *Decisiveness*—developing the ability to decide on an appropriate decision methodology

(3) SUSTAIN RESULTS

- *Building organizational capability*—developing additional capabilities within yourself and within the team
- *Developing talent*—developing the pool of talent that starts with yourself
- *Personal dedication*—developing the ability to "walk the talk"

(4) THE CORE

- *Passion for the business*—developing strong allegiances to the business

---

these competencies. For example, a good leader is trustworthy and an ineffective leader is not. Some differences were context-sensitive; that is, the ability to ascertain the appropriate competency for the given situation. The group felt that effective leaders appeared to be aware of (and sensitive to) the dynamics of their environment and therefore able to invoke appropriate traits/behaviors. Failing to understand the need for building the confidence of subordinates, for example, might lead an ineffective leader to become authoritarian or autocratic, thus worsening the situation. It is evident from this that the most critical of all leadership competencies is the demonstrated ability to be in touch with the needs of the immediate environment—the people, the task, and the organizational structure within which the job must get done.

Agreement as to the key competencies of an effective leader was not perfect. One group member outlined the 11 leadership competencies adopted by her organization (see Table 20.4). These are not identical to those listed above although they are highly congruent. This really doesn't matter. What does matter is that each organization attempts to delineate the leadership competencies that they believe to be critical for all IT positions. Furthermore, not everyone need attain uniform mastery of all leadership competencies. In fact, this would rarely be the case. It is important, however, that employees understand the target leadership competencies for their current position as well as their future position. Each member of IT can then examine their own mastery of various competencies to determine where to focus their leadership self-development efforts. The next section outlines how to do this.

4   Establish a Program to Develop IT Leaders

Once leadership has been established as a critical activity and key competencies have been delineated, it is necessary to implement a leadership program. Without an orchestrated program, it is difficult to ingrain leadership within the fabric of the organization. Over time, an effective program will strengthen everyone's leadership qualities. This follows the belief that everyone has "a champion within" who needs to be released.

One group member outlined the leadership program in place at her organization. This organization believed that IT leadership must be described, assessed, measured, supported, and rewarded at all levels of management. Leadership must be seen as a critical part of every IT job. To achieve this, they embedded leadership within seven key business processes. These processes are listed below:

- *Interview.* Leadership attributes are assessed at "Day 1"—that is, at the first interview stage of a prospective candidate. This assessment consists of self-assessment, peer evaluations, and scenario analysis.
- *Resource deployment.* Whenever resources are to be assigned, the requirements of the leadership opportunity are matched with the leadership skills of the employee.
- *Skills development.* Templates were developed for each level of each profession within the IT organization that included the required skill level for each leadership trait.
- *Personal business commitment.* Each IT employee goes through a process to identify the achievement of his or her skills plan as one of his or her personal commitments to achieving the overall business objectives.
- *Promotions.* Leadership mastery is evaluated as part of the performance appraisal of every IT employee.
- *Professional certification.* This outlines a specialized set of skills to enable employees to be certified at different levels of leadership mastery. The leadership skills are a subset of the overall skills requirements for that profession.
- *Executive resources.* Those people with executive leadership potential are identified through this specific program to assume development and/or key leadership roles within the organization.

It can be seen from this program that leadership has been made an integral part of all human resources processes. Success is possible only when leadership is made an explicit part of the functioning of the organization.

CONCLUSIONS

For IT to assume full partnership with the business, it will have to take a leadership role on many vital organizational issues. Interestingly, this leadership role is not the exclusive prerogative of senior executives—it is the duty of all IT employees. Effective leadership has enormous benefits. To realize these benefits, leadership qualities should be explicitly recognized, reinforced, and rewarded at all levels of the IT organization. This only happens when a concerted effort is made to introduce leadership activities into the very fabric of the IT organization. Leadership is everyone's job.

REFERENCES

Bass, B.M. (1985) *Leadership and Performance beyond Expectations*, Free Press, New York.

Bass, B.M. and B.J. Avolio (1990) "Developing transformational leadership: 1992 and beyond," *Journal of European Industrial Training*, **14**, 21–27.

Bennis, W.G. and B. Nanus (1985) *Leaders: The Strategies for Taking Charge*, Harper and Row, New York.

Drath, W.H. and C.J. Palus (1994) *Making Common Sense: Leadership as Meaning-making in a Community of Practice*, Center for Creative Leadership, Greensboro, NC.

Hemphill, J.K. and A.E. Coons (1957) "Development of the leader behavior description questionnaire," in R.M. Stogdill and A.E. Coons (eds), *Leader Behavior: Its Description and Measurement*, Bureau of Business Research, Ohio State University, Columbus, OH.

Hosking, D.M. (1988) "Organizing, leadership, and skillful process," *Journal of Management Studies*, **25**, 147–166.

Jacobs, T.O. and E. Jaques (1990) "Military executive leadership," in K.E. Clark and M.B. Clark (eds), *Measures of Leadership*, pp. 281–295, Leadership Library of America, West Orange, NJ.

Katz, D. and R.L. Kahn (1978) *The Social Psychology of Organizations*, 2nd edn, John Wiley & Sons, New York.

Richards, D. and S. Engle (1986) "After the vision: Suggestions to corporate visionaries and vision champions," in J.D. Adams (ed.), *Transforming Leadership*, Miles River Press, Alexandria, VA.

Schein, E.H. (1992) *Organizational Culture and Leadership*, 2nd edn, Jossey-Bass, San Francisco, CA.

Yukl, G. (1998) *Leadership in Organizations*, 4th edn, Prentice Hall, Englewood Cliffs, NJ.

21
Best Practices in IT

There is a lot of interest in companies these days in being "the best". Whether in information technology (IT) itself or in business in general, corporate leaders are striving to be "best in class" or "best in the world". They believe that to succeed in the new world economy, their companies must meet world-class standards of excellence in work practices, products, and services. Kanter (1995) notes that the pressures of the global economy are forcing firms to a perspective of "world-readiness" *even if* they choose to focus their efforts locally only. She defines this as:

- meeting best-in-world standards;
- searching for the best ideas and technologies; and
- having world-class employees and partners.

But transforming these high-level management ideals into daily practice in an IT organization frequently loses much in the translation. As Wiarda and Luria (1998) note, "the mythology often gets in the way of common sense." All this has left IT managers wondering. Are "best practices" just another management fad? Can their organizations truly benefit from seeking and adopting the best available practices? Who can tell whether a practice is really "the best"?

This chapter looks at where the true value can be found in all the hype about best practices. First, it examines the concept of best practices, and what IT managers are trying to achieve by using them. It then presents a framework for thinking about the many different issues involved in being a best practice organization. Finally, the problems and challenges involved in using best practices in IT are discussed and an action plan is suggested for how to get started in identifying and using best practices.

WHAT *ARE* BEST PRACTICES?

Focus group members and researchers use a wide variety of terms when they speak about best practices in IT, including: knowledge management (Davenport, 1997); benchmarking (Murray et al., 1997); quality assurance; metrics (Koch, 1998); and process improvements (Heibler et al., 1998). As a result, there is considerable disagreement about what best practices actually are.

The term "best practice" frequently (but not always) refers to a "best process"—whether it is an improved method of developing software or an improved business process using IT. One focus group member defined best practices in IT as ones that "effectively integrate people, process, and technology to do something for the organization." Sometimes, the term is used to refer to the identification, promotion, and transfer of best practices *within* IT. At other times, it is used to mean the best organizational and technical practices to support business objectives (Freeman, 1998).

What we *know* about best practices is that:

- *Practice* is *"what organizational members actually do"* (Szulanski, 1993). It is the "stuff that happens in organizations every day—people working together to achieve practical outcomes and building practical know-how in the process" (Senge, 1997). In other words, practice is not what the organization's manuals say goes on, it is *what actually happens to get the job done.*
- *Best* can be either a practice that is best in the world, according to objective standards (Kanter, 1995) or it can simply mean what's best for a particular business at a particular place in time (Heibler et al., 1998).

We also know that there are strong links between certain best practices and an organization's financial performance (Menke, 1997a; Fitz-Enz, 1997; Kulandaiswamy et al., 1997). In addition, the research shows other positive outcomes of using particular practices such as: software excellence, customer satisfaction, flexibility, competitive advantage, quality decision-making, effectiveness, and efficiency (Heibler et al., 1998; Koch, 1998; Murray et al., 1997).

The challenge of best practices is therefore finding the *right* practices to achieve these results. This requires thoughtful analysis because, with change happening in organizations at an unprecedented rate, it can be counterproductive to seek enlightenment about the future from studying the specifics of what some other organization did in the past. Fitz-Enz (1997) believes "the only hope one has of preparing for the future is to find practices that are so fundamental, so near bedrock, that they will play as effectively fifty years from now as they do today." *True* best practices, he states, are to be found in the management of organizations and *not* in the outcomes of these fundamental management practices. Real best practices therefore are the *beliefs* that drive a process. Thus, he defines best practices as:

... an enduring commitment to a set of basic beliefs, traits, and operating strata-
gems. These are the constant context of the organization: the driving forces that
distinguish it from all others.

For example, a constant focus on adding value in everything can be a best
practice because this practice is transferable to other departments and organizations; creating a database to track customer transactions is not a best practice
because it is specific to an individual business unit's situation.

Focus group members agreed that best practices in IT should emphasize
fundamentals and have a level of universality. They also felt that strong links
to performance measures such as productivity, quality, the organization's ability
to respond, and satisfaction are essential in a best practice. In addition, they noted
that a best practice should be defined, systematic, teachable, repeatable, and
simple.

Drawing on all these perspectives, for this book we will define a best practice
in IT as:

Something that people in IT actually do that supports larger corporate values and
objectives and that is generic, measurable, and transferable to others.

A BEST PRACTICES FRAMEWORK

The conflicting demands on IT by organizations to be efficient and effective, and
to spearhead new business processes can confuse the issue of best practices even
further because different practices are used to achieve each of these goals
(Hildebrand, 1997). What's needed, therefore, is a way to order and think
about best practices so that there can be agreement on how and where a practice
fits with what IT is doing.

From this point of view, three distinct levels of best practice emerge as
important (see Figure 21.1):

1. *Best strategic practices*. These are the key practices to get right because they set
   the context for everything else that is done in a company. If an organization is
   not strategically well positioned, it will be difficult to get the desired results
   from any of its other practices.
2. *Best processes*. At the next level, generic processes ensure that quality decisions
   are made. Processes provide the links between what people actually do (i.e.,
   practices) and the performance of the organization (i.e., being the best). Thus,
   it is the presence of the right processes that show some of the strongest links
   to an organization's financial performance (Menke, 1997a).
3. *Best work improvement practices*. This is the level that people most often
   associate with best practices in IT (Szulanski, 1993; Heibler et al., 1998). It
   focuses on the specific things that organizations do to improve how work is

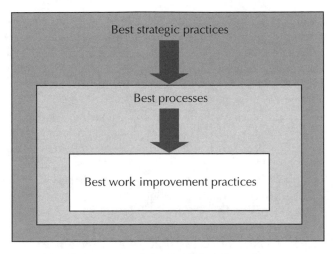

Figure 21.1 *A framework for best practices.*

done. However, without the context of the values and processes of the two previous levels, it is extremely unlikely that: (a) the right things will be identified to be changed or that (b) the people involved will be motivated to change their practices permanently so that better ones can be adopted.

Each of these levels of practice is discussed in more detail below.

BEST STRATEGIC PRACTICES

Streeter (1998) points out that sometimes a best practice mentality blurs strategy with tactics. Without a clear strategy of what makes a company different, there is a danger of "competitive convergence" where companies start to adopt the same best practices and thus to compete in the same way. This is why comparisons with other organizations (e.g., through benchmarking) should only be used within a top-down strategic business plan framework (Murray et al., 1997). Leaders who articulate their core values and then spell out "mission orders"—clearly and simply—help their organizations to succeed because individuals then know what they need to accomplish. With the context clear, "individuals don't need to run back to the boss every time something changes because [they] understand the boss's intent" (Korchinski, 1998).

Another reason why it is important to understand fundamental values and strategies is to facilitate creative approaches to processes and work practices. Unless everyone is very clear about what these are (and what they are not), it is unlikely ideas will be produced that will break away from prevailing schools of thought (Sweetman, 1997).

At this level, best practices focus on facilitating *understanding*. For example, knowing the root drivers of industry change will enable an organization to articulate values and strategies that will be most likely to deliver practices that will affect performance. Similarly, awareness of best results, how and why these results are being achieved, and the organization's unmet needs will establish a productive context for growing best practices (Menke, 1997a).

Some best strategic practices that have been demonstrably linked to improved organizational performance include *for senior managers* (including the chief information officer [CIO]) (Baumbusch, 1997; Wheatley, 1998; Anonymous, 1997):

- identify and communicate your organization's basic beliefs and values;
- understand the drivers of industry change;
- frame decisions strategically;
- communicate the strategic plan;
- measure the contribution of a decision to strategic objectives;
- adopt common terminology—within the organization, within the industry, and with supply chain partners;
- develop a technology strategy;
- coordinate long-range business and technology plans;
- have a comprehensive project strategy that focuses on value, effective planning, and resourcing;
- manage the portfolio of projects.

For IT managers (Korchinski, 1998):

- create and drive a culture of IT excellence;
- create multiple links with end-users to ensure effective partnerships;
- empower staff to make judgments and accomplish their jobs;
- establish a positive climate where everybody is allowed to make honest errors and learn from them;
- facilitate out-of-the-box thinking.

BEST PROCESSES

Best processes ensure that the IT organization has the *capacity* to adopt new work practices. That is, an organization must have the technical and managerial competence, and the resources, to recognize, assimilate, and apply new ways of doing things (Szulanski, 1993). Good processes not only create capacity, they also help to focus an organization on where improvements need to be made and on what types of best work practice are needed. While a process actualization (i.e., implementation) must be monitored regularly, the core processes themselves and their fundamental goals will not change often.

At minimum, IT organizations need to implement processes for doing the following.

Infrastructure Management

There must be a process to deliver a cost-effective infrastructure that meets technology standards and provides reliable services (Hildebrand, 1997). Features that contribute to a best process include:

- a high performance data center and reliable network uptime;
- reliable, up-to-date PCs and network access;
- establishment and management of technical standards;
- attention to the business costs of running the infrastructure.

Service Delivery

IT must have a means to demonstrate its ability to satisfy its customers—both its internal customers and its end-users. Effective features of this process include:

- using customer logic to evaluate service (see Box 21.1);
- continually looking for metrics that demonstrate a strategic link, operational excellence, and customer impact (Koch, 1998; Heibler et al., 1998).

Box 21.1   Customer logic (Kanter, 1995)

- Focus on providing value to the customer.

- Optimize mobilization of resources.

- Use multiple sources to deliver value.

- Focus on relationships and the totality of a customer's dealings with the company.

- Concentrate on differentiation and variation.

Management of the Development Process

IT needs to manage its development process rigorously to ensure quality and on-time and on-budget delivery. This process should also ensure that new business and development practices are evaluated and integrated. Demonstrably effective elements of this process include:

- rigorous management of software development (Menke, 1997a);
- assessing and managing risk (Dutta and van Wassenhove, 1998);

- use of a formal development process (Menke, 1997b);
- adoption of usability engineering practices (see Box 21.2);
- comprehensive measurement.

People Management

An IT organization needs a process to keep its personnel motivated and happy. This will include a means of recruiting and maintaining expertise, empowering people to do their job, and developing their skills. Some effective practices within this process include:

- developing *absorptive capacity* (i.e., managerial competence, resources, basic skills) to recognize and absorb new practices (Szulanski, 1993);
- emphasizing two-way communication with staff (Fitz-Enz, 1997);
- promoting innovation and prudent risk-taking (Korchinski, 1998).

Knowledge Management

This process facilitates collaboration and learning and captures a company's collective experience, know-how, and wisdom, making it available to anyone who needs it (LaPlante, 1997). An effective knowledge management process should:

- provide infrastructure for collaboration—including mechanisms for exchanging ideas, cross-functional groups and teams, and opportunities to develop relationships outside the organization (Kanter, 1995; McClenahen, 1997);
- provide adequate resources for implementing and maintaining the knowledge management process (Davenport, 1997; Kleiner and Roth, 1997).

Box 21.2   Usability engineering

Learn about your users. Take an initial "low tech" approach to development. Focus on the characteristics of the people who will be using the system and their role in the company.

Know their work. Use a combination of interviews and site visits where a team member can shadow a user for a day, to help the team build an understanding of the users' work.

Set usability goals. Set usability goals for the project based on what is learned about users and their work. These should be prioritized and used to guide design and testing processes.

Design multiple interfaces. Concurrently, a number of prototype interfaces should be designed and evaluated. Systems people, end-users, and human sciences people should all participate in this. Different design techniques that could be used are:

- *Parallel design*—different groups develop different alternatives in parallel.

- *Participatory design*—the end-users are involved in design.

- *Iterative design*—a design is created, tested, and adjusted to obtain optimal results.

Evaluate usability. Set up a lab environment with a work space, the prototypes, a set of business tasks, and two video cameras (one to capture facial expressions and verbal comments, and the other screen activity). Hold several walkthroughs and continuously improve the design. This approach highlights problems very quickly. Users enjoy it and feel important to the process.

Use iterative development. Use an iterative development approach to enable the creation of one project component while other pieces are still being designed.

Build in intrinsic performance support. Supplement the emphasis on usability with a constant consideration of the users' need for support from the first day of design.

Collect feedback from actual field use. When the project is fully developed, link it to e-mail so that pilot participants can communicate with the project team quickly and easily.

Relationship Management

Relationships are an essential part of best practices at all levels. Markus and Benjamin (1997) point out that "change flows across relationships." Without good relationships in place, it will be impossible to transfer best practices within IT, from IT to business, or between business units. Therefore, IT must develop a process to develop, maintain, and manage its relationships. Practices that work well in this process include:

- developing multiple links with users at all levels in the organization;
- having formal processes for obtaining regular feedback from end-users (Freeman, 1998);
- co-locating users on development projects.

How well these processes are actualized, assessed, and continually improved will depend on the effectiveness of an organization's strategic practices, IT management's ability to communicate *why* certain processes are important, and their

ability to make explicit linkages between a process and organizational performance.

BEST WORK IMPROVEMENT PRACTICES

Once the context and processes have been established, there are four steps
involved in identifying best work improvement practices.

1   Focus

Not all processes and practices can be improved at once. It is better to concentrate your efforts on one or two specific processes and improve their practices.
Doctor and Swanborg (in Hildebrand, 1997) suggest that organizations have a
hierarchy of practice needs that should be addressed sequentially.

At the most basic level, organizations should take the technology they already
have and work to optimize it. Thus, managers should concentrate first on the
infrastructure management process and its work practices. While this is not a
glamorous process, users definitely know when this basic level of computing is
not well done, and business can be greatly affected by its absence. Interestingly,
even at this level, researchers at MIT have found that IT groups build better
infrastructures, more closely attuned to business needs, when there is a clearly
articulated business vision. Low-cost and reliable infrastructure can best be
achieved by such practices as technical standards, and redesigning work practices
to cut down on the cost of support and improve the quality of service.

Second, IT managers should work on providing superior service delivery and
software development (Koch, 1998). In these processes, having service-level
agreements, using measurable benchmarks, and getting users to do measurement
are all effective practices. Managers should also concentrate on delivering projects on time and on budget. This requires improved staff skills, so practices in the
people management process should also be a focus at this time.

At the highest level of the organization's needs hierarchy are processes that
create value through using technology to enable business change. This cannot be
done unless IT has built up credibility in the company through its software
development, service delivery, and infrastructure management processes. Close
collaboration between business and IT and mutual learning are essential at this
level. Therefore, IT managers should work on practices in the knowledge management and relationship management processes.

2   Analysis

Identifying best work improvement practices involves analysis to ensure the right
things are addressed and the practices introduced are not "paving the cow paths".
To identify areas for improvement, consultants recommend starting with a Best

Practices Audit, where IT managers actively listen to their customers, try to understand their needs, and ask the unasked questions (Heibler et al., 1998). Listening appears to be key to being open to new possibilities that break the mould (Kanter, 1995). To begin an audit, organizations can look at their *products* or *services* (e.g.: How can we improve our help desk?) or they can focus on *functions* (e.g.: How can we improve IT staff-recruiting?) But group members and the experts agree that the best approach is to start with the *process* involved (see above).

In other words, specific problems should be assessed as part of the process. This helps eliminate industry limitations on thinking and enables a much broader range of potential solutions to be introduced. For example, help desk problems could be reframed as part of the service delivery process. IT staff-recruiting is part of a people management process that attracts, develops, manages, and retains people. One IT manager analyzes problems by gathering a wide variety of user comments and then sifting them to separate facts from opinions, guesses, and assumptions. This helps get at the root causes of a problem where opportunities for change can be properly framed.

3   Determine Possible Sources of Best Practice

While best work practices can come from sources external to the organization, focus group members commented that many good ones come from *within* the organization. These have the advantage of being more immediately suited to the organization's purpose and context. The challenge for managers is to create a means to gather these ideas. Looking for improvements that have been developed internally within IT is also a good source of new practices. One organization gave its people enough freedom to research and experiment when they saw an opportunity for improvement. The result was an award-winning application, which set new standards in system usability and created a best practice in usability engineering. (This practice has been included as Table 21.1 to provide a more detailed example of an effective best practice.)

Benchmarking is frequently cited as a source of best practices. This involves comparing a company's financial and operational performance against that of other similar organizations (Murray et. al., 1997; Wiarda and Luria, 1998). This rather daunting task is made easier by benchmarking consultants who maintain data on a wide range of company practices. Group members who had used benchmarking services found them helpful identifying how efficient their organizations are compared with others and where they could be reducing their costs. Unfortunately, they have not found such services as helpful in evaluating their organization's effectiveness and the value of its processes. One member noted: "there isn't the same ability to apply metrics in this area. It's tough to collect data and companies aren't so willing to share."

Table 21.1   *Additional recommended IT best practices.*

This table includes a number of measures and practices used by focus group members and/ or recommended by best practice experts. They are provided here because they are more specific than the practices mentioned in the chapter and because many have not been demonstrably linked to organizational performance.

IT structure and management

- create centers of excellence
- adopt human resource asset management
- have a quality assurance function
- develop a change control function
- train project-managers

Knowledge management

- categorize best practices
- document learnings from post-project audits
- provide frameworks for learning
- facilitate communication and collaboration over time and distance
- support the help desk
- create learning histories

Tools and processes

- use a metadata tool providing process models, object flows, and organizational charts
- introduce stage-gating
- identify internal IT processes (e.g., business model management, application development process)
- create templates
- use email for project feedback
- develop user profiles

Software development

- articulate a system's link to the organization's key strategies
- appoint full-time project-managers
- ensure user participation
- have formal project planning, estimating, and scheduling
- assess risk
- use prototyping
- make applications and infrastructure scalable
- hold regular status reviews
- do walkthroughs and code inspections
- use common coding standards
- use formal estimation procedures
- have formal handoff procedures
- test with an independent group

- log post-implementation problems and track their resolution
- analyze sources of error

Metrics

- monitor customer satisfaction—end-user and internal user
- monitor process satisfaction
- monitor employee satisfaction
- use value-added per employee for overall performance (i.e., sales minus the cost of purchased parts, materials, and services)
- use function points
- use a productivity index (a composite of time, effort, and size)
- track project estimates and actuals
- count percent of projects on-time and on-budget
- count number of defects

A process for benchmarking (Wiarda and Luria, 1998)

- Determine what functions to benchmark.

- Define appropriate metrics.

- Identify best practice companies.

- Measure your own and best practice performance.

- Estimate performance gaps; set goals.

- Monitor results.

Sweetman (1997) suggests that benchmarking against best practices in a particular industry sector is not always the best way to find valuable new practices. A better way is for organizations to determine the outcome they want and then find out who is best at achieving it, regardless of the industry. For example, if IT wants to provide good customer service, it should turn to an industry where customer service is paramount and adapt techniques from it.

4   Continual Improvement

Finally, managers should never be completely satisfied with their practices. They must constantly scan the whole environment for new ideas and problems that need to be addressed. They should look for the things a process is *not* doing as well as evaluating those it is. In doing this, they should not only rely on internal experts, but also bring in people who *don't* understand their business to get a fresh perspective on the process. To ensure continuous improvement, IT managers should create mechanisms that make linkages between problems and opportunities, which facilitate identification and adoption of best internal practices.

IMPLEMENTING AND TRANSFERRING BEST PRACTICES

Once a new and better practice has been identified, it must be effectively implemented in order for an organization to realize its benefits. This is easier said than done. As noted above, practices developed in a particular firm may not be applicable to other companies (Fitz-Enz, 1997). Even within an IT department, problems can arise in moving a practice from the "good idea" stage to the stage where it is used as a matter of course.

Focus group members noted that unless there is some motivation to adopt them, best practices may never become wholly accepted. Continual encouragement and rewards are essential. Some people prefer a direct approach; for example, "You don't get paid if you don't follow the best practice." Others suggested that organizational rewards should be re-evaluated to incorporate new practice use. For example, if the organization wants people to document and update their practices, there must be time and resources available for doing this. Peer recognition is also a strong motivator. However, the bottom line is still that a practice must *demonstrably* improve such things as productivity, quality, or responsiveness. In other words, for a best practice to be permanently adopted, people must see a clear link between the practice and the overall goals of the organization.

Szulanski (1993) points out that there are actually four steps involved in ensuring a best practice is transferred into regular use:

1. *Awareness*—making sure that people are aware of the existence of the practice, and why and how the practice works.
2. *Exchange*—ensuring that the people to be using the practice have the knowledge and the skills to use it (e.g., the proper training and support resources).
3. *Adaptation*—getting a practice working with people and addressing the unexpected problems that inevitably arise. This stage is an opportunity to explore and modify a new practice. Therefore, procedures must be in place to detect and resolve problems with it. Motivation practices begin to play a role at this stage and continue in to the next.
4. *Routinization*—shepherding the new practice into the day-to-day routine of the organization. It is critical that a significant number of people begin to use the practice regularly. This is more likely to occur if rewards are predictable, there is a good relationship between the people requiring the change and those adopting it, and the practice reinforces company-held values.

It is also important that organizations recognize that new members will need to be introduced to its practices. If the organization's staffing is stable, then mentoring or apprenticeship may be enough to transmit knowledge of its practices to newcomers. Otherwise, more formal means, such as training courses or manuals, will be necessary.

Resources are another key to an effective transfer. Markus and Benjamin (1997) note that all too frequently IT organizations are looking for magic bullets that, once developed, will automatically solve a problem without any additional effort. Senior management must reinforce the reasons for the practice and take an active interest in its adoption at all stages. Staff must be assigned to assist in the exchange of information and in solving problems during the exchange and adaptation stages. As well, people must be given opportunities to practice, in addition to training. Focus group members agreed that practices are best transferred by *doing*.

BEST PRACTICES FAQs

Focus group members discussed a number of common questions and concerns associated with the use of best practices:

- *How do I know a best practice when I see one?* It will come to your attention through your continual scan of your environment both internally and externally. You will recognize it because it relates to a process you have identified as needing improvement. There will be clear, measurable links between it and organizational performance, and it will be consistent with the organization's overall values and strategy. The practice itself will be well documented, and the rationale for its use will be unambiguous. It will also yield positive, measurable results in a test situation.
- *How much of a best practice should be devoted to technology?* Approximately one-third of any practice should be technical. The other two-thirds should be focused on the people and organizational issues involved in the practice (Davenport, 1997).
- *What is the biggest single problem associated with best practices?* Many companies know the practices they should be using, but do not actualize them well (Menke, 1997a; Markus and Benjamin, 1997). For example, they might recognize that having a formal development process is a best practice and they might actually have the process documented, but it is not actually used or it is not used as it was intended. Thus, the company doesn't get the value it should from the practice. Experts believe that many organizations could gain significant value just from spending time working on the practices they actually have in place, but know they don't do well (Menke, 1997b).
- *Is there a downside to best practices?* Becoming best at something can mean that an organization can fall prey to arrogance, orthodoxy, and elitism (Kanter, 1995). Best practices are not a magic wand that can radically solve all an organization's problems. Often, companies over-do comparisons. Fitz-Enz

(1997) states, "there is nothing wrong with knowing how someone else does something, but usually after a very cursory examination we go way overboard in adopting the benchmark's method." Finally, there is risk involved. Not all practices may work in your environment. Experimentation with new practices will lead to some mistakes and loss of productivity (Hildebrand, 1997).

CREATING A BEST PRACTICE ORGANIZATION

This chapter has examined three different levels of best practice in organizations and a number of critical elements associated with each. However, clearly not all these elements can be addressed at once. Creating a best practice organization involves effectively integrating three things: research, capacity, and work skills. This involves a management commitment dedicated to the continuous improvement of IT processes and practices. Managers wishing to identify and implement best practices in their IT organizations should start with the following steps:

- *Assign resources.* Staff must be devoted to identifying and implementing best practices. IT managers must also allow people the time to learn new practices.
- *Create the context.* Make sure that the corporate and organizational strategy has been established and communicated. Look for and remove barriers that inhibit the development and transfer of best practices (e.g., time pressures, lack of rewards). Provide motivation for people to use existing best practices. Make sure to balance people issues (i.e., organizational, personal, and cultural considerations) with technology implementation.
- *Start with things you **know** you should do, but you don't do well.* There is a wealth of opportunity here without getting into complicated research. Look for good internal practices. Different parts of your organization may already be doing certain things extremely well. For example, one focus group organization found a best practice for introducing new employees to IT in another country in a different part of the firm.
- *Identify and develop metrics.* Metrics are important, so measure regularly. Continually look for better measures. Wherever possible, use standard measures to facilitate comparability. However, make sure you are measuring what you want to focus on. As pointed out above, many of IT's current measures emphasize efficiency over effectiveness.
- *Plan transfers.* Communicate *why* certain practices are important. Link each practice to organizational objectives. Create a formal transfer process and monitor the adoption of each new practice. Ensure that new employees are also introduced to the company's practices.
- *Evolve.* The development, management, and maintenance of best practices is an ongoing process that deserves attention from senior management at all steps along the way. Strive for a level of universality in practices that will focus on the fundamental truths behind them. At the same time, recognize that

specific implementations will evolve over time. Patience and perseverance are essential.

CONCLUSION

The field of best practices in IT is an extremely large and confusing one. While it can be viewed narrowly as "tricks of the trade" pertaining to software development and operations management, this is not the most productive approach for IT managers to take. Practitioners and experts are unanimous in agreeing that the true value of best practices comes from linking them to a company's strategic, financial, and operational performance. This chapter has presented a framework for thinking about best practices in this way and an inventory of those practices that have been demonstrably shown to positively affect performance. While they are not magic bullets, best practices, intelligently administered by IT managers, will yield both immediate and long-term results for those who use them.

REFERENCES

Anonymous (1997) "Ten practices by the best strategic planners," *Training & Development*, **51**(4), April, 35.

Baumbusch, R. (1997) "Internal best practices: Turning knowledge into results," *Strategy & Leadership*, **25**(4), July–August, 44–45.

Davenport, T. (1997) "Known evils," *CIO*, **10**(17), 15 June, 34–36.

Fitz-Enz, J. (1997) "The truth about best practices: What they are and how to apply them," *Human Resource Management*, **36**(1), Spring, 97–103.

Freeman, E. (1998) "Get out of your office!" *Datamation*, **44**(2), February, 72–77.

Heibler, R., T. Kelly, and C. Ketteman (1998) *Best Practices: Building Your Business with Customer-focused Solutions*, Simon & Schuster, New York.

Hildebrand, C. (1997) "The nature of excellence," *CIO*, August.

Kanter, R. (1995) *World Class: Thriving Locally in a Global Economy*, Simon & Schuster, New York.

Kleiner, A. and G. Roth (1997) "How to make experience your company's best teacher," *Harvard Business Review*, September–October.

Koch, C. (1998) "Value judgements," *CIO*, **1**, 1 February.

Korchinski, D. (1998) "Marines whip managers into shape," *The Globe and Mail*, 17 July, B21.

Kulandaiswamy, S., S. Dutta, and L.N. van Wassenhove (1997) *1996 Best Practice Survey: Analysis of Results*, Working Paper 97/38/TM, INSTEAD, Fontainebleau, France.

LaPlante, A. (1997) "Sharing the wisdom," *Computerworld*, **31**(22), 2 June, 73–74.

Markus, M.L. and R.I. Benjamin (1997) "The magic bullet theory in IT-enabled transformation," *Sloan Management Review*, **38**(2), Winter, 55–68.

McClenahen, J. (1997) "Asia's best practices," *Industry Week*, **246**(17), 15 September, 28–34.

Menke, M.M. (1997a) "Essentials of R&D strategic excellence," *Research-Technology Management*, **40**(5), September–October, 42–47.

Menke, M.M. (1997b) "Managing R&D for competitive advantage," *Research-Technology Management*, **40**(6), November–December, 40–42.

Murray, M.A., R.A. Zimmermann, and D.J. Flaherty (1997) "Can benchmarking give you a competitive edge?" *Management Accounting*, **79**(2), August, 46–50.

Senge, P. (1997) "Communities of leaders and learners," *Harvard Business Review*, September–October.

Streeter, W. (1998) "Uncommon sense vs. 'best practices'," *ABA Banking Journal*, **90**(1), January, 19.

Sweetman, K. (1997) "Unleash the genie," *Harvard Business Review*, **75**(2), March–April, 10–12.

Szulanski, G. (1993) *Intra-organizational Transfer of Best Practice: Predicting Difficulties*, Working Paper 93/88, INSTEAD, Fontainebleau, France.

Wheatley, M. (1998) "Lighten up," *CIO*, **11**(9) (Section 2), 15 February, 34–42.

Wiarda, E.A. and D.D. Luria (1998) "The best-practice company and other benchmarking myths," *Quality Progress*, **31**(2), February, 91–94.

22
Managing the Virtual Workforce

Only a few years ago, the staff of most information technology (IT) organizations consisted of full-time, dedicated employees and a few contract staff. Today, it is a radically changed world for IT staff as well as their managers. Staffing options such as outsourcing, telecommuting, partnerships and alliances, and a global workforce are all being utilized by companies as they grapple with the economic challenges and technology options confronting them. New organizational structures and interorganizational projects mean that staff may be reporting to not one manager, but several different ones. IT managers are also being expected to enable, through information and telecommunications, a large number of other company staff, anywhere, anyplace, anytime. In short, today's employees are rapidly becoming a *virtual workforce*—available when and where they are needed, gone when they are not.

These trends are only the initial responses to a number of new realities that are affecting organizations: the economy; changing relationships between employers and employees; and new workforce demographics. IT is clearly both the driver and the facilitator of these changes. Technical advances in communications and groupware mean that organizations can bring together the best available staff whenever they want, wherever the staff happen to be. Time and distance are being shrunk more and more every day.

As a result, the nature of work itself is being changed, and IT managers are in the forefront of this transformation. As leaders of technology change, they are more aware than others of the potential and the impacts of IT, and thus are often expected to manage it for their company. As managers of a highly mobile group of professional knowledge-workers, they must cope with the challenges of managing this resource effectively. As partners in transforming their organization with the business, they are expected to create an environment to obtain maximum value and productivity from *all* staff.

IT managers are therefore examining new ways of enabling and doing work and asking difficult questions that challenge the old model of work and jobs. For example, why hire in-house experts when they can be called in on an *ad hoc* basis when needed? Why build expensive offices when staff can telecommute from home or a satellite office? Why pay expensive North American salaries when the same skills can be found elsewhere in the world for a fraction of the cost? In short, what are the real benefits of a full-time, centrally located workforce?

This chapter first discusses the nature of the virtual workforce and looks how work is changing in the modern organization. Then, it looks at the progress companies are making toward a new paradigm of resource management and some of the problems they are facing in implementing it. Finally, it examines how companies can prepare for the coming changes to work and makes recommendations to IT managers about how they can anticipate their organization's needs and develop an effective virtual workforce.

WHAT IS A VIRTUAL WORKFORCE?

The concept of a *virtual workforce* should be distinguished from that of the *virtual organization*, although the two are clearly linked in their approach to accomplishing organizational goals. A *virtual organization* is a network of partners that operates across traditional organizational boundaries to get work done and to exploit new opportunities. It is a *structure* of a company and its relationships—whether with companies, governments, or individuals. A virtual organization is concerned with *what* work the company does internally (i.e., core competencies) and what work should be done through other organizational arrangements (e.g., outsourcing, partnerships). Management's responsibility is to determine what work is of distinctive value to the company and what can be obtained in the external marketplace (Rayport and Sviokla, 1995).

A *virtual workforce* is one that is present in effect, but not in form. It is a means of organizing *staff* to achieve flexibility and innovation (Cheesbrough and Teece, 1996). Increasingly, it is being used to assemble "just in time" resources to accomplish a specific objective. A virtual workforce is the means through which a company gets its work done. It consists of *people* and their working relationships with a single company. It is composed of people with a variety of different work arrangements with a company (e.g., contract, telecommuting). Management's responsibility is obtaining the appropriate people for a particular task and ensuring that it gets done.

A virtual workforce can therefore consist of many different types of worker, including:

- *full-time staff in a center of excellence*—employees with specialized skills who are assigned to jobs on a project-by-project basis;
- *part-time/contingent staff*—employees who work less than full-time hours or as needed;

- *mobile staff*—employees who work in customer locations or while traveling on business;
- *telecommuting staff*—employees who work some or all their time from a home or satellite office;
- *global staff*—employees working in locations around the world;
- *contract staff*—individuals who are hired to do a particular job;
- *consultants*—specialized individuals hired for their particular skill, usually in a leadership or advisory capacity;
- *outsourced staff*—individuals who work for a firm with which the company has a partnership;
- *staff from allied organizations*—individuals from other organizations working on a joint venture;
- *matrixed staff*—individuals who report to more than one manager for different reasons.

The list above highlights several challenges of managing the virtual workforce. *First*, it is highly varied. This list documents only some of the more common working arrangements currently in use. The companies in the focus group were all experimenting with a number of these arrangements and some more idiosyncratic ones as well. *Second*, manager–staff relationships are evolving rapidly and traditional managerial approaches to staff may no longer be appropriate. *Third*, the current working environment for many managers and staff is confusing and therefore highly dependent on individual relationships. *Fourth*, there are huge challenges in communicating with and integrating the work of such disparate types of staff. *Fifth*, while the virtual workforce is not limited to IT staff, IT managers typically are dealing with most, if not all, of these types of staff already, and thus are leading the organization in these changes. All these issues emphasize the fact that there is a fundamental shift in the nature of work that must be more clearly understood before a virtual workforce can be effectively managed.

Yesterday's job

- Value defined by position in the organizational hierarchy.
- Reports to one manager.
- Well-defined responsibilities.
- Clear career path.
- Narrow wage ranges, regular increases.
- Rewards linked to position or seniority.
- Benefits packages.

- Work in corporate offices.

- Regular working hours.

- Managers are coordinators.

- A job is for life.

- Limited access to corporate information.

- Limited understanding of strategies and costs.

THE CHANGING NATURE OF WORK

Bridges (1994) analyzed the transition to new types of work in his book *Job Shift*. He notes that the "job", as we have known it, is disappearing and will not be part of tomorrow's economic reality. He suggests that this is because traditional jobs are change inhibitors that limit an organization's ability to be flexible and responsive. In the future, he believes, instead of a single job with an organizational role and defined responsibilities, most people will have a number of jobs (similar to today's "projects") with flexible roles and clearly defined outcomes. In other words, instead of a "football team" workforce where everyone has a position and the plays are charted and orchestrated, companies will develop "volleyball teams" where anyone can hit the ball over the net and everyone has to be ready to help do so (see Box).

Tomorrow's job

- Value defined by contribution to group.

- Reports to everyone in the group.

- Must be able to do whatever needs to be done and shift focus rapidly.

- Careers are managed individually.

- Wide range of compensation, more emphasis on share earnings.

- Rewards linked to outcomes delivered.

- Benefits are the work itself.

- Work where the customer is or where needed.

- Flexible working hours.

- Managers are coaches and business process owners.

- Individual skills and capabilities are security.

- Wide access to corporate information.

- Wide understanding of strategies and costs.

The rules for dealing with this new workforce are still evolving. Bridges (1994) stresses that there are no "silver bullets". Empowerment, self-directed teams, re-engineering, total quality management, telecommuting, job-sharing, networking, and flattening the organization and other "flavors of the month" in business are not going to work in and of themselves. Instead, organizations will have to manage their way through the change.

The challenges of managing a professional, knowledge-based virtual work-force are even greater than managing a more structured virtual workforce. Quinn et al. (1996) point out that managing and developing a *professional intellect* is a specialized skill that has numerous pitfalls for the unwary. They note that professionals possess four different levels of intellect:

1. *cognitive knowledge*—basic mastery of a discipline;
2. *advanced skills*—how to translate book-learning into effective execution;
3. *systems understanding*—the ability to solve larger and more complex problems and to create extraordinary value;
4. *self-motivated creativity*—the will, motivation, and adaptability for success.

In today's organizations, it is the last level that is critical to success and that must be nurtured, because groups that possess it can outperform others with greater resources. In this way, "organizations . . . can simultaneously thrive in the face of today's rapid changes and renew their cognitive knowledge, advanced skills, and systems understanding to compete in the next wave of advances" (Quinn et al., 1996).

In short, in addition to managing a wide variety of different types of worker in a totally changed work environment, today's IT manager must also nurture his or her professional IT workers to enable them to cope with rapid technological change while delivering consistent, high-quality output.

TODAY'S VIRTUAL WORKFORCE

Their experiences in coping with an increasingly virtual IT workforce have made the focus group participants keenly aware of the problems involved in its management. They had the most problems with work that was done outside the office—regardless of the formal employment arrangements (e.g., whether an employee or a contractor). Bringing outside workers into the office seems to cause much less disruption to traditional ways of working. Participants pointed out that a worker's relationship with the company appears to change when work is done outside the office, particularly when he or she works from home.

Human factors are a key limiting factor to home-based work. "Many people don't have an appreciation of the issues involved," one manager noted. These boil down to three important areas that companies must address:

- *Control.* The processes and control systems in an organization must change to keep up with the changing nature of work and the workforce. Managers have concerns about people working non-standard hours, the funding of home-based equipment and telecommunications, security, productivity, and insurance. Because many of these have not yet been adequately addressed in organizations, home-based work is not as widely used as it might be.
- *Technical issues.* The technical architecture of the organization has to support a variety of working arrangements. IT is the "glue" that links the workforce together. Typically, decisions still need to be made about what equipment and software should be made available and how it can be used. Managers are also concerned about maintaining corporate standards when a large number of home-workers are used.
- *Communication* is a significant problem in any team-based work. While in theory, teams can be effective without face-to-face contact, experience has shown that teamwork suffers without co-location. Companies that have tried it—even with teams in offices located in two different cities—note that it doesn't work well on IT development teams because of the high degree of integration required between individual's work.

Because of the huge risks involved, those companies that are using home-based workers are carefully selecting them and "hand-crafting" jobs for them (e.g., structuring work around a specific deliverable).

Human factors are also central to changing work arrangements within the organization as well. One manager remarked that these were the hard part of managing the virtual workforce and that companies need a great deal more investment in this area. *Compensation* was an important issue. Employees and contract staff typically earn different incomes for the same work. This can be demoralizing for full-time staff, if they do not see the benefits they receive as making up for the differential. *Measurement based on performance* is fundamental to the new type of work, but is foreign to most permanent employees. Neither management nor staff have a firm grip on how to measure by deliverables as yet. Finally, *knowledge and its communication* become vital when work itself becomes virtual. One manager noted that, as his organization becomes more virtual, the environment in which people work is actually becoming more controlled and less virtual to ensure that people are working and communicating together effectively.

In short, the reality of the virtual workforce in most organizations today is considerably less than the vision. Most companies, particularly IT organizations, are experimenting with a variety of different kinds of work arrangement, but doing so cautiously. They are very aware that, with the proper policies to facilitate and manage it, virtual work is not ready to be implemented in any major form.

PREPARING FOR THE VIRTUAL WORKFORCE

Nevertheless, forum participants were conscious of growing pressures in their organizations to promote virtual work. Most noted that there is a high demand within their organizations for alternative work arrangements. Staff look at other companies and begin to push for such things as information access and more flexible and mobile work. Management, too, see a number of benefits, such as lower staff costs and lower real-estate costs. Altogether, they note that there is a strong push for companies to become "more creative" in how they manage the workforce. At the same time, however, the pull of caution keeps them from moving into this new world too fast.

The focus group therefore focused on things IT managers could be doing to help them prepare their organizations for the world of virtual work. There are two areas that need to be developed to facilitate virtual work.

1   Technical Infrastructure

IT provides the technical "glue" that enables new forms of working and operating. As a result, IT managers must be aware of the technical issues involved and have a solid plan for the technical support of virtual work. Some of the things IT managers can be doing to prepare their organizations technically for this shift include:

- *Setting standards and addressing technological concerns.* Organizations need to begin to seriously explore their communications goals and their implications. For example, if the goal is to enable communication "anywhere, anyplace, anytime", this has several policy implications, such as for security, access, and hardware and software standards that must be made explicit. Decisions must be made about how to handle these issues and supporting/controlling technology implemented.
- *Creating a strong communications infrastructure.* Effective communications is the backbone of any virtual workforce. As workers at all levels move out of the office, whether to homes or to customer locations, they will need access to information and a strong support network of computer applications (e.g., calendaring, email, database access). Identifying and addressing these needs is a prerequisite to the development of a highly mobile and flexible workforce. Studies have found that communications can have both a strong positive and a strong negative influence on firm performance (Gupta et al, 1995). Problems

with voice and data communications, data and document transfer, and limited price/performance payoffs are all correlated with poor firm performance. On the other hand, effective data/document transfer capabilities and enhanced voice and data communications were positively related to firm performance. Interestingly, this research shows that communications *abilities* are more powerfully related to firm performance than communications *problems*, suggesting that companies should focus on providing their mobile staff with as much communications capability as possible.

- *Implementing groupware.* Software to enable teams to collaborate at a distance is still in its infancy. However, many organizations, such as Ford and Boeing, have used it effectively for major design projects (Rayport and Sviokla, 1995). Remote work may not always be desirable in software development, but being able to link directly with other team-members and to exchange ideas with them gives organizations the ability to get familiar with groupware's capabilities and to gradually discover ways to use it advantageously as opportunities arise.

2   Organizational Practices

Focus group participants stressed that technology is of less importance in facilitating virtual work than human and organizational factors. Unless management is aware of these issues and the policies are in place to deal with them, it is unlikely that virtual work will succeed. IT managers need to raise the profile of these issues within the company and to discover ways to make the new working arrangements function effectively. Some of the ways organizations can prepare themselves include:

- *Developing more working options.* While companies may not be ready for full-fledged virtual work, many are looking at creating more flexible in-working conditions. Most IT organizations allow some work from home when appropriate. Four-day work weeks are also popular. Such arrangements require limited adaptation of work environments and human resource (HR) policies, while addressing some of the demand.

- *Experimentation.* To develop effective virtual arrangements, companies will have to explore a number of options with interested "guinea pigs" (i.e., managers and workers). Cross (1995) notes: "today's market ... allows us the luxury to consider options none of us thought possible a few years ago." He has had great success with a variety of creative outsourcing arrangements for both IT development and operations. Other companies have had more mixed results. A forum member noted that a homework trial in his company failed because management didn't understand the issues involved and couldn't figure out what the people were doing. There are a large number of issues to be addressed with the different kinds of virtual work. Formal and informal experiments, carefully monitored from all perspectives (i.e., staff, management, productivity, communications) can be extremely valuable in helping to shape future organizational policies.

- *Involving senior management.* Senior management, and especially HR, must be made more aware of the issues involved in virtual work. Getting them involved in the decision-making associated with alternative working arrangements will help to shape broader company policy with regard to virtual work in the longer term.
- *Developing consulting skills.* Forum members noted that workers with good consulting skills were better able to adjust to new working arrangements and expectations. Cross (1995) believes that these skills will be essential to the IT workforce of the future, no matter what their formal working status is. This is because consulting skills stress relationship management, project-oriented work with clear deliverables, and a strong business and managerial orientation. Training and developing these skills will therefore facilitate whatever new working arrangements the organization chooses to implement.

While many organizations are clearly not ready to make the great leap into the unknown world of virtual work they can, through these preparations, ensure that when they are, their people, technology, and policies are ready to support them.

RECOMMENDATIONS FOR MANAGEMENT

Although the working world is still a significant way from becoming virtual, there is a growing body of research and accepted practice on how to effectively manage virtual resources in a number of areas. These have been collected below as recommendations for managers planning to enter the virtual workplace:

- *Separate task management from resource management.* Increasingly, organizations are establishing centers of excellence for particular staff skills to ensure that people issues such as skills development, career management, and compensation are effectively and fairly dealt with. Resource managers are responsible for obtaining the appropriate resources—from whatever source—and for their management. Task managers can then focus on getting the work done. While resource and task management cannot be totally divorced from each other, in that they are dealing with the same people, there is a clear consensus that separation leads to better use of resources and more attention to the issues of people management.
- *Develop integration functions.* Coordination of work and conflict resolution are critical activities for systemic innovation (i.e., projects whose benefits can only be realized in conjunction with other related and complementary projects). These functions are best handled by integrated internal management processes because it is highly unlikely that independent companies or individuals will be motivated to share information or cooperate as completely as needed for such

complex work (Cheesbrough and Teece, 1996). Participants echoed this senti-
ment when discussing the benefits of offshore work. The interactions and
communication that are needed make it very difficult for offshore programmers to be part of a development team. These problems highlight the need for
improved internal integration functions if virtual work is to be managed well.
To ensure this happens, integration needs to be made *explicit* in every aspect of
IT work. Formal integration mechanisms should also be established whenever
interdepartmental or interorganizational teams are involved.

- *View sourcing as a strategic business process.* Like any business process, acquiring
technical skills is a *process* that must be planned and managed (Chatterji, 1996).
It needs ongoing coordination, control, and continuous improvement through
learning and feedback. Corporations that don't do this can run into problems
with their virtual workers (e.g., a reluctance to share information or to be
responsive to each other). Maccoby (1996) points out that core skills, strategic
innovation, and major new directions are best sourced from inside the organization. Basic knowledge, pre-competitive research, and the development of
prototypes, are some types of work that can be sourced outside the company.

- *Limit the number of sourcing partners.* Supplier management can be a big head-
ache, as many firms that have moved to outsourcing have discovered (Cross,
1995). While contracts may deliver cost savings, many of the problems
integrating outsourcing activities with other work fall back on the contracting
company. However, if a company uses a single outsourcing provider, it can
become dependent on that provider—an equally daunting prospect. BP Exploration resolved this conundrum by getting a consortium of outsourcers to
work together to provide a seamless mix of services on a worldwide basis and
to collaborate on problem-solving (Cross, 1995).

- *Be careful how you measure success.* Focus group managers pointed out that
consultants are often considered "successful" because, while they deliver what
they have been contracted to do, they don't have to deal with the consequences of their work. Choosing clear deliverables is certainly one key component of measurement. However, as IT work becomes more complex, such
things as evaluation against expectations, general knowledge, and relationship
management skills are also important measures for individuals. Success should
not be too narrowly measured. Cross (1995) notes that when BP Exploration
initially outsourced IT work, "we mistakenly set cost reduction as the most
important target for our suppliers to achieve. [Later], we shifted the emphasis
from costs to service responsiveness, quality, and customer satisfaction."
Compensation systems are ways that success is rewarded in organizations.
Participants and researchers are unanimous that compensation must be re-
crafted to reflect what is valued in companies. Learning how to pay for
value delivered, rather than on an hourly or a salaried basis according to
hierarchical position, is fundamental to changing compensation. When professional IT staff are considered, compensation systems must also recognize
"soft" performance measures. Intuition, professionalism, and risk-taking are

just some of the skills that are coming to be valued in the new IT workforce.

- *Don't give up on virtual teamwork.* Participants were highly dubious about whether work from home or remote locations could be effective. "We've tried home work on teams but it didn't work because so much communication was required," said one manager. Another expressed concern about being able to replicate a team environment in a virtual way: "The most effective communication is still face-to-face . . . Many of the dynamics of communication are lost at a distance—even with videoconferencing." Nevertheless, virtual work teams have been effectively used in organizations with very productive results. Ford has used a virtual international team to develop a new car. The team established common, global specifications and a complete information-based representation of the product. This enabled them to develop a global car with a global appeal (Rayport and Sviokla, 1995). Boeing has used a similar approach (with team-members from three different companies) to develop a new aircraft engine (Malhotra et al., 2001). These examples demonstrate that effective virtual teamwork is possible, if difficult, to achieve and that it has some very real benefits to the organization.

- *Use virtual work to achieve flexibility, not competitiveness.* Use of external workers is critical for companies and, in the future, it will be difficult to avoid. Already, highly skilled and innovative technologists are demonstrating that they want to work for small, leading-edge companies, rather than more general IT organizations (Cross, 1995). Nevertheless, it is also critical that companies retain certain skills in-house or they will risk losing their competitive advantage. "When we decide to go in major new directions and develop . . . for new markets, it behooves us to pay the price internally so that we can gain and maintain continuing competitive advantage" (Maccoby, 1996). In short, while an external workforce is useful for obtaining certain skills, unless a company develops critical parts of its value chain internally, it will risk losing competitiveness (Cheesbrough and Teece, 1996).

- *Communicate, communicate, communicate.* Finally, no matter how the workforce is organized, managers should ensure that communication is their number one priority. "How [professionals] communicate and what they voluntarily communicate are as important as the advanced knowledge [they] may have" (Quinn et al., 1996). In addition to formal mechanisms of communication, management should therefore create a range of informal opportunities to force communication to take place. Because communication is so central to many of the challenges of managing a virtual workforce, this is probably the single most important area for management to focus on. Whereas previously in offices communication has taken place naturally, with a virtual workforce managers must work to engineer communication. Tactics such as forcing people to overlap on different teams, keeping hierarchical roles purposely ill-defined, using the compensation system to encourage information-sharing, and having team evaluations are all methods that are recommended for motivating communication (Quinn et al., 1996; Despres and Hiltrop, 1996).

CONCLUSION

This chapter has shown some of the directions in which work is evolving and how IT managers can prepare their organizations for it. Most companies are clearly not ready for full-scale virtual work. However, as corporate leaders, IT managers have both the responsibility and the opportunity to develop the creative and innovative practices needed to make the virtual workforce an effective reality in the not-very-distant future. Managing a virtual workforce will require a considerable shift in thinking. Traditional approaches to staff management and tried-and-true HR policies are not going to be effective in the future workplace. As they are on the leading edge of these changes, IT managers will not only have to act as corporate "canaries" determining which new techniques are safe and which are risky, they will also have to inform, motivate, and at times push other parts of the organization to adapt to new ways of working.

REFERENCES

Bridges, W. (1994) *Job Shift*, Addison-Wesley Publishing, Reading, MA.

Chatterji, D. (1996) "Accessing external sources of technology," *Research • Technology Management*, March–April.

Cheesbrough, H.W. and D.J. Teece (1996) "When is virtual virtuous?" *Harvard Business Review*, January–February.

Cross, J. (1995) "IT outsourcing: British Petroleum's competitive approach," *Harvard Business Review*, May–June.

Despres, C. and J.M. Hiltrop (1996) "Compensation for technical professionals in the knowledge area," *Research • Technology Management*, September–October.

Gupta, Y.P., J. Karimi, and T.M. Somers (1995) "Telecommuting: Problems associated with communications technologies and their capabilities," *IEEE Transactions on Engineering Management*, **42**(4).

Maccoby, M. (1996) "Knowledge workers need new structures," *Research • Technology Management*, **39**(1).

Malhotra, A., A. Majchrzak, R. Carman, and V. Lott (2001) "Radical innovation without collocation: A case study at Boeing-Rocetdyne," *MIS Quarterly*, **25**(2), June, 229–249.

Quinn, J.B., P. Anderson, and S. Finkelstein (1996) "Managing professional intellect: Making the most of the best," *Harvard Business Review*, March–April.

Rayport, J.F. and J.J. Sviokla (1995) "Exploiting the virtual value chain," *Harvard Business Review*, November–December.

23
The IT Measurement Matrix

In 1993 the authors convened a focus group of senior managers to look at measurement in their information technology (IT) organization (McKeen and Smith, 1996). At that time, many business executives were feeling that IT had contributed little or nothing to the corporate bottom line and that IT services were too expensive and could be bought cheaper elsewhere. IT organizations were therefore emphasizing measurement to demonstrate the value of their contribution to overall corporate performance.

Nearly a decade later, measurement continues to be a critical issue for IT managers and organizations. Three persistent problems still have to be resolved:

- IT investments are often unrelated to business strategy;
- payoff from IT investments is inadequate;
- relations between users and IT specialists are poor; therefore there is little trust between the groups (Bensaou and Earl, 1998).

As well, measurement is more important than ever before because IT investment has become vital to the long-term survival of a business. Increasingly, how a company estimates its value is a critical determinant of how it allocates its resources in IT, and these are, in turn, a key driver of the organization's overall performance (Luehrman, 1997). Unfortunately, many companies are still not getting the performance they expect from their IT investment, often because they are finding it difficult to estimate the future value of such investments (Strassman, 1997). For all these reasons, we felt a second look at the challenges of IT measurement was warranted.

This chapter shows how our understanding of measurement in IT has grown and developed over the past decade. It begins by looking at the purpose of measurement in IT. Then it looks at the different types of measure required for a complete understanding of how well IT is performing. Because of the complexity of IT work, no single measurement approach is likely to address all the questions executives are looking to answer. Instead, this chapter proposes a matrix of measures is needed and suggests the types of measure that should populate each cell of the matrix. Finally, the chapter explores ways to develop or improve a company's IT measurement infrastructure to make it more useful and effective across the board. While it does not discuss specific measures in detail, as a guideline for further investigation Tables 23.1 and 23.2 list measures that this group, individual members, and measurement experts have recommended.

WHAT IS THE PURPOSE OF MEASUREMENT?

Traditionally, IT has been viewed as a cost center, so managers monitored their organizations to track and improve efficiency. Thus, most of the measures tracked IT expenses (e.g., IT budget, training costs, telecommunications costs), or the efficient use of computer equipment, (e.g., number of MIPS, central processing unit (CPU) hours, and the availability levels of different types of equipment). Projects were measured similarly, according to their return on investment (ROI), number of function points or lines of code delivered, or their actual versus budgeted costs.

As our understanding of IT measurement has matured, three problems with these traditional forms of measurement have become apparent. First, they have no connection to the drivers of the business (Young, 1998). Thus, they are virtually meaningless to most business people (Fabris, 1996). As one chief information officer (CIO) put it, "My math was absolutely correct and my measurements unassailable [but] I missed the point ... I was busy making sure we were applying equipment efficiently when I ought to have been trying to help our people work better" (Dyle, 1995). Furthermore, although these metrics highlight cost reductions and improved performance of IT resources, they do nothing to address the *additional* value that IT is bringing to business through improved competitiveness and better ability to exploit business opportunities. Because they don't link to how IT is making the business better in some way, such bits-and-bytes metrics give businesses no real understanding of how IT is contributing to overall business value. A second problem is that IT work is largely knowledge work, so the amount of money or time invested in it is not always correlated to the value it achieves. Therefore, measuring effort and cost leaves us no further insights into business value.

Third, at a time when companies are actively seeking breakthroughs in performance through such techniques as total quality management, re-engineering, and employee empowerment, they are also recognizing that transforming themselves into the agile, competitive, and knowledge-based organizations of the future cannot be accomplished merely by monitoring and controlling measures of past performance (Kaplan and Norton, 1996). In short, the value of IT is becoming not only what has been delivered in the past, but what it is contributing to the *future* of the organization through such things as new products and services, improved employee capabilities, and improved process capabilities. These are now understood to be the drivers of long-term value in business (Kaplan and Norton, 1996).

Thus, while the fundamental question behind IT measurement is still *"What value are we getting for our IT investments?"*, today companies are beginning to define "business value" in different ways than in the past and to look for it in different places. Clarity about what IT contributes to business value is therefore critical because this enables organizations to properly allocate their resources to those things that will drive their business strategy forward. Unfortunately, how business value is to be measured continues to be problematic. How do you measure process capabilities, for example? The key measurement problem confronting IT managers today therefore seems to be: *"What measures do we use to determine the business value of IT?"*

WHAT SHOULD BE MEASURED?

As our understanding of business value has evolved and broadened over time, what we measure about IT work has changed as well. Whereas 10 years ago, metrics were primarily financial, today, focus group members and experts alike recognize that a much broader range of measures are needed:

> Financial measures tell the story of past events [but] they are inadequate for guiding and evaluating the journey that information age companies must make to create *future* value ... [There are] difficulties in placing a reliable financial value on such assets as: employee skills, flexibility, data bases and systems ... which are the very assets and capabilities that are critical for success in today's and tomorrow's corporate environment (Kaplan and Norton, 1996).

Stewart (1997) agrees:

> Companies are in business to make money and, ultimately, their success or failure is expressed in financial terms, but the language of management is increasingly nonfinancial ... Financial accounting provided tools and measurements for industrial capitalism ... capturing most of the value of a product through the costs of materials and labor. But in the economy of knowledge, it doesn't come close.

As these facts dawn on business and IT executives, they are looking further afield for metrics that will reflect a broader and more balanced view of the business value of IT. They are actively seeking to identify the "right" measures that will link IT contribution to the value it is delivering to the business. There is also recognition that these measures might be different for different organizations.

Table 23.1   *Measures recommended in this chapter.*

CURRENT IT OPERATIONS AND SYSTEMS

How well are we doing right now?

- Overall IT performance
- Current IT costs
- Operations performance
- Development performance
- Project performance
- Activity-based costing

Are we doing the right things?

- Internal satisfaction with efficiency, responsiveness, credibility of IT
- Service levels
- Problem resolution quality
- Professionalism of technicians
- Analysis of current problems: trends, baselines, improved actions
- Response times
- Backlogs
- Abandoned calls
- Service survey
- Service management measures

How well are we positioned for the future?

- Operations-benchmarking
- Quality of technology infrastructure
- Quality of information infrastructure
- Speed of knowledge transfer
- Ability to connect with data, experts, and expertise
- Stocks of knowledge
- Bureaucratic drag (time to market)
- Process and system information value-add
- Overall information load.

IT STRATEGIES

How well are we doing now?

- ROI
- Contribution to improved financial results
- Cost savings
- Improved revenues
- Improved productivity
- Value of alliances

Are we doing the right things?

- Balanced scorecards: financial, customer, internal processes, and learning and growth measures.
- Strategic customer satisfaction
- Performance against customer perceptions of value

How well are we positioned for the future?

- IT contribution to new products and services
- IT contribution to improving the purchasing experience and personal relationships with customers
- IT contribution to company image and reputation
- IT contribution to ease of doing business.
- Company use of IT relative to competitors' use.

IT OPPORTUNITIES

How well are we doing now?

- IT flexibility
- IT responsiveness
- Process to assess and implement opportunities
- Ease of doing business with IT
- Perceptions of red tape
- Information completeness
- Simplicity/Complexity of internal processes
- Quality of IT access to information.

Are we choosing the right things?

- Effectiveness of the project evaluation process
- Formal project investment evaluation
- Options valuation
- IT employee satisfaction
- IT retention
- IT productivity

How well are we positioned for the future?

- Measure of what people know
- Measure of how much the organization uses of what people know
- SEI's people capability maturity model
- IT knowledge capital
- Wellness: retention, absenteeism, employee satisfaction
- Productivity: applications and production support
- Assets: people resource management skills and processes, experience, quality and quantity of skills, recruiting skills.
- Knowledge maps
- Radar charts of knowledge
- Categorization of skills and identification of gaps.

Table 23.2   *Measures used by group members.*

___

OPERATIONS

- Daily processor workload
- Online availability
- Daytime status of CPU, tape, DASD, and batch resource consumption
- Errors
- Information security statistics
- Pinpad failures
- Weekly and monthly online availability and response times
- Number of quick fixes
- Weekly and monthly outages
- Phone statistics: number of calls, average speed of answer, abandon rate
- Point of sale outages
- Service-level reports
- Major mainframe and network problems
- Major outages on the weekend
- Weekly help desk report
- Non-compliance report
- Capacity usage
- Online availability and response times
- LAN availability
- Critical application availability
- Number of forms requested by type
- Service-level reports by vendor
- Monthly network service impacts
- CPU, DASD, tape drive, mainframe, network (by vendor) controller availability
- Tape drive errors and tape mounts
- Number of print jobs, rolls of paper
- Number of service calls placed each month by location
- Call statistics
- Service calls on equipment
- Telecommunications utilization: number of calls, number of minutes
- Cellular usage

PRODUCTIVITY

- Application service request tracking and backlog
- Time sheet reporting by individual and project
- Project management office report on project status

PLANNING AND BUDGETING

- Monthly operating expenses
- Operating expense forecasts
- Operating expense analysis
- Annual budget by accounts
- IT capital expenditures

- Asset book values
- Asset depreciation expiries
- Monthly chargeouts
- Development project costs and hours
- Development project forecasts
- Actual versus budget report
- Monthly payments to vendors
- Monthly cash flow
- Information security volumes
- Information security violations

HUMAN RESOURCES

- Vacations and absences
- Budgets
- Headcounts
- Recruitment status
- Overtime report by employee
- Monthly issues report
- Organizational chart
- Self-study library usage
- Staff list
- On-call report by employee
- Health and safety report
- Education hours by education method
- Education costs by education method
- Education costs
- Education hours
- Education days per employee
- HR budget
- Compensation report
- List of courses taken by employee
- Service levels of employees
- Retirements

FINANCIAL MEASURES

- Benchmarking statistics
- Number of days on projects compared with plan
- Effectiveness as assessed by stakeholders
- IT integration costs (actual versus plan)
- Stakeholder satisfaction
- IT budget versus actual
- Product recovery
- Percentage of IT billable time
- Production support unity cost
- Development unit cost

continued

Table 23.2   *(cont.)*

STRUCTURAL MEASURES

- Repair support
- Application production support
- % help desk calls
- Wait time to help desk queue
- LAN and application servicing availability
- Telephony availability
- Email serving availability
- Network availability
- Mainframe availability
- Growth in number of green technologies
- Decrease in number of red technologies
- Products/services
- Number of hits on the website
- Quality of achievement plans
- Number of achievement plans completed

HUMAN MEASURES

- IT retention
- IT new hires
- IT absenteeism
- IT overtime
- IT employee survey
- Application development productivity
- Production support productivity
- People resource management ability: variance to target-staffing
- Experience
- Quality of training
- Quantity of training
- Number of hires versus plan
- Number of days spent on priority projects

CUSTOMER/PARTNER MEASURES

- Questionnaire on IT innovation
- Number of hits on website
- Number of R&D projects undertaken
- Number of R&D projects implemented
- Quality of business partner relationship
- Number of hours charged to call in
- Project on-time delivery—partners
- Partners' application availability
- Partners' service completeness survey
- Partners' service effectiveness survey
- Partners' business orientation survey

In addition, Luehrman (1997) suggests that managers need different metrics for different *activities*:

- *Operations*. Managers need to determine the value of their ongoing services and existing systems.
- *Current strategies*. They need to better understand how well their strategies are doing as they are being implemented. For example: *What is the value being delivered by our new outsourcing arrangements, or our IT architecture?*
- *Opportunities*. Managers need to determine the potential future value of new ways of using IT (e.g., proposed IT projects).

Since IT work encompasses all three of these areas, it is no surprise that we have yet to find a "one metric fits all" for the value of IT.

The experts have not been reticent about making suggestions for new measures (see Kaplan and Norton, 1996; Earl and Feeny, 1994; Stewart, 1997; Bensaou and Earl, 1998), so there is no dearth of measurement ideas for IT managers to choose from! The challenge is to make sense of where they fit in to an organization's measurement needs. Interestingly, the feature that all these approaches to measurement have in common is *relevance*. In our previous book we suggested that this was key to any effective metrics program. We wrote that business and IT executives wanted IT metrics to answer three questions:

- How well are we doing the things we are doing now?
- Are we doing the right things for our business?
- Are we positioning ourselves well to compete for the future?

These questions can be asked of each different type of IT work: operations and systems, strategies, and opportunities. For example, existing IT operations and systems can be assessed not only according to how cost-effectively they are being done at present but also according to whether or not they are being done in the best way possible and how well they will support the organization's future needs. Similarly, current IT strategies can be assessed not only as to whether they are the best way to support the company's current business needs but also as to how well they will support the company's future needs and what value these strategies are delivering to the company at present. In addition, companies need to know how well they are managing their IT opportunities. They want to understand how effective IT is in identifying and acting upon these opportunities now, whether it is selecting the right opportunities, and how well they are positioned to take advantage of opportunities in the future. Table 23.3 shows how these questions might be linked together with the different types of IT work to form a matrix of measures needed for IT.

The next section of this chapter looks at ways of populating this matrix with measures for IT operations and processes, IT strategy, and potential business opportunities that IT might support.

Table 23.3   *A measurement matrix for IT.*

	How well are we doing in IT now?	Are we doing the right things in IT?	How well is IT positioning the company for the future?
IT operations and systems	A	B	C
IT strategies	D	E	F
IT opportunities	G	H	I

THE MEASUREMENT MATRIX

Assessing Current IT Operations and Systems

How Well Are We Doing Now? Measuring the effectiveness of current systems and operations (Cell A in Table 23.3) is probably the least interesting area of measurement because it has been measured to death. It is also the easiest area to measure because there are quantifiable things involved, such as costs, response time, and CPU cycles, which are relatively straightforward to count and to compare. Thus, by far the majority of the measures traditionally used in IT fall into this cell, including metrics for: overall IT performance, current IT costs (e.g., development, training, capital expenses, etc.), operations performance, development performance, and project performance. (For a detailed list of these measures see McKeen and Smith, 1996.) While these are useful for tracking trends in efficiency, they tell nothing about whether or not this performance is effective or whether it will be adequate for future needs.

Most IT organizations collect more than enough measures in this area, so the goal here is to improve them and make them more meaningful and accurate. All companies need to know how efficiently their systems, computer operations, and IT organizations are performing. However, cost and time metrics need to be better integrated to make this information more understandable to business. One way to do this is with activity-based costing (ABC) (Turney, 1991). ABC was developed to replace conventional cost systems since automation has made indirect costs (aka. overhead) a significant cost factor, in addition to labor and materials. It can be used to accurately measure both the *costs* and *performance* of activities (e.g., systems) and cost objects (e.g., products or customers), making it a very flexible measurement system for evaluating current work.

Are We Doing the Right Things with Our Current Systems and Operations? This is a question (see Cell B in Table 23.3) that many customer satisfaction surveys have tried (and usually failed) to address because the diversity of client perspectives make it extremely difficult to answer general satisfaction questions in any meaningful way (Pastore, 1997). However, the satisfaction of the regular users of a company's IT products is still a key measure of the efficiency, responsiveness, and credibility of an IT department. Today, IT managers are realizing that "customer satisfaction" is a more complex measure than had been previously assumed because IT has not one, but at least three different sets of customers: internal users of existing systems and services, internal management for whom IT is implementing new IT strategies and systems, and external customers who use company products and services in which IT plays a key role.

Newer approaches to current customer satisfaction are therefore more focused and business-centric. These include:

- *Internal customer satisfaction.* Meaningful customer satisfaction must be related to a particular business context. Measured properly, it reveals whether or not IT is doing the right things with its service levels, problem resolution, and current systems. For example, the promptness, quality of resolution, and technical professionalism of help desk services contributes greatly to customer satisfaction at this level. Metrics could also be put in place for such things as: recurring problems, response times, backlogs, and number of abandoned calls. IT ability to turn these measures into improved action will be noted by users and result in improved satisfaction. One focus group company uses a five-tier approach to measuring internal customer satisfaction with current operations, with each tier being a different target audience. Different measures are used because each group has a different role (e.g., bill-payers, application-owners, users). Analysis of problem patterns is also key to improving satisfaction in this cell. A simple method of identifying problems is to ask each user about the quality of service received when he or she signs off for the day. Aggregate measures can then be used to establish trends and baselines of service and to promptly flag and address areas of declining customer satisfaction (Pastore, 1997).

- *Service management measures.* Today, many IT organizations have service-level agreements for their customers that guarantee and measure the performance of individual technical components (e.g., servers, mainframes, communications links). However, with service management measures, information systems (IS) managers create metrics that are business-centric (i.e., that relate to services as their customers see them, rather than as IS sees them). For example, email is a service that relies on a variety of technical components, such as applications, servers, and network ports. When any one of these technologies is not working, the customer perceives the service as not working. A service management measure groups these components together and measures the *overall* availability of the service. This not only provides business with service-level agreements they can understand and live with, it also helps IS to justify new equipment expenditures by relating them to business value. As one focus group manager explained, "IT is now able to justify existing or new technology expenditures based on what business values. You don't have to ask for money for a server or a switch, but to improve the email service." Another manager commented, "With end-to-end measures, we can now discuss the 'business risk' of decreasing application support. This is a terminology our customers can relate to and use to make business decisions."

How Well Do Our Current Systems and Operations Position the Company for the Future? Many companies attempt to assess the relative position of their operations (Cell C in Table 23.3) through external benchmarks against other companies. This works better in operations that are more easily compared, than with systems and processes. Benchmarking is supposed to indicate how a company's costs and performance compare, and whether or not improvements are needed. Certainly, a poor benchmark report can be a catalyst for improvement in IT, but the IT managers in the focus group remarked that they had yet to find a company that has scored in the bottom three-quarters of the field! As a result, for them, benchmarking has become an excuse for maintaining the status quo, rather than a driver of improved performance.

A more useful measure of how well an organization's existing systems and operations position it for the future is to assess the quality of its technology and information infrastructure. Stewart (1997) writes, "Even the smartest people in the world need a mechanism to assemble, package, promote and distribute the fruits of their thinking ... The efficiency, the agility with which a company can augment human capital [with its infrastructure] is the true measure of its effectiveness in the Knowledge Age." A company's ability to do this breaks down into two components:

- the *speed* with which knowledge can be transferred to others in the organization;
- the *ability* of the organization to connect people to data, experts, and expertise, including bodies of knowledge on a just-in-time basis.

Infrastructure maps the knowledge of the organization, indicating where to find it when it is needed, and increases the speed with which knowledge can be moved around the organization with telecommunications, hardware, and software. Ideally, information should flow quickly and easily around functions, but be made available only when it is needed. Suggested measures include: stocks of knowledge, measures of bureaucratic drag (e.g., time to market), and assessment of the information value-add of processes and systems. Effective infrastructure can actually decrease the overall information load on employees' desktops. For example, Hewlett-Packard has improved productivity by pushing less information on employees (e.g., standard reports, handouts, manuals) and making more information available on an as-needed basis. By using a variety of practices to "dumb-down" certain information management processes, the company estimates that it has saved between 25% and 30% of the average cost of supporting a typical employee on a client–server network (Stewart, 1997).

Table 23.4 *A measurement matrix for IT operations and systems.*

	How well are we doing in IS now?	Are we doing the right things in IS?	How well is IS positioning the company for the future?
IT operations and systems	Activity-based costing	Service management measures	External benchmarks
	IT costs	Internal customer satisfaction	Infrastructure effectiveness (speed and access)
	Operations effectiveness Development performance	Online monitoring and trend analysis	Information load

In summary, for current IS operations and systems, the measurement matrix might look like Table 23.4.

Measuring IT Strategies

The second row of the matrix (Table 23.3) assesses the value of the IT strategies (for projects, services, and infrastructure) that the company has and is implementing. Again, the three questions on value can be utilized.

How Well Are These Strategies Working Now? This (Cell D in Table 23.3) measures the traditional bottom line by looking at how well the strategies implemented by IT are resulting in improved financial results for the organization. Although this is a backward look at the benefits delivered in terms of cost savings and/or improved revenues, it also looks forward by cautiously projecting benefits into the future. The most common way of doing this is to calculate ROI, which calculates the financial benefit to the company of a particular investment in IT in the past and in the future. There is no "right" measure of how well an IT strategy is working financially. In fact, Kaplan and Norton (1996) state that these measures *should* vary according to the business strategy that a company is trying to achieve with IT. Thus, if the goal is increased revenues, then measures such as revenue growth and mix should be used. However, if the strategy is to reduce costs or improve productivity, then measures of strategy effectiveness should be appropriately different.

A newer aspect of IT strategy assessment, which companies are just learning how to assess, is the value of relationships, alliances, and joint ownerships. Luehrman (1997) writes, "When a company participates in joint ventures, strategic alliances, or makes large investments using project financing, it shares ownership of the venture with other parties. ... Managers need to understand not simply the value of the venture as a whole but also the value of their company's interest in it." This type of metric is increasingly relevant as IT organizations are establishing outsourcing relationships and other innovative alliances with companies to develop new systems or to deliver infrastructure or technical support. The methods of doing this are somewhat technical; nevertheless, it is important to recognize that such measures are available and are important in evaluating the effectiveness of the overall IT strategy.

Are We Doing the Right Things with Our IT Strategy? While measures of financial impact are useful to assess IT strategy, they show what has happened *after the fact*, when it is too late to do anything about it. Therefore, Kaplan and Norton (1996) suggest that companies also look at *leading indicators*, which measure what is happening now (Cell E in Table 23.3). For this, developing a "balanced scorecard" is extremely useful because it seeks out drivers of future performance clearly linking strategy to business value. Several companies in the focus group are in the process of developing balanced scorecards. Scorecards are based on a set of about 20 measures developed internally by management, which assess a strategy from four different perspectives: financial, customer, internal processes, and learning and growth, giving senior managers a comprehensive view of a strategy's value. While measures selected will vary, they should highlight indicators that inform companies about the progress of their strategy and provide causal paths from all measures to financial objectives. If metrics do not result ultimately in improved financial performance, this should be a signal to senior management that they are not looking at the right things.

Other companies are taking a simpler and less complex approach to assessing strategy by identifying who in the business organization should be responsible for working with IT to develop and implement IT strategy, and then focusing on satisfying them. As IT *strategic customers*, these people are responsible for determining corporate priorities and ensuring that the company achieves value for its investment. One focus group manager remarked that this method had reduced the number of IT customers from 4,000 to 48, making it much easier to concentrate on strategic initiatives. All other users of IT are referred back to these key business customers. By having a process for focusing IT, a company ensures that it is working on the right things and that it is measured on what the company considers important.

Another focus group company uses a different mechanism. Since it believes that business value is largely in the perceptions of its customers, IT staff work with their primary customers to identify value criteria before a project starts. These form the basis of how IT will be measured. When other users complain about what IT is or isn't doing, IT staff can then redirect their concerns to the appropriate business person pointing out that they are working according to criteria established by the business itself. This approach has been remarkably effective in focusing users and IT alike on what is truly important to the business's overall strategy.

How Well Are Our IT Strategies Positioning Us for the Future? As management looks further into the future, measures must change again. Strategies that

Table 23.5   *A measurement matrix for IT strategy.*

	How well is IT doing now?	Is IT doing the right things?	How well is IT positioning the company for the future?
IT strategies	ROI and other financial measures	External customer satisfaction	Contribution to customer acquisition
	Measures to assess the value of alliances	Balanced scorecard	Comparison with competitors
		Prioritization process	IT strategy
		Business-defined value	

may have been very effective in the past, and that continue to be in the present, may not be adequate for longer term success. Ultimately, long-term success in business is about attracting customers. Customers are attracted by:

- products and services including functionality, quality, and price;
- customer relationships including quality of purchasing experience and personal relationships;
- image and reputation;
- ease of doing business (Kaplan and Norton, 1996; Stewart, 1997).

IT strategies can contribute considerably to each of these factors. Thus, in Cell F of the matrix (Table 23.3) current IT strategies should be assessed according to how well they promote and enhance these attributes for different types of customer.

A second type of assessment should look at the company's use of IT relative to its competitors. Some focus group companies are already doing this. Because this cell emphasizes comparing the *added value* IT is delivering, rather than its costs and performance, such assessments provide a very different basis of evaluation of IT work than has typically been done in the past.

Overall, for IT strategy the measurement matrix might look like Table 23.5.

Measuring IT Opportunities

This is probably the most difficult area of measurement for most IT managers because it is the least tangible and most uncertain. Nevertheless, the better job a company can do of understanding the future, the better prepared it will be to face it.

How Well Are We Doing with IT Opportunities Right Now? The ability to quickly and effectively take advantage of opportunities is often described as IT flexibility or responsiveness (Cell G in Table 23.3). It is determined largely by the processes an organization has in place to assess opportunities and move them through to implementation. An IT organization that is "easy to do business with" enables a company to respond rapidly to new opportunities using IT (Stewart, 1997).

To measure how well it responds to business queries and opportunities, IT should first assess its information and services. Does it know what information its internal and external customers value, what information drives the business, where it is, and who has it? Can it provide that information on a just-in-time basis? Second, do its processes speed the delivery of new IT products and services to its customers? A common complaint about IT is that its processes are so full of red tape that they prevent business people from using IT to take advantage of opportunities. IT should assess how straightforward and easy to understand its processes are and the degree of bureaucracy it is perceived to have. Third, does IT have processes, information, and expertise in place to enable it to find out what it needs to know? This could be a network of experts, just-in-time training, or a research and development team.

Are We Responding to the Right IT Opportunities? This is a challenging question that organizations have been trying to deal with for many years with varying degrees of angst and success (Cell H in Table 23.3). The common approach in investing in IT projects has been to *not* value new projects formally until they mature to a point where an investment decision can no longer be deferred and then to have a steering committee meet to decide whether or not to go ahead with the project. The problem with this approach is, as most CIOs can attest, that: "The absence of a formal valuation procedure often gives rise to personal, informal procedures that can become highly politicized" (Luehrman, 1997). As IT investments grow ever-larger and ever-more central to their business strategy, companies are recognizing that this approach is inadequate for their needs.

One of the focus group organizations has developed a formal project investment evaluation (PIE) process (based on the work of Robert Benson of The Beta Group) to help it determine where it will invest. This is a structured process that compares the central elements of each proposed IT project with the key factors associated with the company's business strategy. Each proposed project's contribution to corporate strategy is then scored, and this score is used to rank initiatives and assign resources accordingly. This process has enabled everyone in the organization to understand the criteria on which IT projects are selected, clarify IT priorities, and focus on the most important corporate strategies.

Another method of evaluating IT investments is options valuation (Luehrman, 1997; Amram and Kulatilaka, 1999). Luehrman (1998) explains, "A business strategy is much more like a series of options than a series of static cash flows. Executing a strategy almost always involves making a sequence of major decisions. Some actions are taken immediately, while others are deliberately deferred, so managers can optimize as circumstances evolve. The strategy sets the framework within which future decisions will be made, but at the same time it leaves room for learning from ongoing developments and for discretion to act based on what is learned." Options valuation is a new process that enables companies to make more refined comparisons of potential opportunities because they incorporate both the uncertainty inherent in business and the active decision-making required to take full advantage of its IT opportunities.

Employee satisfaction is a different means of determining whether or not a company is taking advantage of the right opportunities. Satisfied employees are a *precondition* for increasing productivity, responsiveness, quality, and service (Kaplan and Norton, 1996). With knowledge-workers, satisfaction and empower-ment are critical to getting desired outcomes (Stewart, 1997). Since employee satisfaction, retention, and productivity lead to improved results, IT managers should assess these factors within their own organizations.

How Well Is the Company Positioned to Take Advantage of Future Opportunities? The final cell in the measurement matrix (Cell I in Table 23.3) addresses the IT organization's ability to develop the skills and competencies of its staff to be ready to adapt to change and take advantage of future opportu-nities. Whether you call it human capital (Stewart, 1997) or learning and growth (Kaplan and Norton, 1996), the capability of IT staff to provide effective solutions to future business problems is critical to the future success of the organization. Therefore, in order to know how well it is positioning the company for the future, IT must develop a way of measuring these capabilities. There are two elements that can be measured: what people know that is useful to the organ-ization, and how much the organization uses of what people know. To date, metrics in this area have been missing or inadequate. As yet, most companies have invested virtually no effort in identifying or measuring outcomes or the drivers of their capabilities and are not linking their strategies to competencies.

However, progress is being made. Some companies are experimenting with new measures, such as innovation abilities, tenure, experience, learning, skills and knowledge. One focus group company is working with the Software Engineering Institute's (SEI) "capability maturity model" for people. This adapts its framework for managing software to managing and developing an organization's workforce and help it attract, develop, motivate, organize, and retain IT talent (Curtis et al., 1995). Another company has developed a complete scorecard of IT knowledge capital, including measures of:

- wellness—retention, absenteeism, and employee satisfaction;
- productivity—application development and production support;
- assets—abilities in people resource management, experience, skills (quality and quantity), and recruiting.

Knowledge mapping is a further way of measuring competencies. Bohn (1994) outlines an eight-stage model of identifying what an organization knows and,

Table 23.6   *A measurement matrix for IT opportunities.*

	How well is IT doing now?	Is IT doing the right things?	How well is IT positioning the company for the future?
IT opportunities	Ease of working with IT	Project investment evaluation	Knowledge maps
	Time to process opportunities	Options valuation	Employee competencies
	Quality and quantity of information available	Employee satisfaction	Knowledge capital scorecard

more importantly, doesn't know. Stewart suggests developing radar charts for key capabilities. People's skills can also be categorized, enabling IT managers to identify competency gaps and develop strategies to create them.

In summary, the measurement matrix might look like Table 23.6. While measuring opportunities is difficult, it is also the area of IT measurement that will add the highest value to the company. Therefore, it is worth pursuing and developing metrics in this area, even if they are imperfect.

DEVELOPING A BETTER MEASUREMENT INFRASTRUCTURE

Focus group members were unanimous in their agreement that metrics were only one part of an effective measurement program. Equally, if not more important than the measures selected, there is an effective measurement infrastructure (i.e., the environment and processes that support IT measurement). They had the following advice for other IT managers seeking to improve measurement in their organizations.

Think Through the Consequences of Measurement

"You get the different behaviors depending on what you measure," was the consensus of the group. People will work toward the measures selected. For example, if you measure people only according to how well they meet their objectives, you will get a group of "single-minded" silos, rather than teams. Therefore, managers must balance the measures they select and be careful to incent the kinds of sharing and teamwork behaviors they value. Balance *between* measures is also important. For example, one manager noted that a system availability measure without an accompanying successful batch-processing measure could result in support personnel stopping batch-processing to make the system available, leading to the system containing "old" data. The availability target would be achieved, but at the expense of some lost value to the business.

Make Sure the CIO Knows His or Her Responsibilities

The CIO's role and actions are crucial to ensuring whether or not the IT function is perceived to add value. A CIO has three responsibilities in this area. First, he or she must build a demonstrable track record of delivery. More than any other single measure, this is fundamental to the perceived value of IT (Bashein and Markus, 1997). Second, he or she must focus IT efforts on facilitating key corporate strategies. Third, he or she must be able to spot and create opportunities for the value-added use of IT (Earl and Feeny, 1994). While the measurement matrix in itself can facilitate these efforts, the CIO must lend the weight of his or her position to each of these organizational emphases by actively monitoring each of these areas and providing the necessary support and resources to address any fundamental problems that are revealed.

Establish and Follow Best Principles

Measurement *principles* are more easily transferable between organizations than best practices. When examining the measurement practices of other companies, understanding why something works and what distinguishes it will help to highlight the principles on which it is based. These can then be adopted into your own organization, but adapted to your particular context (Bensaou and Earl, 1998). Stewart (1997) has identified three principles of measurement that should guide a company about what to measure:

- *Keep it simple.* Don't use too many measures.
- *Measure what's strategically important.*
- *Measure activities that produce intellectual wealth.*

Assign Accountabilities

A measurement program will not be work unless management assigns accountability for the results. Focus group members went further and stated that an organization *shouldn't* measure if someone is not available to deal with the findings generated.

Identify Measures and Their Uses

Not all measures should be reported to senior management. Focus group members strongly suggested distinguishing between diagnostic measures that screen for the general level of health in a certain area, and analytic measures that are designed to help uncover causes of a particular problem. Each type of measure has a purpose. Only diagnostic measures should be reported to the business. Analytic measures should be used internally only.

Use Business Language

In order for a measurement program to work, people must understand what is being measured and why. Measures should not only be linked to business objectives, they should also be phrased in business terms; for example users would rather see whether or not an IT process or service is available, rather than the number of CPU cycles, even if the end result is the same. Interestingly, this also encourages IT staff to see their work as part of the business process, rather than as purely technical in nature.

Recognize that Measurement is an Ongoing Process

It's well known that, over time, metrics programs frequently lose momentum, wither, and die. "When metrics programs go astray, it's usually because what is being measured is no longer a key indicator of success," states measurement consultant Howard Rubin (Fabris, 1996). For example, whereas 10 years ago many of the focus group companies used function points to assess IT productivity, today no-one is using them. "We stopped using them," said one focus group manager, "they take too much time and we weren't learning anything new." An effective measurement program will change over time as new metrics are developed and business strategies change.

Avoid Complexity

As time goes on, complexity will creep into a measurement program, destroying focus and adding effort. Periodically, therefore, disciplined efforts must be made to eliminate some measures. All the experts suggest limiting an IT report card to between 5 and 30 measures (Young, 1998; Kaplan and Norton, 1996; Simons and Davila, 1998). Whichever number your organization selects will mean that many metrics currently in use will be abandoned. This, too, is an important part of measurement. Managers need to recognize what they *don't* need to know as much as what they do need. They also need to constantly seek feedback from their customers and their employees about what's important in their measurement program.

Experiment with Metrics

"A measure need not be perfect to be effective," states Stewart (1997). He suggests that organization introduce more trial and error into their metrics programs. This is one of the best ways to develop new measures for new needs. Experimentation with different methods of presenting metrics can also be worthwhile, Radar charts, dashboards, and color-coding have all helped to make measures more meaningful in recent years.

CONCLUSION

Today, it is not enough to simply count CPU cycles and cost-justify projects. As IT becomes more and more critical to the realization of business strategy, managers must also be able to demonstrate the business value of technology. Because of the type of work done by IT professionals, the amount of effort and money expended in developing it does not always equate to the value received by a company. As a result, IT managers must look at different ways of determining value.

This chapter has shown that, for IT, business value is a multi-layered concept with elements of past, present, and future impact. Therefore, no single metric will be able to communicate what management needs to know. A more meaningful approach is therefore to use a matrix of measures, selecting an appropriate suite of measurement tools and individual metrics for each type of IT work and management need. As we learn more about measurement in IT, it is likely that individual tools and metrics will change. However, because the principles underlying the measurement matrix will remain valid longer, IT managers will be able to use it to drive and organize their thinking about measurement as the field evolves.

REFERENCES

Amram, M. and N. Kulatilaka (1999) *Real Options: Managing Strategic Investment in an Uncertain World*, Harvard Business School Press, Boston.

Bashein, B. and M.L. Markus (1997) "A credibility equation for IT specialists," *Sloan Management Review*, Summer, **38**(4).

Bensaou, M. and M. Earl (1998) "The right mindset for managing information technology," *Harvard Business Review*, September–October.

Bohn, R. (1994) "Measuring and managing technical knowledge," *Sloan Management Review*, Fall.

Curtis, W., W. Hefley, and S. Miller (1995) *People Capability Maturity Model*, Software Engineering Institute, Carnegie Mellon University, September (www.sei.cmu.edu/cmm-p/).

Dyle, W.F. (1995) "Your bloody ROIT," *CIO Magazine*, 15 September.

Earl, M. and D. Feeny (1994) "Is your CIO adding value?" *Sloan Management Review*, Spring.

Fabris, P. (1996) "Measures of distinction," *CIO Magazine*, 15 November.

Kaplan, R. and D. Norton (1996) *The Balanced Scorecard*, Harvard Business School Press, Boston.

Luehrman, T. (1997) "What's it worth? A general manager's guide to valuation," *Harvard Business Review*, May–June.

Luehrman, T. (1998) "Strategy as a portfolio of real options," *Harvard Business Review*, September–October.

McKeen, J. and H. Smith (1996) *Management Challenges in IT*, John Wiley & Sons, Chichester, UK.

Pastore, R. (1997) "Service ace," *CIO Magazine*, 1 August.

Simons, R. and A. Davila (1998) "How high is your return on management?", *Harvard Business Review*, January–February.

Stewart, T. (1997) *Intellectual Capital: The New Wealth of Organizations*, Doubleday, Toronto.

Strassman, P. (1997) *The Squandered Computer: Evaluating the Business Alignment of Information Technologies*, Information Economics Press, New Canaan, CT.

Turney, P. (1991) *Common Cents: The ABC Performance Breakthrough*, Cost Technology, Hillsborough, OR.

Young, D. (1998) "Score it a hit", *CIO Enterprise Magazine*, 15 November.

Index

Note: Page references in italics refer to Figures; those in bold refer to Tables